African Upheavals Since Independence

Other Titles in This Series

Apartheid and International Organizations, Richard E. Bissell

Ethnicity in Modern Africa, edited by Brian M. du Toit

Botswana: An African Growth Economy, Penelope Hartland-Thunberg

Zambia's Foreign Policy: Studies in Diplomacy and Dependence, Douglas G. Anglin and Timothy M. Shaw

South Africa into the 1980s, edited by Richard E. Bissell and Chester A. Crocker

Crisis in Zimbabwe, edited by Boniface Obichere

The Arab-African Connection: Political and Economic Realities, Victor T. Le Vine and Timothy W. Luke

An African Experiment in Nation-Building: The Bilingual Cameroon Republic, edited by Ndiva Kofele-Kale

Regionalism Reconsidered: The Economic Commission for Africa, Isebill V. Gruhn

Bibliography of African International Relations, Mark W. DeLancey

Westview Special Studies on Africa

African Upheavals Since Independence
Grace Stuart Ibingira

Grace Ibingira seeks the fundamental causes of
the widespread upheavals (at least thirty-eight army
coups in the past fifteen years) in African states
today and finds them in the inadequate colonial preparation of African leaders for the responsibilities
of independence, the earlier practices of "divide and
rule," and the "winner-take-all" policies of those who
inherited power from the colonizers. Foreign intervention, he asserts, has often added yet another destabilizing element.

From his unusual position as a one-time Ugandan
cabinet minister, close associate of overthrown regimes
in Ghana and Nigeria, prisoner in a maximum-security
facility in Uganda for five years following the 1966
revolution, and now outside observer, Dr. Ibingira
proposes principles that would lead toward national
and regional stability in Africa. He places a new
emphasis on the role of leaders in African unrest.

Grace Stuart Ibingira, legal consultant to the
UN Development Programme, served in the Ugandan government as a member of parliament, minister of justice,
minister of state, and secretary general of the Uganda
People's Congress. He was Uganda's ambassador to the
UN until he resigned from government service in January 1974.

The Secret Fears of a Tyrant — Confrontation with Justice
(Grace Stuart Ibingira)

African Upheavals Since Independence

Grace Stuart Ibingira

Westview Press / Boulder, Colorado

I dedicate this book to all those leaders among mankind, whoever and wherever they are, who act upon the
realization that the ultimate survival and well-being
of the human race can neither depend on mutually assured destruction among the great powers nor on the
repression or exploitation of the weak by the powerful,
either within a nation or between nations, but on an
enhanced degree of mutual tolerance and empathy for
each other in a diverse, interdependent world.

--Grace Stuart Ibingira

Westview Special Studies on Africa

Copyright © 1980 by Westview Press, Inc.

Published in 1980 in the United States of America by
     Westview Press, Inc.
     5500 Central Avenue
     Boulder, Colorado 80301
     Frederick A. Praeger, Publisher

Library of Congress Catalog Card Number: 79-13636
ISBN: 0-89158-585-0

Printed and bound in the United States of America

Contents

List of Tables.   x
Preface   xi
Acknowledgments   xvii

Part 1
The Nature of the Colonial Legacy   1

1. Introduction   3

   The Concept of Preparation: Myths and
      Realities   6

2. Uganda   11

   Colonization and Consolidation   11
   The Approach of Independence and
      Its Problems   24
   The Independence Settlement   30

3. Nigeria   37

   Colonization and Administration   37
   The Unbalanced Amalgamation of North and
      South in 1914   38
   Regional Power Versus National Unity   40
   The Lack of Leadership Experience for
      Independence   47

4. Ghana   51

   Colonial Administration: Local and Central
      Governments   52
   The Demands for Federalism   56

Part 2
The Politics and Practices of Winner-Take-All
   and Their Consequences   61

5. Introduction   63

6. Uganda: Fundamental Causes of the
      1966 Revolution   65

   The UPC's Resolute Determination to Obtain
      and Exercise Absolute Power   66
   Efforts to Impose a One-Party System   68
   Parliamentary Battles for Reform of
      the Electoral Law   72
   Monopoly and Misuse of the Security
      Forces   76
   The Misuse of Police Powers to
      Promote the UPC   94
   Efforts to Monopolize Government Power . . .   99
   The Revival of Primordial Fears 111

7. Uganda: The Immediate Causes of the
      Revolution 135

   The Exposure of Clandestine Involvement
      in a Foreign Conflict 136
   Accusations of Profiteering from the
      Conflict 139
   The Likely Removal of Idi Amin and
      Its Consequences 140
   The UPC Stand on Ocheng's Motion 140
   The Constitution and Its Restraints 147
   The Seizure of Absolute Power 149
   The Unrestrained Executive and Its
      Effect on National Unity 162
   The 1971 Coup D'etat 175

8. Ghana: The Centralization of Power 185

   Eliminating the Regional Assemblies 185
   Crippling and Eliminating the Opposition . . 187
   Emasculating the Judiciary 192
   The Rubber-Stamp Legislature 194
   The Autocratic Presidency 196
   The Consequences 198
   The Busia Administration 200

9. Nigeria: The Effects of
      Winner-Take-All Policies 205

   The Elimination of Action Group
      Opposition and Leadership 205
   The Struggle to Create More Regions 209
   Control of the Public Service 211
   Census Controversy: The Struggle For
      More Numbers 212

Last Attempts at Recovery: The
December 1964 Elections 214
Regional Elections in Western
Nigeria, October 1965 217

10. Poverty, Subversion, and Instability . . . 221

Poverty 221
External Subversion and Local
Instability 232
The Apparent Exceptions to
Instability 241

Part 3
The Future: Some Lessons and
Some Basic Principles 245

11. Alternatives for Africa 247

The One-Party System 247
Military Rule 255

12. The Military Regime of Idi Amin
in Uganda 269

The Devaluation of Human Life 270
Chaotic Foreign Policy 274
Economic and Social Ruin: Expelling
Asians and Confiscating Their Property . 277
Why Amin Survived 282
Idi Amin in Perspective 287
Uganda's Future 293

13. Some Basic Principles 305

The Philosophical or Ideological
Premise of Government 305
Leadership 307
Recognition and Acceptance of Diversity . . 316
Accepting the Idea of Responsible
Opposition 319
Constructing a Sound, Viable Constitution . 321
Guaranteeing Basic Human Rights 324
Providing "Catch-Up" Programs for
Backward Areas 329
Emphasizing Common Interests 329
Promoting Meaningful Regional Cooperation . 330
Developing an Enlightened Foreign Policy . 332
Conclusions 334

Notes 337

Tables

2.1　Uganda's Colonial Legacy . . . .　22

2.2　The Roots of Ugandan Nationals
　　　Based on the 1959 Census . . . .　27

3.1　Nigeria's Colonial Legacy . . . .　40

6.1　Electoral Results for 1961, 1962 . . . .　70

8.1　Ghana: Preindependence Election
　　　Results, 1956 . . . .　189

10.1　Some Social and Economic Indicators
　　　of the Contrast Between Some Developed
　　　Countries and 15 African States . . . .　223

11.1　Army Africanization on Independence . .　264

11.2　Black Africa: Occurrence of Coups,
　　　1963-1978 . . . .　266

13.1　Ghana: Directions of Import and Export
　　　Trade, 1964-1970 . . . .　331

Preface

One of the memorable landmarks of twentieth-century history is with little doubt the decolonization process, the liquidation of global empires since the end of World War II. Equally spectacular was the African part of this process. Never before in the history of mankind have so many states attained their independence in such a short period of time as in black Africa, beginning with the independence of Ghana in 1957 and continuing until 1964.

But barely over a decade later more than thirty-seven governments in black Africa have been forcibly overthrown by the military, in a number of instances more than once within a single state. Nearly half of the independent states are under military rule. With the exceptions of Gambia, Botswana, Mauritius, and perhaps also Senegal (where originally there were multiparty rulers), the one-party system dominated the continent before it was challenged and then adopted by the armed forces that took power. The new leaders' great promises of what the benefits of independence would be, matched only by the high expectations of their followers, have in many instances given way to instability, uncertainty, repression, and fear. What went wrong? Why? How?

A good deal has been written about the causes of this instability and the military coups. I have tried to summarize these causes in this book. In particular, I have addressed myself to two of the most popularly claimed causes: poverty and foreign subversion. And yet I remain unmoved in my belief that all the proposed causes, significant as indeed they are, generally speaking have hitherto played only a catalytic role.

In my opinion the most crucial and basic causes of Africa's postindependence instability are twofold. The first cause lies in the manifest defects of the colonial legacy to each of these states. Most notable

was the total failure of colonization to combine within
a given colony ethnic groups with compatible characteristics; instead the colonial frontiers were drawn purely on the basis of alien strategic and economic interests. Aggravating this shortcoming was the patent
failure of colonial powers to give Africans meaningful,
sustained long-term training in wielding political
power to meet the needs of and resolve conflicts within
these artificial multiethnic colonies.

The second basic cause of instability has been the
strong preference for autocratic rule, which has been
practiced by many postindependence leaders against a
background of heterogeneous societies. This autocracy,
manifesting itself in the "winner-take-all" philosophy
of those who inherited power from the colonizers, has
tended to alienate a good many groups within the state
by making them feel excluded from the new state structure. This often forced such groups to seek equity
and redress outside the young institutions of the
state, and they resorted in particular to more primordial communal identities, particularly ethnic, ideological, and sometimes religious ones. The result was
repression as the national government sought to eliminate these centrifugal tendencies without providing
adequate or just alternative solutions to their causes.
Protests and demands -- reasonable and unreasonable --
by diverse groups became necessarily clandestine, which
only invited further repression. Violence and instability became inevitable, as the "we/they" perceptions
among the heterogeneous peoples were heightened by a
political climate in which those who wielded power
monopolized it indefinitely or for life.

My account falls naturally into three unequal
parts. The first tells of the background to independence and deals with the principal defects of the legacy of colonial rule that laid the foundations for a
stormy postindependence period. The second and main
part of the book seeks to demonstrate how the philosophy of winner-take-all, held and practiced by many
postindependence leaders and operating on a defective
colonial inheritance, has made instability often inevitable. In both the first and second parts, the
experiences of three states are discussed: Uganda
(principally), Nigeria, and Ghana.

In the case of Uganda there is a fairly detailed
treatment of hitherto unknown events and facts that
led to the Obote revolution of February 1966, when he
seized absolute power, which in turn laid the foundations for his forcible removal by the army in 1971.
The ruthless centralization of power is traced through
three areas of government: the governing party (the

Uganda People's Congress); the central and local governments; and, most crucial perhaps, the army and
police.

With respect to Ghana, the winner-take-all con-
centration and monopoly of power is traced through
President Kwame Nkrumah's rule. We look at the principal landmarks of this process, beginning with the
elimination of regional assemblies, effectively emasculating the constitution in order to provide legislation that would ensure a rubber-stamp legislature and
a compliant judiciary. Important measures that but-
tressed the autocratic presidency, such as the Preventive Detention Act of 1958, are also discussed, as is
their ultimate consequence, the forcible end of Nkrumah's rule.

For Nigeria, this monopoly of power and its adverse results are traced through the principal crises
during Prime Minister Tafawa Balewa's rule. It begins
with a discussion of measures devised to destroy the
opposition's Action Group party in 1962. The unreasonable response to demands for the creation of more
regions to better represent the heterogeneous nature
of Nigeria, the control of public service, and the
census controversy are also included. Finally, one
of the worst examples of the ruthless monopoly of
power, the fraudulent national election of December
1964 and the regional general election in western
Nigeria in October 1965 and their consequences are
discussed.

Through these same countries, it is sought to
demonstrate that without sound principles for running
multiethnic states that give every community a sense
of belonging, neither one-party nor military rule has
provided the tools to bring the stability their advocates claimed they would. The choice of these three
particular countries was not altogether accidental.
Ghana has a special place in Africa's postindependence
history, primarily because it was the first black
African state to become free (in 1957) and therefore
offers the longest perspective on independent nationhood. Nigeria, with about 250 ethnic groups and a
population of over 70 million, is Africa's most populous state and one of its richest states, and it readily shows the fundamental problems of government that
may not be so clearly identifiable in smaller states.
In addition, the Nigerian experience is important
because it offers demonstrable proof that multiparty
systems in themselves offer no assurance of stable
democratic rule, being as open to abuse as the one-
party system. Uganda provides my principal base because I have been very closely involved in its major

political and constitutional development and can discuss its problems from direct personal knowledge. With
a population of about 12 million, including some thirty-two ethnic groups, it represents a typical, fair-
sized African state.

The third and final part deals with the lessons
that can be drawn from the cases discussed and outlines
some basic principles that seem to be necessary to
enhance prospects for stable rule in Africa. Arthur
Lewis, a one-time economic adviser to President Nkrumah
of Ghana, having watched the West African political
scene closely, validly remarked more than ten years
ago that "the fundamental political problem in Africa
is neither economic policy nor foreign policy, but the
creation of nations out of heterogeneous people."[1]
The basic principles I discuss are intended to provide
the means for creating the necessary common identity
and mutual tolerance within a multiethnic state. The
account is rooted both in my personal experience and
in the experience of many other African leaders, whose
statements and actions I cite extensively throughout
this account as the best evidence for the matters
considered.

I was a founding member of the Uganda People's
Congress (UPC) and was its secretary-general and senior
cabinet minister. In February 1966, however, that was
abruptly and brutally ended. My then close colleague
and friend, Milton Obote, for whom and with whom I had
worked so hard for Uganda's independence, fulfilled
his long-time ambition of seizing absolute power by
unlawfully abrogating the constitution and locking up
five senior ministers -- including myself -- who he
rightly knew would have resisted his move. Thus a new
repressive government was introduced on the peaceful
Ugandan political scene that progressively worsened
until it became a living hell under Obote's onetime
principal hatchet man and eventual successor, Idi Amin.
As I endured that deprivation and anguish for five
years, events were taking place all around that touched
me deeply. I saw the disintegration of whole families
of blameless political prisoners, their children becoming delinquent and their wives being seduced purposely to hurt the prisoners further. Almost every
month I saw new political victims brought to detention,
most of them innocent peasants -- often of advanced
age -- who knew little or nothing about the power Obote
cherished. In deep anguish, I witnessed the treachery
of some favor-seekers and flatterers, who once had
urged me as secretary-general of the UPC to stand firmly against Obote's budding dictatorship, but who now
loudly extolled Obote's success while condemning me for

high treason. That the charge did not exist in fact
nor even in law was evidenced by their total refusal
to put me on trial.

In May 1966 on Obote's orders the Ugandan army,
under Idi Amin's direction, slaughtered a few thousand
largely defenseless Baganda peasants because some of
them had feebly tried to protest the abrogation of the
Ugandan constitution. Not a single soldier was punished for this excessive abuse of arms; instead, many
were promoted (including Idi Amin) as a reward for a
job well done. In the solitude of my bare prison cell,
where I had a few filthy blankets for a mattress and
the rough concrete floor for a bed, I could not but
repeatedly ask myself what had gone wrong. Why had
the idealism of our struggle for independence been
abandoned for such repression? Events elsewhere in
Africa gave me added reason to ask myself these questions. The heroes of the African independence struggle
had fallen or were falling into violent disgrace. In
Nigeria, Chief Obafemi Awolowo, a veteran nationalist
and leader of the opposition, was serving a long prison term for allegedly attempting to overthrow the
federal government; Prime Minister Tafawa Balewa of
Nigeria had subsequently been assassinated with some
of his colleagues, unleashing a horrendous civil war.
Within two days of my own arrest, President Kwame
Nkrumah of Ghana had been overthrown by his army.
Elsewhere, leading ministers whom I knew well, whose
names had been household words in the preindependence
struggles, were being detained, assassinated, or were
fleeing into exile. I decided then to write this
book as a candid, personal retrospection on the causes
of our initial failures. This is my contribution to
the understanding of our misfortunes, without which
we are a people without a memory and are consequently
apt to repeat the same mistakes.

No one can ever wish to share both extremes of
fortune, to move as I did from the commanding heights
of a senior cabinet ministery and party leadership to
the misery and trials of a five-year imprisonment in
a maximum security jail. Yet once it came, I found
that it permitted me a high degree of perception into
the basic causes of our upheavals never before possible. I understand better the abuse of power -- especially by those who have never been its victims, or
who having once suffered have forgotten what it was
like. Above all, I understand what it is like to be
the object of a ruthless, misdirected authority.

The fact that I confine my account to the experiences of only three English-speaking states does not
mean that the rest of Africa is different. There is

abundant evidence that what is discussed in these
pages is a phenomenon of continental proportions. Obviously, because of the immensity and diversity of
Africa the causes of upheavals discussed here have to
be rooted in the particular circumstances of each
state. But the basic similarity of these causes
throughout the continent is unmistakable.

G. S. Ibingira

Acknowledgments

This book was made possible by the assistance of individuals and institutions that deserve special mention and my deep appreciation. First, I would like to thank my good friend Bradford Morse, currently the administrator of the United Nations Development Program, who introduced me to that unique place, the Woodrow Wilson International Center for Scholars in the Smithsonian Institution, Washington, D.C., which was ideal for my research and writing. Dr. James Billington, director of the center, could not have been more helpful or understanding in providing me the facilities and assistance for doing my work. His staff at the center were equally helpful and pleasant. The Woodrow Wilson Center partly financed the writing of this book. The Rockefeller Foundation, through a generous and extended fellowship from 1975 to 1977, made it possible to complete my work without undue haste. A special word of appreciation is due to Westview Press, who undertook the publication of this work. Finally, I owe a special debt to my wife, Monique, whose patience and loving care enabled me to accomplish the task.

Despite the invaluable assistance from all the above, none of them was directly involved in the research and writing of this work, which remains my sole responsibility. Indeed, my appreciation of their assistance is all the more because in this book I may have expressed opinions contrary to their own. However, in helping me to write it, they have actively demonstrated the true spirit of that cherished freedom of expression.

G. S. I.

Part 1

The Nature of
the Colonial Legacy

1
Introduction

It is not an overstatement to say that the
principal purpose of African colonization was the
material enrichment of the European colonizers,
and that the welfare of the indigenous people was
often irrelevant, or at best secondary, to the
colonizers' needs. Yet it is constantly argued
in justification of colonialism that the colonizers
were equally motivated to promote the welfare of
the indigenous peoples. Such great proconsuls of
colonial rule as Lord Lugard claimed that the mission of colonization was a "dual mandate":

> Civilized nations have at last recognized
> that while on the one hand the abounding
> wealth of the tropical regions of the earth
> must be developed and used for the benefit
> of mankind, on the other hand an obligation
> rests on the controlling power not only to
> safeguard the material rights of the natives,
> but to promote their moral and educational
> progress.[1]

How genuine was this "dual mandate"? In the
first place, it was self-imposed and unilateral on
the part of the colonizers, for although it is true
that in some cases a colonial power was invited by
a local ruler to assume jurisdiction -- as did
Kabaka Mutesa I of Buganda -- it is on the whole
equally true that the majority of African societies
did not invite colonial rule, that they did not have
a say in meaningfully formulating the terms of this
"dual mandate." Consequently, its terms were disproportionately in favor of the colonial rulers.
Admittedly, some of its principles were constructive,
such as promoting the moral and educational progress
of the "natives." And yet the level that these

3

worthy goals attained was largely determined by a
fundamental desire to make the colonies viable and
profitable. Nowhere was it considered in the founding and consolidation of these empires that the
indigenous people were to be systematically trained
and educated in the art of governing themselves, or
that they were destined to be independent in some
new state structure after a long and purposeful
training in self-government.

Furthermore, the claim that the dual mandate
was "to safeguard the material rights of the natives"
has very important qualifications and exceptions.
The naked exploitation of Africans in such areas as
South Africa, Rhodesia, and, to some extent until
shortly before independence, Kenya, provides real
reservations to this claim. Besides, who determined
the fairness of the prices Europe had to pay for the
"abounding wealth of the tropical regions"? An economic system both domestic and international had
been established by European powers in which they
alone, to the exclusion of the African, determined
the price of Africa's raw materials. The result was
a system of unjust economic enrichment for the colonizers that subsisted into the postindependence era
and provided the young African states with the grievances and justifications to demand a new economic
order.

Often attempts have been made to distinguish
between different types of colonial rule in Africa.
Some, like the French, have been said to have ruled
colonial people "directly" through French administrators, while others, like the British, were supposed to have ruled "indirectly" through the indigenous systems of government. Furthermore, it is said
that the French aimed at transforming their colonials
into Frenchmen, unlike the British, who preserved
the local identities of the ruled. Contrasts go on
and on. But was there really a lasting fundamental
difference in the nature of colonialism as practiced
by the different European powers? Empirical reality
seems to prove the contrary as these differences
often become more academic than real. For instance,
the claim that the British ruled their colonials
indirectly can be misleading. While it is true that
they made greater use of local institutions where
they were well established, there was no doubt in
the minds of both the ruler and the ruled that the
actual power was with the colonizer. Moreover, part
of the typical routine of a British administrator
was to tour his area, hold large public gatherings
of the people and their chiefs with whom he communi-

cated <u>directly</u>. On the other hand, the French, who
supposedly ruled directly, did not altogether ignore
the services and uses of traditional rulers in governing their people. While administrative circles
were <u>purposely</u> constituted without regard to tribal
boundaries, on the ground that any other course might
encourage "separatist traditions," from the 1950s
onwards French colonial administrators began using
chiefs with local support among their people.[2]
Because the number of Frenchmen available to administer a vast empire was necessarily limited by the
great expense of staffing a colony, France had to
rely on indigenous chiefs for governing the colonies
and to this extent, an element of indirect rule was
unavoidable.

Again, the capacity of French assimilative
colonial policies to turn blacks into Frenchmen
should not be exaggerated. It is ture that a small
black elite was transformed into Frenchmen. As
early as 1848, some 12,000 Africans in Senegal had
become French citizens who could send representatives
to the Parliament in Paris. And yet, nearly a century later, there were only 78,000 black French citizens in Senegal and only 2,400 in the rest of the
French West African empire.[3] Given the fact that
over 85 percent of the populations in these territories lived and still live in their ancestral home
areas and that the literacy rate even now, a decade
and a half after independence, is less than 25 percent
in Senegal and the Ivory Coast, the overwhelming
majority of Africans remain African. Similarly, the
English claim of not creating "British Africans" is
not without some limitation, because there were some
elite groups produced in British colonies in Africa
and Asia who were as British as some French African
colonials were French.[4]

For the preponderant majority of Africans, colonial rule was fundamentally the same, not only in
its operation but also most especially in its legacy.
To all the ethnic groups or nationalities who had
previously lived as a sovereign people, it meant the
loss of sovereignty. Everywhere there was denigra-
tion of local culture. Local populations were divided.
There were those who stood their ground and fought
heroically against overwhelming odds with spears
against guns, like the Ashanti in Ghana, the Banyoro
in Uganda, and the emirates of northern Nigeria;
there were others who chose to collaborate with the
invading colonizers to advance their interests, as
did the Fanti in Ghana and the Baganda in Uganda.

And, much later, there were the nationalists who
agitated or fought for independence from colonial
rule.

One of the most adverse consequences of colonization was the arbitrary partitioning of Africa by
the colonizing powers in their scramble for an empire.
The boundaries of the present African states were
drawn in European capitals with predominantly political, strategic, and commercial interests of the
colonizers in mind, almost totally disregarding whether
any ethnic group was cut up into pieces by the new
frontier lines. The problematic legacy was that the
ethnic groups of an overwhelming majority of African
states, except where they border a geographical impediment like the sea or desert, are split up into
different states on all the four corners of the com-
pass. The colonizers completely disregarded which
nationalities or ethnic groups might or might not
live compatibly together within a given boundary.
There was no consideration of the fact that African
societies had systems of government and social organization as diverse as the groups themselves. Notwithstanding the relative homogeneity of a few African
colonies like Botswana, Lesotho, Swaziland, and
particularly Somalia, when the process of African
partition was complete, there were within each colony
many diverse ethnic groups with their own distinct
cultures and political systems, ranging from groups
who knew only loose extended families as a system of
administering themselves to groups with relatively
sophisticated centralized kingdoms. As our examples
will show, some of those grouped together in one
colonial entity were inveterate enemies in precolonial
times. Thus the new Africa was made up of artificial
entities that were to form the future independent
states.

Having thus created and shaped the colonies, to
what extent did the colonizers develop and promote
methods to foster intergroup, interethnic harmony
among the diverse nationals they had forcibly and arbitrarily brought together? To what extent were these
colonial peoples conversant with and trained to administer the national institutions intended to regulate
and resolve interethnic competition and conflict? To
what extent were they in fact prepared to share a common nationhood on independence?

THE CONCEPT OF PREPARATION: MYTHS AND REALITIES

There is some controversy as to whether European

colonial powers <u>deliberately</u> prepared African colonies for independence. Among some academics the British system is credited with having been more benevolent, leaning toward a greater devolution of power to colonials than others. Distinguished colonial administrators like the late Sir Andrew Cohen, while claiming there was a process of preparation for independence, conceded that the colonial powers had erroneously assumed unlimited time within which to do it. But there are others who persuasively argue that the idea of preparation was an afterthought.[5] What is the truth? It is the central argument of this book that there was no well-conceived, systematic preparation of the colonies to shoulder the responsibilities of nationhood. There was therefore little foundation to help withstand the destabilizing problems of independence. In any given state there are two types of resources: human and material. The material legacy of colonial rule was not insubstantial; some of the positive, statistical records of colonial rule will be discussed later on. It is this material record of the infrastructures of the new states that apologists for colonialism cite in its defense. And yet it should not be forgotten that in order to exploit the resources for their own benefit, the colonizers had to establish an infrastructure and the natives had to be trained and educated in order to make the venture profitable and worthwhile. It is significant that even great missionaries who espoused the conversion of the "dark continent" to Christianity as their primary goal were in reality engaged in a dual mission. As the famous David Livingstone put it, there was a prospect before them of "opening Africa for <u>commerce</u> and the gospel."[6] If one wishes to refute the charge that the primary reason for developing the colonies' material resources was <u>not</u> mainly to benefit the colonial powers, and that the beneficial results to the Africans were <u>not</u> largely consequential, one has to show that Africans were indeed fully prepared for independence, prepared to manage the modern infrastructure left behind, and systematically trained in the art of government to better manage their multiethnic communities.

There can be no doubt that the most important resource of any state, developed or developing, is its people. The degree to which they are trained to manage their affairs in private and public life ultimately determines the extent to which they can develop and enjoy the material resources of their country. If, as was predominantly the case with the African states, people were denied the opportunity to exercise

and share responsibility and power at the highest
levels of government, which determine the stability
of the state, and if the future leaders of Africa
played a passive, marginal, or merely supportive role
throughout the colonial experience, it logically follows that such a people -- especially having been
brought together in such an artificial manner -- run
a great risk of a destabilizing postindependence experience. The new leaders' main qualifications were
their anticolonial sentiments, but that was no sub-
stitute for acquiring the art of good government or
knowing the uses and limits of political power. It
is this lack of sound preparation for the crucial
functions of government together with the inclination
of many postindependence leaders to monopolize power
at all costs that have more than anything else accounted for most of the instability in postindependence
Africa.

Once the foundations of a stable government are
negated, it becomes secondary to talk of the blessings
of material inheritance from colonial rule. For instance, of what wholesome benefit was the infrastructure left by colonial rule to the more than one million
Nigerians who perished in that country's civil war?
The railways and roads may have been useful to transport contending armies as they slaughtered Nigerian
citizens on either side and the hospitals may have
saved the lives of the combatants only so that they
might be strong enough to kill again. Of what value
was the material legacy to the thousands of Ugandans
who have perished since the 1966 revolution? What
benefits did such material legacies confer on the
thousands who have been arbitrarily detained and reduced to nonpersons in the land of their birth across
the length and breadth of Africa as a result of bad,
inexperienced government?* The precondition for enjoy-
ing the material blessings of colonial rule was availability of leaders experienced in good government,
which did not exist. Indeed, because of bad government, rather than becoming an asset the benefits
sometimes carried seeds of discord and conflict as
postindependence leaders sought to monopolize them
rather than share them equitably throughout their

---

*By mid-1979 it was estimated by the United Nations
High Commission for Refugees that there were more than
4 million refugees in Africa fleeing domestic upheaval,
some 3 million from independent African states and
about 1 million from the Southern African conflict.

societies.

For this reason I will focus subsequent discussion predominantly on the shortcomings and problems that were created by the excessive delay of colonial powers in meaningfully involving Africans in learning how to govern a modern, multiethnic state.

Although I will dwell on these shortcomings, it is important to mention two fundamental positive aspects of colonial rule that permeated the entire colonial experience of most states. The first was the introduction of a set of values and ideals that had successfully governed a metropolitan society: liberty, justice, and representative government. The fact that the African was denied these in varying degrees does not detract from the fact that he was taught of their existence. Indeed the whole challenge of colonial rule was based primarily on the Africans' insistence to be permitted to live by these values and ideals. This is not to say that the ideals of Western society, rooted in the Christian teachings though they are, are not without shortcomings, but at their very best they contributed the fundamental philosophical guideposts by which most postindependence leaders have tried or have claimed to try to steer their nations.

The second positive legacy was the inculcation of a sense of orderly government, even if it was basically for the benefit of imperial rule. I do not mean to imply that there was no order in precolonial times, which would be absurd; I am simply recognizing the establishment of an ordered society based on modern, if alien, concepts of government. Again, even if the African did not participate at the policy-making levels, he could not fail to be positively touched by this experience through the many decades of colonial rule.

Let us now look at the fundamental flaws of the colonial experience as reflected by experiences of the Republics of Uganda, Nigeria, and Ghana.

2
Uganda

COLONIZATION AND CONSOLIDATION

On 1 April 1893, Sir Gerald Portal raised the
Union Jack formally to establish a British protectorate over Buganda. This event followed the many and
varied pressures coming from explorers like Morton
Stanley who had been impressed by the kabaka's court
in 1875, Protestant missionaries who preferred to see
Buganda under the British flag, England's outright
competitive ambition to colonize, and the desire to
deny this source of the river Nile to other nations.
But it was not until 1914 that Uganda as we know it
today, with its thirty-two ethnic groups, finally
took shape as a colonial protectorate.

As was the case with all colonial powers, the
process of colonization in Uganda was effected through
two complementary methods that by their very nature
and mode of application were to sow the seeds that
eventually embittered nationalists and the masses
against colonial rule. The first was the method of
persuasion, in which the ruler of a kingdom or chief
of a people was persuaded to accept British protection,
to cede his territory, and in effect to surrender the
sovereignty of his people in return for "protection."
In many instances the chiefs, illiterate and without
any knowledgeable or objective advice, simply surren-
dered their people and livelihood to the colonizing
power after vague, meaningless promises. Indeed, so
immoral and deceitful was this method that even one
of the leading promoters of British colonization in
Africa, Lord Lugard, had to term it "the farce [empha-
sis added] of acquiring jurisdiction by Treaties."
He argued, "it was surely more justifiable for the
European powers frankly to found their title to intervention upon force . . . instead of assuming they
themselves derived the right of intervention through

11

cession of sovereignty, under the guise of 'treaties'
. . . which were not understood . . . and which rarely
provided an adequate legal sanction for the powers
assumed."[1] In spite of this, British colonization
was widely based on such treaties, both among the monarchial groups in the South and the peoples to the
north and east of Uganda. But if the majority of indigenous peoples were blind as to the nature of treaties they signed, there were some who understood their
significance, like the Baganda. Lord Lugard had to
concede:

> In Uganda the case is different [from most of
> tropical Africa]. There the people most fully
> understand the nature of a written contract and
> consider nothing as absolutely final and binding
> unless put on paper. They are very clever and
> far seeing, and every clause of the treaty made
> was discussed for several days amongst themselves
> before it was presented to baraza [meeting] for
> the signature of the King and Chiefs.[2]

British colonial jurisprudence, through a consistent chain of judicial decisions dating from 1926 in
Swaziland, declared throughout the African dependen-
cies that the British Crown could never by bound by
any treaty concluded with indigenous rulers, because
such treaties had no force in law.[3] In effect, such
treaties strictly speaking were not worth the paper
on which they were written. In international law
they were even fraudulent because, as Oppenheim states:
"Although a treaty was concluded with real consent of
the parties it is nevertheless not binding if the consent was given in error, or under a delusion produced
by a fraud of the other contracting party."[4] Here
the end justified the means. To the colonial power,
these "treaties" effectively facilitated the subjuga-
tion of alien independent peoples without firing a
shot. To the colonized, however, it provided one of
the foundations for grievances and mistrust against
the colonizers when, upon acquiring jurisdiction,
they refused to be bound by the promises they had
made in such documents, as is discussed later.
       The second and ultimately the most decisive mode
of establishing colonial rule was, of course, the use
of superior military force. Not all the rulers of
the indigenous peoples welcomed the British. Kabarega,
the omukama (king) of Bunyoro stood his ground and
fought bravely against them. The British armies were
essentially made up of mercenary troops from other
African groups, such as from the southern Sudan and

in particular from Buganda -- the kabaka having allied
himself with the British to destroy his traditional
adversary, the omukama of Bunyoro. After a series
of military campaigns, Kabarega was defeated and his
kingdom was terribly devastated by war and famine.
Part of his territory was annexed to the kingdom of
Buganda as a reward for the military alliance.[5] Bunyoro's bid to recover these lost territories was
later to constitute one of Uganda's most intractable
political problems. Although the campaigns against
Kabarega constitute the only overt military conquest
of a people in Uganda, force was used in many areas
and on numerous occasions to make the people accept
British rule. For instance, in 1911, force had to be
applied against the Acholi when they resisted some
aspects of colonial rule in what is usually called
the Lamogi Rebellion. Kakungulu, a Muganda warrior
acting as a British agent in colonization, had to
fight to establish British rule in Lango. In the
kingdom of Ankole (which was expanded under British
rule by incorporating a number of smaller kingdoms),
the ruler of Igara disemboweled himself rather than
meet the omugabe (king) of Ankole whom the British
had recognized as the overall ruler. Perhaps what
was most important about the use of force by the
colonizer was not that it was used -- which was for
relatively brief periods -- but the reality of its
presence and the fact that it could be used against
any resistance. In acknowledgment of the superiority
of gunpowder over the spear and arrow, the diverse
ethnic groups submitted to imperial rule.

As was stated earlier, the fundamental purpose
of colonization was for the benefit of the colonizers
by providing access to raw materials and markets, or
by denying colonial territories to their European
rivals. The type of administration in the colony or
protectorate was therefore to be geared towards this
end. A system of government had to be established
that above all ensured order and stability. The British were at a disadvantage because so few of them
had to administer such extensive territories. However
it would have been uneconomical for the British to
staff parts of the governments due to the greater expenditure it would have involved. Lugard, hard put
to find a formula, came up with the doctrine of indirect rule, as discussed before, which was as effective for colonial administration as it was detrimental
to the future prospect of national unity with Uganda's
independence. Two systems of government, central and
local, were established, and the deliberate decision
to exclude Africans from participation in the struc-

tures of the central government was the most fundamental defect in the preparation for Uganda's emergence as a united state on independence.

Let us now examine the growth of the national legislature and the relegation of Africans to their local ethnic group governments.

The Legislative Council

The Legislative Council, comprised of the executive and legislative branches of government, was the embryo of the sovereign parliament once the colony received independence. During the colonial tutelage, it was the center from which all policies concerning the administration of a colony emanated. Thus, the extent to which the indigenous people were involved in the Council was an important indicator of whether or not the colony was sufficiently prepared to run its affairs on independence.

The Ugandan Legislative Council was established in 1921. Its composition was exclusively expatriate, consisting of the governor of the protectorate and a few of his right-hand advisers. The nonofficial organs that sought membership were essentially representatives of alien commercial interests, like the Ugandan Chamber of Commerce and the Ugandan Planters Association. Representatives of the Asian immigrant community, itself an arm of colonial exploitation, joined the unofficial membership. For more than a quarter of a century after the Council's formation there was not a single African in what was to become the future sovereign legislature.[6] As we shall see later, the indigenous people's relationship with the Legislative Council was one of obedience to and aid in the implementation of its policies in their respective ethnic group areas. It was not until 1946 that for the first time three Africans were nominated by the governor to the Council (one from the kabaka's ministers, another from the katikkiros [premiers] of the western kingdoms, and a third from among the secretaries-general of the eastern province districts).

No one can say the colonial administration was unaware of the adverse effect of the Africans' nonparticipation. The governor clearly observed in 1946 that "few of them have any understanding of what the government is doing and why it is doing what it is."[7] But this was precisely the intention of government: to deny Africans from different ethnic groups the opportunity of meeting together and of participating in the formulation of policies that affected their common destiny.

Much later, due to the international changes after World War II, the exhausted colonial powers had lost their will to hold on to restive empires now experiencing awakened local nationalism, and more sincere attempts were made to induct Africans into the government. There were repeated enlargements of the Legislative Council to include interests that were more especially African. With the expansion of membership in the Council came also its increased powers to legislate for the protectorate. In 1954, the number of unofficial members was increased to seven Asians and seven Europeans nominated by the governor. However, there were to be only fourteen Africans (of whom eleven were to be indirectly elected by the councils of the districts, acting as electoral colleges). In 1955 a reform-minded governor, Sir Andrew Cohen, introduced the ministerial system of government to replace the old executive council of the legislature. Three of the five ministers drawn from public life and appointed by the governor were Africans. In assessing his policies towards the end of his tenure, Sir Andrew Cohen said, "The most important achievement of the country during the last five years has been the real progress made in giving responsibility to Africans in all the main spheres of public life. The aim of all our efforts, the building up of the country towards the goal of self-government in the future is now clearly understood."[8]

Despite this, the measures to introduce Africans to the national government were still most inadequate. It was of marginal value to appoint African ministers who, having acquired a little experience, were not elected by the people. Experience thus acquired was rendered valueless after new general elections returned popular African nationalists whom the colonial administration had declined to involve in government. For this reason, the African representatives in 1957 pressed the colonial administration "to make the necessary constitutional provision in order to have a House three-quarters of whose members are elected." In moving the motion, the African member correctly argued that the purpose was to make the Africans of this country "look upon Uganda's Legislative Council, not as an alien one but as their own Council."[9] Largely because the African nationalists had little faith in the good intentions of the colonial administrators, despite the fact that they had hardly become conversant with the true nature of a central legislature, they began to agitate for self-government. In April 1957 Bamuta moved the first motion in Uganda's history demanding independence within a year. It was followed by many others that demanded the widest possible franchise for self-government. Although the colonial administration rejected these repeated demands as premature, the pressure by Africans from within and without the Council was unyielding. In 1958 for the first time ten African members of the Council were directly elected. It is again significant that these members were not the ones chosen by the governor to be ministers or deputy ministers, to be trained in handling executive responsibility, but instead he appointed nominated Africans to his ministry. By this date (1958) -- only four years away from independence -- not only was the Legislative Council still not a representative legislature within the colonial definition (the legal prerequisitive being that at least one-half of its membership be elected by the people),[10] but the future leaders of an independent Uganda were still being effectively kept out of the government.

The peaceful struggle by nationalists continued, and in 1961 there was at last a general election based on universal adult franchise that resulted in an over-whelmingly African elected membership. For the first time a leader of a political party, the late Ben Kiwanuka of the Democratic party (DP), who had never set foot in the Legislative Council, was chosen to be Uganda's first chief minister. (He later served as prime minister under the internal self-government constitution.) Thus it took sixty-eight years after the establishment of colonial rule and forty years after the introduction of the Legislative Council to get African leaders involved in the process of exercising power through the central legislature. Independence was only one year away. There had to be a more representative general election before independence (Buganda having boycotted the 1961 elections), at which time (May 1962) the DP government was defeated and a new government was formed by Milton Obote, leader of the Uganda People's Congress (UPC), in coalition with Baganda representatives. Ugandans were exercising executive powers for the first time, less than five months before independence.

Given the fact that most of the thirty-two ethnic groups had been independent of each other in precolonial times, the Legislative Council and its central institutions would have been the most appropriate and natural arena for these ethnic groups to unite in and learn to work together, sharing both the benefits and obligations of a common destiny. Thus it was an appalling failure of the colonial power to have deliberately kept the Africans outside these institutions almost right up to the time of independence. This,

of course, was the proverbial policy of "divide and
rule," for it was the best way to stifle unified African nationalism. This defect of the colonial legacy
is one of the twin pillars that has clearly contributed
to the instability of postindependence Africa. True,
one may plausibly argue that even if there had been
African participation in the central legislature at
its inception, there would still have been no guarantee that intra- and interethnic conflicts would not
have sparked off instability after independence. One
could further cite the interethnic problems still experienced by countries that have had this background
for a century and more, like Canada and Belgium, for
example. This argument is faulty. We are not discussing the total elimination of interethnic or intraethnic frictions or rivalries, which is an impossibil-
ity in human affairs. We are talking about the
acquisition of a shared experience by leaders of
diverse groups over a sufficiently long period of time
to provide them with a realistic understanding of the
problems involved if all are to share a common country.
Such experience, attained under the impartial supervision of an alien rule, had the potential of establishing standards, traditions, and conventions and
of promoting an unwritten code of morality among the
diverse leadership, which in the ultimate analysis
would have been crucial to ensuring the sanctity of
national institutions and constitutions. The absence
of such experience and the relative inhibitions it
would have produced partly explain the widespread ease
with which independence leaders abrogated constitutions
and seized excessive powers for themselves, often setting in motion a chain reaction within the state that
later led to their own forcible removal.

Local Government

    The most effective way to divert the attention
of African leadership was to accord exaggerated importance to local governments and thus make them appear
good enough to attract the educated and enlightened
African leaders. For administrative purposes, as far
as practicable each ethnic group was formed into a
unit of local government called a district. Such
was the case with Lango, Acholi, Ankole, Busoga, Teso,
Bunyoro, and the kingdom of Buganda. Where the ethnic
groups were not sufficiently large or viable, a con-
tiguous number were aggregated into a single district,
as was the case with the West Nile district, which
had six distinct groups; the Kigezi and Toro districts,
with three groups each; and the Bukedi district with

six groups. In the districts that were nearly ethnically homogeneous, this unit of local government seemed
in fact a nation in a fundamental sense. The ethnic
groups had been generally distinct in precolonial
time and the formation of districts by ethnic group
ensured that their dealings with other districts or
groups with the protectorate were minimal, and were
never accorded the seriousness they deserved for a
people destined to emerge with common citizenship.

Engrossed as they were in their ethnic group
local governments, the African leadership were never
given, even at this low level, sufficient opportunity
to learn the art of government. They remained merely
instruments to carry out orders of the colonial administrators. The kingdom of Buganda, because of its
size and wealth, had on the face of it more latitude
to administer its own affairs. In 1900 its constitution was set down in an elaborate agreement with the
British Crown.[11] The kabaka was recognized as the
"supreme ruler" of the kingdom, but the governor could
depose him (as he did in 1953) if he was seriously
prejudicial to imperial policy or if he did not accept
the governor's advice. For administrative purposes
the kingdom was divided into twenty counties, with
each county (saza) headed by a chief. The chief would
be selected by the kabaka's government but had to be
approved by the representative of Her Majesty's government, who had the power to demand his dismissal.
The duties of such a chief were to execute colonial
policy, which included administering justice over the
Africans in his county, assessing and collecting taxes,
repairing the main roads, and general supervising of
local affairs. The kabaka's principal ministers were
his premier (katikkiro), the chief justice (omulamuzi),
and the treasurer (omuwanika), all of whose appointments to be effective had to be approved by the governor. In addition, there was the lukiko, Buganda's
parliament, consisting of chiefs and kabaka's nominees,
which was to discuss and help formulate policy for the
kingdom's administration. Overseeing this administration was the resident, a colonial representative of
the governor, through whom the policies of the protectorate government were channelled to the kabaka's
government for implementation, and the demands of the
Baganda were transmitted to the governor. Although
there were some modifications many decades after 1900
-- especially in 1955 -- this remained the fundamental
structure of Bugandan government.

A similar administrative organization, at its
inception implemented with the help of Baganda chiefs,
was established in the smaller kingdoms of Ankole,

Toro, and later Bunyoro.[12] As in Buganda, there was
a principal minister who functioned as the ruler of
each of these smaller kingdoms. But the comprehensive local government organization for these three
kingdoms and the rest of the country was formalized
under Native Authority Ordinances beginning with 1919.
A system of chiefs was established to aid colonial
administration. The principal colonial representative in the district was the district commissioner,
who as the administration progressed was aided by
heads of departments in his area, e.g., agricultural,
veterinary, medical, geological, and public works
officers. The duties of a chief were considerable
in all these areas.[13] He had to maintain order in
the territory within his jurisdiction and could employ
any person to assist him in carrying out the tasks
imposed upon him. He had power to issue specific
orders, including the obedience to native customs,
the prohibition or restriction against the carrying
of arms, and the requirement of able-bodied male
Africans to work in maintaining projects of a public
nature for the benefit of the community. But he was
totally under the control of the district commissioner,
who had magisterial powers to try him for noncompliance
with superior orders and to dismiss him. It was sometimes a humiliating experience for an elderly chief,
widely respected, to be disgraced publicly among his
people by a youthful colonial officer new to the public service. Despite these limitations on the chiefs,
on the whole their positions were worthy of ambition
among many relatively enlightened Africans to whom
the Legislative Council and the branches of the central
government were largely closed.

It was not until 1949 that the African Local Government Ordinance established a district council for
each administrative division, where chosen (not yet
elected) representatives of the inhabitants of the
district could have a chance to discuss the policy
measures that affected their people. In 1955 more
comprehensive legislation was enacted to introduce
meaningful African participation into local government,
taking effect a year later, forty-one years after the
Ugandan protectorate was fully established as a precise, geopolitical entity in 1914. Yet local government is an invaluable ground for training people in
the art of government, both local and national. If
colonial rule had assured democratic and effective
local governments from the beginning, this might have
helped to offset the destabilizing effect of an inexperienced central government after independence.
However, this was never done. Indeed, so effective

was the colonial policy at stifling African participation in their government and keeping them effectively divided that less than ten years before independence
the Wallis Commission, which recommended the reforms
in local government on which the 1955 legislation was
based, had to remark, "There is scarcely any feeling
yet among Africans for Uganda as a unified country
with a sense of common interest and common purpose."[14]

General Development

Education. One of the principal benefits of
colonization was, of course, education. When the explorer Morton Stanley first met Kabaka Mutesa of Buganda in April 1875, the Buganda ruler was already
promoting the study of Arabic around his court. The
Arabs of Zanzibar, who had been trading in ivory,
slaves, and cloth in Buganda since the reign of Kabaka
Suna, had introduced the reading and writing of their
language. But the spread of Arabic was arrested and
later practically eliminated with the advent of Christian missionaries into the kingdom, both Protestant
(1877) and Catholic (1879). Through energetic and
dedicated effort the Christian missionaries initiated
the task not only of spreading the ability to read
and write through their converts and churches, but
also of building schools, beginning in Buganda and
later spreading throughout the whole protectorate.
By 1900, schools were already being built. So effective was this missionary effort, relatively speaking,
that none of the members of the Ugandan Parliament,
district councils, or staffs of the civil service did
not have part of his education in a missionary institution by the time of independence in 1962. It is,
however, a demonstration of the indifference colonial
rule attached to educating the African that more than
a quarter of a century had to elapse from the beginning of the missionary effort before the protectorate
government decided to get involved in the education
of the African. Even then, the effort was limited
essentially to subsidizing missionary schools until
several years later when the government had to found
and promote its own educational institutions.
But there was a negative legacy in this otherwise
noble endeavor of Christian missionaries that was to
affect Ugandan politics adversely in decades to come.
The two groups of missionaries initially came from
either Britain (Protestants) or France (Catholics).
The two powers were traditional adversaries and this
affected their rivalry in the scramble for the African colonial empire. The missionaries were not immune

from the conflict between their respective origins and consequently each group harnessed support among its African converts to contend with the other. In fact, so acute had been this local conflict that a civil war was fought between the two groups in the latter years of the last century. It took the armed intervention of Captain Lugard, representing the Imperial British East Africa Company, to impose peace, siding with the victorious Protestants. A legitimate sense of grievance remained among the Catholics who felt cheated out of a fair share of positions in the Bugandan hierarchy and later in the other provinces of the protectorate, as is discussed later.

The highest college of learning, Makerere, did not award degrees to most students until the late 1950s. Even then, many African students had to go overseas for academic degrees in such vital subjects as agriculture, veterinary science, engineering, and related technological fields. At the time of independence only about 10 percent of Uganda's lawyers were African and the university taught no law. Consequently, the judiciary was almost exclusively expatriate with not a single African judge on the High Court. There was a predominant bias towards the arts when the pressing problems of development required a substantial emphasis on scientific and technical subjects. Local governments controlled primary education and later lower secondary education as well, although missionaries continued to own and run a significant portion of the schools. Governmental commitments in other fields notwithstanding, as the enrollment figures in the various levels of schools show in Table 2.1, education was not the high priority it should have been. In 1930 it was no more than 3 percent of the total budget; in 1940 it was no more than 8 percent of the total expenditure, and in 1960, within two years of independence, it was less than 20 percent. Obviously, it was neither free nor compulsory as only a small percentage of the population went to school.

Moreover, the syllabus in these schools never consciously sought to create an awareness of common nationality among the pupils, which would have been invaluable at this receptive age. The education system was geared, in effect, to the production of manpower to support the more efficient running of the colonial protectorate, and not to the development of potential leaders endowed with a correct awareness of their common future irrespective of their diverse ethnic or religious backgrounds.

TABLE 2.1 Uganda's Colonial Legacy

A. Education as of Independence, October 1962[a]

	Primary	Junior Secondary	Senior Secondary	Teacher Training	Technical
Number of schools	2,352	339	28	35	49
Number of pupils enrolled	387,966	25,942	4,580	3,372	2,858

B. Public Health as of June 1962

	Doctors Registered	Licensed	Dentists	Midwives	Nurses	Pharma-cists
Number of professionals	479	73	73	1,156	1,354	72

Total number of hospital beds = 6,675

C. Miles of Classified Roads as of October 1962

	Ministry of Works Bitumen	Gravel	Local Authority	Total
Number of miles	738	2,605	10,780	14,123

D. Licensed Motor Vehicles as of 1962

	Cars	Commercial Vehicles	Public Service Vehicles	Motorcycles	Total
Number of vehicles	22,244	9,583	611	7,175	39,613

E. Production and Sales of Electricity as of October 1962

	Sales Local	To Kenya	Power Station Use and Transmission Losses	Total Generated
Millions of kwh	228.79	188.90	35.34	453.03

F. Articles Handled by Post Offices in 1962

	Letters Internal	External	Intransit	Parcels Internal	External	Intransit
Thousands of items	15,660	8,628	7	77	91	0.2

TABLE 2.1 (Cont.)

G. Telephone Service in 1962

	Call Offices	Direct Exchange Lines	Extension Telephones	Other
Telephones in use	63	7,682	7,416	504

H. Ugandan Government Revenues and Expenditures for 1920–1960 (in Sterling)

Year	Revenue Less Imperial Loans	Total Revenue with Imperial Loans	Total Expenditures (with Loan Service)	Education Expenditures
1920	777,084 (9 mos.)	---	616,151	4,687
1930	1,412,241	1,412,241	2,047,092	65,065
1940	1,870,914	1,870,914	2,065,941	150,008
1950	10,603,043	11,036,702	8,000,382	566,306
1960	22,337,241		26,940,286	5,185,649

[a] These figures exclude the few schools that catered to non-Ugandans.
Source: Ministry of Economic Affairs, *Statistical Abstract for 1962* (Entebbe, Uganda: Government Printer, 1962).

Public Service. It was a measure of insufficient preparation for nationhood that at the time of self-government and independence almost all the vital positions in public service that were to sustain the independence government were filled by British officials and not Ugandans. There was not a single African district commissioner heading even a local district administration. At the time of self-government in 1961, all heads of important government departments were expatriate. The top echelons of the Army -- of which more is said later -- and the police were British nationals. It is true that during the five years or so preceding independence, there were more serious attempts to put Ugandans in responsible positions. But the acceleration of the process of creating a truly African public service had to await the independence government.

The private sector fared no better. Although the colonial government after 1900 had introduced coffee and cotton as leading cash crops, and although the African peasant farmer produced most of these cash crops on small holdings scattered throughout the country, the commercial life and benefits were firmly in the hands of expatriate companies. The Asians, originally brought to East Africa from the Indian subcontinent for railway construction, were now used

by the colonial administration to promote commerce
and trade in the protectorate. In the process, however, the African was exploited as he remained on the
periphery although his products were the heart of a
growing wealth for aliens who, as middlemen buying
his produce cheaply, exported them at handsome profit.
The economy followed a classical colonial pattern.[15]
On the one hand there was a small, relatively sophisticated sector catering to the expatriate class and
a handful of the African elite, and on the other hand
there was an overwhelming rural sector of African
farmers little touched by the money economy. The
country provided an exclusive preserve that functioned
as an imperial market for British products. Because
Britain had limited resources to expend on an extensive empire and because it jealously guarded against
the encroachment of other external capital and skill
into the colonies, it followed that the pace of development was relatively slow. Yet after more than sixty
years of stable rule, the British left behind, on the
whole, a substantial level of overall development.
The data in Table 2.1 indicate the basic range of
this colonial inheritance.

THE APPROACH OF INDEPENDENCE AND ITS PROBLEMS

The independence of the British empire in Asia
-- India, Pakistan, Ceylon, Burma, and Malaya -- was
a most encouraging signal to African nationalists
that emancipation could not be long delayed. Whatever serious doubts there might have been were banished
by the independence of Ghana in 1957, the first black
African country to become free. Suddenly, the issue
in Uganda became not whether the country would be
free but who was to inherit the mantle of power from
the departing colonialists and what security there
would be for each of the diverse ethnic groups in
the new state. Earlier we discussed the strength
and fundamental nature of ethnic group identity.
Most of these ethnic groups were in existence long
before colonial rule. Since the colonial system
kept them alive through indirect rule and the policy
of minimal interethnic contact, the idea of Britain
bequeathing a new state uniting all the diverse groups
with a government of nationalist politicians from
the different groups, some historically enemies,
generated intense fear in the country, most especially
among the group that had most to lose, the Baganda.

Bugandan Separatism

The Baganda, consisting of about 16 percent of
the Ugandan population, form the largest ethnic group.
As mentioned earlier, at the inception of colonial
rule the British found it expedient to base their
colonial government in this kingdom with the result
that in the early years of the protectorate Bugandan
agents in the service of the government were in most
districts of the country. The kingdom had a long and
proud history. As early as 1874, Morton Stanley, the
explorer, recorded how he was impressed by Kabaka
Mutesa's court, and to "have witnessed with astonishment as much order and law as is obtainable in semi-
civilized countries."[16] While Buganda had accepted
colonial rule, it was not about to have a local African politician of untried experience and integrity
inherit power upon independence. Accordingly, it set
out to seek its independence unilaterally more than
a decade before Uganda received its own. The colonial
government, however, was resolved to leave Uganda as
a single unitary state. Therefore, in 1953 Kabaka
Mutesa was banished to Britain by Governor Cohen principally because the kabaka and his government would
not retract their demand for a timetable for Buganda's
separate independence. Although Mutesa was reinstated
and his prestige enhanced with a new Anglo-Bugandan
Agreement in 1955 that granted the kingdom more autonomy, rather than diminishing, the fears increased
for the Baganda. Partly because of vigorous opposition to unilateral independence by nationalists from
other ethnic groups and partly because of the humiliating way Nkrumah had dealt with the Ashanti king in
Ghana after independence, Buganda became more than
ever determined to secede. They made it clear in
their memorandum to the British colonial secretary in
October 1960:

> Public pronouncements made on various occasions
> by people likely to be leaders of a future Uganda
> are not conducive to the idea of unity as Her
> Majesty's government envisages it. In order to
> avoid another "Katanga" in this country immedi-
> ately after Uganda's independence, Buganda has
> decided and is determined to go it alone.[17]

This and subsequent demands were rejected by the British government. The climax came on 31 December 1960,
when in a highly emotional atmosphere the Bugandan
Lukiko (parliament) declared the kingdom independent
as of the new year of 1961. Although this was a

futile gesture, rejected by the governor, it was now
manifest that urgent steps had to be taken to devise
a constitutional formula for a single Ugandan state
that would remove Buganda's fears on independence.
It will remain a debatable point whether or not Buganda was justified to want unilateral independence.
This question is discussed later, but we can state
here objectively that the nature of colonial administration was such that the need for a separate existence was strongly felt among the diverse peoples --
and especially among the largest and richest. Uganda
existed as a single state primarily in the eyes of
the colonizers who operated its central institutions
and planned for its overall development. However,
to the majority of Africans their true governments
were their ethnic (tribal) local governments with
which they had dealt most often as they had done even
before colonization. It came more naturally for the
individual and his leaders to identify with this basic
ethnic group, having been born into it, than with the
institutions of the central government or the overall
Ugandan structure as no African had exercised any
serious responsibility there until only one year before independence. In seeking its own survival, Buganda therefore had a logical case; however, its
choice of a solution -- secession -- was unrealistic
and consequently unwise. The reasons why secession
was unacceptable are discussed later.

The Western Kingdoms and the Districts

As independence loomed closer the smaller kingdoms of the western region (Ankole, Bunyoro, and Toro),
both emulated and opposed Buganda. Although they
could not seek secession because they were not viable,
they organized a pressure group against the colonial
administration to ensure the safety of their cultural
institutions in the coming new state. Through the
leaders of their local administrations, they sought
to make Uganda a federal union upon independence and
combined forces with Buganda on this point. But they
were unequivocally opposed to Buganda's bid for unilateral independence; together with representatives
from the rest of Uganda, they condemned the movement
in October 1960 and urged the colonial rulers to
keep Uganda united. These smaller kingdoms as well
as the other districts, while desirous of a single
state, wanted to be assured that they would not lose
out to wealthier Buganda. Yet, in the context of the
whole protectorate, though the Baganda were the largest single ethnic group, they were a real minority

representing only 16 percent of the population, as can be seen in Table 2.2. Their fears were consequently the fears of a minority group in the context of Uganda.

Thus there were fears among the diverse peoples of the protectorate that intersected. The power and fundamental pull of these ethnic fears is demonstrated in part by the fact that no political party dared defy them under the banner of immediate independence. Except for condemning Buganda's attempt to secede, which all non-Bugandan leaders did, the politicians were naturally influenced by the demands of their native groups. All leading parties had to concede, at least

TABLE 2.2   The Roots of Ugandan Nationals Based on the 1959 Census
(nationals making up less than 0.5% of the population and all aliens excluded)

Tribe	Total	Percentage of the Nation
Baganda	1,044,878	16
Banyankole	519,283	8
Basoga	501,921	8
Iteso	524,716	8
Bakiga	459,619	7
Lango	363,807	5.6
Bagisu	329,257	5
Acholi	284,929	4.4
Lugbara	236,270	3.7
Batoro	208,300	3.2
Banyoro	188,374	3
Karamajong	131,713	2
Alur	123,378	1.9
Bagwere	111,681	1.7
Bakonjo	106,890	1.7
Badama	101,451	1.6
Banyole	92,642	1.4
Madi	80,355	1.2
Kumam	61,459	1
Samia	47,759	0.7
Bagwe	36,130	0.6
Sebei	36,800	0.6
Kakwa	37,828	0.6
Bamba	34,506	0.5

Total population of all Nationals and Aliens: 6,449,558

Note: (1)   The Banyarwanda population of 378,656 (5.9%) was grossly exaggerated by inclusion of Rwanda Nationals, which was not distinguished here. It is therefore, excluded from the above table.

(2)   The current population (1978) of nearly 12 million still reflects the same composition.

in principle, the right of each group to seek their own safeguards in the independence settlement.

Political Parties

If we seem to have concentrated our discussion on the characteristics and demands of the ethnic groups with the approach of independence, it is because they dominated the political scene more fundamentally than did the political parties.[18] The first nationalist party, the Uganda National Congress (UNC), was not formed until 1952, half a century after the formation of the protectorate. Due to a variety of weaknesses, the UNC disintegrated. There were several small and relatively inconsequential parties, like the Progressive Party (1955), the United National Party (1960), and the United National Congress (1960). The parties, however, that influenced Uganda's future on the eve of independence and after are the Democratic Party, the Uganda People's Congress, and the Kabaka Yekka.

The Democratic Party (DP). Founded in 1954 and now headed by a leading Ugandan lawyer, Benedicto Kiwanuka, the DP had its origins directly in the injustices of colonial rule. It was launched by Roman Catholics who had been systematically discriminated against in both central and local government jobs since the Buganda intra-Christian wars of the last century. Although at its founding the party was essentially based in Buganda, it grew to embrace the whole protectorate, using its religious appeal to cut across ethnic loyalties. Six years before its rival was born, it was already fighting against discrimination in the Buganda kingdom administration, which kept DP membership out of public service. Since secession was barred, perhaps more than any other single factor the dread of the DP taking over power on independence led the protestant leadership of Buganda into forming an alliance in 1961 with the UPC, as is discussed later.

The Uganda People's Congress (UPC). Under the leadership of Milton Obote the UPC was formed as a result of two parties merging, the remnants of the Uganda National Congress and the Uganda People's Union (which had been predominantly non-Baganda). The UPC was formed in March 1960 with an avowed socialist policy but in truth there was up to the time of independence very little difference in basic policy between the UPC and the DP. It is quite astonishing

that this party, which formed the independence government in 1962, was formed as late as sixty years
after the British administration was established in
Uganda and inherited sovereign power when it was only
two and a half years old. It was therefore too rash
to condemn out of hand leaders of different ethnic
groups when they demanded safeguards in the independence struggle as these political parties and their
leaders were to them unknown and untested. All the
same, the UPC fitted the role of a nationalist party,
having the advantage that a few of its leaders had
been members of the Legislative Council since 1958 or
earlier and had taken part in debates demanding independence. After losing the first general election in
1961 to the DP, which formed the internal self-government, the UPC resolved to form an alliance with the
traditional leadership in Buganda in order to defeat
the DP and deny it the inheritance of the independence
government. This alliance was to appreciably determine the nature of the Independence Constitution and
the subsequent course of Uganda's stormy postindependence history.

The Kabaka Yekka (KY).[19] The overwhelming majority of the Baganda had boycotted the 1961 general
election while still holding out for more powers from
the British government. When wise counsel prevailed
and Bugandan leadership decided to be integrated into
the future state, they had only two practical alternatives: to form an alliance or to join either the
UPC or the DP. Only in this sense could they get
sufficient leverage to bargain for some autonomy at
the 1961 and 1962 conferences in London.

Obote, as leader of UPC, had never been enthusiastic about the Baganda. In and outside of the Legislative Council he had at times threatened to crush
them by force should he ever be in a position to do
so. Even when it was manifest after the defeat of
the UPC in the 1961 general election that his party
could not do without Buganda, it was only after much
pressure from his closest colleagues that he accepted
an alliance with the traditionalist government of
Buganda as the only viable option to power. We shall
dwell on this UPC/KY relationship in detail later.
However, it should suffice here to say that a UPC/
Buganda alliance was formed after a series of meetings
between Obote and myself (representing the UPC) and
representatives of the Bugandan government. During
these meetings we agreed that the UPC would support
the Bugandan demands at the 1961 Constitutional
Conference -- the details of which are included in

the discussions of the Independence Constitution --
in exchange for Buganda's support of the UPC in an
effort to unseat the DP. Thus, the UPC/Buganda
alliance went on to represent the majority of the
Ugandan population at the First Constitutional Conference in London in 1961, at which time the UPC supported Buganda's demands for reasonable autonomy and
safeguards for its cultural institutions, such as the
kabakaship. The internal self-government constitution
consequently reflected this arrangement, despite the
DP's strenuous efforts at the conference to deny some
of Buganda's demands, especially the option of the
Lukiko to sit as an electoral college to return all
of the twenty-one Bugandan representatives to Parliament.
     After the 1961 conference and in anticipation of
the preindependence elections and the independence
conference of 1962, the traditional Bugandan government formed a political movement, the Kabaka Yekka
(KY) which means "for Kabaka alone" -- about which
the Baganda, with their throne and traditions, were
overwhelmingly rallied. The Baganda denied that the
KY was a political party, largely because their government had a recent history of discrediting and
destroying political parties. But what is in a name?
For practical purposes it was a political party. Although the KY published no manifesto comparable to
those of the UPC or the DP, its objectives were as
well known. Simply stated, the KY was to uphold the
institutions and traditions of their kingdom. The
KY opened party branches, sponsored candidates, and
contested general and local elections, winning decisively in most of them. In May 1962, twenty-one
of their representatives formed a coalition government
with the Uganda People's Congress under Obote's leadership to lead the country to independence.

THE INDEPENDENCE SETTLEMENT

     The Ugandan Independence Constitution had to
meet two basic requirements that took into consideration: the strength and durability of the ethnic
identity of the several groups; the colonial policy
that had kept African leadership out of the unifying
institutions; and the new political parties, outwardly
vociferous and impressive, which were not yet able to
affect the fundamental thinking of the people. The
first requirement was that power had to be shared
between the center of government and the regions,
particularly between Buganda and the western kingdoms.

Second, although the center had to be strong enough to govern the new state, there had to be clauses entrenched in the constitution that restricted it from misuse of power. A commission was therefore appointed in December 1960 to examine these relationships and propose a basis for a new constitution. This commission, called the Munster Commission after its chairman, was one of the most important in Uganda's political and constitutional history and its proposals were enshrined in large measure in the Independence Constitution as they also had been in internal self-government.[20]

Before outlining the basic features of the Independence Constitution, it is important to mention that all significant groups in Uganda took part in its formation: the DP in opposition, the UPC in government, with representatives of all the districts and kingdoms in attendance. The atmosphere was free and frank under the chairmanship of the British authorities who, despite the faults we have cataloged, were now the impartial umpires seeking a fair, practicable settlement before they withdrew.

A federal union is one in which the central as well as the regional governments each have a sphere of operation, independent of the other.[21] Technically speaking, one could classify Uganda a federal union at the time of independence. This is because the constitution granted the kingdoms some exclusive powers to meet their fears. However, as these were principally relating to their traditions and customs, they were not considerable powers and it was false to make them seem so. In truth, however, because of the preponderant executive and legislative powers of the central legislature, Uganda was more of a semi-federal state. Let us give a few details.

Buganda

The Bugandan Lukiko was given exclusive power to legislate: (1) in matters relating to kabakaship, including succession and the rights and duties of the kabaka; (2) the public service of Buganda; and (3) Buganda public holidays.[22] Legislation regarding "taxation and matters relating thereto," which would have been an important exclusive power, was in fact made conditional to the agreement of the central government. Financial independence is a true measure of the extent of regional power; however, Buganda was to be heavily dependent on the central government, not only for the recurrent expenditures to maintain existing government obligations but also for their

expansion and development. The exclusive revenue
from graduated tax, rent for nonagricultural land and
property, market dues, fees, and fines could never
suffice. It is important to note that the central
government retained financial control over all the
monies given to Buganda to run extensive services and
that the officers of the central government had to be
satisfied that the monies had been properly spent.
On the other hand, the constitution gave exclusive
power to the central legislature over finance, including not only banking, money-lending, and control of
credit and insurance, but also external and internal
loans, including loans for the kabaka's government.[23]

Although Buganda had demanded an independent
judiciary with its own high court, there was created
by constitutional fiction a Bugandan High Court, whose
judges and their tenure of office were in fact entirely controlled by the central government.[24] The judges
of both the Ugandan and Bugandan High Courts were constituted of one and the same people. When they were
dealing with Bugandan cases, however, they had to
administer justice in the kabaka's name. Buganda's
attempt to have exclusive control of its own police
force had been rightly rejected, for as the Munster
Commission had warned, such a power could provide
opportunity to create tribal armies. While the kabaka
was to have a police force, it was to be under the
operational control of the inspector general of the
Ugandan police force.[25] Denied substantial independent sources of revenue and the control of its internal security, and with its concurrent legislative
power subjected to that of the Ugandan Parliament when
in conflict, it is obvious that Buganda was very dependent on the central government. Moreover, it was
stipulated that the executive power of the Bugandan
government was to be "so exercised as not to impede
or prejudice the exercise of the Executive Authority
of Uganda."

The only exclusive rights of the smaller kingdoms
referred to the traditional institutions of their
rulers and their customs.[26] They were to have "cabinet" governments with a chief minister (katikkiro)
and three additional ministers each, who were responsible to their elected kingdom assemblies. For practical purposes all their other relationships with the
center, barring minor exceptions, were like those of
the districts of the northern and eastern regions.
All these regional administrations were given responsibility to administer a wide range of services,
shown below, that gave their people a sense of involvement in nation building but at the same time placed

the ultimate responsibility in the central government.
It should not escape mention that all regional governments were now based on democratically elected regional councils for the districts and assemblies for the
kingdoms in order to maximize the people's involvement
in nation building. The services included the following:

1. Education Services: (a) primary schools, (b)
   junior secondary schools, (c) farm schools (up
   to the first eight years), (d) rural trade
   schools (up to the first eight years), and (e)
   homecraft centers (up to the first eight
   years).
2. Medical and Health Services: (a) dispensaries,
   health centers, subdispensaries, and aid posts;
   (b) maternity and child welfare services; (c)
   school health services; (d) control of com-
   municable diseases, including leprosy and
   tuberculosis, subject to the overall responsibility of the minister of health; (e) rural
   ambulance services; and (f) the provision of
   environmental hygiene and health education
   services.
3. Water Supplies: the construction and maintenance of rural water supplies, subject to
   international obligations and to the approval
   and supervision of the Ugandan government.
4. Roads: maintenance and construction of roads,
   other than roads maintained by the Ugandan
   Ministry of Works.
5. Prisons: in addition to general mandatory
   powers, the prison administrators were given
   permissive functions, covering an extensive
   range of subjects, if they felt competent to
   perform them.[27]

The districts were each entrusted with the general
duty "to assist in the maintenance of order and good
government within the area of its authority." The
provisions of the 1955 ordinance, which entrusted
local governments with the responsibility of maintaining law and order, were repeated. With the consent of the Ugandan government they were empowered
to set up police forces for the execution of this
responsibility. These administrations were empowered
to make laws with respect to (a) any matter for which
they were required or permitted to make laws, (b) personal and customary laws, (c) public security, and (d)
functions they were required or permitted to carry
out. But all these were powers delegated from the

center, which had the ultimate right to withdraw or
curtail them if abused.

Power at the Center

A Ugandan Parliament was established as the sovereign legislature of the new state. It consisted of
the governor general, representing the Queen in purely
a ceremonial role, and an elected National Legislative
Assembly, consisting of eighty-one elected representatives, from whom a Cabinet was formed, headed by a
prime minister with a majority in the Assembly. Perhaps the most important safeguards for the so-called
federal states, like Buganda, was not their exclusive
legislative competence, which as we said was quite
limited, but the restraint put on this national parliament when passing certain types of legislation
affecting these regions.

There were intricate and detailed provisions
stipulating the conditions under which the Parliament
could alter the constitution affecting the federal
states, even if such amendments were national in
character and consequence. For example, Parliament
could not legislate abolition of the option of indirect elections for Buganda's twenty-one representatives to the National Assembly; it could not alter
the content of Buganda's executive authority; it
could not vary provisions relating to the police
forces of Buganda and Uganda; it was denied power to
make alterations in the sources of Buganda's financial
provisions; and it could not change the privileges
of the kabaka unless the Legislative Assembly of the
kingdom of Buganda, by resolution of not less than
two-thirds of all its members, signified its consent
that any act of Parliament touching on these matters
should have effect in Buganda.

There were similar provisions for the relations
with the other federal states. No amendment to the
Charter of Human Rights could take effect in any federal state unless it had been ratified in each state
by a two-thirds majority of all members of its Assembly.[28] Parliament was denied the legal right to alter
the constitutions of the federal states described in
the Ugandan Constitution. Finally, a bill for an act
of Parliament altering any other provision of the
constitution could not pass into law unless it had
been supported on second and third readings by votes
of not less than two-thirds of all the members of the
National Assembly.

On the face of it, such restrictions on the national legislature may appear too restrictive and

therefore unwise. But it should be observed that the
central legislature was not <u>denied</u> a power; it was
only required to fulfill certain procedural criteria
of consent by the prescribed majorities of those affected. Potentially, therefore, the central legislature was very powerful. An example from Ghana illustrates this point. Although the Ghanaian Independence
Constitution was not federal, it gave reasonable devolution of authority to regional assemblies. The
Parliament could not vary such powers or any others
entrenched in the constitution unless a two-thirds
majority were in support both in Parliament and the
regional assemblies. Once Nkrumah's Convention People's party had the prescribed majority at the center
and in regions and wanted a change, the constitution
was amended and regional assemblies abolished constitutionally. It is immaterial to this argument to
determine whether or not this was desirable. But if
the constitutional provision had simply stated a
prohibition (as opposed to granting a power subject
to procedural requirements, which it did not), it
would have been far more restrictive. The difference
between Ghana and Uganda here was that, unlike the
CPP, the UPC was too weak to muster the necessary
majorities in the regions to reform the constitution
so instead of seeking the necessary majorities through
the political process, its leadership opted to take
the short cut of abrogating the constitution by force.

Moreover, the central legislature had other significant exclusive powers to make laws.[29] These included: external affairs; defense; the internal jurisdiction, powers, practice, procedures, and organization
of the courts; the public service of Uganda; and all
medical and veterinary services. The powers of the
central government, therefore, under the independence
settlement were not inconsiderable. The crucial
issue was to be how and why the UPC government would
use them, for that was to determine whether or not
this constitution survived.

The independence settlement had been designed
to meet the realities of the country's history and
its diverse people. It was not unworkable. But
unfortunately its successful operation presupposed
a degree of integrity and skill that its heirs did
not possess. Because there had been no sufficient
period under colonial guidance to try it out, to
have the various groups adjust to the distribution
of its powers and checks, to evolve a mechanism of
resolving any political conflict in its operation,
it could not withstand the machinations of leaders
bent on seizing power at all costs.

3
Nigeria

COLONIZATION AND ADMINISTRATION

The Federal Republic of Nigeria with about 70
million people and over 250 ethnic groups is Africa's
most populous state and one of the leading members
in the Organization of African Unity (OAU). But the
imperfections of its colonial inheritance have substantially contributed to its violent upheavals that
occurred only a few years after independence. What
were these imperfections? In what ways did the British colonizers impose and maintain them? What role,
if any, did Nigerian leaders themselves play in their
perpetuation, both before and especially after independence?
    British contact with coastal Nigeria dates back
several centuries to the days of the slave trade. Although British colonization began with the annexation
of Lagos in 1861, it was not until the beginning of
this century that Nigeria as a geopolitical entity
was established. The colonization process took the
two principal forms: acquiring jurisdiction through
unequal treaties with local rulers (especially in the
South), and outright military conquest of the northern
Moslem emirates, using the West African Frontier Force
in 1902-1903. There were two distinct colonial entities: the North on the one hand, and the South, with
its protectorate and colony, on the other. The inhabitants of both were fundamentally different.[1]
    Although the country had more than two hundred
minority ethnic groups (some of whom were to lead
separatist movements to establish their own regions,
as we shall see), there were four predominant ethnic
groups in Nigeria. In the North were the preponderant
Hausa, a people with ancient traditions and civilization. Their city-states of Kano and Katsina had become leading commercial centers of trade with Morocco

37

by the Middle Ages. Kano could trace its history
through forty-eight kings dating back to 999. About
the thirteenth century the Fulani immigrated from the
east and joined the Hausa, and both groups became
converted to Islam. It was the Fulani Moslem reform-
er, Usuman dan Fodio, however, who established the
Islamic empire of the North through a holy war (Ji-
had), which he waged in the region to a successful
conclusion by 1831. This Fulani/Hausa empire was
administered on priciples analogous to European feudalism, although its main religions and cultural links
were with the Middle East. The two principal rulers
of this empire were centered at Kano and Katsina.
Below them were local rulers, known as emirs, who in
turn headed a pyramid of officials of district and
village heads. It was largely the descendants of
these rulers that the British conquered in 1902-1903
and nearly sixty years later granted independence
together with other Nigerians.

In the western part of southern Nigeria, the
Yoruba people were predominant. At the advent of
British rule they were split into four states and were
on the decline principally because of the disruption
of slave wars. Some of their groups at Ilorin had
been overrun by the northern expansionism before
colonization, and demands for their return to western
Nigeria on independence was to form one of the most
divisive issues that emanated from precolonial history.
The Yoruba were a monarchial people and some of their
kingdoms, such as Ife, had long and illustrious
histories.

The predominant group in the southeast, the Ibo,
were very distinct from both the Hausa/Fulani and the
Yoruba in the fundamental sense that they did not
have the central authority of these monarchial systems,
but instead administered themselves through scattered
extended families.

THE UNBALANCED AMALGAMATION OF NORTH AND SOUTH IN 1914

In January 1914 Sir Frederic Lugard, then governor of Nigeria, amalgamated the two areas, the North
and the South, under one governor-general and with
this act laid the foundations of one of the worst
colonial errors in the country's history. There was
no conception of a future independent Nigeria, no
plan for the predominant ethnic groups and numerous
minorities -- with very different histories -- to
attain mutual accommodation, nor, of course, for any
future government. Because colonial administration

was considered indefinite, what concerned Lugard
in the administration of Nigeria, consequently, were
the solutions of the administrative problems of the
moment in order to make colonial rule more efficient.
 Nigeria on unification consisted of two provinces: The North, with an area of 255,700 square
miles; and the South, with only 76,684 square miles.
The populations had been grossly misrepresented, with
the North put at 9 million and the South erroneously
at only 1.5 million less. In a country of 250 ethnic
groups only two unequal regional centers of power
were being created -- one for the preponderant Fulani/
Hausa empire in the North and the other for the South.
Yet, this would have been the right time to have
divided the North into several more regions, which
would have made states of the future self-governing
federation. This could only have been envisioned
with a definite long-term program. This program, of
course, was nonexistent. The creation of more regions,
especially from the vast North, was rejected deliberately for purely short-term administrative reasons.
As Lugard reported regarding this exercise of amalgamation: "The simultaneous creation of 4 to 7 new governments, the distribution from existing secretariats
of the records belonging to each, and the absence of
buildings for public offices, would all add to the
difficulty and postpone effective amalgamation for
many years."[2] For the future benefit of Nigeria, it
would have been preferable to postpone amalgamation
until these practical difficulties were overcome
rather than to effect it with such preponderant imbalance, jeopardizing future stability. The failures
inherent in this unbalanced amalgamation were further
enhanced by Lugard's own systematic plan of keeping
the natives divided as the most effective way of governing them. Candidly, he reported in 1918 "that
safety in so vast a country controlled by a handful
of British, lies in the maxim Divide et Impera."[3]
Not only were the North and South different in their
precolonial history, but British colonization, which
brought them together, did so by accentuating differences in size of territory, population, and administration. When Lugard conquered the North, the South
had already been exposed to Western education and
influences for half a century. Moreover, the North
was kept more or less an exclusive preserve of Islamic
culture, discouraging the advent of missionaries for
many decades. This denied it the benefits of their
Western education when it was becoming the yardstick
for advancement in the new Nigeria. Table 3.1 illustrates the unbalanced development. The doctrine of

TABLE 3.1   Nigeria's Colonial Legacy

Education and health are used to illustrate the uneven development of Nigeria throughout the colonial experience. It should be remembered when looking at them that the population of the North equaled or exceeded that of the East and West *combined.*

A. Primary Education as of Independence, 1960

	Northern Region	Eastern Region	Western Region	Lagos Region
Number of schools	2,600	6,451	6,540	112
Number of teachers	10,054	44,478	40,115	2,160
Pupils: Boys	206,443	896,334	687,215	39,479
Girls	76,405	534,180	437,573	34,989
Total school population	282,848	1,430,514	1,124,788	74,568

Source: Nigerian Federal Ministry of Education, *Digest of Education Statistics,* 1960.

B. Secondary Schools as of Independence, 1960

North		East		West		Lagos	
No. of Schools	Pupils	No. of Schools	Pupils	No. of Schools	Pupils	No. of Schools	Pupils
41	6,264	113	22,137	700	101,249	29	5,714

Source: Federal Ministry of Education, Lagos, *Annual Abstract of Statistics, 1963,* p. 166.

C. Hospital Beds as of Independence, 1960

Type of Hospital Beds	North	East	West	Lagos
General hospitals and nursing homes	59	4,847	3,200	760
Special hospitals	16	523	1,080	727
Infectious disease hospitals	15	82	57	192
Maternity centers, clinics and rural health centers	642	2,240	2,033	300

Source: Adapted from Federal Ministry of Health Statistics, *Federal Republic of Nigeria Annual Abstract of Statistics, 1964,* p. 173.

indirect rule flourished in the North, although it met mixed success among the Yoruba and failed among the Ibo, who rejected the introduction of institutionalized chiefs to make it work.

REGIONAL POWER VERSUS NATIONAL UNITY

Theoretically Nigeria had become one colony. But only its colonial administrators who centrally initiated and administered it could conceptualize its unity, as they related all facets of regional and central government to a common geopolitical entity. However, to the indigenous people and to the majority of their leaders, the real state was the regional structure, North, South, East, and West. It was the native administrations of these regions that affected the Africans in their daily lives and engaged indigenous leaders while Nigeria with its central institutions of the executive, legislative, and judiciary, manned decisively by alien rulers as they were, remained remote and rather exotic. For nearly half a century after amalgamation, there was no central institution that united the North and the South until the Richards Constitution of 1947.

Once it was certain that the British were prepared to grant Nigeria independence, a fierce struggle understandably ensued -- not against the colonizer but between the nationalist parties that represented these diverse peoples -- first to determine how much power each region would control, and later to determine who would inherit the central government on independence. It is fitting to mention briefly the leading Nigerian political parties whose views shaped the Independence Constitution and decisively influenced postindependence developments.[4]

Leading Political Parties

The National Council of Nigerian Citizens (NCNC). The NCNC was formed in 1944 from a collection of associations, clubs, and labor and ethnic unions with the express purpose of obtaining independence for Nigeria within the Commonwealth; it advocated a "socialist commonwealth." Although it was a nationalist party at inception (with Herbert Macauly, a Yoruba, as president; and Dr. Nnamdi Azikiwe, a leading nationalist and an Ibo, as its secretary-general), it increasingly became identified as an Ibo-dominated party and it alienated the Yoruba. Nationalist as he was, some of Dr. Azikiwe's pronouncements could not but confirm the label. In 1949 he publicly asserted; "It would appear that the God of Africa has specially created the Ibo nation to lead the children of Africa from the bondage of the ages. . . . The martial prowess of the Ibo nation at all stages of human history has enabled them not only to conquer others but also to adapt themselves to the role of preserver."[5] With such an approach, the NCNC could speak principally only for the Ibo as the other predominant groups became resentful and formed their own parties.

Action Group (AG). The Yoruba's answer to the
Ibo-dominated NCNC was the formation by Obafemi Awolowo of the Action Group in 1951, a political party
deriving its strength from the Egbe Omo Oduduwa
(formed in 1948), a Yoruba cultural organization.
Although its membership was to be theoretically national without regard to religion or ethnic orgin,
the party was a regional and ethnic one, predominantly
geared to cater to the Yoruba of West Nigeria. They,
like the NCNC, were dedicated to the immediate end
of British colonial rule.

The Northern People's Congress (NPC). The North
hurriedly formed the NPC from a number of cultural
groups to contest the first all-Nigeria elections of
1951, being acutely apprehensive of their late start
in Western-type politics, an area where the rest of
the developing nation had a definite edge. The stand
of this party on all the major issues that faced an
emerging Nigeria, as we shall relate, had a decisive
influence on the future shape and stability of the
country. Because the party's leadership was drawn
mostly from the traditional rulers and because of the
relative backwardness of the North, NPC policy was
generally the most conservative of all Nigerian parties. To excape southern domination, a legitimate
fear, the NPC unfortunately sought protection in excessive and sometimes unreasonable demands for regional
autonomy within a united Nigeria (just as the Ashanti
in Ghana and the Baganda in Uganda had done). These
demands largely determined the federal nature of
Nigeria.
The leaders of these political parties, denied
an effective role in the central institutions of the
colony, devoted their energies to building more regional power that resulted in further dividing Nigeria.
The division became clearer than ever in 1950 -- only
a decade before independence -- when they met at the
General Conference to review the Nigerian Constitution.[6] Three divisive issues emerged that were to
vitiate the country's stability for decades to come
and were largely a result of colonial lack of fore-
sight. Let us look at them briefly.

Representation in the Central Legislature

Lugard, as we said, had created a Nigeria in
which one region, the North, was greater in population
and territory than the rest combined. His successors

had the power to reform the structure but chose to
maintain it. When it became clear that the British
intended to depart, there was acute anxiety and fear
among the people in the South, represented largely
by the NCNC and the AG, that the North might permanently dominate the new state. The South, therefore,
sought alternative formulas that would give them security. First, they proposed the division of the North
into more states to meet the wishes of many minorities
there, which we shall consider later. Because the
North resisted this, they then sought a division of
powers between the two houses of a bicameral parliament, where representation in the Senate would be on
the basis of the number of regions in Nigeria and not
by the population as in the House of Representatives.
On the other hand, because the North was the least
touched by the modernizing influence of the colonial
experience, it felt convinced that if it did not control a future central government to enable it to redress the balance of development, it would be perpetually dominated by the more enlightened southerners.
Its leaders in the NPC, therefore, demanded to have
at least 50 percent of the seats in the Nigerian
central legislature and often threatened to secede
if their demands were not met. Because of their preponderance and tenacity, they were given this concession and with it -- unlike in any other federation --
the assurance that their region was to dominate the
nation in perpetuity. This violated a fundamental
prerequisite of sound federalism, which rejects the
existence of one member in a union being so predominant as to dominate the rest combined.[7]

Financial Sources for the Regions

Unbalanced development had ensured that the
largest, most populous part of the nation, the North,
received the least financial resources. The northern
provinces contributed 42 percent of the central revenue
and yet, according to the prevailing allocation of the
central government revenue, on a per capita basis it
received 4 shillings, 2 pence. On the other hand,
the West, which contributed 27 percent, received 9
shillings, 8 pence; and the East, contributing 31 percent, received 10 shillings. From the point of view
of taxation, the North contributed 3 shillings, 10
pence per person; the East, 2 shillings, 3.5 pence per
person; and the West, 2 shillings, 8.5 pence. It
therefore seemed undeniable that the North, which was
overtaxed, received the least funds on a population
basis and quite legitimately had to demand a more

equitable formula for revenue sharing and taxation.[8]
A committee of experts had to draw up a compromise,
making a substantial part of yearly grants dependent
upon the number of adult male taxpayers within each
region and recommending ₤2 million to the North for
past deficiencies. This sum, however, was not enough
nor could it compensate for half a century of colonial
neglect.

Revision of Boundaries and the Minority Issues

    Some of the most bitterly contested issues be-
tween the leading Nigerian nationalists involved the
persistent demands to revise regional boundaries and
concerned the protection of minorities in all regions,
which the colonial structure had done little to correct and much to perpetuate. The AG demanded a return
of Ilorin (inhabited by the Yoruba) from the North to
their fellow Yorubas of the West. The North refused
to yield an inch of its territory as Lugard had incorporated it on amalgamation and governor Macpherson
supported it. Each of the predominant ethnic groups
demanded more regional power at the Lagos conference,
the North taking the lead, and set the stage for a
federal Nigeria, which was initiated under the Macpherson Constitution of 1951. It was this demand for
regional power that greatly heightened the fears of
minorities within each region and unleashed the persistent demands for the creation of more regions in
the federation. As Mr. M. G. Ejaife, a representative
from the West, rightly observed: "If a region as
large as the North can have such fears as make them
hesitate to concede their points, it is understandable
that minor tribes in Nigeria must be anxious that
adequate and unmistakable provisions are made to safeguard their survival, and the assurance of a place
for them in the New Nigeria."[9]
    Every region had many minorities and we look at
them because their treatment both under colonial and
especially independence rule contributed to national
instability later on. The northern region had three
principal minority separatist movements. First, in
the southern part of the non-Moslem North, the Tiv
people were steadily demanding their autonomy and
separate state under the leadership of J. S. Tarka.
They formed the United Middle Belt Congress (UMBC)
that initially included the largely Yoruba provinces
of Ilorin and Kabba and proposed a middle belt state
comprised of its minorities. But after the Constitutional Conference of 1957, the AG and the UMBC made a
deal under which the UMBC would renounce claims to

the Yoruba provinces of the North, which the AG wanted
for the West, and in exchange, the AG would support
UMBC claims for a separate state. The second minority
groups in the North were the Yoruba of Ilorin, whom
the AG had successfully courted, and who formed an
alliance that won parliamentary seats to the northern
House of Assembly. The third separatist group was in
Bornu. Though Islamic, the Kanuri of Bornu had a
separate tradition and in 1958 it allied with the AG
against the NPC.

It was in the West, however, that the most dynamic minority separatist movement developed among the
Edo-speaking peoples of the renowned kingdom of Benin,
which had a glorious history comparable to any Yoruba
monarchy. The people here, in 1953, formed the Benin
Delta Peoples' party, aimed at the creation of a Benin
Delta state, with the oba (king) as its leader. Its
name was changed to become the Midwest State Movement,
an outwardly nonpartisan organization whose primary
objective was the creation of its own state. In the
eastern region too, there was minority separatism.
The city states of the Efik and Ijaw peoples had a
long and illustrious precolonial history and resented
the domination of the preponderant Ibo.

All these minorities had existed largely as independent distinct groups before colonization, with different languages, customs, and social organization. On
colonization, they had been put together in each region
with a predominant group that cared little for their
interests and controlled all the power. As long as the
colonial rulers were still in control, constituting impartial arbiters of last resort, the minorities could
live, though uneasily, with their majority rulers. But
the prospect of the departure of the colonial arbiters
struck considerable fear among them as they sensed they
would not receive justice. Thus their demands for separate regions proliferated as independence approached.

Findings and Recommendations of the Minorities
Commission

The British set up a Minorities Commission in
1957 to inquire into the fears of these minorities
and to recommend the ways of allaying them. Its
findings, because of their lack of accuracy, were as
significant in enhancing the prospects of instability
in the country as had been Lugard's uneven amalgamation more than four decades before. To start with,
its terms of reference clearly discouraged the creation
of more states when they said "if, but only if" no
other solution seemed to meet the need, then as a last

<u>resort</u> were they to make detailed recommendations for
the creation of one or more new states. The Commission's membership was exclusively British. The Commission noted that in the three regions "all who gave
evidence wanted a new state rather than constitutional
safeguards of another type."

The Western Region. Actions of the regional government pointed to the deliberate intention of obliter-
ating the separate language, culture, and institutions
of the midwest. Midwesterners were referred to by
derogatory epithets in the western region. Areas of
complaint covered discrimination in the maintenance
of public order, discrimination in the economic field,
provision of public services, parliamentary seats,
conduct of elections, chiefs and local government
councils, and domination on important regional boards,
such as the Production Development Board and the Finance Corporation and the Marketing Board.

The Eastern Region. Similar fears were found
regarding the holding of public posts and services,
economic and social discrimination, local government,
and chiefs. Public order was an issue because the
NCNC party goons of Dr. Azikiwe, the "Zikist National
Vanguard," were used to subdue the opposition by violent means.

The Northern Region. This area harbored comparable fears among the minorities. Moreover, there was
additional fear of religious intolerance among the
non-Moslems and fear of Moslem law, which was discriminatory in nature. The United Middle Belt Congress
pressed for a middle belt state allied to the AG,
covering the Yorubas of Ilorin, Kabba, and Benue. In
the plateau province, the Biroms were strongly in
favor of a new state. Both the AG and NCNC, it is
important to note, were disposed toward the creation
of more states, provided it was done in every region.
But the North hotly defended its indivisibility.[10]
Moved principally by practical considerations of
administration, in a singular act of ignorance about
the power and tenacity of ethnic identity, the Commission recommended against the creation of any new
states in Nigeria before independence. This was the
recommendation the British government wanted to hear.
It ensured a federation in which not only one region
by virtue of its preponderant size had permanent ascendency, but also the unambiguous wishes of most
minorities for new regions in the federation went
unheeded. The Commission recommended provisions of

fundamental human rights in the constitution but
this was not enough to allay minority fears. These
could be -- and were -- often ignored by regional
majorities committed to the policies of the winner-
take-all philosophy, as we shall see, which only
intensified the demands for new regions in the postindependence period.

THE LACK OF LEADERSHIP EXPERIENCE FOR INDEPENDENCE

     To the immense structural problems of the Niger-
ian federation, which came formally into being with
the constitution of 1953, was added the serious draw-
back of the inexperience in government of the Nigerian nationalist leaders who were to inherit leadership
on independence. Their opportunity for working together to run the federation had been limited. They
had been unable to get the feel of government from a
central focus through prolonged legislative and executive experience in the federal government or to learn
how to handle power for Nigeria's diverse peoples. As
was the case elsewhere, the vigor and enterprise of
the nationalist leaders was channelled consistently
into their regional ethnic governments, which had the
tendency -- desired by the colonizers -- to keep a
united Nigeria out of focus nationally.
     Not only did the North and South come together in
a common legislature as late as 1947, but the Richards
Constitution, which introduced a majority of Nigerians
to the legislature that year, ensured that only four
were directly elected, these being the only ones who
could speak for the people. Even when regional legislatures were established for the East, West, and North
in 1951, they were predominantly composed of indirectly elected representatives. Consequently, a few of
the Nigerians who were at this time appointed to ministerial office at both federal and regional levels
had little assurance that when the era of universal
franchise came they would not be defeated and their
experience lost to the country. It cannot be overemphasized that the first Nigerian prime minister,
Tafawa Balewa, and a fully indigenous council of ministers did not come into existence until 1957, only
three years before independence. It was at this time,
too, that the eastern and western regions became self-
governing in internal matters, to be followed by the
North two years later. Therefore, the Nigerians had
only three of the sixty years of colonial rule for
serious experience in the art of exercising real power.
Heads of government departments, the army, and the

police were all expatriate. Of the few hundred Nigerians in fairly senior federal government posts, only
twenty-eight came from the most populous region.[11]
Such experience as had been attained by nationalists
in government had been unevenly shared, as indicated
previously. For this reason even the demands for
self-government and independence were seldom unanimous.
For example, in 1953 Chief Anthony Enaharo moved a
motion in the Nigerian House of Representatives demanding self-government for Nigeria in 1956. While it was
vigorously supported by all major southern nationalists, it was unequivocally rejected by the North as
premature because it felt a desperate need for longer
colonial rule to catch up with the South. The leading
northern spokesman, the Sardaunan of Sokoto, stated
their case:

> The North are the best judges of their own situ-
> ation and we feel that in our present situation
> we cannot commit ourselves to fixing a date for
> the attainment of self-government. . . . It is
> true that we politicians always delight in talk-
> ing loosely about the unity of Nigeria. Sixty
> years ago, there was no country called Nigeria.
> . . . In 1914 the North and South were amalga-
> mated though the administration of the two sec-
> tions are distinctly different. . . . Since then
> no serious attempt has been made by the British
> or by the people themselves to come together and
> each section has looked on the other with suspi-
> cion and misgiving.[12]

After reviewing the poor colonial record on the unification of Nigeria, the Sardaunan rejected the motion
saying, "with things in their present state in Nigeria,
the Northern Region does not intend to accept the invitation to commit suicide."
   But the pace of constitutional development had so
quickened in the 1950s that the Richards Constitution
of 1947 was revised after only two years while the
North had expected to gather experience under it for
nine years. When Nigeria attained independence in
1960, therefore, the independence leaders inherited a
deeply divided country troubled with conflicts that
predated the colonial powers that had governed them by
the credo of "divide and rule." The federation was
fated by its colonial experience to a stormy postindependence period due to (1) the inherent imbalance where
the least developed region had assured ascendency; (2)
the primordial pull of ethnicity, where individuals
sought protection in their established ethnic groups

and not in the fragile institutions of the new state; and (3) the native leaders' lack of experience in sharing power and administering Nigeria jointly.

One cannot help but ask what would have happened if (1) Lugard had created a Nigeria of comparable regions, splitting up the North, and (2) responsible self-government had been granted the future leaders of independent Nigeria for the last half of colonial rule (three decades), the British retaining ultimate responsibility for external affairs and defense, intervening in government only when necessary. Such things would probably not have eliminated the tensions inherent in most multiethnic societies, as the experience of older nations indicates. But they would have given the country and its leaders an even chance for success. Quite probably they would have made interethnic tensions containable by building more trust between different groups, they would have averted the subsequent horrendous civil war because leaders would have learned the uses and limits of power, and they would have necessarily cultivated the indispensable quality of tolerance, with a colonial presence at hand to check abuses and assist in formulating any adjustments.

4
Ghana

The Republic of Ghana, called the Gold Coast until independence, occupies a respected position in
Africa for two reasons. <u>First, it was the first black
state to become independent from colonial rule</u>. Second, its first head of government, Kwame Nkrumah, led
Ghana's independence struggle, later playing a significant role in African and Third World affairs. If
there was to be substantial evidence of sound preparation for independence by the colonial power, it is
here that one should find it. By independence in
1957, it had been under colonial rule for more than
113 years. What are the facts?

Although British jurisdiction took a foothold
on the coast in 1844, for more than three decades the
administration of the area was affected by other colonial commitments in West Africa. Consequently, at
times it was ruled jointly with Sierra Leone (1821-
1850 and 1866-1874) and at other times jointly with
Lagos (1850). It was not until 1874 that the Gold
Coast was declared a distinct colony with its own
colonial administration that continued uninterrupted
until independence. When its consolidation as a
political, geographical region was completed, British
influence had been implanted unevenly throughout the
country. It was strongest in the coastal areas because this was the position from which inland expansion had taken place and it had experienced external
contact for centuries. In the middle of the country
lay the Ashanti, who for more than a century had val-
iantly fought incessant wars resisting British pene-
tration until they were conquered in 1896 and annexed
as a British possession in 1901 with the help of
coastal troops, such as the Fanti. With the conquest
of the Ashanti, the way was open for British expansion
northward, which led to the last act of colonization
in the Gold Coast, the acquisition of jurisdiction

over the northern territories that embraced diverse
ethnic groups who were largely Moslem. A total of
more than thirty-four principal ethnic groups had
been put together by the British as the inhabitants
of the embryonic Ghanaian state. In what manner were
they given an opportunity to share in the administration of the colony and to acquire ample experience
for running it on independence?

COLONIAL ADMINISTRATION: LOCAL AND CENTRAL GOVERNMENTS

     As already stated, one of the distinct character-
istics of British colonial rule was decentralization
of authority. As far as possible each ethnic group,
together with its neighbors, was placed in an administrative unit that administered the daily affairs
of that particular group. This unit was under the
immediate control of a British administrative officer
who would transmit colonial orders and laws to the
people through a hierarchy of indigenous chiefs or
traditional rulers. Although attempts to introduce
indirect rule on the northern Nigerian model never
worked here, local administrations of African masses
were considerably dependent on the indigenous systems
of chieftaincy. Consequently, ethnic groups were
kept essentially separated, each preoccupied with affairs in its ancestral area, although at the same time
united in the overall structure of the central colonial government, seemingly remote and run exclusively
by colonial administrators.
     In the Gold Coast, therefore, the story was fund-
amentally the same as in the rest of the British African empire. Although the Legislative Council was
established here in 1874 to administer and develop
the colony and there were no British settlers claiming
to monopolize political power (as happened in South
Africa), it took seventy-seven years for an African
to exercise limited executive responsibility in the
Gold Coast government. When Kwame Nkrumah's party
won the first general election in February 1951, it
was the first time for an African, not only in Ghana
but in all black Africa. His government and party,
who hitherto had merely played a secondary role in
the government of their own country, were to inherit
power on independence and had only six years in which
to learn the extremely complex art of governing a
diverse multiethnic community.
     It is true that more Africans had been involved
in the colonial administration here than in any other
British black colony. As early as 1889 the first

African had been <u>nominated</u> by the governor to become
a member of the Legislative Council. In the early
days of British rule, indeed, there had been an unusual degree of Africanization of government administration. In the nineteenth century there had not only
been African district commissioners, but also a number
of the most senior posts were held by Africans and
persons of mixed European and African blood, of whom
Governor Bannerman was a leading example. But this
was not a deliberate policy to instruct the indigenous
peoples systematically in the art of government.
Rather, it was an expediency because the unhealthiness,
heat, and mosquitoes of the area made conditions in the
initial stages of colonization extremely hazardous
for most British colonial administrators. By the
beginning of the twentieth century these health obsta-
cles were manageable, and the initial policy of Africanization was discontinued. For more than five decades to come all the decisions and policies that
mattered in the Gold Coast were initiated and implemented by colonial administrators, the indigenous
people playing only a supporting role. Nkrumah was
not exaggerating in 1956, only a few months before
independence, when he observed: "Africans were not
only excluded from government but also from almost
all sections of commerce and business including the
retail trade. Until recently not only the public service, but the commercial and business life of the
country was in the hands of strangers and people from
overseas."[1]

The reforms did not arrive until after World War
II, and by then the dominant nationalists had lost
their patience for giving them a long trial run. In
1946 the Burns Constitution (named after the incumbent
governor) was introduced to meet nationalist demands
for independence. However, its concessions were inadequate because effective power still rested with
the governor and Africans were still essentially in
an advisory capacity. Discontent errupted, and rioting and disturbances swept through the streets of
Accra. The governor had to set up the Watson Commission to investigate the causes of the unrest and to
propose remedies. In 1948, more than a century after
British colonization began and more than half a century after colonial administration was operational
in all Ghana, this Commission could still report,

> The Constitution and government of the country
> must be reshaped so as to give every African of
> ability an opportunity to help to govern the
> country, so as not only to gain political exper-

54

> ience, but also to experience political power.
> We are firmly of opinion that anything less than
> this will only stimulate national unrest. Gov-
> ernment through advisory committees [under the
> Burns Constitution] as a measure of reform in
> our view is quite unacceptable.[2]

The colonial administration responded to this by
setting up the Coussey Commission to formulate a more
acceptable constitution under which the first general
election on universal adult franchise was based. Once
it was clear that the British intended to hand over
power to indigenous leaders, an intense struggle ensued among the diverse groups in the country to determine which ones would inherit this power. For those
who would not inherit it, it became imperative to obtain sufficient safeguards for their respective groups
in the future self-governing state. Why were these
demands made for federalism, for entrenched rights in
the Constitution, and why were threats of secession
made in case no devolution of power was conceded?
Substantially for the same reasons as in most other
colonies. We repeat, although the colonial experience
had put the diverse ethnic groups together, colonial
rule ensured that each group maintained its precolonial identity, with minimal intergoup/interethnic
dealings, especially in matters of government.
It has been strongly argued that there was no
tribalism in Ghana. For example, the rivalries between the Ashanti, Brong, Fanti, and other southerners
-- who constitute nearly 47 percent of the whole population -- were not considered tribal problems as they
all belong to the Akan linguistic group.[3] In my view
this is quite misleading. Empirical data demonstrates
that some of the most intense and historically bitter
rivalries were between groups that belonged to the
same linguistic or ethnic classification, and that
each group viewed itself as generally different and
distinct. Thus historically, for example, the Ashanti
and Fanti were traditional adversaries even though
they belonged to the same larger Akan group. For
example, the following exchange in the Legislative
Council was not a joke but reflected the true perceptions of the dramatis personae, who were all Akan.

W. E. Arthur [CPP rural member from the colony] : I
    want to remind my brothers from Ashanti that they
    were not taking part in the administration of
    this country in the early days and it was only
    as late as 1946 that they were invited to take
    part in the government.

Krobo Edusei [a leading CPP minister from Ashanti]:
    Talk Nonsense.
W. E. Arthur: I am talking sense Mr. Speaker, they
    must understand that Ashanti is a conquered ter-
    ritory . . . (Interruption -- Some honorable mem-
    bers: Shame! Shame! -- uproar)
Nana Boakye Danquah [a leading Ashanti chief]: On a
    point of order Mr. Speaker, the last speaker has
    said that the Ashantis were conquered and I would
    like him to prove to this House in what way or
    manner they were conquered. We were never con-
    quered.
W. E. Arthur: We all know the history of this country
    and that --
Bediako Poku [CPP]: On a point of order, Mr. Speaker.
    An expression has been made by the Honorable
    Gentleman who just sat down that the Ashanti were
    conquered. If the Ashantis were conquered, he
    should know that the Ashantis also conquered the
    people of the colony in those days. The Ashantis
    were not conquered by Fantis! (Uproar).

In Uganda, as said before, the traditional rivalry
and conflict between the Baganda and Banyoro was well
known notwithstanding that both belonged to the Bantu
linguistic group. Given this setting and the divisive
nature of colonial rule, therefore, political parties
proliferated to bargain for the different group interests. Before we consider the struggles for power that
ensued, it is fitting to mention the principal parties
that were to influence the course of Ghana's history
during and after independence negotiations.

The Convention Peoples Party (CPP). The CPP was
the dominant party that led Ghana to independence and
was in power until its leader, Kwame Nkrumah, was
overthrown in February 1966. Originally Nkrumah had
joined the United Gold Coast Convention (UGCC) at the
invitation of its leader, Dr. Joseph Danquah, to help
organize this party. But, having established a substantial following in his own right, Nkrumah broke
away on 12 June 1949 to form his own party, the CPP,
of which he became chairman, K. A. Gbedemah, the vice-
chairman, and Kojo Botsio, the secretary. There is
no question that the CPP emerged as the most dynamic
nationalist force on the political scene, embracing
membership from the whole country. Yet even at its
most popular time, it had serious challenges from the
Ashanti and the North. Although it was national, it
is fair to say that it drew its overwhelming support
from the southern groups of the colony.

The National Liberation Movement (NLM). This
was the political vehicle for the Ashanti through
which they sought to win preindependence elections,
to inherit political power, and to demand a federal
form of government that would ensure the Ashanti identity and interests in the Independence Constitution.
It was formed in September 1954 under the leadership
of Bafuor Osei, of the asantehene's (king of Ashanti)
court and Dr. K. A. Busia, who later became leader of
the opposition.

Northern People's Party (NPP). The diverse
chiefdoms of the northern region, which had been long
neglected by colonial rule and had acquired their own
identity, now formed the NPP in June 1954 under S. D.
Dombo Duori-Na, an educated subchief, and Mumuni Ba-
wumia, secretary to the most powerful chief in the
northern protectorate. Its avowed aims were to ensure
respect for the cultures of the northern peoples and
their material development. There was a strongly
felt determination to end southern contempt for the
North.

Togoland Congress (TC). The TC was formed in
1951 by the Ewe leaders S. G. Antor and Kojo Ayeke.
After the defeat of Germany in World War I part of its
colony of Togo was administered by Britain and the
other part by France. The British administered their
portion with Ghana, although its inhabitants, the Ewe,
resented this and persistently clamored for union with
the other, larger French Togo. Consequently, this
party's aim was both to secure autonomy and eventually
to integrate with French Togo.
Three particular parties, therefore -- the NLM,
the NNP, and the TC -- clearly represented substantial
minority group interests in opposition to the CPP, and
as the preindependence elections show, in 1956 represented no less than 43 percent of the total votes
cast. To what extent did the independence settlement
cater to such diverse interests? Was it justified to
meet their demands for some decentralization and autonomy?

THE DEMANDS FOR FEDERALISM

Although the 1954 general election -- again won
by the CPP -- had been thought to usher the colony
to independence, the opposition demands for some regional autonomy became so serious that the British
decided on another final election, held specifically

over the issue of whether or not the Gold Coast was
to be a federal union on independence. The CPP, which
favored a unitary state, won with 56 percent of the
votes cast, but it is significant that in the regions
where federalism was advocated, the opposition parties
had majorities. Thus of the twenty-six seats contested
in the northern territories, the NPC had fifteen and
the CPP eleven seats; out of the twenty-one seats in
Ashanti, the NLM and its allies had thirteen and the
CPP eight seats; out of the five seats in southern
Togoland, excluding that part of the colony that made
up the Trans-Volta/Togoland Region, the Togoland Congress and its ally had three seats and the CPP two
seats. Therefore, with the exception of the colony
area embracing the western, eastern and Accra regions
-- where the CPP had decisive victories -- the majority in the three other regions favored a federal system of government.

But Nkrumah's arguments in rejecting federalism
were not without merit. In the first place, the election results had to be considered as a whole. In
that case, the CPP policy for a unitary government
had been endorsed with its electoral victory of seventy-one seats to the opposition's thirty-three. Second,
Nkrumah pointed out that for a small country like Ghana, it might be too burdensome to have a federal
structure with a bicameral legislature, regional governments, and an expensive public service to support
them. But it was mistaken to dismiss the demands for
federalism on the ground that it was not until after
1954 that they were made. The group interests that
these demands sought to protect were as ancient as
the societies themselves, many predating the colonial
experience. The demands for federalism as a method
to protect such interests came so late partly because
the regional parties that articulated them were not
formed until 1954 and partly because the CPP's desire
for centralized authority, which denied regional autonomy, did not clearly emerge until a few years before
independence. For instance, it was not until the
Van Lare Commission of Enquiry, which investigated
representational and electoral reform demarcating
electoral districts in 1953, that the CPP government
clearly came out in favor of cutting down on Ashanti
parliamentary representation. While the northern
territories were to get twenty-six instead of the
original nineteen seats, the colony and Trans-Volta
regions were to get forty-four and thirteen, respectively, instead of an original combined total of
thirty-seven seats, and the Ashanti were to have twenty-one with an increase of only two seats. Not only

was this vigorously and correctly attacked by the
Ashanti as unfair, but it convinced them more than
ever of the need to demand regional autonomy as a
safeguard against potentially hostile CPP central
power. It was significant, too, that the combined
forces of regional and ethnic appeal could compel
such CPP luminaries from the Ashanti, like Krobo Edusei, to support the NLM demands for more seats.

But when the protracted negotiations for the Independence Constitution were finally concluded (though
sometimes characterized by opposition boycotts and
persistent demands for federalism), a new unitary
constitution was produced. This constitution ensured
a strong center, entrenched some vital institutions
of the state and their respective powers, and met
the demands of federalists halfway by promising to
establish regional assemblies that would enable the
different regions to enact subsidiary legislation
and to administer some services in their areas in
order to give their people a sense of participation
in nation building.

We can summarize these constitutional safeguards
as follows: Section 32 of the constitution provided
that no bill to amend or repeal any part of the constitution shall become law unless supported by a two-
thirds majority of all the members of Parliament on
the third reading of the bill. Section 33 laid down
special procedures for altering regional boundaries
and names of regions; Section 34 forbade the compulsory acquisition of property save under law, and gave
a claimant a constitutional right to adequate compensation and access to the law courts to determine his
rights; Section 35 provided for bills affecting chiefs
to be referred to the regional Houses of Chiefs;
Sections 66 to 69 provided for the office of chief,
Houses of Chiefs, and their functions. Provisions
included the establishment of the branches of the
executive (Section 6) and the legislative (Section
20). To ensure that it was the representatives of
the people who governed, Parliament was to meet at
least once a year, and it was to be dissolved at least
once every five years (Section 47 [3]) to be followed
by a general election within two months of every dissolution (Section 48).

The impartiality of the judiciary was assured by
Sections 54 to 57. It was further provided that after independence, regional assemblies would be established to cater to regional interests (Sections 63
and 64).

Despite Nkrumah's subsequent rejection of this
constitution (due to its provision for a weak execu-

tive and his British-born attorney general's support
of this view), it remains an objective fact that the
constitution was sound and was tailored to meet the
needs of a multiethnic society on independence.
While the British may certainly be blamed for having
failed to provide Ghanaians with ample experience in
the art of government, it is wrong to assert that
they bequeathed an unworkable constitution. The failure came primarily because the independence government, which inherited the power, loathed sharing it
with any other institution or group in the state.
It is one of the most glaring examples of winner-take-
all practices in postindependence Africa, as we shall
see.

Part 2

The Politics and Practices of Winner-Take-All and Their Consequences

5
Introduction

We have already concluded that the administrative
legacy from the colonial past was most imperfect and
carried within it the seeds of potential conflict and
instability after independence. But even if "independence arrived already crippled by the colonial past,"[1]
there are serious questions still to be asked in search
of the true causes of the instability and violence that
have swept across Africa since independence. Was the
collapse of the independence regimes and institutions
inevitable? To what extent did the methods that the
political leaders adopted contain tensions and conflicts in the wake of independence? Were they appropriate or self-defeating?

It is the core of my argument that the practices
of the "winner-take-all" philosophy held by many independence leaders contributed more than any other
single factor to the unleashing of the instability
we are to talk about. By "winner-take-all" I mean
that belief and practice where those politicians who
inherited power on independence in these plural states
(or sometimes those military or civilian leaders who
replaced them) proceeded by all means, available or
contrived, fair or foul, to concentrate all (or a dis-
proportionate share of) power, resources, jobs, and
patronage in their hands and for their supporters for
all time, to the detriment of groups of different political, religious, ethnic, or regional background
within the state. Because of the differences in local
circumstances from country to country and in the style
and temperament of the diverse leaders, a wide range
of strategies and methods have been devised to pursue
this winner-take-all policy. The results, as our
examples show, have been devastating.

Before dealing with its application, let us answer the question: why has this winner-take-all policy
been so widespread in independent African states?

One may argue that it is basically because African
indigenous systems of government, whether they were
based on clan heads, chiefs, or kings, invariably
tended to be a monopoly of power. This should be the
most cogent argument of those who claim the African
rejection of multiparty politics was because it was
alien to African systems of government. There is some
truth to this, but I am convinced this view can be
exaggerated as a cause. There were always serious and
meaningful consultations by the rulers and their advisers; if the leaders ignored this, they risked being
deposed or dethroned. Moreover, as argued later, because there was more homogeneity in precolonial societies, definitions of or deviations from the norms of
society seldom caused the sharp conflict or differences that they do today in our multiethnic states.
In my view, the greater cause of winner-take-all practices lies in the interaction of defective colonial
legacies and the self-interest of the leaders. On
independence the leaders lost one of their most important unifying forces, the colonial power as an object
of common opposition. However, because they had had
insufficient cooperative experience in running the
country during the colonial era, and because their
followers had had even less interaction (since over
85 percent of each ethnic group habitually lived in
its ancestral home), mistrust and uncertainty about
the intentions of different leaders for the well-being
of others became inevitable soon after independence.
As a result many leaders in power felt secure largely
only in the company of their kinsmen or related ethnic
groups. But these initial fears, which may have been
understandable, became exaggerated and exploited by
those who sought a monopoly of the benefits of power,
encouraged to unreasonable extents by the close supporters who wanted to enjoy the fruits of independence.
This, of course, alienated those groups or parties
about whom the leaders had felt insecure and had kept
out of government. When they reacted with protest
and opposition, this only provided the grounds for
an even greater monopoly of power and the more determined exclusion of those already kept out. Let us
take, for our first example, Uganda.

6
Uganda: The Fundamental Causes of the 1966 Revolution

Apolo Milton Obote, as leader of UPC, inherited the independence government on 9 October 1962. On 22 February 1966, he abrogated the constitution and concentrated power in his own hands. His declared reasons for this seizure of power are considered in detail later. However, they were allegedly to forestall Kabaka Mutesa's attempt to employ foreign troops to overthrow the government and to prevent a number of his leading colleagues, whom he arrested, from promoting instability in the party and country. Nothing could be further from the truth. It is wisely said in jurisprudence that a case should never be decided without hearing both parties (audi alteram partem). The case for Obote's seizure of power, which unleashed Uganda's instability, has been exhaustively stated by him and his supporters since 1966 in the press, in the Parliament, in court cases, and in varied literature.[1] But there has been to date no coherent explanation or an alternative interpretation of what truly happened.

In 1967 while in exile, Frederick Mutesa II, the former kabaka of Buganda and president of Uganda, wrote a book giving a sketchy explanation of what had happened, largely omitting the real story except for his battle with the Ugandan army.[2] I can only think of one likely reason for such an omission and that was fear for his relatives and friends still living in Uganda, some of them in prisons at the time. Obote had demonstrated his ruthlessness by unleashing his army on largely defenseless civilians. Accurate disclosures that credibly contradicted his reasons for his seizure of power might well have triggered retribution against any of Mutesa's relatives, friends, and allies within his reach. But why did Obote abrogate the Ugandan Constitution and seize dictatorial power? It is my considered opinion that even without

65

the Ocheng motion (considered later) -- which censured
him in Parliament on 4 February 1966 and sparked off
the revolution a few weeks later -- there would still
have been some revolutionary upheaval in the country
in the subsequent months because of his relentless
and increasingly ruthless efforts on all fronts to
monopolize power and eliminate all opposition, inside
and outside the UPC.

At the heart of the Ugandan revolutions of 1966
and 1971 was the insatiable desire for a monopoly of
power by the UPC leadership. The independence settlement had left a separation of powers between the executive, legislative, and judiciary branches of government that assured the ordinary citizens against
arbitrary misuse of power, in addition to giving some
limited autonomy to the ethnic groups without weakening
the central government. Soon after independence the
prime minister set out to concentrate power in his own
hands through methods that involved abuse of authority
and resulted in instability. It is appropriate to
examine this process of unsurpation and abuse through
four basic areas of government: (1) the ruling party
and its philosophy, (2) control of central and local
governments, (3) the forces of law and order and their
functions in the new state, and (4) the primacy of the
executive branch and the emasculation of the legislative branch after 1967.

THE UPC'S RESOLUTE DETERMINATION TO OBTAIN
AND EXERCISE ABSOLUTE POWER

Some of the most effective pressure exerted
through the Legislative Council in the African colonies'
demands for self-government and independence was to use
the very standards of democracy as practiced in Britain, such as universal adult franchise and representative and responsible government. Obote was one of
the most articulate advocates of a democratic system
in Uganda and his public pronouncements up to independence (and indeed up to the 1966 revolution) bear this
out. But in fact while he was outwardly espousing
this, he was privately preparing to use brutal illegal
force, not against the colonialists, who had already
agreed to leave anyway, but against any Ugandan political party other than the UPC that inherited power.
A few months before independence, as minister of justice responsible for constitution affairs, I accompanied him to London to press the British government to
advance Kenya's independence date. In our free time,
Obote introduced me to the first secretary of a cer-

tain European embassy in London with whom he had had
a long-established contact. When we later returned
to our hotel, my astonishment was immense as he categorically told me he had made preparations to overthrow the DP government by force if the UPC lost the
preindependence elections in April 1962. The diplo-
mat's country, according to him, had already agreed
to provide the necessary training and materials, such
as arms. As a founding member of the UPC party who
had sat in on all its meetings and as its legal adviser who, with the late John Kakonge, had largely
drafted the party constitution and manifesto, I knew
it was never the UPC party policy, in private or public, to seek unlawful seizure of power from the government, although we would do everything permitted
by law to win elections. This assertion, the first
to put me on the alert, was to be followed by many
more serious statements and actions. After becoming
prime minister, Obote would often confide in some of
his close colleagues (like B. K. Kirya and myself)
that he would never under any circumstances relinquish
power voluntarily. He would then quote from John Milton's Paradise Lost, relating how Lucifer, having been
deposed from heaven, told the other fallen angels,
"to rule is worth ambition though in hell. It is
better to rule in hell than to serve in heaven." The
implication was unmistakably emphasized that it was
preferable to turn Uganda into chaos in order to stay
on top than to lose to another party in a peaceful
election.

Of course, all (or most) political leaders want
to attain, hold, or exercise power. But what happens
when the objective is to attain and hold power at all
costs and for all time, as was Obote's real ambition?
Conflict and violence sooner or later become inevitable, especially when there is a powerful opposition
as there was in Uganda. Most of Obote's close colleagues in the party and government looked at him
initially as an honorable man, especially as his statements seldom betrayed his real intentions. Similarly,
Parliament and the country at large were prepared to
give support to his administration. He had a chance
to become a great Ugandan leader; although not charis-
matic, he was intelligent, articulate, and a nationalist. The country he inherited, though multiethnic
and historically divided, after more than sixty years
of orderly colonial administration had evolved a
tradition for order and respect for law and established
authority. But, quite rightly in his calculations,
Obote foresaw a future political struggle, a possible
challenge from the DP and the KY, and he chose force

to deal with that challenge rather than persuasion
and political contest. Thus, he determined the
country's future instability and official violence
from which it has not yet recovered.

In a country with deep-rooted interethnic and
intraethnic cleavages as in Uganda, the leadership
may have (among others) two options for handling the
population. The first option involves maintaining
or accentuating ethnic divisions in order to resolve
or shelve problems or to keep power, in the old classical colonial mold of "divide and rule." Obote
employed this tactic constantly. The second and preferable option is one of continuous effort at genuine
persuasion and compromise. He was hailed by many,
especially outsiders, as a conciliator because he
compromised with Buganda to attain independence. However, this temporary conciliation was in fact forced
upon him privately, I know, against his will by some
of his senior colleagues in the party, largely because
it was the only way to defeat the DP and inherit the
mantle of power on independence. The tactic of divide
and rule was useful to his ends both because it kept
his potential opponents busy fighting each other, as
well as because it consequently gave him precious
time, as he had hoped, within which to build and exploit ethnic relations favorable to him in various
departments of government. His duplicity became the
curse both of the party and later the government. The
more he extolled the virtues of national unity and
attacked tribalism in public, the more he exploited
and accentuated ethnic divisions in private.

EFFORTS TO IMPOSE A ONE-PARTY SYSTEM

We discuss later the nature of one-party systems
as a whole, but for the moment it should be noted
that there is real merit in a one-party system only
if it is genuinely representative of society and has
sound leadership and objectives. There would therefore have been nothing inherently wrong in aspiring
to establish such a system in the country. It has
added significance, however, for a leadership resolved
to seize and monopolize power because it ensures the
absence of acknowledged, legitimate opposition. Yet
it was difficult to establish a one-party system in
Uganda without serious threats of instability. While
Obote often quoted Tanzania's one-party system and
Ghana's CPP in private to justify it at home, he preferred to ignore the fact that the Tanganyika African
National Union (TANU) was for all practical purposes

the only serious party of the overwhelming majority
of Tanganyikans, dating from preindependence elections.
In contrast, in the context of Ugandan politics, the
UPC was quite uncertain of its strength. Despite the
crossings to the government side, however, of elected
DP and KY members in Parliament and district councils
in search of better material prospects, the DP and
the KY still had impressive followings. Any attempt
to impose a one-party system, therefore, was bound to
be resisted with unpleasant consequences. But in
Obote's calculations any resistance to the one party
at some future date would be crushed by his army.

Consequently, while touring his home district he
issued a public statement on 7 January 1964 that advocated creation of a one-party state in Uganda, partly
because "organized opposition against the government
is a typical capitalist notion and concept," and partly
because the opposition outside Parliament was "irresponsible, opportunistic and subversive."[3] Not only
were these reasons distorted but they were never discussed either within the policy-forming organs of the
UPC or the cabinet. I was acutely aware of the Nigerian misuse of federal power to install Akintola and
destroy the Action Group in western Nigeria and its
violent results. Thus, in fear of a similar prospect
at home, I immediately issued a public statement making the important reservations, that while we might
work for a one-party system, the UPC would never introduce it through force and legislation. It would come
through the free choice of the people in elections.[4]
Notwithstanding this mitigation, which Obote resented,
there were vigorous and public protests from the DP
and the KY. To understand why it was destabilizing
to impose a one-party system one needs to know the
relative strength of parties in the country.

The UPC was a poorly organized party and its
strength rested more on the individual following of
its leaders from the different areas than on effective
organization and coherent philosophy. It is significant, for instance, that during the first crucial
elections that led to self-government in February 1961,
the party had for its headquarters campaign effort one
old duplicating machine, one Land Rover (donated by
President Nyerere), and a few typewriters, manned by
a few upaid personnel. This was not the fault of the
then secretary-general of the party, John Kakonge,
who was responsible for the day-to-day administration.
It was rather the fault of Obote's relative disinter-
est or inability as a leader of the party to canvass
more support for its proper organization. But the
development of Uganda also had ensured relatively more

attachment to local leadership. Consequently, individual candidates in both local and national elections
won mostly by their own effort. As the results of the
1961 and 1962 general elections show (see Table 6.1),
UPC was clearly in a minority, though the largest
single goup. It could neither compare with the CPP in
Ghana nor the TANU in Tanzania, which were increasingly
Obote's models.

The independence government could only be formed
in coalition with twenty-one Bugandan representatives.
Outwardly, the UPC seemed to have done better in district councils. Within a year of independence all
local governments in district councils, including the
three western kingdoms, were UPC dominated. It was
only Buganda that remained impregnable. Despite this
favorable showing, paradoxically the UPC was experiencing more internal problems as a party. The apparent decline of official opposition led to considerable
in-fighting within the party. The larger it grew, the
more fragmented it became. It was difficult and often
impossible at that time to enforce discipline and a
common policy.

Practically in every district or kingdom there
was serious intraparty conflict among UPC followers,
which though rooted in diverse causes would have been
containable with better party discipline. But Obote's
style was to keep the party divided to enable him to
play one faction off against another. The Acholi district in the North, despite the fact that Obote had
wooed its sons in the security forces, was for a long

TABLE 6.1   Electoral Results for 1961, 1962

Year	Party	Votes Obtained	Parliamentary Seats Won
1961	DP	515,718	43
	UPC	494,959	35
	Others	87,900	3
1962	UPC	537,598	37
	DP	496,854	24
	KY	400,000 +	21

Note: See the Report on the Uganda Legislative Council Elections, 1961, p. 17; see also the official report
on the general elections of April 1962.

time so badly divided as to paralyze its local administration. The district was ethnically homogeneous
but was divided on a religious basis between Catholics
and Protestants and on a subregional basis between
East and West Acholi. Often it defied central government (UPC) policy. Despite the urging of the UPC
central committee to unify Acholi leadership, Obote
preferred to keep the Acholi fighting each other since
a unified Acholi would worry him as it would be capable of producing rival leadership with greater support
in an already ethnicised army.

In Toro, a rival UPC group, "Kagorogoro," under
Rwambarali set up its own party organization with
Obote's secret consent and material support to oppose
the lawfully constituted party government of Samson
Rusoke. In Kigezi, not only was the party handicapped
by the rivalries among the three ethnic groups (Bakiga,
Bahororo, and Banyarwanda) but it was also deeply divided by the rivalry between Lwamafa and Bikangaga,
its leaders of national stature. Similarly, in Ankole
there were two UPCs, one under Bananuka and another
under James Kahigiriza, who was in government. The
story of factionalism applied to all districts.

On the other hand, the DP and the KY, though
their numbers in Parliament had been reduced through
the crossing of their members to the government side,
were still firmly established among the people. It
should be explained that the most common reason people
switched to the government as they did was to seek
rewards from the government either in state corporations or by appointments to government commissions in
order to bring in extra income and influence, for
example.[5] But once a member changes his party, it
is quite uncertain to what extent, he carries his
constituents with him. They certainly do not share
meaningfully in the material rewards he personally
gets, and it is more likely that the majority would
still support their original party. One could sense
this in the solid support for the opposition found
in public meetings of the constituencies of former
members of the DP. As for Buganda, there was absolutely no question that it was solidly in support of
the KY. The Baganda MPs, who switched to the UPC,
had never been elected directly by the people but had
been indirectly elected by the Buganda Lukiko. They
had no proven or credible electoral support, although
admittedly many were sound men; they were conditioned
by the nature of the Buganda society and government
of the time.

Given the still basically strong opposition and
the disorganization and indiscipline within the UPC,

it was imprudent to impose a one-party system. Yet
such are the politics of the winner-take-all philosophy. With the circumstances in Uganda at the time,
the most realistic approach would have been to offer
the DP and the KY positions in a national government
with a merger of all the parties, just as the Uganda
People's Union had merged with the Uganda National
Congress to form the UPC. Obote was in a strong position to do this for, despite their basically strong
potential, the opposition was a bit demoralized by the
constant defections of its MPs to the government. The
offer was never made because while Obote wanted the DP
and the KY to cease to exist, he was apprehensive to
accept their members in large numbers into his party.
He preferred to have his cake and eat it too. As we
shall later see, the KY was crippled in January 1966
and the whole opposition banned in December 1969 after
an attempt on Obote's life.

PARLIAMENTARY BATTLES FOR REFORM OF THE ELECTORAL LAW

    In any politics of the winner-take-all philoso-
phy, it is always a basic requirement that the party
in power monopolizes the electoral system. Thus, a
political battle now ensued, launched by the DP and
the KY, to reform the electoral law and ensure equal
opportunity to all parties in elections. A brief history of this contest indicates some of the clearest
evidence of Obote's intentions, if any more proof
were needed by those close to him. The basic electoral
law under which the first countrywide general elections
were held in 1961 was an old colonial ordinance of 1957
(with subsequent amendments). There were several loopholes in this law and as a result there had been widespread malpractices by the DP and the UPC in many parts
of the country, both in national and local elections.
Personation was widespread. Extra ballots in bundles
appeared in some ballot boxes unaccountably. Sometimes after polling in remote rural areas, some ballot
boxes mysteriously got lost. Several electoral districts controlled by the UPC returned minority candidates because electoral boundaries were drawn by pro-
UPC officials showing a patent bias against the DP.
For instance, although the UPC elected a majority of
candidates in the Ankole Eishengyero (district council)
in the 1963 Ankole elections, the DP had polled 7,000
more votes.[6] There was therefore a clamor to remove
these defects, in particular for national constituencies, as they tended to produce unrepresentative
results.

One of the most urgent reforms required was the
elimination of using separate ballot boxes for each
candidate. Because voting was in private, a skilled
party functionary of any party could use a long con-
cealed forceps to transfer dozens of ballot papers
at a time from one box to another in the brief moments
he was alone supposedly casting his ballot. Repeated
in all the hours of polling, thousands of ballot
papers could be transferred this way to a candidate
for whom they were never cast and possibly vitiate the
true verdict of the electorate. Because the 1962 election was supervised by the departing colonial administration it was fair and malpractices equally affected
all parties. But, as the postindependence elections
of several district councils began to show, enthusiastic UPC local officials throughout the country exceeded
their powers and, assured of immunity from above, decisively and unfairly promoted the interests of their
candidates. As Obonyo, a DP member of Parliament,
revealed without serious contradiction, for example,
in the Bunyoro Rukurato (district council) elections,
twenty-four UPC candidates had been returned unopposed
because twenty-four DP candidates had all been disqualified by the UPC officers presiding over the elections. In Lango elections the UPC presiding officers
refused to accept DP nominations. In varying degrees
similar malpractices obtained during the first two
years of independence in Acholi, Ankole, Kigezi, and
West Nile, as well. Obviously the opposition became
most restive.

In addition to all this, Section 45(1) of the
constitution provided for an electoral commission,
whose duties were, inter alia, to demarcate constituencies and regulate elections. It was of the utmost
importance, in a country so deeply divided in many
ways, that the membership of this commission not only
be fairly independent from political bias but that
it also be seen to be so. Yet the commission's chairman as well as all its six members were not merely
silent UPC supporters but regional or national UPC
leaders.[7] How could the DP and the KY expect fair
play? Still, there had to be periodic elections.
This had been unanimously agreed upon in the independence settlement to take place at five-year intervals,
and it was expected. Thus the opposition DP sought
electoral reform supported by the KY after their alliance with the UPC ended.

There were some in the UPC and the Cabinet who
concurred with the need for such reform. The first
two years of his government were Obote's best, although others may think differently. The Cabinet had

moved with integrity and vigor to implement its electoral promises that still rang loud and clear. There
were still the good will and optimism that came with
freedom. Above all, there was relative cooperation
at all the important levels in the country. There
was no question that in the event of a general election in a few years' time, if this momentum were
maintained, the UPC would be returned not because of
massive cheating at the polls but because of its
record in almost every field: education, health, agriculture, employment, etc. But in contrast were the
consequences of legitimized, extensive cheating in
elections, which could produce a hostile and violent
electorate as it did in Nigeria from 1962 onward.

On 1 April 1963 the opposition tabled a motion
in Parliament to reform the malpractices mentioned.[8]
The attorney general, who worked with me as minister
of justice, replied truthfully that government was
"in the process of doing so." As there were no results, Byanyima revived the opposition's demand on
3 October 1963 and categorized the areas for reform.
But I had already replied to him in writing confirming the government's intentions: "I share your views
that the electoral law is faulty, and I am happy to
inform you that my ministry has been preparing a bill
to replace all previous elections laws which it intends
to bring before parliament for debate at the next
meeting of the National Assembly."[9]

Officers at the Ministry of Justice had done an
excellent job in revising and reforming the law, eliminating all loopholes. The draft was considered and
approved by the electoral commission. In accordance
with normal practice, I put the item on the agenda
for cabinet meetings to discuss and make suggestions
before the final draft of the law went for debate in
the National Assembly. The records of the cabinet
meetings would show that this bill was on its agenda
for nearly two months without Obote as chairman ever
calling it forth for ministerial views, despite the
fact that the Cabinet met often and there was no lack
of time. Privately Obote maneuvered for its rejection
and subsequently the draft law dropped from the agenda.
Why? Because the reforms would prejudice UPC prospects. In other words, because the malpractices worked
against the opposition, they had to stay on the statute
book.

In the course of these debates for electoral reform, two things became manifest as to Obote's thinking on the whole issue of elections. On numerous
occasions he made it clear to some of his close colleagues -- especially those active in party organiza-

tion, like B. K. Kirya and myself -- that there was
no possibility of any party replacing him through
elections. Often, he would assert that even if there
were to be a general election in a few years and mira-
culously if the DP were to win, how could they physically remove him from power? He would then recount
the loyalty he had built in the army and police and
assure us of their capability to maintain the UPC in
power even though in defiance of the electorate's
verdict. It was during this period that some of his
close colleagues and founding members of the UPC began
to show increasing anxiety in private as to the probable consequences of this policy, not only to themselves as individuals but also to the country as a
whole. They were later to take a stand against Obote's
moves toward absolutism and pay dearly for it. The
second thing that became apparent, closely connected
with the decision to remain in power at all costs,
was an almost pathological fear of elections. No
device seemed too extreme to postpone them.
     It is quite significant that for several years
after 1963 Obote would not even permit parliamentary
by-elections to fill vacancies of members who had
died, had resigned, or had been detained. By the
time of Obote's overthrow in January 1971, in a Parliament of eighty-two elected members, seventeen seats
were vacant. Some, like that of late Babukika in Kigezi, were vacant for nearly eight years; yet, this
was a time in which Obote claimed outwardly that the
UPC was invincible. There was a persistent clamor
from vacant constituencies, which were in effect dis-
enfranchised, to be permitted to return new representatives but without avail. To exacerbate matters,
the denial to reelect not only pertained to constituencies known to represent the DP, but even UPC strong-
holds like Sebei, of the late Chemonges, which had
been vacant for five years up to Obote's overthrow.
It did not do Obote or the UPC credit when the only
place he would give the electorate another chance in
by-elections was in his home district of Lango. His
cousin, Martin Aroma, was quickly returned there in
place of Abdala Anyuru, who resigned to become chairman of the Public Service Commission. But why reject
by-elections? The answer basically was partly in
Obote's profound sense of insecurity, as is dealt with
later.
     As there was no positive response from government,
the opposition revived their demands for electoral reform almost a year later in September 1964.[10] By this
time there had been a cabinet reshuffle and Cuthbert
Obwangor, a dedicated and senior member of the party

from Teso, had become minister of justice in charge
of the electoral law. A man with a large following
in the party and a staunch believer in government by
electoral mandate, Obwangor vigorously promoted the
reforms I had left in the ministry and even introduced
his own amendments to improve them. But like my own
bill, his never saw the light of day because Obote
killed it. A year later, on 13 September 1965, a KY
member of the opposition, Daudi Ocheng, with DP support introduced a similar demand for electoral reform
but it was by now already clear Obote was neither
interested in elections nor in electoral reform. The
more these demands were made the more he circulated
the view in UPC top circles that elections were a dis-
traction from the task of nation building and that the
masses were only interested in services by the UPC
government. In other words, the ground was being prepared for a one-party system and the elimination of
genuine periodic elections.

    There was no reason for this view to the group
that opposed him in the party. The UPC could win e-
lections anytime and to evade them would be strength-
ening the opposition parties and inviting instability.
Outwardly, with typical duplicity, the prime minister
would reaffirm his commitment to governing by the will
of the people through elections. It was a typical
falsehood when, having actually abrogated the constitution in 1966 and evaded a general election, he reported to the UPC in 1968 that in September 1965 he
had proposed to the UPC central executive committee
his desire to have Parliament dissolved for a fresh
election. He stated that this was opposed by his
ministers (whom he was later to imprison without trial
for five years) because they expected to lose. The
issue was never discussed. In any event, the political strength of these ministers was so clear that they
could have had no fear in an election. It was because
of their strength in the party that he never moved a
vote of no confidence in them, which would have been
appropriate to demonstrate his support in the UPC.

MONOPOLY AND MISUSE OF THE SECURITY FORCES

Politicizing the Armed Forces on an Ethnic Basis

    Rightly -- but for wrong ends -- the prime minis-
ter attached a more important premium on the Ugandan
army than on any other department of government. It
is essential to give a brief history of the army in
order to understand its later development. When the

British ruled East Africa (Kenya, Tanganyika, and
Uganda), there was one army for these territories,
the King's African Rifles (KAR). It had a unified
British command but the troops were recruited from
the three respective territories. They had the same
standards and a common history with pride in their
performance during World War II against the Italians
in Ethiopia and the Japanese in the Burma campaigns.
But equally, as in all colonial armies, there was
also a dark past of suppressing nationalist uprisings,
like the Mau Mau in Kenya, to uphold colonial rule.
On independence, the KAR was split up and divided between the three states. Uganda inherited one battalion of 1,000 men who constituted the national army
called the Ugandan Rifles. One aspect of the disastrous unpreparedness for independence was the fact
that in 1961 there was not a single Ugandan commissioned officer. As Obote told the country, "before May 1,
1962, that is the date on which I formed this present
government, there were no Ugandan full officers in
the Ugandan Army."[11] The troops were commanded exclusively by the British. It was only a short time before
independence that two noncommissioned officers (NCOs)
rising from the ranks, Shaban Opolot and Idi Amin,
were commissioned just before the first Ugandan officer ever trained in a military academy at Sandhurst
arrived in the country. It is important to note that
despite the absence of indigenous leadership in the
army, the troops were disciplined. The absence of a
bitter protracted struggle for independence in Uganda
or mass political parties of long duration, and the
British tradition of divorcing the army from politics
ensured that on independence the Ugandan army was
united and unweakened by ethnic rivalries and divisions
that were to become its curse under Obote's government
and later.

The DP government under Ben Kiwanuka during internal self-government, to its eternal credit never attempted to politicize the military on sectional interests. But immediately after independence Obote set in
motion steps for the rapid expansion of the Ugandan
Army and its politicization in a negative sense along
ethnic lines. For the first five years of independence
it was the fastest expanding army on the African continent, growing yearly at the rate of from 48 to 50
percent.[12] Why? Considering the pressing need for
services in education, health, agriculture, and the
infrastructure, what exceptional peril faced the country to warrant such rapid development of the army?
It is my considered opinion that although there were
real security problems of an external and internal

nature, none justified such rapid expansion. The actual, though secret, reason most people never knew
was Obote's preparation for the eventual use of the
armed forces in seizing absolute political power.
This fact more than any other consideration determined
the speed of expansion and the predominantly regional
nature of military recruitment. This view is demonstrated by examining the actual security problems that
faced Uganda on independence, both internal and external. These problems did not in fact necessitate this
rapid expansion, although they warranted serious attention through political and diplomatic methods, which
Obote knew, and a relatively low increase in security
forces.

Internal Security

It is true that there were endemic and potentially
serious problems of a security nature on independence.
There was a secessionist movement, Rwenzururu, in the
kingdom of Toro, whose members (the Bamba and Bakonjo)
wanted to be separated from the kingdom because they
had long resented Batoro hegemony. There were killings
of people and destruction of property. But, even at
its height, the local conflict in this remote frontier
area of southwest Uganda bordering Zaire never seriously threatened internal security, nor did it require
the attention of a quarter of a battalion of the army.
It needed a political solution and at this stage Obote
tried to seek one, with moderate results.
There were the incessant cattle raids among the
Karamojong of northeast Uganda, either among themselves
or between them and other cattle people, the Turkana
of Kenya, across the frontier. These raids, using
mostly traditional weapons of spears but also some
firearms, involved the participants capturing cattle
from their opponents, sometimes with consequent loss
of human life, though in small numbers. A well-trained
and armed part of the national police force numbering
nearly one thousand, called the Special Force, was
primarily responsible for maintaining order here.
Occasionally, it would call in the aid of the army.
It was not, however, the primary work of the army to
maintain law and order in Karamoja. Even when it was
part of its functions, only a few platoons were deployed or needed.
But there was the potential problem of Buganda.
A referendum, according to the independence settlement,
was to be held in two of the counties in Buganda (which
the British had given to their Bugandan allies after
the conquest of Bunyoro on colonization) to determine

if the inhabitants wanted to stay in Buganda, have a
district of their own, or join the Bunyoro kingdom.
This settlement had been imposed by the British during the constitutional conference in 1962 over Bugandan protest.[13] As the date for the referendum approached, the Bugandan government began to settle
hundreds of its own people in the contested counties,
many of whom were veterans of World War II, with the
intention of reversing the preponderance of Banyoro
in the forthcoming referendum. There was as a consequence a stirring up of emotions as all sides campaigned for support, a prospective threat to internal
security. But partly due to the central government's
administration of the counties before the referendum,
and partly due to the use of the extensive police
powers in the area, disturbances were relatively minimal, and the referendum was held with the counties
opting to go to the Banyoro without serious security
incidents.

The long-term possible threat from Buganda, however, could have been an attempt to secede from the
rest of the country. The kingdom had a well-known
history of particularism under British rule and in
December 1960 had declared itself "independent," although this was sheer vituperation as Buganda had
absolutely no means to implement it. But its history
provided anyone who wanted to provoke a revolution,
however unjustified, with a perfectly plausible ground
as its past intransigence was well known and could
be, as it was, quoted as justification. And yet the
purpose of the Munster Commission, the constitutional
conferences, and the independence settlement were to
a large measure to search for a formula by which to
integrate Buganda into the country. I was convinced
this had been done and the subsequent upheavals in
the country since 1966 when Obote seized absolute
power and Buganda ceased to exist, have reinforced
this conviction. There was a real opportunity for
the UPC to integrate Buganda peacefully and eventually
in fact to control its government, as it did with the
other kingdoms under the independence settlement.

However, as will be shown later, Obote dreaded
the prospect of Buganda's coming into the UPC en mass.
Consequently, he intended to keep the Baganda at arms
length with the exception of the few he could use,
and he anticipated (rightly) a resurgence of their
primordial fears and possibly their desperate attempts
at secession, even if it was with his provocation.
This aspect genuinely inspired his policy toward army
expansion. In any event, having decided to eliminate
all opposition by law, he could reasonably expect

vigorous opposition from both the KY and the DP leading to likely internal upheaval. We can therefore
say there was objectively no probable, internal threat
to security that warranted rapid army expansion, except in opposition to Obote's excesses. Indeed, two
completely well-armed battalions and a substantially
well-trained police force would have been adequate
for national security. This would have been most
desirable also for releasing scarce funds to satisfy
electoral promises to the masses, which had been numerous on independence and were beginning to be dis-
honored.

External Threat?

Was there a real external threat to Uganda to
justify the type of military buildup? The policy of
Obote towards the Sudan and the Congo (now Zaire) was
sometimes sound but at times a source of concern.
Take, for example, first the Sudan. At the time of
Uganda's independence in 1962, the civil war in the
Sudan between the Arab Mohammedan North and the black
Christian South was in full swing. Because of artificial colonial frontiers, there were several Ugandan
ethnic groups in the North, in the West Nile, and the
Acholi districts, who had their kinsmen across the
border as nationals of the Sudan engaged in what
Ugandans rightly considered an armed struggle for
their legitimate rights. Obote, therefore, as a northerner with a bond of kinship to them and as an African quite commendably decided to give assistance of
sorts to the southern Sudanese with the full support
of his party and the DP. Uganda became one of the
havens in the countries surrounding southern Sudan to
which tens of thousands of Sudanese refugees could
flee to safety.
Shortly after independence Obote made an official
visit to the Sudan, then under General Aboud, to establish good neighborly relations. For several years,
however, the relations between the Sudan and Uganda
were not easy. Often, the Sudanese army pursued
Southern guerrillas (Anyanya) deep into Uganda territory in the north. At times they abducted southern
Sudanese or destroyed property several miles inside
Uganda. Sometimes, though Obote was skilled in covering up, the situation was both humiliating and dangerous as Uganda never really answered back in kind.
Opposition members of Parliament, particularly Martin
Okelo and G. Oda from the northern areas affected,
often attacked government inaction in the National
Assembly.[14] But there was a limit to what Uganda

could do. Because it was a fact that Uganda gave
sanctuary and some support to the southern Sudanese
insurgents, it could not protest too loudly or else
evidence could readily be produced of Uganda's com-
plicity. The country's approach to the Sudanese
problem, therefore, was through diplomatic and not
military pressure. The Sudan was aware that Uganda
was the source of the White Nile, which was its life
line as well as that of Egypt. Although there was
the Nile Waters Agreement controlling the river's
flow, the danger of a hostile Uganda dishonoring it
would always remain. This possibility was strengthened by the good relations that existed between Uganda
and Israel, since the Israelis were training the Ugandan army and were the arch enemies of the Arab world.
It was consequently in the interest of the Sudan to
act with restraint towards Uganda. These facts and
possibilities were in Obote's possession, and to some
extent, he used them. Arming to meet a Sudanese
threat, therefore, would have been a ruse. In any
event, if the army was being expanded for that purpose
then it was a woefully inadequate exercise. The Sudan
was the only dependency in Africa to emerge into independence with a highly professional and fully Sudan-
ized army.[15] As Obote and I saw on his official visit
to Khartoum, the Sudanese army was so far ahead of
Uganda militarily that to try to match it would have
been disastrous to our economy, and in fact we never
did. The expansion of the Ugandan army, though dramatic, fell far short of what would have been reasonably
required to meet a serious Sudanese armed threat.

Uganda's relations with Zaire were difficult because of the civil war still raging at the time of
Uganda's independence. The two countries have a border
of over 700 miles and several ethnic groups live on
either side of the frontier dividing the two states.
There was no fundamental cleavage, no traditional enmity, as had existed between black Uganda and the Arab
Sudan over the southern Sudanese issue. However,
because of Obote's personal involvement in the Congo
war (as we shall discuss fully later), the Congolese
army attacked Ugandan frontier posts while pursuing
either Ugandan troops fighting for the rebels or the
rebels themselves as they fled to sanctuary in Uganda.
Obote then had a pretext for justifying the creation
of a third battalion, the second battalion having been
created ostensibly to contain the Karamoja cattle
raids. According to him, the danger to the state was
so urgent that only people with military experience
from World War II were to be recruited to eliminate
the delay involved in training.[16] Without any compunc-

tion, he ensured that this battalion of nearly 1,000 men was approximately 90 percent from the northern ethnic groups who made up less than 25 percent of the country.

The composition of the first battalion inherited on independence had been approximately as follows, on a percentage basis:[17]

Acholi	35
Iteso (the only substantial non-northern group)	30
Lugbara	20
Other West Nile groups	10
The rest	5
Total	100

(Note the absence of Obote's Lango group as a significant factor at this time.)

The preponderance of ethnic groups from the north in the first battalion was a creation of the colonial rulers for their own purposes. But Obote quickly grasped its potential and proceeded to develop a national army many times larger than he inherited, but still emphasizing the predominance of the same groups as the colonialists had done. If there were genuine reasons to expand the army so fast, which is contested, what was the criterion for recruiting its personnel? The answer to this question leads to the heart of Obote's real intentions and the true cause of the Ugandan revolutions of 1966 and 1971.

To eliminate different southern ethnic groups, Obote advanced a variety of reasons through his spokesmen. The Baganda were said to be poor fighters, reluctant to join the army, and looked down upon it. That is why even in colonial times they were never recruited. This was very false. This kingdom had been established and maintained by force of arms, and military service had always been looked upon as a symbol of social prestige. Nearly 100 years before independence, one of the white explorers to reach Buganda, Morton Stanley, recorded how favorably he had been impressed as he "saw about 3,000 soldiers of Mutesa nearly civilized."[18] This was only a palace guard, for the total army reached about 30,000. The British were aware of this military capability, especially having witnessed it closely in their joint

operation with Bugandan troops in which they defeated
the valiant nationalist, Kabarega of Bunyoro. As
they did with similar powerful groups in their colonies (as with the Ashanti in Ghana), therefore, they
never recruited the Baganda into the army but directed
their enterprise into the professions, civil service,
or profitable agriculture. The military was reserved
for those not considered a political risk at the time.
These happened to be the ethnic groups of the North.
The only exception to the rule was during the two
world wars when recruitment was from the whole protectorate. It is significant that in World War II, the
majority of African officers from east and central
African commands were Bugandan.[19] Nevertheless, over
the decades the British policy took hold and the Baganda accepted the situation as they sought other
alternative civilian occupations.
    The situation with the kingdoms of Ankole, Bun-
yoro, and Toro was similar. These all had a tradition
of military power. Bunyoro, in particular, was at
its zenith long before colonization and the rise of
Buganda and had been the most powerful kingdom in
East Africa.[20]
    Then there was the excuse that because the Bagan-
da and the so-called Bantus generally tended to be
shorter than the northerners, the northerners were
recruited partly because they met the required height
of 5'8". This requirement was absurd and was a relic
of the colonial past; however, Obote found it convenient to keep because it served his purpose. As members of Parliament became suspicious and probed more
about recruitment in July 1963, the minister of defense defended the height requirement: "I cannot
accept that the height of our soldiers should be reduced. We do not want people who look like totos
[small children]."[21] Needless to say some of the
best soldiers have been short. The Japanese and Viet-
cong readily come to mind. Yet another excuse was
advanced in Parliament that "after calling up all
ex-servicemen, Baganda did not come because they were
stopped by their politicians and therefore they should
not complain that the army is entirely of people from
the North."[22] This, I know, was patently false as
proved by the thousands of young Baganda who turned
up the few times recruitment was held in Buganda. An
articulate Bugandan representative, Ali Kisekka, who
was later to become Obote's minister, substantially
stated the truth on the whole issue of biased recruitment:

At present our army is composed of people mainly

from one region [the North] . . . . Stability
hinges on many factors. One of these factors I
think is to try as much as possible to make our
army portray national unity. . . .
Why can our Minister of Internal Affairs not
introduce a quota system in our army? . . . An
honourable friend yesterday did say that this
situation arose because it was only in the North
where you find people who are most suited for
military activity. . . . They have not told us
whether in those olden days before the coming of
the British protection we had to go to the North
to get soldiers to keep our kingdom. We kept it
with our own military people and this happened
not only in Buganda but in other kingdoms [inter-
jections].

He then attacked the tactics of recruitment,
which are elaborated later.

Today when they (the army recruiting teams) go
to the North, they spend there two or three
months recruiting, but when they come to Kampala
they spend here one day and they recruit mainly
those whom they have directed to come to Kampala
because they failed to recruit them in the North.
When they go to Masaka (in Buganda) they spend
there half a day to recruit only about three
people -- two of them probably being those Northern people who are living in Buganda. When they
go to Mbarara (Ankole -- South Uganda), they
spend there half a day to recruit only about
three people. This sort of recruitment must be
stopped. They must give us quotas.[23]

E. Lakidi (Acholi, North) interjected, "You cannot
fight." Ali Kisekka replied: "It was because the
Baganda were great fighters that the British people
feared to recruit them in the Kings Rifles. They
knew that if they had recruited Baganda in the army
the British would not have ruled this country for
fifty years." Twice, as a member of the Cabinet and
secretary-general of the UPC, I asked the ministry
of defense for a breakdown of the army, district-by-
district, and was denied it although I had other private channels to its access. Clearly, the reason for
the denial was the fear of confirmation of the allegations that recruitment was heavily in favor of one
region. As a challenge, while minister of state
responsible for the public service, I compiled a list
of all Ugandan senior public servants by rank, reli-

gion, ethnic group, qualification, and case history.
It was a laborious, comprehensive exercise to show
there was no nepotism. I distributed the report to
all parliamentarians and demanded a comparable report
be made for the army. Of course, it was never done
and everybody knew the reason was fear of exposure of
the blatant and unjustifiable recruitment of the army
on an ethnic basis by a government that daily attacked
tribalism and urged national unity.

When pressed by parliamentarians to answer persistent charges of recruitment on ethnic grounds,
Obote denied its existence and insisted recruitment
and promotion were made on merit. To illustrate his
tactics we can quote what he said on one occasion to
"answer effectively the stupid allegations that there
has been some discrimination in the promotion of officers. . . . Promotion to Captaincy since May 1, 1962,
16; promotion to Major since May 1, 1962, 2; promotion
to Lt. Colonel since May 1, 1962, 2."[24] He dared not
list the troops recruited. It is obvious the answer
did not address the question. It was not how many in
each rank were promoted that was asked, but from which
groups they came. The obvious answer, to give a hypothetical example, would have been: promotion to Captaincy, 2 Acholi, 1 Langi, 3 Lugbara, 1 Musoga, etc.
There was no legitimate reason for withholding such
important information except that it would have exposed
an alarming bias to one region and exposed himself.

The contention still remains that the potential
conflict with the Congo, which had been sparked off
by Obote's secret support of the rebels, did not warrant the military expansion. But assuming it did,
there was no proper reason for restricting recruitment
predominantly to the one region where Obote came from.
Alarmed by this bias, several people, including myself,
tried to bring pressure for fairer recruitment from
all ethnic groups. It worked to a small extent as was
witnessed by the recruitment of the second battalion
based in Karamoja. But even that seemed too much for
his plans. The recruiting team would later announce
its itinerary throughout the country, region by region,
over the radio and in the press. They would call upon
young men wishing to join the army to meet them at
specific places and times. But as I checked in the
field myself, an ominous pattern had evolved. In the
east, west, and in Buganda, the notice tended to be
too short, thus ensuring that a substantial portion
of potential recruits would get the information too
late. Alternatively, sometimes the recruiting team
altered the announced date and venue for recruitment
without informing the public. Naturally, when they

arrived there were no recruits and they left. Occasionally, on the days they made a genuine appointment in order to cover their tracks or because of mounting pressure and criticism, the selection process was so unusually demanding that out of the hundreds at each spot, they enlisted a handful, if any at all. But in the northern region it was different. Many weeks in advance of any recruitment, officers did everything possible to ensure a massive turnout of young men at the appointed time and place at which time there would be a generous recruitment.

The linchpin of Obote's strategy was the politicization and particular ethnicity of the Ugandan army. He reasoned that if he filled the army with northerners (some of whom he was linked to by bonds of kinship -- real or imagined) and if he granted them privileges beyond those of any other department of government, they would be willing to do his bidding not merely in maintaining the security of the state under the constitution but at any moment of his choice. Obote felt they would support him in the abrogation of the very constitution by which he had ascended to eminence. The army therefore was not just to uphold the constitution but it had to place the prime minister above it. Loyalty, then, was ultimately neither to the state nor to the constitution, but to the individual incumbent, Obote, as head of government. But as we shall show later, this dangerous doctrine, though outwardly successful in the initial years, was doomed to failure. In the first place no region was really ethnically homogeneous. The anthropological terms, Nilotic (for the northern people) and Bantu (for the southern people), were quite superficial and misleading. There are several distinct linguistic and ethnic groups in the North as there are in the South.[25] Besides, historically there was no enmity between the northern and southern peoples of the country. On the contrary, traditional hostilities and battles were fought between close neighbors within the same ethnic group, such as occurred between the Langi and the Acholi, both Nilotic, and between the Baganda and the Banyoro, both Bantu. Obote's plan, therefore, of playing groups against each other was bound to fail partly because it was based on a false understanding of the country's history, especially because there was no unifying philosophy for all these groups as he preferred to keep them divided.

The second reason why this ethnicized army failed was because ultimately Obote did not trust any of the other northern groups except his own. He paid them lipservice because he still needed them in order to

buy time to recruit more of his own kinsmen and give
them positions of command. I had personal knowledge
of this as secretary-general of UPC. For example,
twice I had been dispatched to the Acholi district
to meet political leaders there and resolve their
internal disputes, which had divided and paralyzed
the district administration. My proposal to end the
crisis and unify the district, which was submitted
to and was accepted by the UPC executive committee,
was never implemented because Obote wanted to keep
the Acholi UPC leaders (e.g., Otema Alimadi and Peter
Ola) fighting each other. Thus Otema Alimadi was removed from the political scene to become ambassador
to the United States. This left Peter Ola, who was
more compliant and ineffective, in charge of Acholi
UPC. Divided between the UPC and the DP (then within
the UPC itself) the Acholi district was so weakened
that Obote was able to use some of its leaders and
troops to his ends without their posing a challenge
to him or effectively opposing some of his wild plans.
His encouragement of the West Nile fragmentation along
the same lines was equally pronounced. He reasoned
that if he was going to use troops from these groups
he had to keep their political leaders sufficiently
divided so as not to pose him a challenge, hoping to
carry them along under a loose umbrella of a common
ethnic identity that in truth did not exist in many
cases.

It must remain a matter of historical significance that some of the most determined opposition to
Obote's entire rule came from the very groups he was
seeking to mislead with ethnic appeals. Leaders of
stature, like M. Okelo and G. Oda from the West Nile,
A. Latim and H. Obonyo from Acholi, opposed him to
the end. As Obote became more confident and began to
discard those he had used among these groups in favor
of his own kinsmen, they discovered the truth and
turned against him. The false theory of an ethnicized
army crumbled, as is related later.

To camouflage it all, the national leader constantly condemned tribalism and urged the nation to
unite. Increasingly, however, Obote's actions were
beginning to speak louder than his words. In April
1965, he threatened a group of his leading colleagues
(including W. W. Nadiope, the vice president), saying
that he could use the Ugandan army and police to wipe
them and their supporters out. He then claimed he
personally had the loyalty of about 80 percent of the
army and 65 percent of the police. But what was the
basis of that loyal support? Clearly it was the loyalty of kinship and regionalism, reasons not worthy

of a national leader in a plural country.

There were two possible alternatives for recruiting an army in such a country. The first alternative,
which bears considerable merit, is what the Muganda
representative demanded in Parliament: a system of
quotas for all groups. Equitable representation in
the security forces would promote rather than hinder
public trust in government. The forces, when recruited
on a sectional basis, tend to be looked upon as "alien"
and in a crisis, such as the 1966 and 1971 revolutions,
tend to be looked upon as occupation forces by areas
other than those from which they were drawn. The end
result is ultimately self-defeating.

The second alternative system for recruitment
was for a party espousing a socialist philosophy, as
Obote's UPC did, to recruit the thousands of bright
young school-leavers who could not find places in
higher education or employment but who were strong
supporters of the UPC government and its objectives.
This would have been the best way to ensure support
and loyalty of the army. Indeed, it was the course
President Nyerere took for Tanzania after the mutiny
by recruiting TANU party members. True, such recruitment would have been roundly attacked, perhaps by the
KY and the DP, who would rightly have demanded equal
opportunity for all nationals. But this would have
been more defensible for a nationalist progressive
government than to have based recruitment of national
defense forces -- on whose loyalty the very existence
of the state and its basic institutions depended --
on sectional ethnic considerations with their obvious
potential for internal challenges and conflicts. Why
did he not recruit UPC youths? The reasons plainly
concerned ethnic origins and not fear of attack from
the opposition. The strongest support for the party
had not been in the North where he came from, but
clearly in the eastern region among the so-called
Bantus. Among the Basoga, for example, the second
largest ethnic group in the country, the UPC had enormous support. It had returned seven UPC members, the
largest number from any single district. There was
also extensive support in Bukedi and Bugisu in the
East, and Kigezi in the southwest. With the exception
of Lango and part of Karamoja on the other hand, the
DP had a strong showing in the North. And yet, in
spite of this, recruitment for the army from the East
was only marginal, while it concentrated in the North.
There were two main factors influencing Ugandan politics: ethnicity and religion. As the DP was largely
based on religion, it was Obote's calculation that
the pull of ethnicity would be stronger than that of

religion and with the added patronage he lavished on
the army, Nilotic identity would transcend the Catholicism of the DP. It worked for a time but at a great
cost to the country, as is later related. In this
regard, Obote was a tribalist and must be judged by
what he actually did and not what he publicly claimed.

The secret decision to use the army for maintaining power in the future produced other undesirable
side effects. Certainly, it was thought mistakenly
that relaxing discipline in the armed forces might
endear the UPC government to the troops even more.
Consequently, discipline declined steadily; in the
beginning it declined imperceptibly but later declined
rapidly and to an alarming extent. One vivid illustration of this occurred in 1964. In January of that
year, following one another in quick succession, the
armies of Tanganyika, Uganda, and Kenya mutinied in
their respective territories. In Uganda at Jinja
barracks, fifty miles from Kampala, troops manhandled
their officers and demanded more pay and better conditions of service. When the minister responsible
for them arrived to size up the situation he was
roughed up, locked up, and forced to sign an agreement
for the government to endorse the terms set by the
soldiers. It was the civilian government's first experience in dealing with a hostile army. There was an
outcry for discipline and dismissal of all those who
had violated regulations and army discipline in order
to set an example for the rest of the army and avoid
repetition. But to justify the reenlistment of the
mutineers, Obote later minimized the incident, saying
that there had been only "a sit-down strike." This
was patently false. The situation had been so serious
as to justify hasty appeal for British troops to fly
into the country and disarm the mutineers, which they
had done with efficiency in a predawn surprise raid.
(The British troops had been invited and came to quell
the mutinies in all three states.) Jomo Kenyatta in
Kenya and Julius Nyerere in Tanganyika had the muti-
nous leaders tried and jailed and the rest were dismissed from the army. However, almost all the mutineers in Uganda came from the very region whose
support Obote had set out to purchase at all cost.
Therefore, he publicly dismissed the mutineers only
to invite them back into the army privately and grant
them all their demands. Assured of such treatment,
discipline went steadily downhill as the soldiers felt
they could get whatever they wanted, however unreasonable.

In May 1966, the Ugandan army crushed Buganda
and thousands lost their lives. Whether or not using

troops against a largely defenseless citizenry is
proper is not material for this argument. Even if
troops had to be used to crush a rebellion, their
discipline was absolutely essential, especially considering that they were acting among their own nationals. But they went on a rampage; they raped, looted,
and generally terrorized the civilian population
around Buganda. There was a public and international
outcry against the excesses. Obote had to observe in
October 1968: "since May 1966, Uganda's Armed Forces
have been blamed as having been undisciplined, unruly,
and virtually in control of government."[26]
The lack of discipline was to continue, despite
denials, until it posed one of the greatest difficulties President Amin or any other leader had to face.
Thus, the proud tradition of a good and valiant national army was prostituted and manipulated by a
political leadership that put the seizure and retention of absolute power above any other consideration.
David Martin, in his book about Idi Amin (nearly
half of which in fact is about Obote), rightly con-
demns the horrendous loss of human life that followed
under the military government.[27] Obote emerges as
the hero and Amin, the villain. He glosses over the
tenacity with which Obote defended, politicized, and
programmed Amin to use the army for his personal ends,
launching the process of indiscriminate killings. He
criticizes several military commanders by name who,
as reputed Obote supporters, had been able to stop
Amin from taking over but failed to do so. It is
significant that not a single name of an officer from
the South, the so-called Bantus, is mentioned. This
means either that they were not in important positions in the army or that, if a few were, they were
not expected to risk their lives to defend him.
In any event, it is inadvertently a sad commentary
that Obote -- the nationalist leader, the "unifier"
-- was expected in time of dire peril to count on
troops from only a small section of the region, less
than one-quarter of the nation he ruled. But this
was entirely his own choice. Indeed, he cannot dis-
claim part of the responsibility for all those soldiers from Lango and Acholi who tragically lost their
lives because he had misled them into supporting his
personal ambitions, a majority of whom knew little or
nothing about the true nature of the power struggle
among the politicians.

The Choice, Protection, and Promotion of Idi Amin

Few things demonstrate Obote's reckless determi-

nation to regionalize and ethnicize the army as his
choice and support of Idi Amin to head the Ugandan
army. By Obote's own admission after his fall from
power, he had in his possession when he became prime
minister in May 1962 a disturbing record about Amin.
This is so.

As a corporal during the Mau Mau uprising, Amin
was said to use excessive force, even by colonial
officers who were eager to suppress this rebellion in
Kenya. There were reports that he had brutalized and
killed members of the Turkana tribe in Kenya when sent
to stop cattle raids between them and the Karamojong
in late 1961. The Kenyan colonial authorities at the
time demanded his repatriation to Kenya to stand trial
for the crimes, the punishment for which was dismissal
and possible imprisonment. Obote himself confirms that
the army headquarters for the King's African Rifles
in Nairobi had found Amin guilty and had sent his file
to Sir Walter Coutts, then governor of Uganda and commander in chief, to confirm the sentence and to dismiss Amin from the army. Sir Walter had insisted that
the case should not be handled in Kenya but in Uganda
as the protectorate was about to be independent.
Quite rightly, the governor sought the prime minister's
opinion on the case as to whether or not he should
confirm the sentence of dismissal. But Obote firmly
advised that Amin should be kept in the army. Remarkably, after his fall the same Obote had to say lamely,
"Even now I cannot explain why I came to give that
opinion [not to dismiss Amin]. . . . I advised that
Amin be warned."[27]

The truth is that Obote knew precisely what he
was doing. He chose Amin not in spite of demonstrated
ruthlessness but because of it. Amin was the kind of
man he wanted. Though Sudanic and not Nilotic, there
was a sense of common belonging as a fellow northerner
and around him Obote believed he could construct a web
of interethnic alliances within the armed forces to
buttress his own political power. In 1961 he saved
Amin from dismissal against unequivocal advice from
a parliamentary demand for his suspension or dismissal.
In both cases, Amin was saved precisely for the firm
purpose of Obote's using him as a hatchet man against
Obote's political enemies in some ultimate confrontation. Obote's determination to save him for a predetermined reason is all the clearer when one recalls
the ease with which he (Obote) dismissed from the army
several Sandhurst-trained officers, contrary to all
military regulations, when their only crime was either
being suspected of DP sympathies (if they were Catholic) or because they did not come from Obote's region.

The dismissal of Major Karugaba is as good an
example as any of this. Karugaba was the first Ugandan officer trained at Sandhurst in the United Kingdom.
At the time of independence he was already commissioned
and acted as the official escort of the duke of Kent,
who represented the British queen at the independence
ceremonies.

During the governor-general's garden party on
12 October 1962, as I accompanied Obote through state
guests he pointed out Karugaba to me at a distance
and inquired whether I knew him. I replied I did not.
He then confided that the senior British officers were
recommending him to command the army and to retire
Opolot and Amin, who had reached the highest ranks
they could reasonably attain. Obote then told me
Karugaba was a Roman Catholic and as such could not
be trusted and he would not accept him to head the
army. This was, of course, a case of Obote maneuver-
ing adroitly. The major reason was not religion, even
though there were areas and times where it counted.
The minister of defense, Felix Onama, initially a
close confidant of Obote, was himself a Catholic.
The principal rejection of Karugaba was because he
came from the so-called Bantus of the South. But
Catholicism was the only label Obote calculated would
be unacceptable to me because in southern Uganda where
Karugaba came from sharp religious rivalry between
Catholics and Protestants was a dominant political
factor. As I was Protestant, though from the South,
I was expected to endorse Karugaba's eclipse from the
army. I could not possibly accept this assumption.
Karugaba was later removed from the army contrary to
all regulations and against my explicit resistance.
Obote could never forgive me for this initial attempt
to block Amin's rise. Other trained officers like
Major Tom Ongotok from Amin's own district were later
similarly summarily removed.

Shaban Opolot from Teso was made commander in
August 1963 and Idi Amin, his deputy, but only because
of intensive private political opposition by a handful
of UPC top leaders who felt that Opolot, because of
seniority and performance, deserved the top post if
it were to go to a former NCO. This was postponing
the inevitable, however, as Obote continued to groom
Amin and often bypassed Opolot on major issues concerning the security of the country and the expansion of
the army. After the 1966 revolution (discussed later)
Obote finally gave the command to Idi Amin and eventually detained Opolot for over four years without trial.

But there were more than ample warnings given to
him not to keep Amin in the army. After Obote gave

his opinion to retain him, Sir Walter Coutts said it
was an error to keep such an officer in the army and
that the case against him deserved at least a sentence
of imprisonment. He then warned Obote that Amin might
cause him trouble in the future. Colonel William
Chayne, who was commander of the army on independence,
unequivocally recommended against keeping him in the
army and recommended to Obote at least to retire him.
Colonel Tillet, commander until the mutiny, privately
gave strong and unambiguous warnings against his retention. Close colleagues of Obote like myself, who
urged him to heed such advice, earned his enmity.
All this advice fell on deaf ears for a decision had
long been made to keep Amin, not because Obote loved
him but because for the time being Amin could serve
his purposes, there being no comparable northern officers yet to replace him. The secret recruitment
of the mutineers into the army after January 1964
(when they had been publicly dismissed), the rewarding with promotions of police officers who had shot
innocent civilians, as in the Nakulabye incident (discussed later), the sustained effort to flout military
discipline twice to save Amin and dismiss blameless
officers, the awarding of the army's demands with
little reference to the rest of society, and the consistent recruitment of the army predominantly from
one region were all part and parcel of a coherent plan
evolved by Obote to use force based largely on regional
or ethnic grounds as a means of keeping himself in power, even if it meant having to abrogate the constitution. He was to boast, as he threatened some of his
colleagues in 1965, that he could order Amin to mow
them and their supporters down because Amin would obey
him without any question. The real truth is that as
long as Amin would shoot Obote's political enemies on
his instructions, as he did with regard to the Baganda
in May 1966, he was an excellent officer. But when
Amin turned against him when a bloody feud ensued between the two men, then Amin became a tyrant. Of all
Ugandans formerly in public service, Obote has least
justification to condemn and attack Amin. If you harbor a deadly cobra and your friends and neighbors warn
you repeatedly about the dangers, both to them and to
yourself, of doing so, but you persistently ignore such
advice, calling those who tender it envious or ill-
intentioned, and if you continue to groom, nourish,
and protect the snake until it is old and strong enough
to bite or kill those in whose presence you release it
(because you detest them), one day the snake might turn
on you and your household with its deadly venom. Then
you have no one to blame but yourself. This is the

case of Obote with Amin. One can only regret the appalling loss of innocent lives that followed their conflict.

THE MISUSE OF POLICE POWERS TO PROMOTE THE UPC

Despite the internal security problems discussed earlier (of secession movements in Toro, cattle raids in Karamoja, and the lost counties in Buganda), the country had a remarkable tradition of respect for law and order. The police force that maintained it had a long and reputable tradition; its relations with the public were excellent. It was not until the UPC government began to instruct the police to suppress opposition parties and their meetings and to victimize suspected opposition supporters that the public became apprehensive and the police appeared ruthless. Government took numerous steps to bring about this result of which we can only give instances.

Normally all political parties or any organization were by law and the constitution allowed to hold a public meeting. The DP and the KY did so, just as did the governing UPC. It was only when there was a probable risk of a breach of public peace that the authorities took steps to stop the meetings. The existing law, S. 32(2) of the Police Act, empowered the police officer in charge of an area, if in his opinion the holding of a public meeting would result in a breach of the peace, to require the convener of the meeting, assembly, or procession by notice in writing to apply to the local magistrate for a permit. Both the police officer and the convener would then appear before the magistrate who, having heard the grounds for the police officer's fears, might or might not grant permission for the meeting. This system worked well and all political parties had conducted numerous campaigns under it in all the elections to national and local councils held up to 1964. It was fair because it preserved the impartiality of the police in the public eye and the decision was entrusted to an independent person, a magistrate.

Despite all effort, including the crossing over to the UPC of elected members of opposition parties, the DP and the KY were in fact still widely and ominously supported in the country. One only needed to see the vast thousands addressed by DP leaders in the West, East, and North of the country, while the KY remained unchallenged in Buganda. Obote, therefore, decided to vest the power of decision concerning whether or not to hold political meetings in police

officers instead of (as it had been) in a magistrate.
While he did not yet directly control the appointment
or posting of magistrates, because of his control of
public service appointments under a politicized Public
Service Commission, he could control directly the appointments of police officers who were to be in charge
of overseeing political meetings. In February 1965
the Police Act was amended to confer these powers on
the police. Its opposition in Parliament was emotional
and strong. It had now become obvious to the opposition that the UPC government was moving to eliminate
them from existence on all fronts.

The DP leader, Alexander Latim from Acholi, termed
it "very malicious." But it was Abu Mayanja, a one-
time close colleague of Obote in the defunct UNC and
a leading nationalist, who exposed the government's
weakness: "This government which was elected by the
people of Uganda, so sure of itself, is nevertheless
so afraid of the people of Uganda, so terrified that
it is not going to permit them to assemble to listen
to anybody who has got a different point of view."[28]

The opposition then challenged the government to
quote any instances where the present law had failed,
warranting the introduction of a new one. They challenged them to find any instances, for example, where
a policeman, having advised against a public meeting,
had the magistrate ignore his opinion and grant permission, with the result that the meeting was held
and a breach of the peace had resulted. It is significant that no such instances were quoted, because
there were none. If there had been enough breaches
of the peace to justify new police powers, it might
have helped to cover up the UPC's true intentions.
But as the old law had functioned flawlessly, it was
now another unambiguous signal to the opposition that
their days were numbered.

The tendency, as E. K. Mulira put it, was clear:

Where governments in Africa have tried to transfer powers from the judiciary to the police,
those powers have not been used by the police at
their discretion, but have been used by the chief
executives of those countries to destroy their
political opponents. . . . They have used those
powers not only to destroy their political opponents who existed at the time when the bills
were debated and passed in parliament, but even
those people who at that time supported them in
parliament to pass those bills, later on suffered
as victims at the hands of these leaders.[29]

This was both prophetic and accurate, as we shall see. Shortly after the passage of the new law, sure enough, legitimate peaceful meetings of the opposition were banned or disrupted throughout the country. This was obvious provocation inviting instability. It was too much to expect a part of the masses and their leaders to acquiesce submissively to such an outrageous abuse of authority. Place after place was cited where opposition meetings had been disrupted or prevented by the police. There were numerous instances from the East, North, and West where a UPC official demanded to address a DP rally and, on being refused, had the crowds dispersed by the police to prevent the lawful conveners from addressing their followers.

With the overt involvement of the police in party politics, came alarmingly the decline of discipline and the increase of the use of firearms to impose the UPC upon the people. Reports began to come from many parts of the country of excessive force by the police in handling civilians, which had never occurred previously. From the West Nile district, Acholi, Lango, and Bugisu, representatives of the people began to produce accurate reports of such incidents that the government could not contradict. But perhaps the most dramatic and tragic illustration of this new era was what came to be called the "Nakulabye incident," named after the place where the incident happened in the Buganda region. Official violence and loss of human life on an incomparably larger and more brutal scale were to engulf the country from 1971 onward. But Nakulabye is a landmark on the road to that violence, for it marked clearly the determination of a government to encourage and reward members of the security forces to take human life without proper justification but for purely selfish political ends. What followed in later years was only a more extensive application of this same philosophy. A conflagration always begins small.

Nakulabye is a suburb of Kampala, the capital of Uganda. Late one afternoon on 10 November 1964 there was a quarrel -- not unusual in such areas -- between a woman and a Congolese man, who was making amorous advances to her. A couple of relatives joined them to settle the dispute. In a few moments, two police patrol cars arrived with batons and commenced to beat everyone in sight. A little later, armed police arrived and, without asking any questions and without the slightest provocation, at once began shooting at the crowd. Their method is relevant to the deliberate nature of their acts, and we give some detail from sworn evidence:

Victim 1: Kalungi Munyoro, aged about sixty years, was a taxi driver. As he approached where the police were, they stopped him. Before he could fully get out of the car, they shot him at point-blank range with a .303 rifle, without even asking him a single question. He died instantly.

Victim 2: Fabiano Musika was talking to his neighbor when he suddenly saw the security men rushing toward their huts. One of the security men saw him and immediately fired at him, but missed. Musika quickly rushed back into his house, closed the front door, went through the living room and stayed in his bedroom. The police rushed after him, broke open his door, passed through the sitting room and shot him through the chest at point-blank range with a .303 high velocity bullet. He died instantly.

Victim 3: Mr. Mayanja, aged about sixty-two, a Munyoro by tribe, was eating with his wife when soldiers came to their door and ordered him to open it. They then dragged him out, beat him, and then shot him through the head. He died at once. His wife was dragged out and beaten, but not killed.

Victim 4: Keita was a seventeen-year-old Muganda schoolboy. He had just returned from school and was busy helping his mother with domestic chores. Two police officers came to the door and ordered them to open. The mother and eight kids were got out. One policeman loaded his rifle, while Keita was on his knees pleading, and at point-blank range shot him through the stomach. He died instantly.

Victim 5: Silas Matovu, sixty-year-old Mugandan, was in his house when police shot and missed his son, Leo Muwonge, as the bullet flew between his legs. The boy rushed into the house to tell his father, Mr. Matovu. As he was attending a slight wound on his son, one policeman aimed at his heart through an open window and killed him instantly.

Victim 6: Ezama, a young Lugbara schoolboy who was returning from school, saw the group of armed police at a distance and decided to turn into an alley to escape them. One soldier fired at him and missed. Ezama then threw down his motor bike and ran. He encountered two soldiers on the opposite side. They shot him through the back to his death.[30]

All these elderly and young people had no connection with the quarrel that the police had come to settle. Even if they had, they deserved no such cold-blooded murder by a police force that was supposed to protect them. Many more people were seriously injured. The incident caused a public outrage. The manner in which Obote handled this outrage in Parliament did not help our relations. He had to answer. Having prepared his speech he summoned me to his office from the National Assembly, which was in session just one floor below his office. There he gave me his prepared speech to read on the floor of the Assembly within a few minutes. Why did he not have the courage to face the nation and deliver it himself? He explained that he had suddenly made an appointment that required him to leave Parliament buildings at once. But as it turned out, he had no appointment at all and never left his office. I had to bear the brunt of Buganda's outrage by giving an explanation on the floor of Parliament. While promising appointment of prompt inquiry into the true causes of the tragedy, the government did not show remorse commensurate with the brutal murders. I had little choice at so short a notice. I descended to the Assembly and delivered Obote's statement but made it quite clear he prepared it himself and would have delivered it but for a sudden commitment. Typically, he was later furious that I should have mentioned it was his statement, but I was not about to accept responsibility for official murder.

Chris Kantinti, then a Kampala senior magistrate, was appointed coroner to establish the true circumstances of the deaths. His report was unequivocal: all the victims had been "violently and deliberately shot by a group of armed policemen." Then he said, "I accept that a crowd gathered at the scene, as people here usually do for flimsy things. I agree that they gathered peacefully to know what was going on." There was clearly no cause for these brutal murders. Not a single policeman had complained he had been assaulted in any way. If the police had exceeded their powers, it was clearly the government's duty to show the country its disapproval by punishing the offenders under due process of law. But rather than do that, the government showed its gratitude by rewarding the participating policemen with promotions. The officer who had directed the operation was given a trip abroad and promoted to become a regional police commander in the East. He had done a "good job" in teaching the people a lesson and demonstrating the power of the UPC. This incident left a deep impression on many of the people in all parties. It refueled primordial fears and with them came the decline of an effective UPC.

The police had always used "reasonable" or minimum" force in the performance of its duties. Before any member of the Ugandan Cabinet was born, this rule had been established for the police force and it had worked well. It checked excesses without preventing the police to function effectively. But the situation was remarkable now that Obote had granted the police use of "maximum force" instead of "minimum force." It meant that under the law if a policeman killed you while booking you for a traffic offense, for example, he would be immune from prosecution. It was absurd for Obote to give the reason for such a move as police inability to interpret the use of "minimum force" when performing their duties. As he had done with the army, he now moved to condition the police in such a way as to do his bidding, including the blatant use of brutal force on their countrymen as a justified method for keeping the UPC in power at all costs.

EFFORTS TO MONOPOLIZE GOVERNMENT POWER

Controlling the Central Government Public Service

One of the great problems that the independence government faced was to ensure a stable, contented, efficient public service, for upon this depended the translation into reality of all government programs. Above all, the public service had to be loyal in the implementation of government policies. But as the public service became fully Ugandanized, it followed that its personnel could not in reality be indifferent to the political and other major issues facing the country. It was obvious that the service was divided among the parties (the UPC, the DP, and the KY) just as the rest of the population they served. But how does one ensure loyalty? What is its test? Was a good DP or KY public servant incapable of serving a UPC government efficiently? Was it preferable to employ in government services only UPC supporters, however professionally substandard they were? The Ugandan government was confronted with these questions in an acute form because of the shortage of skilled manpower on independence.

The initial position was to continue the British practice in the United Kingdom of maintaining a public (and military) service that did not participate in politics publicly or actively. This seemed by far the best course and in the initial stages of Obote's government, on the whole, it worked well. There is a

reciprocal element in confidence and loyalty. When
the leadership placed confidence in the public service
to perform its duty, the public service generally responded effectively and loyally. But Obote began to
feel that the better alternative was to convert the
entire public service into UPC party members and supporters and to eliminate those who would not accept
conversion. This process, interacting with the general political issues, helped exacerbate opposition fears
that their days were numbered.

All matters of appointments, promotions, dismissals, and related issues concerning the public service
were vested in the Public Service Commission. Although
its membership was appointed by the prime minister, it
was independent in its deliberations and decisions.
The first constitutional amendment of September 1963
changed this position and made the Public Service Commission merely advisory to the prime minister. In
effect, therefore, the tenure of office in the public
service was no longer to be dependent on an independent
body, but on the will of a political leader. The opposition bitterly attacked this move inside and outside
the Parliament as a potential cause of insecurity among
public servants and a prelude to UPC party members taking over public service. At this stage it was an unjustified charge because it was necessary for a young
and unsure government to have sufficient authority to
ensure an efficient government in this transition time.
The crucial issue was how the powers were to be used
and, unfortunately on this ground, there was beginning
to be cause for concern.

In several ministries, able and experienced public
servants were labelled DP and were dealt with unfairly.
Those who were not dismissed (in top echelons there
were relatively few) were superceded in promotions by
UPC supporters or lived in permanent apprehension for
their future. The danger became more manifest as the
UPC began to make political appointments of people the
public service could do without. Alexander Latim of
the DP gave some examples of such appointments and why
the opposition opposed direct ministerial control of
public service appointments. For example:

A gentleman called Miriaduar, who failed in so
many offices -- he became a sort of a typist in
the Provincial Commissioner's office in Gulu, he
failed; he then joined the police force, he failed; he was made a jago (local government chief),
he failed; . . . I campaigned against this man in
Moyo in April. He was brutal. . . . He is now
an Assistant District Commissioner in Moyo, and

he is ill-treating all those men against whom he
was campaigning in Moyo elections. . . . There
was another man called Lou. . . . He made a mess
of every school he went to. This man is now a
District Commissioner or Assistant District Commissioner, and I have many other instances. . . .
Why should the UPC now resort to appointing these
men who have been failures in life, simply because they have supported them in politics?[31]

That was to be the challenge to fair play. This
pattern claimed by Latim touched every district and
kingdom, except for Buganda for different reasons.
It is obviously true that in all politics there is
patronage to reward party supporters after victory.
What, however, is negative and ultimately self-defeating is to carry this to such an extent as to begin
eliminating able, efficient officers and replacing
them with incapable party supporters or goons. The
issue was made acute by the fact that government was
the biggest employer in the nation. And yet Obote
had a logical though unjust reason for it. He had
never been enthusiastic about a well-organized, well-
staffed UPC. It was therefore much neater for him to
employ UPC supporters in the public service and make
them work to build the party with government resources
that the UPC could not do by itself. This assured him
complete control as he alone had the power ultimately
to appoint and fire them, which he did not have under
the party constitution with party officials who were
responsible to the Central Executive Committee of the
UPC. This practice was more pronounced at the district
level, which was also the most sensitive level as it
was closer to the people. A kind of witch-hunt of DP
(and later of KY) supporters in government departments
ensued. In order to appreciate the aggravation, it is
important to remember that the vast majority of those
victimized were in fact never disloyal to the government.
    I will give just a few examples. As minister of
justice, I was responsible for, among other things,
the administration of the lower courts (at the time
called the African Courts), largely administering customary laws and assuming responsibility for policy
regarding the higher courts (magistrates and High
Court). The African courts handled about four-fifths
of all the litigation in the country; consequently,
they touched the people more closely and more often.
In Obote's own district of Lango, the chief judge of
the African Court, a man called Omonya, had served
government for nearly twenty-five years. Obote asked

me to dismiss him on the ground that he was a DP supporter. What was the evidence? The political head
of Lango district administration, Ben Otim (married
to Obote's aunt), had made the allegation and it was
final. It seemed unlikely that a man of such long and
distinguished service would be so rash as to play politics, especially in the home area of the head of the
country's government; but it was not improbable. I
decided to send my principal officer to Lango to make
inquiries. His report, which was thorough, rather than
disclosing any evidence of political involvement, com-
plimented the judge as an outstanding and respected
officer. I took this information to Obote who still
insisted I must fire Omonya nevertheless. I then
drove to Lango myself to make an on-the-spot inquiry.
I interviewed all types of people including the origi-
nators of the accusations. Omonya knew of no evidence
to brand himself as a DP supporter. He decided cases
between parties of all political persuasions but not
one UPC member ever alleged a case had been lost to
a DP follower because of the chief judge's partiality.
No evidence existed whatsoever that Omonya even attended public or private DP meetings. On the contrary, he
was highly regarded in Lango and I drove back to Kampala determined to take a stand against this escalating
danger of witch-hunting. When I gave my findings to
Obote, he threatened to fire me instead. In the end
we compromised. The judge was retired within a year
and with full benefits. The principal reason to remove him had been that he was a Roman Catholic and a
DP supporter by attribution.

A chief minister of one of the "federal" states
wrote to me that I dismiss four of his top judges in
the African Courts because they were DP supporters.
Again on inquiry, they turned out to have been sound
officials, but were supposed to be DP supporters because they were Roman Catholics. This time, I rejected
the request. But the pressures to conduct witch-hunts
of DP or KY supporters in government were widespread
without a firm stand to stop them. There were therefore two competing approaches to the public service.
The first, promoted by Obote, was to put as many UPC
supporters as possible in government posts and eliminate DP and KY supporters, real or imagined. The
second was to take all people equally so long as they
rendered efficient and honest service. In a country
divided by ethnic and religious cleavages, further
handicapped by the scarcity of trained manpower, it
was disastrous to begin promoting sectional party interests in the public service. It would however be
unfair to place the entire blame on Obote. There were

lower UPC officers who were sometimes carried away by
their eagerness to promote the party and exceeded the
proper limits of dealing with opposition members. It
was both absurd and dangerous to say that every Catholic was prima facie a DP supporter, even though the
DP was a predominantly Catholic party. This attitude
had a counterproductive tendency of driving some UPC
Catholic supporters into the arms of the DP. Besides,
the UPC had among its prominent leaders, ministers,
and founders, some leading Catholics. In any event,
even if in his privacy an officer supported an opposition party, so long as he performed his duties well,
that was his inalienable right. But the winner-take-
all philosophy tended to demand total and exclusive
control of everything, as far as humanly possible.

It was the appointment of a leading UPC politician
as chairman of the Ugandan Public Service Commission
(PSC) that elevated the problem to new and more serious
levels. Although the PSC had become advisory to the
prime minister, it could still be regarded as fairly
impartial as its membership was drawn from professional
people of integrity even if some had UPC leanings.
Overall experience was showing that the vast majority
of career public servants, even though they may privately hold other political views, were prepared to
serve loyally under the government of any party. But
on 26 August 1964 Abdala-Anyuru, a UPC member of Parliament from Lango West (in Obote's district), resigned
his seat as Obote had chosen him to become chairman of
the Public Service Commission. Abdala-Anyuru was a
capable, intelligent UPC member and would have made as
good a cabinet minister as most. But to appoint him
to head a body that controlled the fate of all public
servants was most imprudent. It struck terror among
many public employees who feared victimization on political grounds. One can obviously argue that a UPC
man can be as fair as any in such a post. Yet, it was
not only necessary for people at the top to be fair,
but it was also important to appear to be so to everyone, especially in a divided country. The choice of a
UPC member by a UPC government to head the PSC was
rightly not expected to be viewed as fair in the country. The opposition promptly launched a vigorous attack on the appointment. Their leader asserted: "What
the UPC government is doing is trying to see to it
that only members of the party in power get employed."[32]
This was perhaps an exaggeration, but it accurately
reflected how the action was perceived publicly. I had
by this time become minister of state in charge of the
public service. If there were any attacks on government policy, it was my responsibility to defend it.

However, I knew absolutely nothing of Abdala-Anyuru's appointment until one morning a chance remark brought it to my attention. Obote had left the country for a Commonwealth Conference. Both of us shared a common permanent secretary who was also head of the Civil Service. He stepped into my office to inform me he was taking some papers to the president to sign. When I asked what papers he told me they were those confirming the appointment of Abdala-Anyuru as chairman of the Public Service Commission. At this time, although the prime minister actually made the appointment, it had to be signed by the president to take effect. The president, Sir Frederick Mutesa (also kabaka of Buganda) was purely a ceremonial head who had to sign what the prime minister asked him to.

Astonished by the information, I asked the permanent secretary to hold on to the papers while I telephoned Obote in London to discuss the implications of a UPC member of Parliament becoming the chairman of PSC. Clearly, it was the prime minister's prerogative to make the appointment but it was most unusual that he should do so without discussing it with his minister who had to defend its political unpalatability, even just to inform him of his decision. The permanent secretary declined, as he had explicit instructions to take the appointment papers to the president for signature. It was Obote's instruction that the appointment be made and announced before his return. I decided to delay it. I went to the president at once and explained the explosive political implications involved. I pleaded for a stay of his signature until Obote returned and he agreed. On Obote's return no appointment had been made as expected and he was furious. He summoned me to his office and called the minister of works, Balaki Kirya, to attend. When the three of us met, Obote angrily demanded I withdraw my advice to the president about signing the papers for Abdala-Anyuru's appointment. He then gave me three days within which to do it or I would meet unspecified serious consequences. I reiterated that it was his prerogative to make the appointment and that even if I wanted to I could not stop him, but my action in delaying it was to discuss its implications with him. As the minister responsible to defend it, I had a right to be consulted and informed even though I could be overridden. I was not going to retract a step I considered fair and essential. Of course, Abdala-Anyuru was later appointed but the rift between Obote as president of the UPC and myself as the party's secretary-general was regrettably increasing. This rift was principally arising from our conflicting views about

how to direct the policy of unifying and integrating
the diverse peoples of the state. The conflict was
to escalate.

Two other instances show the nature of the conflict that was taking shape. Akena Adoko, Obote's
cousin who later became most notorious as head of the
"gestapo" -- the general service unit -- first came
to me when I was minister of justice to ask for a job,
as he was a trained lawyer. He was offered two posts
successively, first as a magistrate and then as a
state attorney, each of which he soon discarded although they were excellent prospects in a virtually
unindigenized judiciary. He then demanded to be
appointed principal of a law school my ministry had
established to train customary law magistrates. Not
only was this a much more senior post for which he
did not qualify under the normal procedure, but it was
already filled by an able officer I was not prepared
to replace. I resisted this pressure. The next thing
I knew Akena was in the prime minister's office, once
again with me as I had become minister of state, except now he was the head of a super-spy operation,
which gave him more power than any UPC official had
ever wielded, with the exception of Obote.

As minister responsible for the civil service, I
endeavored to keep the PSC free of adverse political
pressures even though Obote had already politicized
it by exclusively appointing to it UPC members. Only
once did I ever intervene to influence an appointment.
The post of deputy commissioner of prisons fell vacant
and had to be filled. This was a responsible position
as the prison system dealt not only with issues of
punishment or reform but also ran extensive countrywide industries. There were two candidates for the
post, neither of whom I knew personally. One, the more
senior Kigonya, was both a Muganda and a Catholic and
therefore had a double handicap. The other, Samson
Achieng, though more junior was a cousin of Obote.
The minister responsible for prisons strongly supported
Achieng. The principal ground given was that it would
be easier for him to deal with a prison staff which was
supposedly predominantly northern, although there was
no proof to substantiate this. I obtained the files
of both officers and on perusal I saw that there was
absolutely no question that Kigonya was not only more
senior but had consistently a better record. I decided to intervene. In a strongly worded letter to
the PSC, I pointed out as minister responsible for
public service that I would not support Achieng over
Kigonya; justice had both to be done and to appear to
be done. Significantly, Obote decided to keep the

post vacant for nearly three years, even after I was
no longer in government. Ironically, after the revolution of 1966, Achieng assumed special significance
in the prison system as he took particular charge of
all of Obote's VIP detainees, including myself. This
made the conditions of detention more difficult. After
the revolution, Obote at last made him the deputy commissioner, as rules of the winner-take-all philosophy
were now in full bloom. Multiplied many times over
in other ministries and local governments, the practice
could not but promote resentment and conflict, with a
tendency to make individuals unduly conscious of their
ethnic, regional, or religious background, which was
not good for the health of the state.

In addition, the practice of hounding opponents
was spreading to the private sector. The case of
Daudi Ocheng was not an exception. Ocheng was one of
Uganda's few agricultural economists and by the time
Obote took over power in May 1962, Ocheng was assistant and likely successor to the expatriate chairman
of the Uganda Development Corporation (UDC), the most
important nongovernmental body in the country. But
because he was a friend of the kabaka (whom Obote had
secretly decided to dispose of as discussed elsewhere)
and despite the fact that he was from a leading Acholi
family in the North, he fell foul of the UPC government and was dismissed from the UDC on Obote's orders.
He took an important job with the Madhvani Group of
Companies. I was present when Obote instructed a
minister to threaten Madhvani with nationalization if
he did not dismiss Ocheng forthwith. He was accordingly dismissed and had to fall back on his own resources. He did not deserve this persecution and had
done nothing to warrant it, although he was later to
become a leading critic of the UPC government, playing
a role that no honest government needed to fear. His
motion to expose some of the unlawful activities of
Obote's government (which we consider later) will always rank as a highlight in the country's parliamentary annals.

Controlling Local Governments

We mentioned the conflict, both intraparty (UPC)
and interparty, that was beginning to build up in the
local governments (or regional administrations, as
they were called). With the advent of representative
government in the early sixties, direct elections to
the councils of these governments were fought with
as much vigor and seriousness as elections to the Parliament. All political parties, as they advocated and

agitated for independence, heightened the significance
of representative government among the masses, in local as well as central governments. The winning party
therefore looked forward to exercising whatever authority the constitution granted the councils without undue
interference and control from the center. The UPC
government early in its life, nevertheless, began to
take steps to ensure and tighten its control over local
governments and their politics. Let us take taxation
as an example.

The issue of assessment and payment of taxes to
local governments was very important. Originally, each
locality had a tax assessment committee that consisted
mostly of chiefs. It should be mentioned that chiefs
here were civil servants and were required to be nonpartisan regarding political parties. They were therefore on the whole regarded as more impartial in assessing taxes than were politicians. But the new government law transferred these powers from the chiefs to
the tax assessment committees "to be constituted in
accordance with written directions issued by the Minister."[33] This by itself need not have been alarming as
it gave the central government authority to ensure
uniform and fair practices of such committees throughout the country. But as it turned out, only UPC party
members were put on these assessment committees. As
a result, widespread unrest and protests mushroomed
over the claim that DP supporters were being unjustly
required to pay higher taxes than UPC members of comparable means. The opposition leaders resisted the
new committees and urged their supporters in some
areas where blatant injustices had been done not to
pay taxes. The government had to pass legislation in
February 1963 making it a punishable offense to incite
people not to pay taxes. Had the opposition DP been
represented on tax assessment committees, even as
minority members, it is highly probable that these
tensions would have been avoided.

But the monopoly of power and positions throughout the whole local government administrations in the
state was such that, although objectively the DP was
substantially supported, they were never given the
opportunity to participate meaningfully in the formulation or execution of policy. They were rendered
second-class citizens in their own country.

This policy tended to spark off conflict in addition in areas where the UPC was governing a multiethnic
district -- as in Kigezi, Bukedi, Toro, and West Nile
-- where one particular ethnic group (or in alliance
with another) sought to impose its hegemony on the
rest, with adverse divisive results. Because the

central government itself shared with the UPC the
policy of monopolizing power, rather than acting as
a restraining influence on local governments it actually promoted and exacerbated the practice, inasmuch
as the top hierarchy in the government and the party
scrambled for support throughout the lower echelons
of the party and government in the state.

The Independence Constitution had empowered Parliament to enact legislation setting down more fully
the powers and functions of the three western kingdoms
and Busoga. We have already discussed the main powers
thus granted. But the debates that surrounded this
legislation and the opposition it aroused among those
affected indicated the local fears. The kingdoms
affected demanded the general power to legislate over
a farther-ranging list of items than was ever contem-
plated by the framers of the constitution. The demands
were made all the harder to reject because three of
the four governments (Bunyoro, Busoga, and Toro) were
led strongly by the UPC and only Ankole was controlled
by the DP at the time. Quite properly, Obote and Obwangor (minister responsible for regional administrations at the time) stood firmly against these excessive
demands. It is therefore ridiculous to suppose that
every act by government in trying to exert and centralize control was detrimental. Some, like this refusal
to grant more power than necessary, were sound. The
failure came, partly, when powers thus retained were
used with manifest partiality and divisiveness by
leaders of the central government.

As I argued in Obote's support:

> While we tried to compromise with history, while
> we tried to move smoothly from the past into the
> future by accepting the reality that the kingdoms
> are to have a certain measure of federal status,
> nevertheless, in anticipating the future, we had
> to state and be firm that only those powers as
> are commensurate with the requirements of a mo-
> dern state and with the peculiar circumstances
> of the kingdoms should be given.[34]

In June 1963, two principal posts of political
leaders of district councils were created. The political head of the local government was to be a secretary-
general and would serve as the head of the majority
group in the council. There was also to be a financial
secretary who would be in charge of the treasury. This
was a democractic development and one welcomed by UPC
supporters who controlled all the district councils.
And yet, within six months, another law was passed

making the appointment of these two principal officers
conditional upon the minister's approval. The previous
legislation had also stipulated that any of the two
officers could be voted out of office by two-thirds of
the council members. But now, even if the council had
such a majority, it could not remove its leaders without the minister's approval. In other words, the right
of the people in every district to choose their political leaders was substantially negated. The government's reason for such central control was ostensibly
to "ensure election by Councils of non-tribal, non-
factional groups."[35] These were noble aims except
that they presupposed what did not exist, that the
minister and the central government would be immune
from these divisions when in fact they promoted and
exploited them.

The powers thus assumed by the center therefore
were double edged. They were not aimed at the DP,
which controlled no council, but at UPC supporters.
By taking upon itself the power to select or reject
principal political leaders in district councils, the
central government was now directly embroiled in local intraparty disputes. In practice it took sides
and therefore made friends as well as enemies within
its own party. If the central authority had been
exercised fairly from the top, it might perhaps have
been beneficial both for the local administrations and
the UPC. But as it turned out, the powers thus assumed
were merely an additional instrument in the hands of
the party leaders who were also the Ugandan government
leaders to manipulate and exploit intraparty conflict
now emerging in the top hierarchy of UPC. With a
party divided from top to bottom, therefore, justice
and fair play came to be guided by the systematic
promotion of sectional interests within the party and
not by the interests of the UPC and Uganda as a whole,
although this had to be paid lip service. More and
more powers were acquired by the central government
to control district councils, as we shall later show,
to the point of making local government a sham. With
the UPC being discredited by its own members and its
unifying force on the decline, more fundamental pulls
of ethnicity, religion, and outright personal ambition
came to the fore to make government at both local and
national levels increasingly problematic.

As was mentioned earlier, government at these two
levels was the biggest employer in the country. Each
local government had a fairly large body of employees
manning all its services. The appointment of all these
employees was vested in a Regional Public Service Commission set up by an act of Parliament. It was most

desirable that government both be and appear to be
fair in these appointments, promotions, transfers,
and dismissals of the local government officers, such
as chiefs who were in such close contact with the
masses of the people. But as with the Public Service
Commission of the central government, the Regional
Service Commission was not only made merely advisory
to the minister in performing its functions, but its
composition was entirely made up of UPC party members
and supporters as well:

> Chairman: Lalobo -- UPC, Acholi
> Members: Mungonya -- UPC, Ankole, Komukoryo --
> UPC, Kigezi, Olema -- UPC, West Nile, Ekurotoi
> -- UPC, Teso, and Wasukulu -- UPC, Bukedi.

Such composition inspired apprehension among a good
many officials who feared they would be victimized
or removed because they were DP, on however flimsy
and wild the suspicion. Local government administrations began to decline in effectiveness because of
such divisive meddling, and the more they declined
the more the central government took more powers to
direct them, yet without amelioration. As early as
23 September 1963, only a year after independence,
the minister of internal affairs was already reporting
to the nation a sad state of affairs:

> Throughout the country there are indications of
> an increase in inter-tribal tension and inter-
> party friction. . . . I would merely warn that
> in my view this inter-tribal friction and party
> quarreling is doing a grave disservice to the
> development of this country. A house that is
> split against itself cannot stand.[36]

From the minister's own district a leading opposition spokesman had charged: "General lawlessness
and hooliganism of the UPC society in West Nile have
had far-reaching consequences in that they have heightened tension between UPC and DP and aroused the dormant
spirits of a peace-loving people."[37]
But why could not the DP be included on such bodies as the regional or public service commissions?
A couple of their members sitting on the commission
and constituting a minority, which in voting would not
have altered a decision, would have been a most useful
restraining influence and ultimately would have been
to the advantage of the UPC administration and party.
The idea of monopolizing power was increasingly so
pervasive, however, that even to suggest such an ap-

proach would have been looked upon as a betrayal of
the party's best interests. The process was therefore to escalate, with a good section of the population (whose combined votes for the DP and the KY in
the last general election far exceeded those for the
UPC) effectively denied a fair share in the rewards of
independence for which they had struggled as much as
the UPC.

THE REVIVAL OF PRIMORDIAL FEARS

Buganda

The manifest efforts by the UPC central government to concentrate all power in its own hands, if
necessary using ruthless methods through the national
police force, and the rapid expansion of the army so
shamelessly on a sectional ethnic basis could not help
but arouse fears long ago held by various groups in
the country concerning the safety of their future.
Not unnaturally, the Baganda, who had for so long
fought for their autonomy, were among the first to
become apprehensive.
The Buganda government, in its bid to secede before independence, had given the British in 1960 as
one of their reasons:

It would be asking too much of the Baganda to
entrust the destiny of their country into the
hands of political party leaders whose experience
has not been proved by time. This could be extremely risky in the light of recent history
which has shown clearly that politicians in emergent countries use parliamentary democracy as a
springboard to virtual dictatorship.[38]

Now they saw symptoms of a dreaded dictatorial regime
steadily creeping toward their doorstep to fulfill
their worst apprehensions.
What had happened to the warm and promising relationship between the UPC and KY? A proper understanding of this relationship and how it was dissolved
is essential to the true understanding of Buganda's
revived fears and their connection with the 1966
revolution.
We said the alliance between the UPC and KY had
been principally formed to defeat the DP and to keep
it from forming the independence government. It was
obviously an opportunistic arrangement in this regard.
But it was a perfectly legitimate political maneuver,

for a government had to be formed and as the strength
of the parties in Parliament stood, it could come
about only through a coalition. Apart from UPC's support of some of Buganda's demands at the constitutional conferences, there had been no other specific undertakings by either side except a general agreement to
work together. There was no written document of any
kind to embody whatever had been agreed upon. And yet
this did not presuppose automatic conflict between the
two allies. The policy of the Buganda government had
been to obtain reasonable authority on some aspects
of Bugandan administration and above all to safeguard
the position of their kabaka in an independent Uganda.
With UPC help these objectives had been attained. As
there was no declared consistent policy guiding KY
administration in national affairs within the coalition, the UPC government policy formed the basis of
national administration for both parties at the center.
The policies of the departments of education, health,
agriculture, commerce and industry, and foreign affairs
became the policy of the KY, executed by ministers
from both groups under Obote's leadership. It is significant to remember, that so long as the alliance
lasted, despite occasional strains, at no time had the
KY in Parliament voted against a UPC-sponsored measure,
disobeying the government whip. This is important because it shows the possibility still existed for the
UPC to control and direct the KY.

The blame for the breakup of the alliance is
shared by both sides but more so by the UPC. Shortly
after forging the alliance and forming the government,
two schools of thought emerged within the UPC leadership about the future of the KY. One group, headed
by Obote, felt that the sole value of the KY had been
to provide a ladder for the UPC to gain power. The
other view, supported by several leading members who
were cofounders of the UPC and had helped forge the
alliance, was that in order to introduce party politics
to Buganda, which had resisted them for so long, and
to integrate the kingdom into the nationalist process,
KY leadership should dissolve the party and direct its
members to join the UPC. In this way, the UPC would
have a good start ahead of the DP in Buganda. I supported this view, but Obote would not have it. He
considered such a substantial move of the numerically
relatively preponderant Baganda as a threat to his
own position. Consequently, he preferred the KY to
remain intact.

In 1963, while I accompanied Obote to New York
where he received an honorary doctorate from Long
Island University, we received a cable informing us

of the first crossings of KY members into the UPC.
Five leading ministers in the coalition had joined
the UPC. As I rejoiced at the news in our suite at
the Waldorf Astoria Hotel, to my astonishment and remorse Obote was visibly angered and resentful about
it. Why? It could not be a genuine crossing over,
he said. One cannot trust the Baganda. They wanted
to control the UPC and this crossing was their spear-
head. Accordingly, he felt the best thing would be
to remain in a state of permanent coalition (referring
to the Conservative party and the Irish Unionists in
the United Kingdom) with the Baganda and their KY intact. I was distressed because this seemed to me to
be losing a golden opportunity to transform Buganda
into a UPC stronghold. Given time and proper strategy
it seemed feasible. Buganda as a region under the UPC
party constitution would have been subject to the UPC
central executive committee, which was the directorate
of the party. It would have been practical to open
party branches in the kingdom with the support rather
than hostility of Bugandan leadership. The Baganda
masses would have been open to UPC party propaganda
that aimed at building a unified, just, humane socialist society in a relaxed atmosphere. All the UPC
needed was to buy time for a purposeful conversion
within the kingdom.

The KY had been formed as an essentially ad hoc
organization to enable the Baganda to contest elections
within four months after the 1961 constitutional conference. It was never intended by its authors to be
a permanent body.[39] However, organizations create
vested interests of sorts and it soon became apparent
that some KY leaders were now changing their minds and
wanted to make it permanent. To some of us in the UPC,
who sought to integrate Buganda, this was an ill omen.
It supported Obote's view, though for different purposes, and raised problems the alliance had never faced
-- and often postponed -- because of their potentially
explosive nature. For instance, could UPC, which was
not only a national party but the ruling government,
afford not to actively seek party membership in Buganda? If it did, what would happen when the KY controlled the Baganda masses? A clash between two
allies in the field would be inevitable. The party
functionaries in lower cadres on either side would not
appreciate the need for considerable restraint nor the
consequences of exacerbated interparty tensions and
conflict. Indeed, these fears were to be realized with
sad and costly consequences. When UPC officials went
to the Buganda countryside to open party branches, they
were often intimidated by KY members. When there were

by-elections for local government and municipalities
within Buganda, the UPC and the KY contested them
against each other. But the relations on the whole
were still sound by the first independence anniversary
in October 1963 and were still within limits for reconciliation.

The government had made a decision to have an
African Ugandan head of state (a purely ceremonial but
prestigious post) by this first anniversary of independence. Although the UPC had made no commitment to the
Bugandan government, it seemed eminently sensible that
if the UPC as the senior partner in the coalition headed the government, the KY as the junior partner should
have the next best position, a constitutional head of
state, which would obviously be filled by the kabaka
of Buganda. Obote sent Balaki Kirya to Mutesa to sound
him out on the offer. When Mutesa showed interest,
Obote and I drove into the Bugandan countryside and
informally offered him the presidency. He was warm
and obviously appreciative.

If there was ever any opportune moment to disband
the KY and give the UPC free reign in Buganda, this
was it. The idea of making their ruler the head of
state made the Baganda both gratified and magnanimous
toward the UPC, which of course had the decisive say
in the choice. Some UPC founders and leaders (including myself, and then Attorney General Godfrey Binaisa,
a senior Muganda UPC official) pressed for the condition that before making Mutesa president, the KY
should be dissolved.* With the kabaka as part and
parcel of a UPC government, there would be no reason
for the KY's existence. This position was strongly
supported by some of the new Bugandan UPC members,
like Dr. Lumu, minister of health, who had contributed
positively to formulate the alliance while he was still
a KY member. Moreover, preliminary soundings with some
important KY leaders showed they would accept the dis-
banding of their party if it was put to them as a quid
pro quo for electing Mutesa president. Since the UPC
had now a working parliamentary majority of its own,
KY leadership was acutely aware of its dependence. In
good time I put the proposal to Obote but he equivo-
cated. Within a month it was plain he had no intention
of demanding the KY's dissolution. Many UPC members,

---

*Godfrey Binaisa, Q. C., is now president of Uganda,
having been voted in by the Consultative Council of
the Uganda National Liberation Front to replace Yusufu Lule in June 1979.

in Parliament and elsewhere, felt we should not just
hand over the presidency to Mutesa without ensuring
a sound foothold in Bugandan politics for the UPC.
We decided to have a showdown on the issue when we met
in the Central Executive Committee of the UPC to endorse the candidacy of Mutesa for president. There
were emotional and angry exchanges, but Obote won.
The KY was to remain intact. What was ironic was that
those who wanted Mutesa to be president (the majority
with the UPC) were the same people who wanted to ex-
tract the condition of the KY's demise so as to open
Buganda for the first time to full-fledged national
political activity.

The position of Obote was both ambivalent and
dishonest. On the one hand he was working toward
making Uganda a one-party state and branding the KY
as an undesirable tribal organization. On the other
hand when the opportunity came to disband it peacefully, he deliberately rejected it and frustrated those
who worked for its realization. Moreover, having worked for the KY's survival, he was unprepared to go all
the way to make the alliance work smoothly. It was
unavoidable that there would be friction and misunder-
standings, not only between the KY and the UPC in the
field but between their respective governments in Buganda and at the center. The Bugandan government
sometimes tended to claim powers it did not have. This
was well illustrated by their claim over all central
government police posts in Buganda and their claim for
greater revenue sources than they were entitled to.
The disputes were submitted to the law courts and Buganda lost on both issues.[40] This was a significant
confirmation of the central government's potentially
extensive control over Buganda under the independence
settlement, contrary to the popular but erroneous belief that Buganda had the power. There were other
numerous areas of an interdepartmental nature where
unnecessary friction between the two governments arose
simply because of an absence of open, continuous contact between the leaders of both governments.

To enhance the proper functioning of the alliance,
the UPC and KY leadership set up a joint committee in
1963 to draw up recommendations that would form the
basis of the alliance in operating the two governments.
The committee consisted of Abu Mayanja, Masembe Kabali,
and Ali Kulumba for the KY, and Paul Muwanga and myself
for the UPC. It reviewed all the areas of conflict and
recommended methods to eliminate or minimize them. Its
report was submitted both to Obote and the katikkiro
(premier) of Buganda for consideration and signature.
The Bugandan government accepted the recommendations.

For several months Obote evaded the committee's pleas
to meet with them and discuss the report. Of course,
it was merely a report and could be accepted, amended,
or rejected by any of the parties. But Obote neither
accepted nor amended it. He simply killed it by pre-
varication, delay, and unwillingness to endorse it.
He gave no reason for this inaction either to the UPC
Central Executive Committee, which had endorsed the
joint committee in the first place, or to the Bugandan
government, with whom he had set it up. Consequently,
once more, opportunity to formulate a sound working
basis with the KY was lost, not unwittingly but by a
calculated and deliberate act of the prime minister.
The Baganda could not but become apprehensive as to
the true intentions of Obote regarding their future.
It was becoming too plain that Obote simply wanted to
use the Baganda and then once he felt strong enough,
to dump them.

The Dissolution of the UPC/KY Alliance. The
moves of the UPC central government discussed above
contributed to a climate that made it impossible to
maintain the alliance. But Buganda had its share of
the blame, as we shall relate later. Obote, now assured of a majority in Parliament without KY support,
swiftly created the atmosphere necessary for dismiss-
ing the KY from the coalition. He reversed his position and publicly demanded its dissolution on 3 August
1964. It was improper, he said, to have a member of a
party (KY) who bore the local title (kabaka) and that
of the president of Uganda, although Obote had agreed
to the situation in order to help fight the DP. He
then vowed he would "kick them [the KY] out" of the
government. From the time of his original refusal to
disband the KY, when there had been an opportunity
and good will had taken place within the UPC hierarchy,
there had been no inconsistency or immediate querying
of his methods by the public. On 6 August 1964, KY
leaders challenged him to call a general election,
warning that "it is to invite trouble for UPC to sit
in parliament and pass legislation banning KY."[41]
Events moved quickly. The same day the Bugandan UPC
regional conference called on Obote to dissolve the
alliance, which he promised to put before the governing Central Executive Committee of the UPC with his
support.
    At this UPC Bugandan regional conference, for the
first time in public Obote bitterly attacked the kabaka. He accused him of being behind the KY -- which
was partly true -- and countered: "If KY tried to upset the government, we would interpret it to mean that

the Kabaka alone meant it to do so."[42] The Baganda
were angered by this attack on the kabaka. Was it
justified? After all, technically he was a constitutional monarch and the attack should have been properly directed to his KY ministers. Yet, this was
just polemics because whatever the rights or wrongs
between the quarreling allies, no one could divorce
the KY from the kabaka, as is discussed later. Nevertheless, on 22 August, the KY and the entire kabaka's
government organized a mammoth protest march through
the streets of Kampala that ended with emotional
speech making at the Clock Tower (an open place for
public meetings). Several speeches were made attacking Obote. Abu Mayanja asked rhetorically: "If Dr.
Obote and some of his colleagues claim to be nationalists, where were they when a number of Baganda politicians including myself were being tortured and
imprisoned by imperialists?"[43] The same day the Baganda warned in a Lukiko resolution: "If anything
happened to the Kabaka, Dr. Obote, himself, would be
responsible."

The following day, four Ugandan government ministers, significantly all from Obote's region, denounced
the UPC/KY alliance and issued a signed joint statement asserting that due to the insult to Obote at the
mass rally: "As from today, Sunday, 23/8/1964, we are
no longer a party to the alliance and we will work as
if there is no such alliance either within the Cabinet
or in parliament."[44] The indignation of the ministers
was understandable but to declare the end of the alliance in reprisal was surely excessive high-handed-
ness. Besides, there was a proper order that the
break of the alliance, as its formation, should have
followed. The responsibility for any such decision
clearly lay with the Central Executive Committee of
the UPC, which had authorized negotiating and making
the alliance with the Baganda and the KY. This committee never met to consider the dissolution of the
alliance. Of the ministers who unilaterally declared
the alliance at an end, only Onama, minister of defense, was a member of the Central Executive Committee.
It was plain, however, that they spoke for Obote and
with his full authority.[45] On 24 August the parliamentary group of UPC members were hastily summoned to
a meeting and were told about the break in the alliance
as a fait accompli. Within the UPC party constitution
the party was preeminent and its organs theoretically
empowered to direct the parliamentary group on policy.
Yet, there had been no Central Executive Committee
meeting to advise the parliamentary group on what
course to follow. It is likely that Obote bypassed

it because its members, most of whom were UPC founders, might have posed some questions he did not want to answer. All the same, on 24 August, he announced the end of the alliance in a statement: "The UPC parliamentary group has studied the speeches made by KY leaders at the meeting held in Kampala last Saturday. The group has concluded that these speeches leave no alternative to the UPC parliamentary group but to bring the alliance to an end."[46]

It was both dishonest and absurd to tell the country that the cause for the breach of the alliance were statements made only a few days previously. As we traced the causes, they were far deeper and of longer duration; the speeches were merely the catalyst needed. Yet the alliance had been a milestone in Uganda's history. Without it, probably the UPC might not have formed the independence government to bring Uganda into the international community of nations on 9 October 1962. It had left the party now outwardly stronger than it ever was. The strength of the respective parties in Parliament now stood: UPC, 60; DP, 16; KY, 14. But the new epoch with the KY now in the opposition was to heighten the bitterness, suspicions, and fears that the alliance had so usefully attempted to remove from the minds of the Baganda.

Buganda's Failure. If we dwell on the wrong policies of Obote that led to the revolution, it is principally because, compared with all the other dramatis personae, he alone had enough authority under the law to promote genuinely integrative programs for the whole country. Just as his failure was decisive toward chaos, so the potential of good policies would have been toward stability. But he was by no means alone to blame. All of us in the UPC must share that blame, as we sat in the Cabinet and party councils and promoted measures whose true implications few cared to examine fully.

The Bugandan government, too, in a fundamental sense cannot escape responsibility for the 1966 crisis. This kingdom had a long and illustrious history. To the advantages of strength and cohesion it enjoyed in precolonial history were added quite impressive matériel and other benefits as the British chose to administer the whole protectorate with Buganda as the center. Almost all aspects of development and modernization started here before they radiated to the other provinces. Education, the key to enlightenment and modernity, was preponderately in Buganda's favor. Despite these blessings, the Baganda failed to grasp the role they seemed so naturally and historically

prepared to play, namely, to provide leadership for
the whole country and be the vanguard in Uganda's
struggle for independence. They looked upon themselves
as a separate nation, which was historically true, but
they totally failed to appreciate the implications of
the unifying nature of the colonial experience that
tied them, for good or for ill, to other diverse Ugandan peoples. The Bugandan governments, in particular
those in power during the entire decade of the 1950s,
completely missed the opportunity to organize the rest
of the country behind them in the struggle for independence at a time the British were becoming receptive to
decolonization in earnest. The few Bagandan politicians who accepted the opportunity and the challenge
were politically destroyed by the powerful traditionalist governments of the kingdom. Such was the first
nationalist party in the country, the Uganda National
Congress, led by Ignatius Musazi, a Muganda, in 1952.
Successive political parties were formed by enlightened
Baganda nationalists only to be rendered ineffective
or destroyed.

The result was a kingdom ruled by powerful but
unenlightened traditionalist separatists. When the
DP was formed in 1954 with a predominantly Bugandan
leadership and a potential national following, it was
rejected and victimized because of its reputed Catholicism. It was in these circumstances that the late-
comers, like most of the UPC leaders from outside
Buganda as late as 1960, stepped forward to form a
viable alternative leadership for the country while
Bugandan traditionalist leaders still pursued blind
alleys to separatism. The greatest evidence of Buganda's failure in my view was its inability to provide viable nationalist leadership to the whole country
on independence when it was eminently qualified to do
so.

The Bugandan administration of Katikkiro Michael
Kintu, in particular, did an ill-service to the Baganda
for which they had to pay very dearly. Through a pyramid of chiefs it had caused the Baganda masses to live
in a fairyland. It had embarked on the costly scheme
of Buganda's futile bid to secede even though the British government had made it abundantly clear, backed
by the might of imperial arms, that Uganda was one
state and it was to remain so until independence. To
perpetuate itself in power the Bugandan government had
whipped up the emotions of its population to support
its empty declaration of independence for Buganda on
31 December 1960. Yet, everyone in the country knew
the declaration was meaningless as the Baganda had no
power to implement it. Governor Crawford had merely

warned them and the following day life went on as
usual with Buganda as part of the Ugandan protectorate.
There was a real chance to put a stop to this
type of policy when the UPC became the senior partner
in the coalition government that led the country into
independence. For the first time in nearly twenty
years Bugandan leadership was genuinely receptive to
working in concert with the rest of the country. Tragically, as we related, Obote had no intention of reha-
bilitating them. He had long ago decided to deal with
them by the brutal force of arms at a time of his own
choosing.
      It is a measure of the inadequacy of Buganda's
leadership at this time that after the first year,
they could not read Obote's direction correctly although it was stamped on every significant action of
government. When they finally did, despite the fact
that they had neither an army nor a well-armed police,
it did not occur to them early enough that they were
giving Obote the pretext he had long wished for and
had been preparing for -- to destroy their kingdom
-- by continuing along their imaginary course.
      On the return from the independence constitutional
conference in 1962, which drew up the final independence settlement and constitution, unashamedly the
Bugandan government told its people it had got back
"all our things" that they had demanded for Buganda
at the conference -- and many of which had been denied
-- including the control of police forces and more
independent sources of revenue. The constitution had
stipulated the holding of a referendum, as we mentioned
elsewhere, in the "lost counties" to determine whether
their inhabitants wanted to remain under Buganda, form
their own administration, or join the Banyoro. It was
a clear, mandatory provision. But on 22 August 1964,
at the height of the UPC/KY controversy, the Lukiko
quite impoliticly passed a resolution that it would
not accept the holding of a referendum in the lost
counties. It was another inconsequential vituperation,
because the referendum was held and the counties went
to Bunyoro without any move by Buganda to stop them.
The "resolution mentality" had become a habit. For
someone who needed a pretext to seize absolute power,
as Obote did, they provided an excellent plausible
ground. In January 1966, the first steps were taken
to contain and cripple the KY by law. An amendment
to the penal code was enacted making it an offense to
use the title, name, or symbol of a ruler of a federal
state to cause disaffection. This was obviously aimed
at the KY (Kabaka Yekka), which bore the kabaka's
title. Although Amos Sempa, a veteran KY leader, des-

cribed the law as "very Obote-like, wicked, malicious," by their procrastination and poor political judgment, the KY leaders had provided their enemies with the needed opportunities to destroy them.[47]

Having realized the hostility of Obote toward them, there were two prudent alternatives. First, the KY should have disbanded shortly after forming the independence government and converted their supporters to the UPC. By itself, it could not effectively protect Buganda's identity. As we have mentioned, with a population of only 16 percent of the whole of Uganda, they were in a real minority. Common sense dictated, therefore, as it did to other ethnic groups, that they seek protection in a larger national party that provided more leverage. Second, if they rejected the UPC after the break of the alliance, the KY should have disbanded and merged with the DP. The history of Uganda's political parties was a history of party mergers and this would have been nothing unusual. It was therefore irresponsible and poor politics for KY leaders to persist in its survival until it was dissolved in machinegun fire and the blood of its largely innocent and defenseless citizenry in 1966.

In March 1965, Masembe-Kabali, its secretary-general, was already lamenting its fate: "This kingdom of Buganda, a very important region in this country, with a famous history, now appears to be like an island. It is an island, it is secluded, it is inbred, it is in fact the greatest paradox that we should still have KY here."[48]

What was the kabaka's role? History cannot pass judgment on others and absolve him from all responsibility. The idea of a constitutional monarch was alien to the African systems of government. The king in precolonial history was vested with executive, legislative, and magisterial powers, which he exercised with the aid of his leading subordinates. Both the ruler and the ruled were used to this system. Consequently it became difficult for the kabaka to divorce himself entirely from direct political decisions. Indeed, in 1953, he had been temporarily exiled by the British because of his political involvement. In the 1955 Anglo-Bugandan agreement that reinstated him, it was clearly stated he was to be above politics and had to become a constitutional ruler. This provision, however, remained a dead letter and the kabaka, though behind the scenes, by force of custom and disposition found it impossible to totally keep out of politics. The Munster Commission had recommended that the best safeguard for the kings in an independent Uganda was their acceptance of positions as constitutional rulers

above political struggles.[49]   But, as in 1955, the
1961 and 1962 Ugandan constitutions, which embodied
this recommendation, were never fully complied with.
Having retained that political power in practice, the
kabaka's use of it contributed to Buganda's difficulties.
     It was his responsibility to choose his own lead-
ing ministers. The decade of the 1950s was important
in the colonial preparations for independence. But
instead of appointing enlightened ministers, he consistently preferred traditionalist, particularistic
people who lacked the vision and grasp of a united
Uganda. The resulting successive particularistic
governments, especially the longest one under Katikkiro Michael Kintu, were unequal to the task of safe-
guarding Buganda's best interests within a united
Uganda. As noted, they harassed and destroyed political parties and denied aspiring Bagandan nationalists
(like Ignatius Musazi, Abu Mayanja, Joe Kiwanuka, Ben
Kiwanuka, Godfrey Binaisa, or E. Mulira) a base from
which to reach out to the rest of the protectorate.
The kabaka therefore bore the responsibility for the
policies of the men he chose to lead the kingdom.
The isolation and insulation of this kingdom from the
mainstream of independence movements, rather than protecting its future provided attractive conditions for
its destruction by its enemies.
     Yet, from my personal friendship with him, I
know the kabaka was resolved to make amends for past
dereliction, and there was evidence to show this. In
the negotiations with the UPC to form the alliance,
there were some die-hard traditionalists who opposed
it. The kabaka himself had reservations about Obote's
suitability to lead the coalition but despite that,
he overcame all objections and the alliance was established. With it, Uganda's independence was assured.
In this regard, therefore, he made a positive contribution to the country's attainment of freedom. Later,
when it became clear that the KY was a liability providing Obote with a pretext to attack Buganda, the
kabaka urged KY leaders to disband it and join the UPC
and so be integrated fully in Uganda's politics. A
few members of the Lukiko and the Ugandan Parliament
heeded his exhortations and crossed over to the UPC.
But the KY had created a leadership that now had its
own vested interests for survival. The kabaka, who
reputedly could not be disobeyed by tradition, was now
defied and the KY survived to face greater confrontation with the UPC.
     Obote gave as his principal reason for illegally
seizing power in 1966 the kabaka's attempt to invite

foreign troops and usurp power. This is discussed
later, but I have already argued that Obote's fundamental objective from the start was to seek a monopoly
of power by the use of arms, if necessary, notwithstanding contrary provisions of the constitution.
Mutesa's actions only a few weeks before Obote launched
his revolution could not have been the true cause but
just the requisite excuse.

Escalation of Intra-UPC Conflict

By early 1964 there was a fundamental rift in the
UPC leadership, both in the party and the government.
Outwardly, it may have seemed to be a clash between
personalities or ambitions, but in fact it concerned
the very basis of why Ugandans became independent.
All UPC leaders had worked hard and loyally for the
party. Before they took power in May 1962 they had
seemed highly motivated and principled, but their
exercise of power had now divided them between those
who sought absolute power at all costs and those who
wanted power without alienating the majority of the
diverse nationals. The struggle between these two
factions sharpened as more and more attempts were
made to acquire or misuse more power.

The issue, simply stated, was whether a governing
party had the right to render those citizens who lost
to it second-rate nationals; whether victory at the
polls meant a monopoly of power, positions, and patronage for all time, especially when a clear majority at
the polls had supported the opposition parties.

Obote's position was crystal clear because of his
unshakable belief in the winner-take-all philosophy.
He was promoting it not only against the official opposition, as examples given show, but even against
those in his party whom he considered an even more
serious threat. It is false to think that this opposition began with the so-called "Ibingira group." John
Kakonge, while secretary-general of the UPC, had put
up sharp opposition against Obote's tendencies to monopolize power and downgrade the principle of collective
decision in the party. Indeed, it was for this reason
that Obote had maneuvered him out of the post of secretary-general and kept him out of the Cabinet on
independence -- although he was to bring him back later
in his attempt to break up the UPC opposition building
up against him (Obote) in Parliament.

There was in fact a disturbing aspect about Kakonge's removal from the secretary-generalship of the
UPC that only a few people knew. During the conference
he had put up an impressive fight to retain his post,

with the backing of the youth wing of the party. Unknown to all others except later to Kirya, Obote had given secret instructions to the police, which was armed and had been brought in ostensibly to keep the peace, to shoot at Kakonge and his supporters if they tried to disrupt the conference. This was not an instruction to shoot blanks or to shoot in the air, but to shoot live ammunition at party members. I did not know of this fact until a month later (certainly Kakonge did not know it), although obviously we had seen armed police around. It was yet another indication of the murderous involvement of law enforcement agencies in party politics and was a serious warning for those close to Obote. Fortunately, the need to fire at these UPC members never arose, as the proceedings were conducted in an orderly manner, though with considerable vigor and heat.

In May 1964, I took over as secretary-general of UPC, not because I opposed all Kakonge's policies but because I felt he had not done enough to build resistance in the UPC against Obote's tendency to grab all power and promote militarism. It had not really been Kakonge's fault; because of Obote's having maneuvered him from Parliament and the deliberate policy to maintain a weak and poor UPC, the secretary-general could do little. But I was backed by a powerful group of UPC founders (W. W. Nadiope, B. K. Kirya, Cuthbert Obwangor, and others) who wished to establish a well-regulated check against excesses in the party and so maintain its credibility among the masses. These were really the men who had put Obote in power and made the UPC what it was with him. They loved it no less than he. But they were convinced the best way to maintain the UPC in power was not only to try to fulfill party promises but also to appear to be fair to all the diverse sections of the population with their eye on future favorable elections.

While Obote favored and prepared for eventual seizure of power by force, his opposition in the UPC worked to nullify this prospect by demanding a broadly-based army, a respect for the constitutional process, and a reasonable place for the opposition. The idea of not destroying the opposition was not merely out of higher moral principles, but it was the result of a practical calculation based on the fact that to attempt to destroy a powerful opposition in a divided country might be too costly to warrant the prospect.

Even by early 1965 the opposition in UPC official reckoning for all practical purposes was meaningless. Obote promoted a convention where invariably any measure, however reasonable as long as it was proposed

by the opposition, had to be rejected. This produced
resistance from his opposition in the UPC. As I told
Parliament:

> I make this appeal to our UPC members: let us
> show the country, let us show all these small
> opposition parties sitting opposite us, that ac-
> tually we deserve the place which we occupy. . . .
> We must resolve for a certain measure of self-
> criticism, permit reason to prevail over emotion
> and not think that people who say something may
> have gone wrong are automatically malicious . . .
> when leading members of UPC refuse to hear the
> truth it becomes a matter of considerable con-
> cern.[50]

Because it was no longer possible to promote vigorous government through open debate by formal opposition, it was obvious the only way left to do it was
within the party. The existence of pressure groups in
political systems is an inevitable fact. It is both
absurd and unrealistic for a party leader to reject
their existence and ignore their aspirations in a party
that has acquired a de facto monopoly of power in the
country as had the UPC. Obote now unleashed a struggle
with all the formidable power at his command -- short
of force -- to eliminate the opposition within his
party. The idea was to put favorite UPC leaders in all
districts, then convene a party-delegates conference
and dismiss the opposition, giving him absolute control
of the party. As it turned out, however, the opposition was so strong and so popular within the UPC that
it controlled not only the Central Executive Committee
but more than three-quarters of the regions. It was
for this reason that even after Obote assumed absolute
power following the 1966 coup d'etat, he dared not call
a meeting of any party organ for more than two years,
despite the fact that the constitution of the UPC demanded the Central Executive Committee to meet at least
once a month, the National Council at least once every
three months, and the annual conference once every
year. Obote feared and expected an open defiance in
all these party organs before the use of force had
neutralized that prospect.
Be that as it may, to Obote, in a real sense, all
the opposition -- that of his own UPC and the traditional one of the KY and the DP -- became one and the
same thing. They were opposed to seizure of absolute
executive power and in support of constitutional government. From this came his attempt later to link the
two, quite falsely, as having been in collusion to

topple him. The consequence of this struggle was to
weaken the UPC further despite its control of all
governments in the country (except Buganda). To the
local divisions, which were natural to every district
within the party, was now added the larger, more national conflict from the top with the "Obote group"
and "Ibingira group" (as they were called) competing
for support throughout the country. Committed to
seize absolute power as the panacea for all Uganda's
problems, denied its attainment through the UPC and
Parliament by the group opposed to and apprehensive
about his excesses, Obote was more than ever convinced
that the use of force was the only way to remove political opposition in and out of the party. Was it justifiable? My answer of course is hardly. Apart from
other considerations of ethics and morality, it created
more problems than it resolved.

The two predominant groups in the UPC acquired
several labels, which were sometimes accurate but more
often misleading. For instance, the Obote group was
termed Nilotic and radical, while the Ibingira group
was called Bantu and moderate. This was oversimplifi-
cation. I have already indicated that no region in
the country was ethnically homogenous. In the North
for example, there were three distinct ethnic groups:
Eastern Sudanic, Western Sudanic, and Nilotic. In the
South, the word Bantu was a linguistic classification
that falsely gave a picture of a unified people among
several distinct, different groups. But it is unfortunately true that these alien labels were used damag-
ingly in private by leaders of both groups to gather
support in forging alliances for their respective
causes, while in public each group extolled the virtues
of national unity and attacked sectional interests. Is
it possible to apportion the blame for this manifestly
diverse tactic? To answer this, one must understand
the history of the UPC first.

The party had been formed by a merger between the
UPU and the UNC, and there is little doubt but that
most of its leaders were highly motivated for the unity
of Uganda. In the UNC Obote, who was its president,
was ably supported by one of the country's leading pio-
neer nationalists, Abu Mayanja, who (though being a
Muganda from the Bantu) had rejected the myopic politics of this kingdom. It was this group that I joined
actively in 1959. Balaki Kirya from Bukedi in the
East was its chairman.

The UPU was the larger and potentially much
stronger of the two parties. Most of its leaders were
far better known and more widely supported in the country than those in the UNC. These were men like W. W.

Nadiope and M. M. Ngobi of Busoga; C. B. Katiti, W. W.
Rwetsiba, and Z.C.K. Mungonya of Ankole; G. Magezi of
Bunyoro; Cuthbert Obwangor of Teso; and John Babiha
of Toro. These men already had proven electoral support, having been elected members of the Legislative
Council. They were overwhelmingly from the so-called
Bantu areas, although there was substantial semi-Hami-
tic support from Teso. Had they been motivated by
ethnic, regional, or linguistic politics, they would
with the greatest ease have chosen from among themselves the leader of the new party after the merger in
1960. Indeed, without the merger, they would still
probably have won any future general election with the
DP and Buganda -- not Obote's UNC -- as their principal
rivals. And yet, quite voluntarily, inspired by nationalism and idealism for the unity of Uganda, they
offered the leadership of the UPC to Obote. But these
are the same men, only a few years later, whom Obote
was to accuse of attempting to create a so-called Bantu group to attack or remove him from office, as if
they had not known who he was in the first place when
they chose him for leadership. They were in detention
by the 1971 coup, and yet they had been instrumental
in making Obote the leader of the UPC and the prime
minister.
     What had happened? It has already been indicated
how once in power, Obote set out to create a national
security apparatus with a manifestly ethnic, regional
bias without a reasonable explanation to justify keeping the masses of his supporters in the other areas
out of the police and army in the regions that constituted more than 75 percent of the country. Because
there was no natural unity for the northern ethnic
groups, they had to be held together in part by the
existence of an external threat to their common interests in the region. Obote, most regrettably, first
subtly but later expressly, constantly pointed out
that this external threat was the so-called Bantus of
the South -- in particular the Baganda -- in order to
unify his northern followers, many of whom (as in A-
choli) had their own reasons for rejecting his leadership.
     It was consequently plain that, in order to pro-
tect the interests of their respective groups, the
southern leaders -- who had been badly disillusioned
by Obote's partiality -- would have to join together
to make what came to be known as the "Ibingira group"
in the UPC. This group, therefore, came into being
as a reaction to Obote's prior formation of a "northern group" in the UPC and the security forces. It was
a tragic defeat for Ugandan nationalism.

But both groups had supporters throughout the
country unconnected with this basic ethnic cleavage.
For instance, the groups in the North that opposed
Obote's local policies, as in Acholi, would invariably
support the Ibingira group. Similarly, the groups
opposed to the Ibingira group in the South would support Obote because of his power to dispense patronage,
which opportunists could not resist. The terms "radical" and "moderate" were both superficial and misleading. Some party functionaries sometimes used them
vociferously to discredit or support a side, but they
were not fundamental to the Ugandan revolutions.

The case of the KY and Mutesa supporting the UPC
is another illustration of an initial good faith that
was abused. Consciously and after considerable debate,
the kabaka and his government in Buganda opted to support the UPC led by a northerner, Milton Obote, in
preference to the DP, which was led by a fellow Muganda, Benedicto Kiwanuka. There had been reluctance
at first because Obote was not that well known, but
in good faith the Baganda threw in their lot with him.
This act alone made it possible for him to form the
independence government. But the hostile manner in
which he proceeded to treat them, especially his unambiguous distaste for their joining the UPC in large
numbers, raised grave questions as we have discussed
elsewhere. The Baganda were preeminent among the
Bantus and their fate sooner or later was bound to
produce a reaction among their neighbors, even if at
the beginning Obote succeeded in isolating them.

Of course, Obote could cite good examples of
many prominent people from most ethnic groups in an
attempt to rebut the charges that he was a tribalist.
He could even shift some of the blame for whatever
had happened to them. For example, the minister who
moved motions in Parliament to perpetuate a state of
emergency and was identified with detaining people
was from the Bantus. At the time Obote ordered the
military attack on Buganda, his cabinet had five
senior Bugandan ministers. Obote could quote the
names of senior officers in all sectors of public service who came from regions other than his own. The
crucial fact to remember, however, is that in most
cases, all these people had no actual power and were
only instruments to implement his will and rubber
stamp his decisions, just as Parliament became after
the 22 February 1966 revolution. They could not oppose his measures, however wrong. The attorney general, Godfrey Binaisa, a Muganda, had to resign against
the 1967 Constitution. But the actual center of power
and decision making had clearly shifted to a small

circle consisting mostly of relatives, like Akena Adoko and Adoko Nekyon, with the addition for convenience
of a few other northern leaders, like Onama. Those
who found it hard to accept this took a stand under a
rather misleading but identifiable label of the "Ibingira group."

The prime minister now resorted to using unusual
and regrettable methods to eliminate his opponents in
the UPC. His first move was to set up a spy operation
headed by his cousin, Akena Adoko, at first called
Protocol and later the General Service Unit, to spy
on his colleagues. Adoko was answerable only to Obote.
The accounts of his department were exempt from government or even informal audit. In its first year
Protocol overspent their budget three-fold, spending
the money not on proper intelligence work but by
squandering it in ways that are improper to recount
here. Although I was answerable for Adoko's department and had to answer for its derelictions in Parliament as minister of state, I was denied any knowledge
of what it did.

It soon became apparent however, that the Protocol section was bribing or attempting to bribe security
escorts, drivers, or domestic servants of leading ministers and UPC officials for the purpose of obtaining
in the minutest detail information on what they did in
their private lives. For any government to run an intelligence agency is both proper and necessary. But
it is abhorrent if such an agency, with all the resources of the state behind it, seeks to hound or
witch-hunt supposed political opponents. As secretary-
general of the party, therefore, I addressed a strong
letter in 1965 to Obote protesting against his use of
government money to pay his kinsmen to spy on party
leaders. The results could only be counterproductive.
When he called the Cabinet to discuss this letter, to
his surprise and annoyance, rather than objecting to
its having been written, several ministers spoke out
in detail of how often Adoko had stalked them even at
the oddest hours of the night. It was now plain that
the cost of opposing some policies of the prime minister was to live under the shadow of a growing gestapo
directed by his kinsmen.

But it was in August 1965 that it became clear
beyond doubt that the UPC and its government were
heading toward some catastrophe. Obote had spent over
a month and a half on a world tour. Shortly after his
return early in August 1965, he convened a cabinet
meeting to report on his trip. What caught and stunned
the ministerial attention, however, was another kind of
report. His minister of defense told the Cabinet that

he had received a most disturbing report the day Obote
returned. Allegedly, the vice-president of the UPC
and Uganda, W. W. Nadiope, and the minister of state
and secretary-general of the UPC, Ibingira, had hired
an unidentified person to assassinate Obote by shooting him as he alighted from the aircraft at Entebbe's
national airport. Before anyone could say a word,
Obote followed, saying that in support of that allegation, he had a letter given to him by senior police
officers that indicated some evil intent. He then
drew from his pocket a note, which he circulated to
the cabinet members. It was supposed to be a letter
written by Daudi Ocheng to the secretary-general of
the UPC, urging him to work hand in hand to hasten
the fall of Obote. But to Obote's annoyance, there
was a swift ministerial consensus that the letter was
a fake and the assassination allegation, too, improbable. Indeed, some of his supporters in the Cabinet
who knew Ocheng's handwriting positively stated it
was not his nor was the purported signature.

I was both stunned and outraged. The whole basis
of the opposition group within the UPC was to uphold
constitutionality and justice. Nothing could have
been further from its intent than the charges just
made as they were patently absurd. If Ocheng were to
plot with me, there was no need to write potential
documentary evidence. We lived within easy reach of
each other as did most parliamentarians when in the
capital, and it would have been easier and more prudent to simply talk about it. At once I demanded a
high-powered investigation to clear the name of the
vice-president and myself, which the Cabinet supported.
A high-ranking police officer was detailed to investigate, which he did, and he came up with a report that
none of the allegations had any basis in fact. Yet
Obote supressed this report because it disturbed his
plans for a frame-up.

But the damage was done. Why did Obote choose
to smear the names of his critics in the party with
such grave and baseless charges? At the time, two
reasons appeared probable. First, from March 1965
he was under pressure from Ocheng and the opposition in Parliament, as is discussed later, to expose
his secret involvement in the Congolese civil war and
his use of the Ugandan army in that process to share
in the booty of war. Because of his prevarications
and partly due to independent evidence, it had become
clear that he was covering up his actions. Consequently, his critics in the party, in particular the
secretary-general, had not used their influence to
block Ocheng's persistent probing. Since a view

had developed that supporting any measure by an opposition member was a betrayal of the UPC, it seemed
attractive to link Ocheng and the secretary-general
as perpetrators of a heinous plot in which the famous
"gold motion" by Ocheng (discussed later) was only a
small part. This supposedly would discredit the motion and misdirect public attention from Obote's actual
derelictions to the possible treason by the secretary-
general and other critics. Besides, Ocheng was a
close friend of the kabaka. To link him with subversion would be to remind the country of Buganda's past
intransigence and thus to create a feeling that Buganda
was again about to do the same. This would prepare the
way to attack the kabaka later. The second view, not
unconnected with the first, was to prepare the secretary-general for elimination. One of the maxims Obote
preached so often to his colleagues to justify any
misuse of power was that "politics is a dirty game."
In a typical maneuver, therefore, by smearing my name
he was putting me on the defensive to justify whatever
elimination plans he had. I had no illusions about
the outcome.

There were few viable alternatives. I thought
of resigning from the Cabinet and the post of secretary-general of the UPC. But this course was unsatis-
factory. It could be exploited as an indirect admission of guilt. On the other hand, having persuaded
so many people to join the UPC, either as members or in
coalition, it would be dishonorable now that danger
seemed close to abandon them and seek personal safety
through resignation. In any event, having spent some
of the best years of my life contributing to the building of a safe, stable, independent state, it was unthinkable to abandon that ideal, not because I was
defeated in an election or had retired peacefully, but
because these very ideals stood threatened. My decision to stay on, to strengthen my group in the party,
and to try to frustrate any attempt to use illegal
force to seize power had a real bearing on the revolution. As the opposition created a powerful but certainly law-abiding and constitutionally-minded section
within the UPC and Parliament, Obote was convinced
that if he did not usurp power soon the opposition
within and without might become too strong for him in
the future. The die was cast; now only a pretext had
to be found.

What might have intensified Obote's tenacious
pursuit of absolute power was his profound sense of
insecurity and, at times, his inadequacy. When he was
elected president of the UPC at its inception in 1960,
he had not been the leader with the widest political

support. Indeed, politicians like Obwangor of Teso,
Nadiope of Busoga, and others from the West had greater
following in the country. He had been chosen by the
party leaders, motivated by high ideals of unity, as a
symbolic gesture. He remained acutely aware of the political power of the men who had made him and their
potential, therefore, to unmake him should they so
choose.

   He acutely resented the idea that another leader
in the country was appreciated or liked by the people.
He would tell me often how he resented the fact that
at some public occasions where all officials met, the
kabaka received thunderous applause from Bugandan
masses while Obote's was negligible. He felt people
despised him. I would try to reassure him that the
kabaka had the applause among the Baganda because
they were his people, that if he went to Obote's district in Lango the position would be reversed. In any
event, I tried to explain, he (Obote) had the executive
power of government while the kabaka's was merely ceremonial. The arrangement was useful because it made
the country governable and gave the UPC time to build
support in Buganda. He rejected this approach. In
his view the way to take that public applause away
from the kabaka was by eliminating him from the scene.

   In addition, he had a prejudice against educated
people. Having left college at Makerere himself without any qualification, he saw in every successful grad-
uate a reminder of his own failure. To be acceptable
to him, invariably, they had to prove extremely obse-
quious, especially if they were leaders within the UPC
or top civil servants. He consistently coaxed Balaki
Kirya, a largely self-made and successful member of
the UPC, to avoid the so-called graduates or intellec-
tuals of the party because they were "dangerous."
Even on the night of 31 January 1966, when Obote pre-
sided over the parliamentary members' meeting, he
pointedly appealed to his leading ministers (like
George Magezi and Balaki Kirya) not to support that
group led by the secretary-general in the UPC on the
patently unfounded ground that it looked down on them
for their lack of higher education, even though these
men were as able -- if not abler -- than most college
graduates in the party. In 1968, he would publicly
attack Makerere University academics who dared speak
out against some of his arbitrary acts of detaining
innocent citizens, like Abu Mayanja and Rajat Neogy,
whose only crime was to be acquitted in a court of law
on charges of sedition. All they had done was simply
to publish an article in Transition magazine, alleging
that the public suspected there was nepotism in judi-

cial appointments. Obote then declared, "we agree you
cannot divide intellectualism from corruption of the
mind, from subversion of the country, from being anti-
Africanism, you cannot. We agree totally."[51]
And yet he desperately wanted to be regarded as
an intellectual as well as an original thinker. In
fairness it could be said he clearly belonged to the
intelligentsia of the country, a class of enlightened
people where the possession of a university degree is
not an indispensable attribute for membership.
Obote's basic political philosphy of winner-take-
all was bad enough for the country. The methods he
used to attain it removed any possibility for its
peaceful realization. His belief that "politics is
a dirty game" became pervasive among his supporters
by the sheer force of example. The party and the
country had attained independence because of a sincere
belief in the pursuit of higher ideals. Political
power is the mightiest instrument within the state.
It can pervert the best ideals or it can promote their
realization. It literally encompasses the power of
life and death. It was therefore profoundly tragic
that in private the national leader, rather than set
a good example, explicitly discredited and corrupted
his political power.
An illustration of Obote in action is in order.
He was most happy when he exploited intraparty or interethnic conflict. For instance he told the kabaka,
then president, that Nadiope, the vice-president, was
after the presidency and was undermining the kabaka,
that he was getting too big for his boots. But Obote
would reassure the kabaka that he supported him. Then
he went to Nadiope with exactly the opposite story,
promising to make Nadiope president in the next elections if he made sure Mutesa was cut down to size and
would stop thinking of himself as king of the whole
country. The point to remember about this is that
these attributions were entirely manufactured by the
prime minister to provoke conflict between Mutesa and
Nadiope. In fact these tactics succeeded for some
time as the two men each believed in what Obote had
attributed to the other. I took it upon myself, having
discovered his methods at some cost, to bring the truth
to the attention of both men, much to Obote's dislike.
Indeed, in late April 1965, one evening at the vice-
president's house, in the presence of five party leaders, he charged that my group was out to topple him.
Challenged to produce evidence, he said, "if you deny
it, why do you try to bring Nadiope and Kabaka together?" It was a remarkable admission of his methods.
Among his leading ministers whom he was later to

detain, he would summon one and show him but not allow
him to read a letter from a pocket inside his coat.
He would then lean forward and quietly confide in him
that another cabinet colleague or leading party official had written the letter to him (Obote) making serious allegations against the minister. He would cat-
egorize the allegations, then implore the minister
not to mention this confidential information to anyone.
He would then summon the person who was supposed to
have written the letter and tell him the same thing in
reverse -- the minister this time was said to have made
the charges. Again, this would be in confidence. If
any of those so approached demanded to read the letter,
he would be told that it was asking too much, as it
was written in confidence. In actual fact, there was
never any letter written by any of the parties involved.
But the desired effect would be produced, as leading
officers in the party began to collide with each other.
Multiplied many times throughout the party leadership
before it was discovered, the system contributed to
serious intraparty conflicts. Subsequently, some of
the ministers he was later to detain faced him. They
demanded that should anyone be charged secretly, as
Obote alleged, all parties involved should be summoned
to meet face to face with the prime minister and other
party officials. Obote refused, and significantly,
the accusations simply vanished.

It was extremely dangerous to attempt governing
a divided country by creating new or playing on old
divisions and rivalries. It is difficult to contain
conflict once it is unleashed because it can have its
own self-perpetuating momentum. The method of "divide
and rule" as practiced in the UPC, therefore, accentuated the divisions on ethnic, regional, religious,
ideological, and party bases, and was another milestone
on the way to national upheaval.

Nonetheless, Obote was an intelligent and fairly
able leader. His achievements stood out all the more
clearly because of his humble beginnings. It was a
tragedy that he sought dangerous tools in absolutism
to support his ego when he did not need them to govern
well or effectively.

7
Uganda: The Immediate Causes of the Revolution

On 4 February 1966, a KY member of the opposition, Daudi Ocheng, moved a motion in Parliament, which Obote's maneuvers had postponed for a year. Ocheng charged him with having used the army to support the insurgents in the Congolese civil war and in the process having enriched himself with looted gold, ivory, and coffee. In addition, there was another charge made by Ocheng that the prime minister with his two ministers were using the then deputy commander of the army, Colonel Idi Amin, to make arrangements to seize power and abrogate the Independence Constitution. This was the most serious parliamentary censure in Obote's nine years in power, not only because of the gravity of the charges but also because of the overwhelming support with which Parliament endorsed the motion, demanding the suspension of Colonel Amin, and instituting investigations into the allegations. Why did Obote react by suspending the constitution, giving Amin command of the army, and assuming sweeping presidential powers? Was it, as he claimed, to save the country from chaos, from a group of neotraditionalists who were fomenting trouble in order to seize power? Or was it because the Ocheng motion, with its possible damaging disclosures, heralded his likely fall from power by a popular vote he was not prepared to countenance?

Given the basic fact that he had long resolved to remain in power at all costs and that he had conditioned the army and police to support this end, any serious move to challenge or censure his leadership had to be eliminated by persuasion if possible and by force if necessary. The Ocheng motion could not be stopped by party or parliamentary maneuvers. Its adverse consequences, therefore, had to be preempted by force and in the process Obote would seize absolute power to ensure once and for all time that none would ever seriously challenge him again -- neither through the party, the legislature, nor the electorate. This was at the heart of the events that followed the Ocheng motion that essentially had posed these basic threats to him.

THE EXPOSURE OF CLANDESTINE INVOLVEMENT IN A FOREIGN CONFLICT

In his first official report to the UPC delegates conference of 1968, in which he detailed why he seized power, Obote extensively argued that whatever support he had given to the secessionists of Eastern Congo (Zaire) in the civil war was authorized by the party and the Cabinet, that such aid was within the framework of the Organization of African Unity (OAU).[1] He never said a thing about the secret, illicit extent of the Ugandan army's involvement in the fighting inside the Congo and that it was this that had caused Uganda to be attacked by Congolese mercenaries and army, both on land and by air. Towards the end of 1964, the situation along the Congo frontier was becoming serious. Often, Uganda was being attacked without fully understanding the reasons why. There had been a civil war in the Sudan in the North and in Rwanda in the South, both along Uganda's borders and involving an influx of tens of thousands of refugees, but none had created comparable tension. Officially, the information the UPC organs and the Cabinet received on these developments in the Congo was scanty and purposely distorted by Obote in order to obtain his predetermined results -- support for government action or condemnation of the Congolese government and its allies.

Although there were a few who supported an open recognition of the Stanleyville regime of Gbenye opposing the Congolese Central government, there was a consistent majority in all the UPC and parliamentary group meetings that opposed any physical intervention by Uganda, instead advocating a search for a way to resolve the civil war through a political (as opposed to a military) settlement under OAU auspices. Obote outwardly supported this view and sent delegations to attend OAU meetings on the matter to seek a political settlement.

Ostensibly in order to handle problems arising from the influx of Congolese refugees, Obote set up a committee of four persons: the ministers of defense and community development, Felix Onama and Adoko Nekyon, and the deputy commander of the army, Idi Amin, as members, and himself as chairman. Only these four men

were "to deal with the dual problem of refugees from
the Congo and the security of Uganda." The persons
picked had been his right-hand men in ethnicizing the
security forces. From now on, the Cabinet and the UPC
became effectively isolated from the Congo problem.
On 13 January 1965, Gbenye met Obote and Presidents
Kenyatta and Nyerere in Uganda and agreed to seek a
political solution to the civil war. There was absolutely no decision or agreement to support the Stanleyville regime by military means on an East African
basis.

Despite the isolation of the party and Cabinet
from the truth, disturbing reports quietly began to
pour in from the frontier district of the West Nile.
Credible information from eyewitnesses indicated a
steady build-up of arms being ferried into the Congo
from Uganda. At times, mysterious aircraft brought
armaments and landed unannounced on airstrips in north-
west Uganda. Obviously Uganda could not promote a
political settlement by fueling the military conflict.
What was worse, however, was the active involvement of
the Ugandan army in the fighting. Acting under Obote's
direct orders, a section of the Ugandan army was
fighting side by side with the insurgents hundreds of
kilometers inside the Congo on several occasions. On
10 February 1965 the Congolese government gave an ul-
timatum to Uganda to pull out its forces or face a
military conflict. Obote predictably denied any involvement. Yet, actual fighting was under the direction of the committee headed by him, though under
the operational control of Idi Amin, and training was
provided for the rebel troops within Ugandan borders
and inside the Congo.

Life in the West Nile district became most insecure as armed Congolese insurgents spread fear and
lawlessness among Ugandans. Naturally, members of
Parliament from the area, with direct and daily access
to what was happening, protested vigorously in Parliament for protection with little avail.

It was against this background that aircraft of
the Congolese air force, probably operated by mercenaries, bombed two frontier towns of Goli and Phaida in
the West Nile district around 16 February 1965. There
was an outburst of rage in the country and urgent questions had to be answered. Why of all Congo's neighbors
was Uganda the only one to be bombed and attacked by
the Congolese armed forces? As usual, Obote had to
misdirect public attention by shifting the nation's
wrath to the United States, which was admittedly the
prime backer of the Congolese government. The United
States, it was alleged -- probably rightly -- had pro-

vided the combat aircraft to the Congo and therefore
was ultimately responsible for the attack on Uganda
on 16 February 1965. A national demonstration was
held against the American embassy in Kampala where the
American flag was burned. Yet, this did not answer
the question of why Uganda was attacked. It was under
these circumstances that Ocheng introduced his motion
in Parliament on 16 March 1965 charging that the deputy
commander of the army, Idi Amin, was in charge of Congo
operations, had banked excessive amounts of money in
his bank account, and that Obote, Onama, Nekyon, and
Amin were involved in making a fortune from gold,
ivory, and coffee, using the Ugandan army to fight inside the Congo. Ocheng demanded an inquiry into these
allegations, as well as the suspension of Colonel Amin
from the army.

Opposition members of Parliament brought some
details to light. Gaspari Oda charged that on 18 January 1965, forty-nine men of the Ugandan army went to
Esebi, nearly thirty miles from Arua inside the Congo,
to fight, organize, and train Congolese rebels.[2]
Martin Okelo, also from West Nile, supported this and
added more details. The Ugandan army was training
about 1,500 rebels in Uluko, close to a refugee camp
near Arua, in Uganda, using Ugandan army military
trucks. On 26 March 1965, a contingent of Uganda's
army fought with the Congolese troops at Vurra customs
on Uganda's frontier, suffering several casualties.
Okelo added, "For months the government, by hook or by
crook managed to conceal from the nation the true picture of what has been going on in our western border
...a great deal of half-truths have been cunningly
mixed up with gross errors."[3] An Italian missionary
resident in the area, Father Montoni, had his own version as to the reason for bombing Uganda. "A Uganda
village bombed whose school was shot at by a Congolese
plane was a hideout for Congolese rebels. They had
crossed the frontier and used Nyapea village as a refuge and it was believed locally this was the reason
for the attack."[4] Again, Obote hotly denied all these
allegations.

But from several eyewitness sources it was plain
that Obote had misled the party, the Cabinet, and the
country, and his conduct subsequent to the Ocheng motion increased this belief. For a whole year, unequal-
led in Uganda's parliamentary history, he sought to
obstruct, postpone, or eliminate Ocheng's motions demanding an inquiry. In September 1965, Ocheng reintroduced his motion. Obote demanded the galleries of
the National Assembly to be cleared of strangers and
then told Parliament in camera that investigations

into Ocheng's allegations concerning Amin were so near
completion that he requested the motion be withdrawn
since he would soon submit his findings to Parliament.
The motion was withdrawn on this assurance.

At the time, it seems Obote was not sure of what
strategy to follow except that he was resolved to cover
up the correct facts regarding his secret intervention.
For instance, he told Joe Kiwanuka, a leading Ugandan
parliamentarian, that the funds in the colonel's account had come from Algeria as aid for the insurgents.
Yet, he said nothing of this to his colleagues in the
Cabinet. Five months later Amin himself came out with
the truth in a statement that the money came from the
rebels to purchase provisions for them in Uganda.
Moreover, Obote had lied to Parliament in September
because there never had been any police inquiry in the
matter.

On 22 October 1965, he wrote to Ocheng that the
motion dealt with security matters and therefore Ocheng
had no business introducing it -- very much like President Nixon's attempt to cover up Watergate crimes
under the cover of national security. The prime minister had real fears that if the party and the country
learned that he had waged a secret war that had resulted in the attack on Uganda while he had told them
another story, it might be a short step to the end of
his career. If the UPC was united, Obote would have
felt more confident, perhaps, but as related elsewhere
serious intraparty strife had developed and there was
a powerful group in the party that opposed his policies
and identified with the secretary-general. The strategy he chose to strengthen his coverup was to link
Ocheng and the UPC secretary-general, not only as
planning to eliminate him but also as being supporters
of the reactionary Congolese government and its American patrons, which was another misdirection and totally
misleading.

When the motion was reintroduced on 4 February
1965, the bitterness and unanimity of the speeches
showed the depth of national anger. As a leading member of the UPC, Abu Mayanja, put it, "Some of us love
this country well enough to die for it. We do not have
any other country to go to, but I have the strongest
possible objection to dying in order that X may get
gold." [Hear! Hear!] 5

ACCUSATIONS OF PROFITEERING FROM THE CONFLICT

Ocheng had alleged that Obote and his committee
of four had obtained considerable quantities of gold,

ivory, and coffee from the Congo. The amount of gold
was never certain. Some who claimed to have seen the
Land Rover that carried it into Uganda said it was
about six tons. It was later admitted by Obote and
Onama that there had been seventeen bars of it, each
weighing about 20 pounds. Parliamentarians alleged
that twenty-two lorries full of coffee and two lorries
of ivory had entered Uganda. If Obote were to be
shown to have benefited from any of this, it would
have been most damaging to his standing. This was all
the more so because of the consistency for a year with
which he hotly denied that any gold ever came to Uganda as alleged or that he personally realized any material benefit from the conflict. But now that his
denials had not put off the motion and he was not sure
how much his adversaries knew, he became desperate
that the process might stumble onto some grave revelations and end his career.

THE LIKELY REMOVAL OF IDI AMIN AND ITS CONSEQUENCES

     Considering that Colonel Idi Amin was at this
time Obote's trusted man in the army, any threat to
remove him, such as was posed by the parliamentary
motion, was also a threat to the prime minister himself. He had built the army the way he wanted it by
using Colonel Amin. Thus far he had not yet shown
any signs of distrusting or wanting to remove Amin.
He had no immediate replacement. The matter was all
the more serious because the then army commander,
Brigadier Opolot -- who had been rendered ineffective
by the reliance on the more trusted Amin -- was known
to have little sympathy for Obote as a result. The
removal of Amin in the middle of a manifestly hostile
political atmosphere within the UPC and outside it
could mean that Obote might be forced out of government by a constitutional process at a time when he had
no one in the army to help him. Amin, therefore, had
to be saved once more, this time through a revolution.
It was a logical and correct calculation except that
it was highly dangerous and cruel for a head of government to invoke a process that legitimized violence and
caused the death of thousands of people.

THE UPC STAND ON OCHENG'S MOTION

     By the time Ocheng put his motion on the order
paper for business in Parliament in January 1965, the
UPC was deeply and seriously divided. It was not

merely a clash of personalities. There was an on-going divisive contest from the top hierarchy down between those who sought a total monopoly of power in the state and in the party, who were identified with Obote, and those who, while resolved to maintain the primacy of the UPC, were strongly opposed to forcible elimination of all opposition (within the KY, the DP, or the UPC), who were identified with the secretary-general. It had clearly emerged by now that Obote had little use or respect for the laws and procedures he was sworn to uphold. He sought to exempt his supporters from the very laws and procedures to which he subjected his opponents and the rest of the country. Let us look at a few illustrations.

The same Daudi Ocheng had moved a serious motion many months back charging that the minister of agriculture, M. M. Ngobi, and the minister of health, E. Lumu, had acquired a coffee-processing factory through corrupt means. These were leading members of the party and the Cabinet. Obote summoned them to his Kampala lodge, and held them that whole day and night under what was in effect house arrest on the grounds that they might interfere with police investigations if left at large. He then immediately instructed the police to carry out a thorough investigation, which they did. The ministers were vindicated; there had been no corruption, although they felt humiliated by the way Obote handled them.

Several inquiries of a similar nature had been held concerning other UPC officials; it was proper that they be made. How then could the UPC be asked to put off a request for an inquiry into allegations on public officers simply because they were Obote's favorites? Or why could Obote himself not be investigated? Five months earlier he had brought the gravest possible charges against the vice-president of Uganda and the UPC and the secretary-general of UPC of an attempt to assassinate him. Although the evidence he produced was patently fabricated, unlike what Ocheng had produced regarding Amin, the two party leaders had been investigated by a competent police officer without loss of time and they had been exonerated. Moreover, if blameless army officers could be dismissed contrary to all regulations, then there was an even greater case as to why another officer, Idi Amin, should at least be investigated in the light of the prima facie persuasive evidence that had been brought to light.

If Obote had been honest and honorable, if he had confided in his UPC top leaders or in the Cabinet at the very beginning when the charges were made, admit-

ting the Ugandan army's involvement in the Congo and
that the money in Amin's account belonged to the Congolese forces, it was probable that, despite the
strains within the party, his colleagues would have
rallied to support him and so would have blocked the
opposition motion. After all, the opposition in Parliament were a mere handful that could not pass any
measure without support from UPC members of Parliament.
It is possible to make mistakes in government, especially when delegating responsibility, and the UPC
would have understood this. But Obote was caught up
in his techniques of misdirection and misrepresenta-
tion. No matter how his close colleagues pressed for
the truth in private, he consistently refused to tell
it to them and branded Ocheng's motion as totally
malicious and unfounded. Several members of the UPC
and the Cabinet, however, possessed independent access
to eyewitnesses from the West Nile and the Congo
frontier, and consequently knew there was some real
truth to the allegations. They decided to get it out
through an investigation.

The practice of debating opposition motions in
Parliament at the time should be well understood in
order to realize Obote's erroneous report to the UPC
in 1968, which stated that the party parliamentary
group had decided to reject Ocheng's motion on 31 January 1966. The Cabinet had to consider all motions
moved by members of Parliament. It would then make a
decision on what the government's stand was -- whether
to support or reject the motion. This cabinet stand
would be sent to UPC back-benchers in Parliament for
their support, and they would vote as so instructed
by the government. Ocheng had submitted two motions
for this parliamentary session. One requested Parliament to rename Lake George, Lake George Rukidi,
after the late ruler of Toro, Sir George Rukidi, and
the other demanded suspension of Colonel Idi Amin and
an inquiry into his bank account. Both motions were
on the agenda when the Cabinet met under Obote's
chairmanship to consider what stand government should
take. It was decided to reject the request to rename
Lake George. But Obote refused to put the second
Ocheng motion before the Cabinet for discussion.
There was therefore no cabinet direction to the UPC
parliamentarians on this particular motion concerning
Uganda's involvement in the Congo.

Late in the afternoon, Obote asked the UPC members
of Parliament to meet after the National Assembly ad-
journed. At about 9 p.m. only thirty members out of
nearly seventy were able to come. It should be said
there was never a stipulated quorum for these meetings.

I was there. The meeting was held to discuss what to
do with the Ocheng motion censuring Amin. A few members, repeating well-rehearsed statements, called for
its rejection. Others, because of abundant evidence
indicating Uganda's involvement in the Congolese civil
war, demanded an investigation and believed there had
been a massive government coverup. It was at this
meeting -- for the first time in a year of consistent
probing and denial -- that Obote remarkably admitted
some gold had come into Uganda from the Congo. The
effect was electrifying. The possibility that much
more remained unsaid was enhanced. There were angry
exchanges between supporters with different views and
some members began one by one to leave. By about mid-
night, I made this observation:

> What is the purpose of this meeting? If it is
> called to advise the parliamentary group on how
> to vote on Ocheng's gold motion, what is the
> recommendation of the Cabinet? Although it was
> on the agenda the Cabinet did not discuss it.
> There is therefore no Cabinet recommendation
> and Ministers discussing this matter now can
> only be taken to express personal not collective
> views to bind this meeting.

I then left, leaving about twenty-five members to continue with Obote in the chair. Later this meeting
made a decision to oppose the Ocheng motion in Parliament, contrary to all established practice. This decision only infuriated a large section of the UPC even
more as they saw it as yet another last ditch attempt
at a coverup. Conveniently, Obote left for a tour of
the northern region and left Cuthbert Obwangor to chair
cabinet meetings.

Whenever the prime minister was away and unable
to preside over cabinet meetings, the normal practice
was for him to designate a cabinet minister to preside
in his place. Government business would be transacted
as usual. If there was any issue the prime minister
felt should not be discussed in his absence -- which
seldom happened -- he would instruct the cabinet chairman to that effect. It is important to mention that
there was never a quorum required for the cabinet meeting to transact any business as cabinet records would
show. When the Cabinet met on February 4 with nine
ministers present and Cuthbert Obwangor in the chair,
therefore, there was absolutely no reason why it could
not consider any issue as a competent body. Considerable pressure from UPC parliamentarians was brought
on leading UPC officials in the Cabinet to make a

formal decision accepting the Ocheng motion in principle. The purported decision to reject it by a handful
of parliamentary members under Obote's chairmanship
was manifestly unrepresentative and obviously contrary
to established procedure.

Obote had built a doctrine where most things proposed by the opposition had to be rejected. Consequently any attempt to support an opposition measure
from the government side was regarded treasonous. And
yet, we had accepted an institutionalized opposition.
Its members were as intelligent, as indigenous, and
as representative of Ugandans as we were. To treat
them as nonpersons and reject almost everything they
proposed had extremely dangerous consequences. The
government's intolerance to criticism that showed
against them was turning inward against UPC members
who held opinions contrary to Obote. To many UPC members, therefore, it had become clear that what was
sacrosanct was not the name of their party, which they
loved dearly, but the principles for which the party
stood. If some of these principles -- because they
were universal -- were supported by the opposition,
they should not consequently be rejected. One such
principle was the precept that all men were under one
law.

On this basis at the cabinet meeting of 4 February
1966, as Obote reported to UPC in 1968, "According to
records it was Ibingira who raised reversion of the
decision taken on the motion by the Parliamentary
Group [i.e. to revive debate on the motion to suspend Amin].⁶ It was plain the majority of ministers
felt there had to be a cabinet direction on the matter
and it had to accept the motion in principle. Ocheng's
motion had been exaggerated out of all proportion. All
it sought was an inquiry while Amin was suspended.
Such inquiry could, as it later did, absolve him and
Obote of all misdeed. Yet it was important that we not
only be, but appear to be, just as leaders. As I said
in Cabinet, "we should demonstrate to this country that
no one is above the law." The Cabinet decided to accept the motion, and in the afternoon so directed the
parliamentary group. It is significant that with the
exception of only one dissenting vote, the National
Assembly voted to accept Ocheng's motion. The debate
of that afternoon remains unique in the courage of the
members to stand up for truth and Uganda's real interests.

A leading minister, B. K. Kirya, once Obote's
alter ego, paid "warm tribute to Ocheng" because he
had spoken "the whole truth." He then went on to show
the party's disillusionment:

When we were debating this motion some time, we
were told in camera that this matter was in the
process of being investigated. Now, any sensible
person would think twice whether the investigation
takes twelve months to get to the final result.
We cannot tell the country that there was any law
missing that would enable authorities to do this.
But if there is a delay, why do we not as a government accept and say that it is unfortunate
that a delay has been caused, rather than say
that because Ocheng brings this motion it is
therefore rubbish?[7]

For my part, as I told Parliament, the issue of
whether gold and ivory had been looted in the Congo
was now superseded by a more ominous one when on 4
February Ocheng for the first time alleged Obote was
using Idi Amin to initiate the abrogation of the Ugandan Constitution. As recounted previously, there was
already evidence that he was planning just that, although it was not certain when he would strike. It
now seemed to me that the time might be much sooner
than I had previously thought. I therefore supported
the inquiry, in an extempore short statement:

It is proper and fitting that anybody in government and outside it, in public or private life,
should not consider himself as beyond the reach
of the law. It is on that basis without much
argument that this motion is accepted. . . .
The investigation of an issue does not necessarily
mean we are going to prove conclusively to be positive. If all the cases which the police have
investigated were actually to lead to convictions,
I think we should spend half of our budget on
prisons. Many may be wrong, but if there is a
prima facie case, if there is a basis upon which
to found a reasonable suspicion, then an investigation is proper. We must accept this not only
on paper, but we must accept to find out the
truth.[8]

Obote, however, was resolved never to accept such
an open inquiry. Suddenly, he said it was not possible
to suspend Colonel Amin because there was no legal provision for such a step; instead, Amin was sent on
leave. This assertion, of course, was patently false.
The Uganda Armed Forces Act of 1964, incorporating all
the preindependence legislation and regulations dealing
with army discipline and conduct of officers was more
than adequate.

Master of misdirection as he was, upon Obote's
return to the capital after the passage of the motion,
he claimed he had "led the country with clean hands"
and accepted holding the inquiry. He proceeded to
appoint an impressive number of judges from the East
African Court of Appeals to do so. Under cover, however, he was preparing troops in a bid to seize absolute power.

On 22 February 1966, after 1:15 p.m., while the
Cabinet met in a routine session to consider the terms
of reference for the Commission of Inquiry into Ocheng's
allegations, armed police burst into the cabinet room
and surrounded all the ministers who sat stunned
and speechless. On Obote's signal, five leading ministers and founders of the UPC were roughly grabbed,
handcuffed, and brutally pushed out of the cabinet
meeting to face five years in a maximum security prison without trial until liberated by the 1971 coup
d'etat.

The grounds for arresting the ministers that Obote
presented in April 1966 to Judge Russell at Gulu were
extraordinary in their falsehood. Until I saw it happen, I would not have believed that such a frame-up
of innocent people was possible from a close colleague.
The principal witness for the state was a member of
Obote's bodyguard, a man named James Makanya Namondo.
He charged, for example, that I had driven him to my
house in Entebbe, taken him into my bedroom and presented him with a revolver, asking him to shoot Obote
while stopped at any Kampala traffic light. Namondo
then alleged he had been present at a meeting including all the five ministers in the house of the commander of the army, Brigadier Opolot, where a vote was
made to overthrow Obote. He had never been to my
house nor was he ever on close or even casual terms
with me or any of the other alleged conspirators. Yet
he had to give entirely fabricated evidence in order
to provide Obote the grounds for overthrowing the
constitution and seizing absolute power.

Soon after the fall of Amin I met Namondo in Kampala among the liberators! In an attempt to get at
the truth I assured him I had no hostility toward him
but wanted to know at whose instigation he had testified against me so falsely, knowing it could have led
me to the firing squad. He was most apologetic and
went on to confirm what I already knew: that he had
been made to give the false testimony by the heads of
the General Service and the Special Branch, admitting
too that everyone concerned knew the falsity of the
evidence. I pointed these facts out to several ministers in the government and the leader of the Tanzanian

intelligence in Kampala, who I wanted to talk to Namondo to get the true story of how the Uganda tragedy had originated. Whether he did or not I do not know.

THE CONSTITUTION AND ITS RESTRAINTS

As we indicated before, the Independence Constitution, while providing for a strong central government and legislature, imposed important restraints on each of them. Above all, the fundamental rights of the people could not be abrogated without a national consensus through a two-thirds majority in the national legislature and in the kingdoms. Even though the four "semifederal" regions of Ankole, Bunyoro, Busoga, and Toro were dominated and controlled by the UPC, their governments were not prepared to surrender all rights and powers affecting the common people to the central government without any restraint. Buganda obviously would not. Parliament itself would not, despite the fact that it was now overwhelmingly UPC. A substantial section of its UPC membership, apprehensive of Obote's insatiable grasp for more powers, were unprepared to support him in removing all restraint from the constitution imposed against assuming more powers. Similarly, within the UPC hierarchy outside Parliament, there was a formidable opinion against vesting excessive powers in the executive because of the increasing misuse of the powers he already possessed.

With this solid backing for the retention of constitutional restraints, and given the unwavering determination of Obote to assume all power, a crisis was ultimately unavoidable. As he put it to me once in a rhetorical question, "What happens when an irresistible force meets an immovable object?" What was so vital was not merely that the constitution preserved kingdoms when he favored republicanism; the issue of kingship was blown out of proportion as an added excuse to repudiate the constitution. The truth is that after independence power had effectively passed into the hands of the people and their kings were solely symbols of their traditions. As I said, even the kabaka's power (who was the most powerful ruler) could be defied by the KY leadership. If the issue in 1966 was simply to remove kings and no more -- which is strongly denied -- most Ugandans would have gladly considered it. But in fact the abolition of kingship was to be, to my mind, a secondary matter. The crux of what Obote wanted was the power to take away the rights of any individual, any group or organization, political, cultural or otherwise, without any re-

straints, without any challenge, either in Parliament,
in the electorate, or in the law courts. The separation of powers among the executive, the legislative,
and the judiciary, which the constitution assured, had
to give way to a virtually unrestrained executive.
This could only come through a revolution as the people
of the country were not going to grant it by free
choice. Precisely these immense powers, as we shall
see, were assumed by him once he abrogated the constitution.

It is most important, in judging objectively as
to whether or not the Independence Constitution was
viable, to remember that at no time was a basic measure of policy of the central government obstructed
or denied implementation by any region -- including
Buganda -- because of a constitutional impediment. A
good example was the transfer of the "lost counties"
from Buganda to Bunyoro. Mutesa, as president of Uganda, had to sign every law before it became effective.
Anticipating that he might decline -- for obvious political reasons -- to sign the legislation authorizing
the referendum and subsequent transfer of the territory
because of his position as kabaka of Buganda and to
save face among his people, the first constitutional
amendment, which I moved in Parliament in 1963 as
minister of justice, provided that if for any reason
the president was unable to sign a bill into law, the
prime minister would do so and the law would take
effect as if it had been duly signed by the president.
That is what happened and there was no crisis. It was
also the only time this provision was invoked.

Obote was later to claim dereliction of duty in
the Bugandan administration, financial malpractices,
and the like, as illustrations of the inadequacy of
the constitution. Two points should be made in this
regard. First, there was no local or regional government in which administrative malpractice and incompetence did not occur at one time or another. There was
a total of fourteen regional or local governments, of
which Buganda was only one and the rest were UPC-con-
trolled. Second, if there were malpractices, the
central government, through its financial power to
withhold important grants or services, had all the
leverage it needed to make any local government comply
with policy, including Buganda. There were enough
powerful levers to deal with Buganda. But they required planning, patience, and good will, none of
which were available at the center. The true cause
of the crisis lay not in the constitution but in Obote's unreasonable desire to remove its meaningful restrictions. This was exacerbated by the UPC's failure

to penetrate Buganda appreciably.

The first serious attempt to remove Idi Amin from the army was thus decisively crushed, and its failure greatly enhanced the position and power base from which he was later to decimate the country. The names of those political leaders who were the first to stand against Amin deserve special mention, especially because it was unfashionable at the time. Among others they are:

Government Side:
B. K. Kirya, Minister of Works
E. S. Lumu, Minister of Health
G. B. Magezi, Minister of Housing
M. M. Mgobi, Minister of Agriculture
G. S. Ibingira, Minister of State
C. J. Obwangor, Minister of Justice
C. Magara, MP
J. R. Kangaho, MP

Opposition Side:
Daudi Ocheng, MP
J. H. Obonyo, MP⎫
A. Latim, MP   ⎬ later murdered by Amin
M. A. Okelo, MP ⎭
B. Byanyima, MP
A. K. Mayanja, MP

THE SEIZURE OF ABSOLUTE POWER

The same day on which Obote arrested the ministers, he announced to the country that he had suspended the constitution, assumed all executive powers in the state, and would be advised by a number of people to be named later. This was patently illegal of course, because the constitution provided no powers for suspension but only amendment, and this was vested in the Parliament. The executive powers of the state were vested in the Cabinet, appointed by the prime minister and advising the president. On 26 February 1966, Idi Amin, who only three weeks previously had been voted suspended by Parliament, was now given the effective command of the Ugandan army. Things moved swiftly. On March 3, Obote assumed the functions of the presidency and dismissed both the president (Mutesa, the kabaka of Buganda) and the vice-president (Nadiope, who was also vice-president of the UPC), although such powers of removal were vested in the Parliament. The charges against the five detained ministers were too vague. First it was because they had conducted themselves in a manner that was threat-

ening the security of the state, without detailing
precisely how. Then it was later alleged that they
were in collusion with the opposition to overthrow
the government. The truth is that there was a perfectly legitimate political struggle going on between its
leaders to influence the policies of the party, not
to abrogate the constitution. When Obote felt he was
losing, he had to employ his ultimate weapon -- Amin
and his army, with all the terror that it meant.
   The prime minister made a great play of Mutesa's
having attempted to ask foreign troops to aid him in
overthrowing the government. This was allegedly the
principal reason why Obote seized power. Did Mutesa
really want to overthrow the government? If he asked
for foreign troops, what were his reasons? For more
than a year before the 1966 crisis I had been telling
him, as a good personal friend, that I was worried by
Obote making preparations to seize absolute power,
impose a one-party system, and preempt any prospect
of a fair election, even though I could not tell when
he would strike. Mutesa was fully aware of how dis-
advantageous the continuation of the KY was as it
provided an ideal target to whip up anti-Bugandan emotions as a prelude to possible physical attack. It
was for this reason that he decided to advise KY political leaders to disband it and open Buganda to political parties. At first it seemed incredible that a
prime minister should plot to "overthrow himself,"
since he was already in power. And yet it was this
seeming improbability that provided Obote with a perfect cover for preparation until he came out in his
true colors. Then it was too late to stop him. The
kabaka no longer aspired to Buganda's secession and
was resolved to meet whatever problems the future held,
within a Ugandan framework. This was no mean achievement for the UPC/KY alliance. I know too, that he
completely supported the constitution.
   It was under the independence constitutional formula that Buganda had been fairly integrated in the
country and the kabakaship had been assured. If he
had wished to exercise executive power he might have
done what Sir Seretse Khama did in Botswana: abandon
the traditional role and launch a political party.
With Buganda's almost unanimous support, no other
nationalist would have beaten him. This was not his
ambition and the post of a ceremonial presidency,
offering him prestige and relatively less toil, was
preferable to him. If he was to fight at all, therefore, he would fight to protect the status quo ensured
by the constitution, not to upset it by promoting a
revolution. Immediately after the Ocheng motion was

passed in Parliament, swift and alarming developments followed, compounded by persistent rumors of an impending coup. Troop movements were ordered from different battalions to report to Deputy Commander Idi Amin for unspecified instructions without the commander of the army's knowledge. Regularly scheduled military exercises were interpreted as moves in perpetration of a coup against Obote, who stayed in the North on the pretext that his schedule had been planned long in advance. This in fact was similar to what he was to do much later when he went to Singapore, leaving preparations behind to eliminate his opponents in his absence. In this case, the idea was that the Ocheng motion having passed, his group in the army should launch a revolution in the capital, eliminate political opponents physically or by detention, repudiate the constitution and invite him to the capital to assume full executive powers. Few people in the country knew how much they owed to the courage of the opposition members of Parliament from the North who moved to neutralize this calamity.

In January 1966, an Acholi parliamentarian had already warned Obote about this:

> There are certain individuals who were of opinion that they could exploit the ethnic groups of our men in the armed forces. I would like to inform, especially those who do not come from where I come, that it would be futile for anybody who calls himself Nilotic to think that he could play the emotions of the Acholi to fight on his side, because they are fully aware of the plight of certain politicians who having failed, . . . have exhorted and resorted to playing on ethnic origin of the men of our armed forces . . . do not count on certain Nilotics to come and support you and maintain you in office indefinitely or for thirty years as some conceited Front Bench Members seem to think.[9]

Despite Obote's efforts, the Acholi were certainly not unanimously for him. Most particularly the DP parliamentarians from Acholi and West Nile, like A. Latim, H. Obonyo, and M. Okelo, who could use ethnicity as a tool to penetrate Obote's monopoly of the army, had to work intensely, drive secretly to several battalions, and plead with the troops not to move on the reckless behest of government politicians. It worked. But the country and especially the capital knew what was being attempted by Obote. The Cabinet under the chairmanship of Cuthbert Obwangor met at least twice

and sent urgent requests to Obote to return to the
capital, but in vain. It was such circumstances,
therefore, that prompted Mutesa to get involved. He
had no executive authority to conduct government business. But the very constitution that tied his hands
was in imminent danger of being abrogated by those
charged to uphold it. It was obviously an impossible
position to be in: on the one hand being required to
be constitutional when constitutionality is in the
process of being repudiated, and on the other hand
taking some steps to ensure the survival of the constitution when he had no legal powers to do so. He
chose the latter course -- to act -- and it was the
more honorable course, even if it did miscarry, partly
because the action was too limited and too hesitant
but especially because the commander of the army,
Brigadier Opolot, who had privately campaigned for the
Ocheng motion to remove Idi Amin, his rival, and had
assured constitutionalists he would block any overt
move to abrogate the constitution, became fainthearted
and faltered in the face of a more bold and desperate
Amin, once the revolution was under way.

    I had some meetings with Mutesa at this time; he
was entitled to consult his ministers. The position
he took was that should there be an actual upheaval
or rebellion in the army when any faction moved to
seize power, it should be stopped so as to uphold the
constitution, and if necessary a precautionary request
should be sent to the British asking them to provide
military assistance to overcome the disorder. As a
former colonial power with which Uganda had parted
without hard feelings and as a fellow member of the
Commonwealth, Britain was a reasonable choice at the
time. It was not the first time that British military
assistance was requested to put down a rebellion in
Uganda. As stated earlier, in January 1964 British
troops had been called in by Obote to quell a mutiny
in the first battalion. The only difference this time
was that Mutesa, the ceremonial president, and not
Obote, the executive head of government, was to make
the request. Technically, therefore, Obote was right
that Mutesa had no legal power to make the request.

    But the request as put was contingent on there
being an overt, internal military threat to abrogate
the constitution that could not be contained by local
means. It is significant that the prime minister
conveniently omitted this point and injected a new
false claim that the request was for foreign troops
to overthrow the government. Mutesa plainly and openly
stated that he had made the request in good faith as a
responsible head of state. But the supreme moment for

which Obote had long planned was at hand and the politicized army under Idi Amin was on top.

On 15 April 1966 in a parliamentary session while surrounded by troops, Obote formally announced, "the constitution we had from October 9, 1962 is hereby abrogated."[10] He then _imposed_ his own brand of constitution, granting himself for all practical purposes the unrestrained, centralized power. Without any members of Parliament having seen the new constitution, they were forced to adopt it.

As he told Parliament, "It is hereby resolved that the . . . constitution now laid before us be adopted and _it is hereby adopted_ this 15th day of April 1966 as the constitution of Uganda." He added, "Fairly soon you will find copies [of the constitution that parliamentarians had never seen but had approved] in your pigeon holes."

At long last he could give some reasons. "The new constitution," he said, "proposed to treat Uganda as one united country . . . one country, one parliament, one government, one people," while the abrogated constitution had the message that "Uganda must be divided so much so that there is no government that will ever be able to govern." Was this really true? It was at the heart of the Ugandan crisis and the crises in many other emerging African states. Was excessive centralization of power the answer for effectively integrating multiethnic groups in the new state or was it counterproductive? We shall return to this issue later in this chapter.

In the most ill-conceived move of its life, the Bugandan Lukiko, with its old "resolution mentality" passed a motion on 19 May 1966 asking Obote's central government to quit the capital, which was in Bugandan territory -- thus, in effect, seceding. Morally, they had a case. The Independence Constitution by which all Ugandans had come together had been unlawfully abrogated and, logically, this meant releasing different groups from the obligations it had imposed. Consequently, if the central government was the first to abrogate it, it had no moral or legal right to tell others to uphold its new one. But the country had left legality and morality behind. What mattered now was that anyone with the military might could impose his will. The Lukiko resolution, therefore, was a godsend to Obote for a longed-for opportunity to crush Buganda.

It has been claimed by Obote that when the first army contingent went to the kabaka's palace it had instructions to search for illegally hidden arms, _using minimum force_. This is false on two counts.

First, the order to the troops could not have been to
use minimum force. After they slaughtered civilians
by the hundreds around the palace in an unequal battle,
not a single soldier was ever reprimanded for the excessive use of force; indeed, many were rewarded with
promotions. Second, there were no illegally hidden
arms in the palace. The kabaka was permitted by the
laws enacted by Obote's government to have a bodyguard
of 120, who were armed with submachine guns and six
automatic rifles, all certified by the Ministry of
Internal Affairs. The declaration that the objective
of the army's palace invasion was to search for arms
was a fabricated excuse for launching a premeditated
attack on the kabaka by Obote. The world was to be
informed by the New York Times of 30 November 1978
(more than ten years later) that it had been in fact
the British-born agent, Bob Astles, the confidant of
Amin and Obote at the time, who had suggested to both
of them that in order to make the invasion of the
palace plausible, they had to hide some arms in it
during the attack and then claim their capture after
taking the palace. This was what was done.

Undoubtedly, there was considerable tension around
Buganda as a consequence of Obote's unlawful assumption
of absolute power and his revocation of the constitution under which the Baganda and others had felt their
future secure. We were used to handling such crises,
and the police forces had always been sufficient to
handle the situation. The introduction of the army
was not because the police had failed to handle the
situation but rather to take advantage of the situation, to destroy Buganda, and to seize absolute power.
It is hard to arrive at the correct figure of those
who died, but they were counted by the thousands
throughout the kingdom. The precedent was now firmly
set to use massive official violence against political
opponents, real or imagined, and it was to rebound
against Obote with tragic and terrifying force after
the 1971 coup d'etat that deposed him.

The Gold Inquiry

Having seized immense executive powers and promoted Idi Amin to command the army, Obote now proceeded
to appoint the commission to investigate the allegations Ocheng had made against them in Parliament. It
consisted of three highly qualified, impeccable judges
of the East African Court of Appeals. It heard evidence in Uganda from 7 March 1966 and submitted its
report on 4 May 1966. Its findings were significant
not for what they said but for what they omitted and

for the conduct of parties before and after submission
of the report. Its conclusions were:

1. That the allegations of the receipt by the
   prime minister, Mr. Onama, and Mr. Nekyon of
   gold, ivory, monies, and other property from
   the Congo were totally unsupported by evidence
   and completely unfounded.
2. That Colonel Idi Amin received approximately
   shs 480,000 from the Congolese revolutionaries
   for which he had duly accounted to them.
3. That Colonel Amin also obtained at least eleven bars of unrefined gold originating from
   the Congo, each bar weighing approximately
   twenty pounds. How and from whom he received
   the gold they were unable to say for certain,
   but they strongly suspected that it came from
   the Congolese revolutionaries. The shs 480,000
   previously mentioned was largely the proceeds
   of the sale of that gold. They were satisfied
   that if there was any looting by Ugandan troops
   from the Congo in the course of the military
   operations, of which there is no evidence, Colonel Amin was not a party to it.
4. They were not satisfied that there was any
   conspiracy, any plot or plots between the
   prime minister, some of his ministers, and Colonel Amin to abrogate the constitution or overthrow the government of the country.

Outwardly, it was a stunning triumph for Obote
and his small group. They had seized absolute power
and abrogated the constitution, but the commission
absolved them from having plotted to do it. But Obote
knew he could never publish this report, which absolved
him. Obote desperately needed massive support in the
country, especially after destroying Buganda. He had
been pointedly accused of having involved the Ugandan
army in the Congo conflict to gain a fortune and in
order to cover this up he had abrogated the constitution and seized absolute power. The simplest and most
effective way to counter this would have been for him
to publish this report, even an edited version of it,
in order to vindicate his name in the country, especially because the commissioners were widely respected.
As he proclaimed himself president on 15 April 1966,
he promised the nation, "A time will come when citizens of this country will debate the report of the
Commission of Enquiry."[11] However, from the date this
report was submitted to him to the time of his overthrow by the army (nearly five years), the report was

never published -- not even leaked to the press --
despite repeated demands by the public and the opposition. No rational explanation of the coverup could be
advanced other than the dread of possible challenge
from those beyond his reach.
     The reasons that the commission never arrived at
the truth seem to be as follows. First, because of
its terms of reference the commission construed the
rules of evidence too narrowly and rigidly. Only direct evidence, testimony within the personal knowledge
of a witness, was admissible. This meant exclusion
of an important body of evidence from perfectly credible sources because of the laws of evidence barring
hearsay testimony. Second, the commission was further
especially handicapped from reaching the truth because
of the fear of witnesses for their very lives. Obote,
aided by Amin, had just seized power and hundreds of
people including leading cabinet and party officials
had been unlawfully seized and imprisoned without
trial. Therefore, it would have been most reckless
for anyone to testify before the commission in a manner that proved the validity of the charges. This
threat applied to resident foreigners and Ugandan citizens alike.
     Nothing illustrates this threat to witnesses more
than the experiences of two men who were closely connected with the gold that came to Uganda from the Congo. The first man, a European by the name of Venter,
was the manager of the Commercial Bank of Africa in
Kampala. According to the evidence he presented to
the commission, which was uncontested by Obote and his
colleagues, he had been requested by Colonel Idi Amin
to fly to Europe on 25 January 1965 to find a market
for gold, which (as he was told) "had been given to
the Ugandan government by the Congolese nationalist
forces to pay for the supply of weapons and ammunition."[12] Amin had then told him that, "ultimately, a
total amount of about <u>five tons</u> of gold was involved."[13]
Amin drove Venter to the airport, but on their way
they stopped at Amin's home where there were eleven
bars of gold, each weighing approximately twenty pounds.
He showed one to Venter. The gold bar had certain
numbers written on it and the name of a company the
witness could not recall. He took down these particulars on a piece of paper and flew to Europe to seek
the market.
     In Brussels Venter consulted Edouard Dervichian,
the managing director of his bank. Dervichian identified the name of the company that was on the gold bar
and advised him that it would be difficult to find a
market for the gold as its ownership would be disputed

by the company that had mined it in the Congo. Venter
then returned to Uganda and informed Colonel Amin that
it was impossible to find a market for the gold. This
was the first time the true account of what had long
been privately known or suspected was becoming public.
These revelations caused a commotion among the public
attending the hearings. The chairman complained,
"we've so many police and they can't keep order."
    Immediately after his testimony, he returned to
his bank. There Venter's offices were ransacked and
some employees roughed up by armed police. His life
was threatened because of his revelations to the commission and that evening he caught a plane and fled
the country. Why was Venter threatened in such a
manner by state law enforcement agencies? Is it likely
that it could have been done without Obote's knowledge?
It is known Obote was following the hearings very
closely. Venter's revelations were the first serious
independent challenge of his coverup and it is incon-
ceivable that Venter was harassed without his explicit
instruction.
    The second case is that of General Nicholas Olen-
ga, one of the military commanders of the Congolese
insurgents under Gbenye before they fell out. As he
told the chairman of the commission, it appeared there
were serious misappropriations of the funds and properties of the Congolese revolutionaries by some of
their leaders, including Gbenye. Indeed, Gbenye, who
was the favorite of Obote, claimed General Olenga had
been dismissed from his group. When the commission
opened, Olenga was invited to Uganda to give evidence.
Asked whether he knew anything about the gold and related allegations, he said on 9 March 1966 that he did
and would give useful information to the commission
if he could obtain his personal documents relating to
the matter from Khartoum in the Sudan. Olenga cabled
for this documentary evidence. On 18 March 1966 the
commission recalled him and the transcript of the evidence is worth verbatim quotation.

> Rankin [attorney for the commission]: General
> Olenga, on the last occasion you were here, you
> said you were unable to say anything until you
> had a dossier from Khartoum?
> General Olenga: Yes.
> Rankin: Have you received the dossier from Khar-
> toum?
> Olenga: They have arrived here now, but they are
> with the security people. I cannot get them from
> the security forces and I have tried four or five
> times to do so, and I have been menaced by armed

men.

Rankin: Can you tell me who in the security forces has got the documents?

Olenga: I have not got the documents but they
have come four or five times to demand them from
me, menacing me at the same time.

The Chairman: I thought he said that he had got
the documents and hidden them somewhere.

Olenga: Yes, I have them hidden and they have
tried to get them from me.

Rankin: Have you read the documents since you
received them?

Olenga: I know them and I have been menaced about
them. I know them and I could tell about them
before they arrived but I have been threatened
about them.

Chairman: We are trying to inquire into whether
gold belonging to the Congolese revolutionaries
arrived in Uganda. We are trying to find what
happened to that gold. If you want to tell us
something you know about it you can do so, but
if you do not want to tell us anything we can't
go on forever.

Olenga: I only want security because the police
came to get me at 2 a.m. in the morning when I
arrived here.

Rankin: Do you know whether any Congolese nationalist gold has come into Uganda?

Olenga: If I have the security I will give all
the necessary proofs.

Chairman: As far as I know until yesterday you
were free to do what you liked.

Olenga: I came here yesterday with four people to
tell about this story. . . . I went back to the
hotel and there were hundreds of soldiers waiting
for me to take me away.

Rankin: Are you willing to answer the questions
of this commission or not?

Olenga: When I asked for these documents it was
to give evidence before this court, but I must
have security. I only ask for security, that
is all I want, and I will give evidence of other
things as well. If they wish they can take my
wife and children away and place them in a residence somewhere -- a diplomatic residence, and
I will give evidence. I will throw light on the
matter immediately.

Justice Miller (member of the commission): Ask
him (addressing French interpreter) if he can
produce these documents.

Olenga: Yes, all!

Rankin: It seems to me, my lord, with respect,
 he is trying to require us to give a guarantee
 which you have no power to give [i.e. of personal
 safety] .
Chairman:We have no power to give any.
Olenga: All my officers with me are in danger as
 well.
Chairman: Tell him (addressing the interpreter)
 that we are not in a position to give him the
 security he wants; we don't know, if he commits
 a crime it is a matter for the police, and if
 he is an illegal immigrant, it is a matter for
 the immigration department. We do not know anything about that.[14]

This was a most unfortunate attempt by the chairman to evade facing the issue of official threats to
this and other witnesses. Why did he not seek or
promise to seek assurance for the safety of witnesses
from the government? Why did he not protest at such
overt intimidation by authorities that was destined
to render any impartial inquiry impossible? If government had violated its promise to protect not to
harass witnesses, what was the purpose of continuing
the commission?

Olenga: I am here at the demand -- at the wish --
 of the government.
Rankin: Absolutely no power, and I think we have
 done our best twice and I don't believe Your
 Lordships could do more than that.
Olenga: They have set a trap for me here, the
 strength of the strongest.
Chairman: What you say here to this commission
 . . . nothing will happen to you. Well, all
 right, we can't go on like that. . . .
Olenga: The night I gave the letter here, I was
 taken away. I want to know whether the others
 are in prison, or in forced residence under
 house arrest.
Chairman: Well, nothing will happen to you for
 being a witness here, if you want to give evidence, do so. If you don't want to give the
 evidence then that is your own. . . .
Olenga: The night I was taken away it happened
 in front of everyone, and this is security, this
 is safety!!
Chairman: Well, I don't know what to say.
Olenga: I have nothing to lose, death is nothing
 to me, but I have pity for my children. . . .
 I am in a state of danger. I don't want to have

trouble with my brothers [i.e. Obote and asso-
ciates]. They are threatening me. . . . I
came here yesterday, quite confidently, and I
spoke, and I would like to know whether it is
the commission which has placed me in the prison
where I am.
Chairman: Well, you can be assured that it is not
the commission that has to do with that at all.

Olenga left the witness stand without any assurance as to his safety and never returned to give that
evidence which was so central to the inquiry. Shortly
afterwards the place where he was staying with his
wife and children was raided by armed troops and there
was a struggle that turned the place upside down. He
was overcome, beaten almost to death, sustaining many
major fractures of his bones in three limbs. He was
then transferred by the same Ugandan government authorities to Moroto hospital over 400 miles northeast of
Uganda where for three months he hovered between life
and death. When he recovered after several months
more, he was transferred to Moroto prison; his wife
and children faced indefinite detention. The technique
of making people disappear had not yet caught on, but
the climate for its existence was surely being shaped
by these government policies.

Another long-denied fact now seemed established
from these hearings, namely, the Ugandan military
involvement in the Congo. It was given in evidence
in camera without challenge that Colonel Idi Amin had
been sent into the Congo to the town of Aru, where he
stayed for about two weeks. A former leading official
of the revolutionary government told the commission
when asked the purpose of Colonel Amin's presence in
the Congo, "According to what Dr. Obote told me, he
was sent there to coordinate with President Gbenye to
fight mercenaries" (who were fighting for the Congo
regime). Although the whole truth was not stated
about the actual clashes that took place between the
Ugandan and the Congolese forces inside the Congo, it
was revealing that a deputy commander of the Ugandan
army should spend so many days in the territory of
another state secretly planning hostile activities
against its government. This has nothing to do with
whether or not Uganda supported the Congo regime, some
of whose policies were insupportable. However, the
implications of becoming involved in the subversion
of another regime whose policy is not liked are so
adverse to the stability of every state that the charter of the OAU as well as international law does not
permit it.

From these few extracts of the transcript we can
draw definite conclusions:

1. That the entire proceedings of the commission
   were held under such an extreme sense of insecurity and fear among potential witnesses
   that no real evidence regarding the accused
   and their connection with the gold could come
   to light.
2. That the threats and intimidation of witnesses
   were directed by Obote's government with his
   instructions or authorization.
3. That the only reasonable ground for such conduct on Obote's part was fear of discovery of
   proof to confirm some or all the allegations
   made by Ocheng in 1966.
4. That the commission in absolving Obote and his
   colleagues was denied access to material evidence which in effect rendered its findings
   seriously misleading.
5. It is because Obote knew that the findings of
   the commission omitted the truth about his
   guilt that he dared not publish them to vindicate himself lest someone out of his reach
   contradict him with proof.

The true story of this secret involvement and its
material rewards is yet to be told. But it is important that in the light of even the little that this
commission was able to elicit, it had been more than
justified for Daudi Ocheng to make his motion, for
the Cabinet to have insisted upon knowing the truth,
and -- in an act of singular courage and responsibility
-- for Parliament to have overwhelmingly supported the
demand for an inquiry on 4 February 1966. It must be
plain, too, why Obote had to seize power. Only under
the new revolutionary circumstances would he have been
able to terrorize witnesses and preempt a fear-free
inquiry into his misdeeds. Yet as I said before, the
Ocheng motion and Parliament's support of it -- though
an important, immediate cause of the revolution -- was
not its fundamental source. They only compelled Obote
to use force earlier than he had in any event planned
to do. A revolution was going to happen quite probably
in any event as Obote refused to hold a general election the following year. His opposition in the DP,
the KY, and the UPC was so powerful and he, so committed to the monopolization of power at all costs that
conflict was inevitable.

X THE UNRESTRAINED EXECUTIVE
AND ITS EFFECT ON NATIONAL UNITY

The Republican Constitution of September 1967,
amending the Revolutionary Constitution of April 1966,
was Obote's dream of what was needed to unify a multiethnic society. The attempts to centralize authority,
which I indicated to have been one of the fundamental
causes of the 1966 revolution, were incomparable to
the vast powers that at his behest Parliament now
vested in him as president. It is convenient to look
at these powers under the following subheads.

Power Over Security Matters

It is normal in many systems of government that
a president is vested with the command of the armed
forces and it was done in Uganda.[15] He had power over
the operational use of the forces as well as the power
to appoint, promote, or dismiss its members. He had
power over internal security and could give the inspector-general of police "such directions with respect
to the maintaining and securing of public safety and
public order as he considered necessary and the Inspector-General had to comply with those directions."
This, without more, would have been reasonable. But
the law added, "the question whether any, and if so,
what directions have been so given shall not be en-
quired into in any court."[16] Such a provision effectively rendered meaningless the safeguards for the
fundamental human rights of the common man to whom
Obote paid lip service. It meant in law that any
X police officer, claiming to act under directions from
the inspector-general of police, could deprive an ordinary citizen of his basic rights with impunity. All
he needed to show in a court of law if challenged was
that the inspector-general was acting under the directions of the president which could not be inquired
into. The powers were widely abused and, rather than
promoting order, they spread fear and resentment among
the people.
For Obote, at last, it was now possible to enact
what the Independence Constitution and its supporters
could not permit, a preventive detention law called
the Public Order and Security Act. It empowered the
president to detain anyone who "has conducted, is
conducting or is about to conduct himself so as to be
dangerous to peace and good order in Uganda or any
part thereof, or that he has acted, is acting or is
about to act in a manner prejudicial to the defense
or security of Uganda or any part thereof."[17]

Some observations can be made about such sweeping
powers. First, the criminal law of the land covered
all the crimes or attempted crimes that threatened
the defense or security of the state or any part thereof. It was inherited from an experienced colonial
power that had to anticipate and contain possible subversion from nationalist agitation for independence.
A tradition, consequently, had taken hold in the living
memory of all nationalists -- and they insisted upon
it -- that every citizen could not be jailed without a
fair trial. The current preventive legislation, therefore, negated this tradition and considerably downgraded the position of the judiciary among the people.

It was misleading to say in justification for
assuming absolute powers that the colonial administration had had them. While it is true that the governor
had had authority under certain circumstances to detain an individual, such power was well defined and
above all used with considerable restraint.[18] In any
event, the existence of such power was one of the
counts in the indictment against colonial rule that
Obote and fellow nationalists so often rightly cited
to justify independence. But it is no exaggeration
to say that in a space of five years he detained more
people arbitrarily than had colonial rulers for a
quarter of a century. It seemed, therefore, a profound act of disillusionment to the people that what
the independence government sought was not to succeed
colonialists in order to provide better alternative
policies but simply to continue or worsen old ones as
they took over the top positions in the state. In
opposing the granting of such powers, a leading nationalist had correctly observed that Obote was "adopting
the very arguments which colonialists used to make in
order to deny us of our freedom. . . . We cannot
justify autocracy, we cannot justify the granting of
dangerous powers which destroy the liberty of the
people of Uganda on grounds that Uganda is backward
and that we can't afford a civilized government."[19]

By January 1971, eight of the original sixteen
(or 50 percent) of the members of the independence
Cabinet were under detention without trial in maximum
security prisons.[20] So were many leading members of
Parliament and leaders of the opposition, like the
first prime minister of the country, Ben Kiwanuka, and
his leading lieutenants, such as Paul Semogerere.
Hundreds of simple, common people poured into Luzira
prison every few months, many of advanced age, to be
released after four, six, or twelve months. While one
could understand Obote's fear, however unreasonable,
to detain leading politicians, it was quite untenable

that hundreds of such peasants and farmers -- a clearly
peace-loving people -- would constitute such a threat
to his government to justify detention, backed as it
was by formidable power. There was a standard charge
against all these detainees: attempting to overthrow
the government. In most cases it was so vague as to
be totally absurd. Where there were some particulars,
as in the case of ministers, the allegations were so
serious and in such apparent detail that they should
have warranted a proper trial. The law required all
detainees to appear before a government tribunal, pre-
sided over by a judge of the High Court once every six
months, to examine the evidence against them, their
conditions of detention, and to make recommendations
to the responsible minister. In virtually all reports
the tribunals made on the ministers and other political leaders, they asked the government to put them
on trial since the charges were covered by provisions
of the Penal Code. The judges rightly argued that
this would absolve the government from the stigma of
accusations of holding people without trial who were
presumed to be innocent. Yet, these recommendations
were rejected on Obote's orders since they were merely
advisory. He had to reject these recommendations
because the charges were manufactured by Akena's Protocol (later General Service) and the police, and
they could never stand up under cross-examination in
a proper court trial. All that happened in the tribunal was that a police officer stood up and recited a
list of charges and then sat down. He could never be
challenged by cross-examination. The officer called
no witnesses to substantiate what he charged. Such
was the travesty of the process. It was significant,
too, that no member of the public except advocates was
ever permitted to attend the hearings of the tribunals.
The press was excluded and hearings always took place
behind the high walls and barbed wire of the maximum
security prison. This was simply to keep the public
from discovering the falsity of the charges and the
innocence of the detainees.

Abuse of detention powers without trial is almost
inevitable because is it such a tempting solution to
the practitioners of winner-take-all policies, though
it is ultimately self-defeating. One of its characteristics is that it gets out of hand. For instance,
while it is true that Obote created it to remove top
leaders and their main supporters, it seems probable
that he was not directly responsible for all the
detentions of many common people even though the ultimate blame was his. But such is the force of example.
Once his subordinates and the police who enforced

these laws saw how he had misused it against his opponents, they were often quick to do the same against their own enemies in the name of protecting the state or the president. A vendetta among individuals concerning purely personal matters, quarrels over beer parties, jobs, girl friends, anything that had nothing to do with the security of the state became familiar grounds for depriving ordinary citizens of their liberty without trial.

Another aspect of the power to detain without trial is to render the individual leader indistinguishable from the state. It is proper that government be empowered to deal with subversion or threats to internal security, but it is questionable to equate all aspects of the security of the state with that of the head of government. It is equally untenable to equate the security of tenure of office of the incumbent executive with the security of his person or the security of the state. And yet this is at the heart of most abuse of the powers of detention. A president or prime minister may fear some influential colleagues or opponents may muster more support than his own in the legislature or electorate and, through a perfectly proper political competition that poses no threat whatever to the state, may force him to abandon some measure dear to him or may even force him out of office. This is a threat to his political position but not to his person or to the state. Because he would have no plausible reason to defy or punish his opponents for such an act, he may proceed to link it to the security of the state or to a physical threat against his person. Although it may at times be difficult to distinguish among these three aspects because they are at times coincident, it is nevertheless true that what has often caused oppression and abuse has been the attempt to protect the tenure of office. Then later, the threat to the person became a logical result of the leader's bad policies and repression.

The standard justification for a preventive detention law, therefore, as advanced by Kwame Nkrumah while introducing his law in Ghana, is that only those who have committed or are about to commit crimes have anything to fear. This is misleading and simplistic. It was Tafawa Balewa of Nigeria, in his unsuccessful attempt to introduce such a law, who spoke more truthfully about it: "Nigerians have every right to feel afraid because it is a power which could be misused and I, as the Prime Minister today, can give no guarantee that such power cannot be misused."[21]

The power of detention without trial struck considerable fear among the citizenry, although it had

not yet been invoked since its function was still being
well served by the use of emergency powers. The freedom to which the masses had so strongly aspired on
independence and that had been guaranteed by detailed
provisions in the constitution was now so uncertain
as to be nonexistent. Deliberate effort was made to
create fear among the masses by the threat of an army
let loose and the specter of detention without trial.
As a leading Muganda representative said, "Most Baganda, including myself live in great fear that needs
only to be experienced to be realized. People are
constantly threatened by army vehicles carrying armed
forces who sometimes point their guns to the pedes-
trians and this creates more and more fear."22 With
remarkable candor, a leading member of the government
admitted the government was promoting fear deliberately:
"It is quite true that we are seeking to exploit the
emotion of fear in the minds of our people. But I
think that all of us would agree that fear does induce
very effective response in the minds and actions of
people."23 This proposition is debatable, even though
Hobbes said much the same thing -- the more fear is
played upon the more people become governable. It is
in this very fear and resentment that seeds for an
effort to overthrow such a regime flourish among oppressed people.

The president was empowered at any time by pro-
clamation to declare a state of public emergency in
any part of Uganda, and this could be effective for
thirty days unless further extended by the National
Assembly.24 Such a power was a prudent provision
since it is conceivable that a sudden calamity or
threat, external or internal, or an act of God may
have to be contained by swift executive action. Whatever the rights or wrongs of the battle against Buganda in May 1966, for example, it was prudent to have
declared a state of public emergency over the kingdom
in 1966. The blatant abuse came when the danger was
passed, order was restored, and yet people had still
to continue under a state of emergency from 23 May
1966 until it was lifted by the army government shortly
after the 1971 coup. Every six months the powers had
to be renewed in Parliament despite a persistent public
clamor that they should be lifted. After four years
of public emergency Obote would even say to the nation
in April 1970, "I report that the security of the
state of the Republic of Uganda is sound and contains
no cause for concern."25 Why then did he still maintain the state of emergency? Largely to instill fear,
partly to enable his security forces to be exempt from
prosecution for any excesses committed on the public,

and partly because of his own inherent feeling of insecurity. Whatever the cause, it never endeared concentrated executive power to the people, nor did it
help to unify them.

Sweeping as they were, the presidential powers
may still have been exercisable with caution if the
incumbent president, required by the constitution to
exercise them in some cases with the advice of the
Cabinet or Parliament, could be held accountable if
he acted alone or against such advice. But it was
further provided that where the president was required
by the constitution "to consult or to consider or to
act in accordance with the advice of any person or
authority, the question whether he has done so <u>shall</u>
<u>not</u> be inquired into in any court."26 This effectively
assured one-man rule. The president, with powers to
declare war, to detain individuals at will, to appoint
all important officers of state, to legislate by sta-
tutory instrument, and to enforce all laws in the
country, was now empowered to do this without being
bound by any advice or consultation with any other
authority in the state. It should be remembered the
raison d'etre for the assumption of such powers was
to effectively unite the multiethnic groups in the
country into one people under one parliament. Because
Obote was deeply influenced by the cleavages in Ugandan politics and since he was not Plato's philosopher-
king, rather than unifying the nation this concentra-
tion of his power effectively nullified national unity
and drove individuals and many leaders to seek protection in their ethnic groups instead of the institutions
of the state.

Power Over Legislation

As the Nkrumah constitutional amendment had done,
the president in Uganda was now vested with some legislative powers for the country:

1. When Parliament was not sitting, he could promulgate such ordinances as the circumstances
   appeared to him to require -- when the Cabinet
   advised him exceptional circumstances required
   immediate action.
2. If Parliament was dissolved, he could promulgate such laws as circumstances required for
   the effective government of Uganda during such
   a period. All such legislation would have the
   same force of law as acts of Parliament.27

The legislature was effectively emasculated and

the primacy of an executive that usurped its powers
was assured. Since the president had the power to
dissolve Parliament at any time and it was he who
could summon it to meet, he was consequently legally
empowered to assume all or many of its legislative
functions by either refusing to summon it or by dis-
solving it at any time. Yet it was Parliament that
was more representative of the diverse nationals of
the republic than a single self-imposed executive.
True, these powers had not yet been invoked, but their
very assumption was not purely for psychological reasons; they were intended to be used. In any event,
the perception of these powers by the masses -- who
considered them unprecedented, oppressive, and dangerous -- could not be effectively answered by claiming
they had not yet been invoked, especially as Parliament
had never failed to perform its legislative functions.

Control of Local Government

     The historical significance of local government
to the people was indicated earlier. It was a natural
and logical link that tied the diverse groups of the
country to the center in the process of nation building. But in a space of only six years, the powers and
functions of local governments had been tampered with
by eighteen major legislative amendments in 1963, 1964,
1965, 1966, and 1967, consistently aimed at vesting
their total control in the central government.[28]
Legislative amendments were so often and so ill con-
ceived that at times they were contradictory, bewil-
dering, and contributed more to confusion and instability than order in most districts. The excessive
central control was all the more resented because now
all the district administrations were UPC dominated.
More confidence in the center was natural to expect
but it was minimal or at times nonexistent because of
the intra-UPC schisms.
     In 1967 a new local government act was passed
giving the power to appoint and dismiss all principal
officers of elected local governments to the central
government. This meant, for instance, that a district
council for half a million people, whose councillors
were elected on a universal adult franchise, was denied the basic right to choose or reject its principal
leaders (the chairman, the secretary-general, and his
assistant) who could be and often were imposed from
the center. This meant that the executive and legislative arms of local government would be in frequent
conflict and this crippled their functioning. It was
clear that when there had been relatively less inter-

ference in the choice of their leaders or control of
their day-to-day work, local governments had functioned
relatively more effectively and responsibly under the
Independence Constitution than under the Republican
Constitution of 1967. The principal function of chiefs
now, especially in Buganda, became the promotion of
UPC membership and the selling of party cards, a function that would have been much easier to assume in
1963 when Obote threw away the chance to demand a
peaceful dissolution of the KY. This meant a decline
in effective local administration that had significantly depended on chiefs.

Self-Perpetuation in Office

The Independence Constitution had stipulated a
periodic general election every five years. It was
a prudent measure. Either without the elections or
with a provision that sought to negate the primacy of
the Ugandans in choosing their leaders it would have
been impossible for the diverse groups to accept the
constitution. But Obote had now preempted the first
general election since independence by abrogating the
constitution and had perpetuated himself in office.
The 1967 Republican Constitution now ensured that both
the executive and legislative branches would continue
for another five years without elections.[29]
Although some provisions were put in the constitution to empower Parliament to move a vote of no
confidence in the president by a two-thirds majority,
no one took them seriously after the experience with
the Ocheng motion in February 1966. Moreover, even
assuming Parliament had the courage to censure the
president, a vote of no confidence in the president
meant automatic dissolution of Parliament. Since the
president had preponderant powers in the conduct of
elections where he could ensure their elimination,
most parliamentarians could not be expected to take
the risk. In any case, with his powers to control
whether or not Parliament was to meet, the president
could frustrate any intention to censure him simply
by refusing to summon the National Assembly into
session while he legislated for the state. As was
done at the center, local government councils throughout the country -- under handpicked leaders -- were
perpetuated by law even if they were long due for
elections. The sense of monopolizing power was therefore heightened at all levels in the state and a
corresponding resentment among those kept out of government was inevitable.

Abolition of Kingship

Although Obote overemphasized the abolition of
the monarchy in the four kingdoms as the great purpose
of the Republican Constitution of 1967, it must by
now be clear that it was an almost consequential reform in reality. The kings were each limited to their
own area and, as already stated, the power in their
kingdoms had effectively passed to the representatives
of the people. While president of Uganda, the kabaka
of Buganda's independent authority was only with respect to appointing the domestic staff at the state
house. In all other matters of state he had to do the
bidding of the prime minister and the Cabinet. The
powers that Obote assumed, therefore, were not from
the kings but were taken away directly from the people,
although allegedly he took them to protect the masses
against the monarchs.

The issue of kingship was very emotional among
those ethnic groups who had them. It is quite significant that even in the reputedly most radical regimes
in Africa few have directly moved to abolish them.
For instance, Nkrumah never dared abolish the kingship
in Ashanti or other chieftaincies in Ghana, although
he effectively and rightly divested the incumbents
of political authority. Chieftaincy or kingship has
survived the revolutions in Ghana and Nigeria, despite
the fact that, as in Uganda only certain parts and
not the whole country had them. This was for good
reason, too. The institution, with modification and
reform, is the only truly indigenous form of social
and political organization to have survived the imposition of alien values from the colonial experience.
Moreover, it was not merely a political role that the
ruler fulfilled, since this had been rightly vested
in the people, but by custom he had intimate cultural
connections with his group. The position of the kabaka among the Baganda is a good example. The Baganda
had told the British earlier:

There is not a single period in our history when
the Baganda had no King ruling over them. The
Baganda have a system of clans and by means of
royal marriages among women of various clans,
and since by custom members of the royal family
belong to the clan on their mother's side, a
situation has arisen in passage of time, whereby
most clans have had a ruling monarch or an outstanding prince as a member of their clan. This
custom has had profound effect on Kiganda society.
As a result the King in Buganda bears a personal

relationship to every single Baganda family in
the Kingdom.[30]

Having in effect deposed the kabaka when he fled
to exile in 1966, it would have seemed more prudent
for the government to keep the institution at the
time. But the constant failure to distinguish between
an incumbent and the position he holds led to the
faulty conclusion that because Kabaka Mutesa was unsuited to the position (which is debatable), the institution of kabakaship per se therefore was bad and
should be abolished. Yet, in the Revolutionary Constitution of April 1966 kingship had been left intact.
Lwamafa, then minister of regional administrations,
had promised installation of a new kabaka and government in Buganda. But in the Republican Constitution
of 1967, Section 80, Buganda ceased to exist as a
kingdom, as did Ankole, Bunyoro, and Toro.
As a mode of government on a global scale monarchy is outdated and on the decline. But this does
not necessarily mean it had to be abolished here at
this particular time if the people it served still
wanted it. It is true that to some extent opinion
was somewhat divided in Ankole and Toro as to whether
they should retain kingship on independence due to
interethnic conflicts. But support for it in Buganda
and also Bunyoro was unequivocal. What was the best
way for the central government to abolish the institution? The April 1966 Revolutionary Constitution had
removed all entrenched clauses from the constitution
that required special and higher voting majorities to
effect constitutional changes, such as the abolition
of kingship. It would have been much fairer for the
central government to have asked the local kingdom's
legislature to pass a resolution by simple majority
to decide whether or not to abolish the institution.
It would have reflected the wishes of the majority
in the kingdom concerned and the central government
would have taken less blame.
Indeed, the issue was not even that kingship was
expensive because in some cases, the people would
have gladly supported their ruler. As a Bugandan
parliamentarian, a doctor of medicine, Sembeguya,
argued:

I belong to Empindi clan and the head of our clan
is Mazige. He is paid nothing except a clan respect. The King must be left in the same position, this much will go a long way to satisfy
the wishes of many people. The complete abolition of kingship and constitutional heads is too

much for those it affects. . . . To abolish it
by a stroke of a pen without assessing the wishes
of the people it affects is to interfere with the
individual freedom because the creation of kingship or clanship was a matter of the people and
not the Central government.[31]

The principal argument for removing kingship was
to create "one people" or "one nation." With the exception of a few bureaucrats and politicians at the
top, could it really be said that the exercise had
promoted such unity among the broad masses of the
people and many of their leaders? Hardly. As Abu
Mayanja who had constantly criticized and defied the
Bugandan traditionalist government even before Obote
rightly warned, "If somebody says you can achieve unity
by abolishing kings I can tell him you cannot destroy
tribalism by a stroke of the pen in that manner."[32]
This was echoed by the former secretary-general of the
KY, Masembe Kabali, "The constitution alone will not
unite all tribes in this country. . . . I am convinced
that if the tribes are going to unite, each tribe must
be able to understand what another tribe or somebody
else says; we must recognize the goodness which exists
in all tribes and we must cultivate tolerance."[33]
Tolerance, however, was anathema to the practices of
winner-take-all politics.
    While kings were being removed in the South, the
president who was now posing as the symbol of unity
was being openly exposed and attacked by fellow northern nationalists like Martin Okelo, who said, "Which
tribe is seeking to colonize Uganda? Which tribe is
trying as much as it can to get key positions in Uganda
so that it dominates the country? Which tribe is trying perhaps, to get abroad as many of its members as
possible so that they get the right people who would
come back to colonize and rule us?"[34] He was obviously
refering to Obote's group and not the Baganda.
    This enforced uniformity in the state was based
on a false notion that the individual is inherently
incapable of reconciling his loyalty for his group to
that which he accords the state. And yet it is of the
essence of life for a member of society to bear multi-
ple loyalties without necessarily inherent contradic-
tions. For example, there is loyalty to one's family,
to one's former school, to one's religion, to one's
clan, to one's ethnic group, to a regional or continental grouping of states, to the United Nations, to
the human race, and -- perhaps even at some future
time -- to a galactic community.[35] The demand that
an individual's loyalty to the state exclusively

monopolizes his attention and aspirations is imprac-
ticable and contrary to human nature. Moreover, the
abolition of kings did not abolish their ethnic groups,
which still had many primordial ties, such as to customs, language, and values. On the contrary, the
diverse nationals were only made painfully more aware
of how diverse they were by monolithic centralism,
while they had thought the prospect of genuine unity
feasible on independence.

Powers Denied

What was equally significant about the 1967 Republican Constitution, was the extent to which Obote had
gone to concentrate even more power in his hands than
was finally accorded. In the original constitutional
proposals submitted to Parliament by the Obote government, the president had been empowered to nominate
twenty-seven members, or one-third of the legislature.[36]
This violated all principles of representative government for which Obote had correctly attacked the colonialists. He himself had justified the abrogation of the
1962 constitution and had condemned the powers it had
given to the kings to nominate some chiefs and councillors to sit in their legislatures. Yet he was prepared
to arrogate to himself even greater powers of nomination that bore even wider implications.

Another extraordinary eye opener was his attempt
at the UPC Delegates Conference of 1968 to force delegates to accept a proposal that a candidate for the
presidency of Uganda would be automatically elected
if he was so proposed by the UPC supreme authority.
This was a travesty of democratic government. It meant
in a country of 11 million people a few dozen individuals, hand-picked by Obote himself to constitute a
UPC delegates conference, could effectively and conclusively elect him president of the republic to exercise those awesome powers discussed. It would be
charitable to say that he showed he could accede to
popular pressure as he withdrew the provision when
some courageous delegates vigorously objected. It is
more pertinent to note that the very fact he could
even propose it indicated the extreme limit he was
prepared to go to in order to stay in power as well
as his deep fear of an open national election. But
it was perfectly consistent with his previous history
in frustrating electoral reforms, avoiding by-elections,
and preempting the 1967 election with a revolution he
engineered from the top.

Other Aspects of Over-Centralized Authority

The full operation of the 1967 Republican Constitution marked the climax of the winner-take-all philosophy under Obote's administration. Although a one-
party system was not officially implemented until 1969,
Uganda was for all practical purposes now a one-party
state. The opposition parties, though still existing,
were persistently denied authority to hold public
meetings in the exercise of their supposed basic rights
of association and speech, even though there was never
any prospect for a breach of the peace. The public
service was now being openly coerced to attend UPC
political meetings. The inspector-general of police,
the commander of the army, Idi Amin, and their ranking
officers had to attend the UPC delegates conferences.[37]
Public funds were being used openly to promote the
interests of the party in organizing its conferences
and paying its officials. The witch-hunting of opposition supporters in government departments was more
than ever fashionable.
    Meanwhile, the abuse of security powers to force
the UPC on an unwilling populace continued. A good
example is the attempt by a progovernment Moslem
faction to use armed force to take over the mosques
and other properties of a more dominant Islamic community. The majority of the Moslems in Uganda, about
6 percent of the population at the time, were organized
under the kabaka's powerful uncle, Prince Badru Kakungulu, as the Uganda Muslim Community. In the political
contests of the early 1960s that led to independence,
this group had strongly supported the UPC against the
DP. As the conflict advanced between Buganda and Obote, however, Kakungulu's support for the UPC cooled.
In order to divide his Moslem followers, therefore,
Obote's cousin, Adoko Nekyon, who had become one of
his right-hand men, formed a rival Moslem group called
NAAM (National Association for the Advancement of Moslems). Despite government patronage or threats his
group could not penetrate Kakungulu's formidable support. The mosques of the Uganda Muslim Community
throughout the country had been built entirely by
private, voluntary effort. Because NAAM had built
none it now sought to oust the owners from those in
existence. A fierce struggle ensued.
    In Kajara county of Ankole, a NAAM member of Par-
liament accompanied by a few provocateurs confronted
a body of Ugandan community Moslems who had gone to
their mosque to worship. They demanded that the peop
withdraw from it and that NAAM should take over possession and worship instead. The owners refused. Th

member of Parliament then by prearranged signal moved
to call in the security forces. Within an hour a
truckload of armed troops arrived and, as at Nakulabye
four years earlier, without asking any questions they
simply took aim and opened fire at close range, killing
over a dozen people as the rest fled. The official use
of violence against all sections of society that opposed the UPC was such that none could raise a finger
against the perpetrators of the murders. The crimes
had been executed in the name of the UPC and were consequently exempt from the ordinary process of law.

THE 1971 COUP D'ETAT

Immediate Reasons

        Obote has advanced two principal causes for the
January 1971 coup that deposed him. The first is that
Idi Amin, his right-hand man for a long time past, as
commander of the army had misappropriated a large sum
of money from defense funds. The president had demanded a full explanation by the time he returned from the
Singapore Commonwealth Conference. Rather than face
the charges, Amin decided to seize power to preempt
an inquiry, and so he deposed Obote in his absence on
25 January 1971. The method sounded so familiar, re-
calling the Ocheng motion and the subsequent seizure
of power by Obote himself. The second principal reason Obote has given was that of foreign subversion,
that is the Israelis -- probably in collusion with
some other western powers -- assisted Amin to pull off
the coup. Are these really the main reasons why Obote
was toppled?
        Amin denies he planned the coup. Instead, he
alleges there was a plot by Obote and his kinsmen in
the army to remove or liquidate Amin and his West Nile
group in the armed forces. Consequently, Amin claims
his supporters moved only in self-defense after Obote
supporters had initiated their move.
        In fact, neither Obote nor Amin is telling the
whole truth about this. There is abundant proof that
for two years before the coup, both men had sharply
split the army largely on an ethnic basis. Obote, as
president and chairman of the defense council, and
Amin, as commander of the armed forces, each had a
substantial following being conditioned for defense
or attack against the other. John Agami, a Lugbara
from West Nile and one of Uganda's earliest trained
army officers, has written an informative account on
this division in the army in his privately published

book, The Roots of Political Crisis in Uganda. Agami
affirms what well-informed Ugandans knew, that Obote
had divided the army on an ethnic basis.[38] He mentions
that Obote had a deep fear and mistrust of Acholi,
which I knew to be true, who at that time were dominant
in the army. To swing them to his side at least for a
while, he had to create yet another "external threat
to their interests," this time of the largely Sudanic
peoples of the West Nile district led by Idi Amin in
the army, conveniently and typically forgetting that
these groups had constituted his essential instruments
to destroy a prior common "external" enemy, the so-
called Bantus of the South in Buganda.

There is now some evidence to support Obote's
other charge that foreign intelligence agencies played
a role in his removal. The Washington Post of 24 February 1978 quoted some former CIA officials who admitted that three Western intelligence agencies (of Israel, the U.K., and the United States) plotted his
removal and assisted Amin. The confession of the
Israeli military officer involved in assisting Amin
with the coup is discussed later. Moreover, there is
substantial circumstantial evidence that the Israelis
and the British were on very close terms with Amin
after the coup. Their diplomats were the most visible
in the capital shortly after Obote's fall. Some senior Ugandan officials at the time claimed they were
witness to the Israeli diplomats' boasts that they had
a hand in picking Amin's new government. The first
state visits Amin paid abroad were to Israel and the
United Kingdom. Despite this manifest involvement of
alien powers, however, I shall argue strongly later
that it was essentially catalytic and supportive in
nature. The basic causes of conflict and domestic
upheaval had already been created by Obote's winner-
take-all policies and the reactions they elicited
from the diverse indigenous groups.

We should mention here that when Obote began to
prefer charges against Amin, charging embezzlement of
defense appropriations, whatever their merit in fact,
Amin knew clearly he was being set up for elimination.
It should be remembered that Amin was one of the very
few Ugandans who well understood the devious and Machiavellian nature of Obote's methods. He knew how the
plans to eliminate Shaban Opolot from the army command
had been hatched, he knew closely how the Ugandan army
had been politicized on an ethnic basis and why, and
he had an insider's view of Obote's laborious preparations to destroy Buganda in 1966. He was largely
instrumental in enabling Obote to abrogate the constitution in February 1966. He had witnessed Obote's

duplicity regarding the Ugandan involvement in the
Congolese conflict and had seen him lock up ministers
who had been his close friends and who had put him
in power. Idi Amin, therefore, knowing what to expect,
had moved to preempt Obote's moves in the armed forces
to save himself and his group. But it is important
to answer the question of why the two dear friends,
Obote and Amin, fell out. We shall return to this for
the basic causes of the revolution.

It is remarkable that the connection between the
1971 coup d'etat and the 1966 crisis with its subsequent constitutions and policies seem to be consistently ignored or played down in assessing the basic causes
of Obote's fall. The causes in fact lay in Uganda's
history and in his assuming absolute power to impose
a winner-take-all philosophy on a diverse people who
had a fairly well-developed sense of justice. Without
Amin's alleged malpractices and his attempt to save
himself in a coup and without any foreign instigation,
it is my considered opinion that there would still
have been several attempts to topple or eliminate
Obote by other indigenous groups. Dissident Acholi
and others in the army had already tried twice before
Amin, and an attempt on Obote's life had been made by
the Baganda in December 1969.

Basic Causes

We must go back to the interethnic and intraethnic
alliances that had been formed by Obote and his critics
within the UPC to find some of the real causes of this
coup. He had established a web of alliances in the
army of all the diverse northern groups under an in-
correctly but effectively labeled "Nilotic group."
There had been two principal bonds he used to hold the
alliances together apart from belonging to a common
region for the six decades of colonial rule. The first,
as we said, was the material benefit in salaries and
other perquisites to the forces. But it soon became
clear that this was a dangerous practice that Obote
could not always satisfy. For example, a lieutenant
promoted to captaincy today may feel more than discontented if he is not made a major next year -- and a
colonel six months after that. He may take exception
against the government if another officer is promoted
to a similar or higher rank, either because he feels
the officer does not deserve it or because he thinks
the government is partial. In any case, the defense
budget, however large, has to be limited; the material
aspect of holding the army together necessarily becomes
finite. The second bond used by Obote to cement north-

ern support in the army, the "alien" threat of the so-
called Bantu group, was now gone. The kabaka had been
living poorly in exile in London, where he later died
under circumstances suspected of foul play. Buganda
had ceased to exist in 1967 as had the other kingdoms
and the opposition group within the UPC had been emasculated with the detention of its leaders in 1966.
The diverse elements in the security forces, therefore,
could have been held together only by a wholesome, permanently unifying ideology that did not exist. The
northern coalition began to fall apart both within UPC
hierarchy and in the army.

Minister of Defense Felix Onama became apprehensive about Obote because Obote was moving more toward
his kinsmen, and as he (Onama) was close to Amin, the
two allied for mutual protection. Onama was not a bad
leader, but like so many others he had been hoodwinked
by Obote's cunning. Indeed, as early as 1965, despite
the fact that Obote was using Onama to ethnicize the
military, he had explicitly told me (as we both discussed my conflict with Obote) that Obote's downfall
would come ultimately because of excessive reliance
on his clansmen. This was prophetic as the president,
now feeling a little surer, replaced the counsel of
his long-time colleagues from the diverse groups with
that of his kinsmen who had done virtually nothing to
merit such positions, whose only qualifications were
kinship -- or as it was called, tribalism. Obote now
used his great powers as president to promote a new
elite in the army comprised of graduates of military
academies largely under the leadership of his kinsmen,
men who felt better qualified than old NCOs like Idi
Amin. The belief that Obote had ever had the major
blind support from the predominant Acholi troops is
misleading however much he wanted it. There had always
been a strong, DP-based opposition in Acholi against
the government. There had also been divisions of East
and West Acholi. All these divisions were reflected
in the army in varying degrees. Only a portion of
Acholis, therefore, could have supported him. It was
a grave tactical error when Acholis were to be treated
and punished as Obote supporters en masse after the
revolution of 1971. This, of course, is hardly a justification for thousands of innocent Langi who met
Amin's destruction merely because they were from
Obote's tribe.

Amin and Onama fell back on their West Nile groups
to weave new ethnic alliances, in particular between
the Lugbara (the largest), Kakwa (Amin's), and Madi.
Because some of these groups also lived in the Sudan
and had fought as Anyanya against the Sudanese govern-

ment, like the Kakwa, they were inducted by Amin into
the army by the hundreds -- later by the thousands.
The pro-Obote group and the pro-Onama/Amin group in
the army and the UPC now sought allies very much as
the Obote and Ibingira groups had done before 1966.
In this regard Obote was at a considerable disadvantage, although outwardly he appeared formidable.

All the causes we discussed as leading to the 1966
revolution were still at play and indeed had been
greatly intensified by the authoritarian nature of the
postcoup presidency. The president had no UPC to fall
back on, despite lip service about its strength. Indeed, Kakonge, a former party secretary-general, had
candidly admitted in 1967, "the entire party was thrown
in disarray" and "the party was disrupted completely"
by conflicts already discussed.[39] A formidable part
of it, which had supported the former ministers now in
detention or had evolved independently because of manifest injustices and rampant nepotism, was available in
the UPC to support any leaders or group that was courageous enough to stand up against Obote. The formal
opposition of the KY and the DP had been abolished by
law in 1969 after an attempt on Obote's life, allegedly
by a few Baganda. And yet, the disarray and disillusionment in the UPC had in fact encouraged support for
these opposition groups in private and their grass
roots support was impressive. Though the parties were
banned, their members and their beliefs remained. Just
as they had been willing on certain principles to support the stand of ministers who resisted Obote' excesses before 1966, they were equally willing to give
moral support to any group in the UPC that would stand
up against him now.

The president had removed the kabaka partly to
inherit his applause among the Baganda; instead he had
reaped a solid wall of hostility and consuming hatred.
Even though the Baganda were not a factor in the army,
the strategic nature of their region at the heart of
the country's life constituted a substantial asset for
any group in the UPC that might seek to topple Obote.
Very shrewdly, some Baganda elders had reached out to
seek allies within the UPC and the army to outflank
Obote. It was in these circumstances, that an uncle
of the deposed kabaka, Prince Badru Kakungulu, and
his leading Moslem supporters purposely and persistently cultivated the friendship of and later alliance with
Idi Amin through their mutual Islamic faith. By the
time Obote detained Kakungulu a year or so before the
revolution, the Amin/Buganda alliance was assured and
Obote's political fate was in real jeopardy. Moreover,
a vast majority of those troops and officers within the

army from the other regions, having labored under
grievances imposed by Obote's winner-take-all policies,
were now ready to support Amin against Obote. Denied
a strong and united UPC support, confronted with formidable opposition from the KY and the DP (though technically abolished by law), and with his linchpin of
the armed forces as divided as the party, Obote was
destined for deposition. It was his policy never to
surrender power; he once had told me that the "house
would have to crumble over his head." Thus he had to
prepare for a desperate last attempt through his faction in the army attempting to seize power while he
was conveniently abroad, in a typical misdirection, to
protect himself in case the effort failed, as it did.
It is said that it takes one thief to catch another.
This time, as we said, he would not be successful because Amin knew his methods too well and was the best
qualified to preempt them.

The Absence of Elections

However unpopular a regime might be, once there
is a prospect to challenge or remove it in a genuine
general election, its opponents are less likely to
resort to the extreme measure of attempting to overthrow it by unconstitutional means largely because of
the serious risks involved. They are more likely to
organize their supporters and await an opportunity
to change the government by the ballot box. If, however, there is objectively no hope of holding an election, or if it would be so rigged as to negate the
popular will of the electorate were it held, there
remains only one method of changing the regime, namely,
its unconstitutional overthrow, however great the risk
and no matter how long it takes. Such was the case
with Obote. Before he went to Singapore, he had announced a date for a general election, April 1971.
Before he left, he had appointed an electoral commission and a new system of elections (which we shall
consider presently) had been officially declared. But
was he really going to hold a general election by April
1971? Or was this going to be another unfulfilled intention, as was the general election he had claimed
he was to hold in 1967 but preempted with his revolution?

There is persuasive evidence that all the talk
about a general election in April 1971 was probably a
smoke screen that would have been superseded, had the
plan to remove Amin and associated political opponents
succeeded when Obote was in Singapore. We have already
discussed Obote's rejections of electoral reforms and

his confidences to close colleagues denigrating the
concept of general elections. We mentioned his unsuccessful attempt at the UPC convention to have the
president elected by the party delegates conference,
which showed extreme insecurity about the prospect
of facing the masses in a general election. Despite
having seized all power, Obote was acutely aware from
intelligence reports of how powerful and widely supported in the country were the groups opposed to him.
It is doubtful that he would have held a general election with this sort of background simply because he
had said so. But there was more.

As part of the "new political culture" he introduced a novel electoral system, called "three-plus-one,"
under which supposedly the April general election was
to be conducted. In the old system, a candidate stood
for election only in one of several constituencies.
Now, every candidate was to be elected by four constituencies. Uganda was divided into four regions. A
candidate would stand in one constituency in each of
them and needed an overall majority to be elected.
He might get overwhelming support from his home area,
called the basic constituency, but he was sure to be
defeated nevertheless if two or more constituencies
in the other three regions gave him minority votes as
compared with his rivals there. The system was both
complex and extremely unfair.[40] Obote extolled its
virtue as a blueprint to eliminate ethnic politics,
since every candidate would have to think nationally
and canvass support from the whole population. This
sounded ingenious and attractive; some observers termed
it original and imaginative. The truth is, however,
that its attractiveness was merely academic and lay in
its untested promise without being rejected by empirical failure, since the elections were never held due
to Obote's overthrow.

How could such a system be fair? More than 90
percent of the population who were to be voters are
scattered in rural areas, covering considerable distances. Experience in the 1961 and 1962 elections
showed that the constituencies as they were then, even
when a candidate had to contest only in one, imposed
a hardship on most candidates because of long distances
involved to reach the voters. Most candidates were not
well-to-do. It was therefore an unbearable burden to
require a candidate to multiply the problem fourfold
by having to stand for election in each of the four
regions. Since most candidates had few resources for
the campaign, it seemed this was a most effective way
of ensuring that only those candidates supported by
Obote would be elected. As president, having merged

the party and the government, he had all the resources of the state at his command to promote or discourage any candidate. The true motive, then, was not in fact nation building, but a device to prevent opposition groups within the UPC from staging successful elections. Indeed, sometime in 1965 a variation of this system had been briefly mooted by Obote -- an electoral system under which the candidate did not stand in his home area among his ethnic group. The real idea as expressed privately at that time was to save some of his supporters in Parliament who, it was known, could not be returned in their home areas. Now it was revised and clothed with the catchword of nation building. And yet even such a system was not foolproof to block anti-Obote groups in the UPC. Because of the opposition in the Cabinet, men like Onama and some of his colleagues would still have been elected. Systems of new alliances between candidates in different regions for mutual support would most likely have sprung up to enable even some poor candidates to be elected. Obote could not be too sure.

The system was equally unfair to the voters. One of the bases of effective parliamentary representation is that there must be effective communication between the electorate and the representative. This is best attained when both communicate in a common language. That was one of the main reasons why candidates stood for election in their home areas. But now it was very likely that two or three constituencies were to have candidates who would probably speak different languages and so require the use of interpreters, as there are at least five totally different languages in the state. This would impose the burden of translation. Of course the use of interpreters in different parts of the country was a practice of daily occurrence for all party leaders who traversed the country to address different groups. But this was always a fleeting exercise and caused no problems as local constituents had their local representative who often acted as interpreter for UPC visiting leaders. Under the "three-plus-one" system, however, such a local representative, intimately conversant with local problems and needs, could be defeated because of a poor performance in two or three constituencies from regions he least understood and that least understood him, even if he was overwhelmingly supported in his basic constituency. In order to work well, the new system should have been preceded by at least five to ten years of vigorous government action to promote a common language, like Swahili, through which the broad masses of the people would have been able to communicate with all or a majority of candidates.

It was in the mechanics of implementing the three-plus-one system, however, that we find real evidence that general elections could not have been held by April 1971 as already promised by government. Experience in the general elections of 1961 and 1962 showed that it required at least four to five months to prepare for a general election. It took two months to carry out the registration of voters; another month would be required to correct registers, then at least an additional month was needed for candidates to campaign. The constituencies were due for revision from their original demarcation more than ten years earlier because of the consequent increases in population. An electoral commission had been appointed, but it could not have accomplished its task of revising the constituencies in under three months regardless of how fast it worked. From the first day of registration to voting in revised constituencies, it would have therefore taken a minimum of eight but probably nine months. At the time Obote left for Singapore in January none of the aforementioned steps had been started. Even without the coup d'etat, he would have returned shortly after 20 January. Assuming that his first act was to put the electoral machinery in motion, although there is no evidence to support this, a general election would not have been feasible before early October 1971. But even assuming that there would have been no revision of constituencies (which would have been a travesty after more than a decade), it would still have required four to five months, which would have meant holding the general election in June 1971.

June was scheduled for the Organization of African Unity summit meeting in Kampala. In fact the actual preparations in the country at the time Obote left for Singapore were not for a general election but for this OAU summit. A multimillion dollar luxury hotel was already being built, along with a conference center for that purpose. Preparations for such a conference require time, skilled manpower, and money that the government could ill afford. It was improbable that on his return Obote would have launched an expensive election process to take place contemporaneously with the summit preparations. It seems reasonable to deduce from all these considerations, therefore, that it was not possible to hold a general election by April 1971 as Obote had promised. His critics and opponents had no illusions about this -- at least those who knew his methods well. Denied a reasonable prospect of changing the government by use of the ballot box, Obote's opponents had only one alternative left, however hazardous -- a coup d'etat against him.

8
Ghana: The Centralization of Power

The winner-take-all practices in Ghana were characterized by a rapid overcentralization of executive
political power, the elimination of opposition parties,
and the emasculation of the judiciary and legislature,
which were accompanied by a repressive police system
in which thousands of citizens were detained without
trial. It is convenient to outline these policies
below.

ELIMINATING THE REGIONAL ASSEMBLIES

The regional assemblies, which had been provided
for in the Independence Constitution as a compromise
solution to meet the aspirations of those who had demanded federalism, were to be set up after independence.
As early as 1955, Kwame Nkrumah had assured the country
that his government was in favor of "a reasonable degree of devolution of power to regions." But within
a year after independence he completely reversed himself and asserted that "the Opposition committed rape
on mother Ghana by forcing these regional assemblies
upon the country."[1] There was no longer tolerance for
even this minimal sharing of power. As he explained,
the constitution had been accepted embodying many "undesirable" features simply because to have resisted
them would have given British authorities an excuse
to delay independence. Now that Ghana was free, the
regional assemblies were to be constitutionally eliminated. The assemblies were established. Because the
opposition parties tactlessly had boycotted their elections, CPP candidates were overwhelmingly elected to
all of them. Their first business after elections was
to pass a resolution in each assembly, carried by a
two-thirds majority as required by the constitution,
abolishing themselves. Was this warranted? If the

assemblies had been empowered to wield considerable autonomy, or if having been in existence for some time they had demonstrated centrifugal, divisive tendencies prejudicial to the safety and unity of the new state, this measure abolishing them might have been justified. But as it was, they neither had extensive constitutional powers since Ghana was a unitary state nor had they proved prejudicial to good government since they had hardly transacted any business. Not only had they just been created but they were all controlled by the CPP governing party, which could be expected to follow the central government's line while still giving local communities a feeling of being involved in nation building and the administration of their affairs. No wonder the national debate for their abolition caused considerable heat and emotion. Dr. I. B. Asafu-Adjaye of the opposition could remark, "The Prime Minister says a rape was committed on mother Ghana [by insisting on the creation of regional assemblies] for the first time when the Prime Minister spoke extempore, he exposed himself, and he has rightly been called a monster by the honorable member for Seky'ere West [Amponsah] ."[2]

Closely connected with the abolition of these assemblies was the emasculation of the chiefs' political influence in local and regional government. On the whole there is little doubt that where traditional rulers are hereditary and not popularly elected, they should be removed from the actual exercise of political power in order to make them acceptable to their people as a whole, it being immaterial whether they supported the government or the opposition parties. None of the national and regional parties, however, was prepared to insulate the chiefs from active politics largely because the institution of chieftaincy was deeply embedded in the people's traditions and still popular. Consequently it could be used by political parties to increase their popular support. As a result, partly to enhance their personal interests, the chiefs took sides, some supporting the opposition (the NLM and the NPP) and others the CPP. But the CPP was not prepared to tolerate any chief supporting another party and steps were taken to eliminate those who were not compliant. Early in 1958, a number of Ashanti chiefs who were pro-NLM, such as Duyan Nkwanta, were downgraded from the position of paramount chief. Others, like Becham who supported CPP, were upgraded. Pro-NLM chiefs were often dethroned, their only offense being to feel sympathy for the opposition, to be replaced by CPP proteges. Legislation was passed to divide Ashanti into two regions, Ashanti and Brong/Kyempim, the purpose of which was to weaken the power of the NLM and the

Asantehene. The financial resources of the Asantehene, which were derived largely from land, were by another legislative amendment (The Ashanti Lands Act of 1958) now taken over by the central government to ensure that the opposition could no longer materially benefit by them and that the Asantehene was politically demobilized.

The Independence Constitution had provided for the establishment of a House of Chiefs for each region in 1958; however, they were denied any meaningful role in governing the nation. As the traditional rulers were discredited and eased out of power, Nkrumah found it irresistible to assume their regalia and titles, such as Osagyefo, the Ashanti title for their king. Having abolished regional assemblies and eliminated the influence of opposition chiefs, the CPP established a system of regional commissions in October 1957 to bolster its power. Presiding over each region was a CPP party member as regional commissioner, a representative of the central government "personally and directly responsible to government for the administration of their regions and for seeing this policy is carried out." With this the fusion of CPP and government was effected at local and regional levels, and although the opposition parties still existed, they had been rendered superfluous in the scheme of things at these levels.

CRIPPLING AND ELIMINATING THE OPPOSITION

It was a fundamental goal of Nkrumah and his close supporters to monopolize power at all costs. True, a few years before independence this was not clearly manifest. Thus in 1954, he could concede, "I well know the benefits of a sound and constructive Opposition in the Legislative Assembly."[3] But there was no doubt after independence about his belief in the monopoly of power. The concept of opposition was discredited as divisive, alien, neocolonialist, and detrimental to rapid development. The minister of information could categorically assert in 1958, "We shall never allow the Opposition to unseat us. The CPP shall always sit here as the government."[4] This meant that no measure would be considered too extreme to introduce if by it the CPP could remain in power. Such a concept nullified any prospect of unseating it in a fair election. Given this absence of a fundamental inhibition in the ruler's conscience against taking drastic measures, there was no constitutional provision of any kind that could ultimately protect the opposition. A series of legislation, considered below, was promulgated to eliminate it and establish a one-party system.

Repeal of Entrenched Clauses of the Constitution

As already noted, even though the Independence Constitution had established a unitary state, it had allayed the fears of opposition groups by entrenching the basic institutions of the state. They could not be tampered with unless Parliament and, in certain cases, the regional assemblies voted for such measures by two-thirds majorities of all their members. But now Nkrumah himself introduced a constitutional amendment in November 1958 to abolish these special procedures for amending the constitution.[5] This meant that any provision of the constitution, however sacrosanct, could be amended or repealed by a simple majority of the members of Parliament in session. Since the CPP had more than a majority the way was clear to reframe the basic law of the state. One of the first moves as noted was the abolition of regional assemblies.

The Deportation Act of 22 July 1957

The Deportation Act was enacted empowering the government to deport from the country anyone declared by it "to be a person whose presence in Ghana is not conducive to the public good." A year later, the act was amended to preclude the right of appeal to the law courts. Prima facie, there was nothing wrong with such legislation as every sovereign state must have a right to expel undesirable aliens. It was in the actual operation, however, that the legislation was abused. It emerged clearly that it was aimed at opposition supporters. While it was theoretically applicable to non-Ghanaians only, several of those deported claimed that they were Ghanaian citizens with demonstrable proof.

The Avoidance of Discrimination Act, December 1957

The basis of opposition parties, as we have mentioned, was regional: the NLM in Ashanti, the NPP in the North, and the TC in Togoland.

There was in addition the Ga Standfast Association, a protest movement that came into being in Accra in 1957 to protect the rights of the Ga people that were allegedly being usurped by other communities resident in Accra. Finally, there the Moslem Association Party (MAP), which was supported by most Moslems in Ghana (totaling approximately 6.5 percent

TABLE 8.1 Ghana: Preindependence Election Results, 1956

	Colony		TVT		Ashanti		North		Total		Percent of Total Votes Cast
	Seats	Votes	Seats	Votes	Seats	Votes	Seats	Votes	Seats	Votes	
CPP	44	179,024	8	55,508	8	96,968	11	66,641	71	398,141	57
Non-CPP	0	42,602	5	46,076	13	127,601	15	82,837	33	299,116	43
NLM	0	26,124	—	—	12	119,533	—	—	12	145,657	
MAP	0	1,814	—	—	1	7,565	0	1,732	1	11,111	
NPP	—	—	—	—	—	—	15	72,440	15	72,440	
TC	—	—	2	20,352	—	—	—	—	2	20,352	
FYO	0	1,230	1	5,617	—	—	—	—	1	6,847	
WYA	0	3,898	—	—	—	—	—	—	0	3,898	
Inds.	0	9,536	2	20,107	0	503	0	8,665	2	38,811	
Totals	44	221,626	13	101,584	21	224,569	26	149,478	104	697,257	100

Source: Dennis Austin, Politics in Ghana, 1946–60 (N.Y.: Oxford University Press, 1970), p. 354.

of the population). We have already mentioned that these groups, in the preindependence elections of 1956, polled 43 percent of the votes cast and won 33 of the 104 parliamentary seats (see Table 8.1).

To eliminate these parties from existence, the CPP government enacted the Avoidance of Discrimination Act in December 1957. In effect, this law prohibited the formation of any party based on regional, ethnic, or religious basis. It meant that all these sectional parties were unlawful and had to disband. Was this justified? Generally speaking, regional or ethnic parties in a young state can provide a vehicle for adverse centrifugal forces and their containment or elimination need not be attacked out of hand. It may be an act in the right direction towards rational unification. But if the purpose of their abolition is to deny the existence of any form of meaningful opposition or the expression of an opposing but justified view in order to assert authoritarian rule as was this case, then the true motive for eliminating such parties is untenable. Be that as it may, the regional ethnic parties disbanded to form a single national opposition party, the United Party (UP).

The Preventive Detention Act, July 1958

In 1958, the CPP-dominated Parliament enacted the infamous Preventive Detention Act, which empowered government to detain anyone without trial for up to five years, and as this could be renewed, theoretically an individual could be detained for life. There had been two immediate causes for this law. First, government alleged uncovering an opposition plot to assassinate Nkrumah, whose authenticity remains contested. Second, the CPP government became intolerant of ordinary process of law. In November 1957, S. G. Anton and Kojo Ayeke were arrested and charged with involvement in the Alavanyo riots in the former trust territory. Although they were sentenced to six years, they were acquitted on appeal on a technicality of a misdirection to the jury by the trial judge. A year later, a similar case occurred and the CPP became convinced that rather than risk the acquittal of dangerous men, it was preferable to have powers of detaining them without trial, even if this was to mean, in actual practice, that many innocent individuals might be arbitrarily deprived of their liberty. At a stroke, this power destroyed the rule of law. The individual could no longer be presumed innocent until proved guilty, since guilt could be assumed without the need for proof and punishment could follow. The judiciary was deprived of its fundamental responsibility to determine and protect people's rights not only between themselves, but importantly, between them and the government or the state. No wonder the passage of this law through Parliament was exceedingly acrimonious.

Nkrumah assured the country that law-abiding citizens would not be affected by this legislation; it was the subversives and fifth columnists of foreign powers who should fear it. He seemed obsessed with a feeling that foreign powers were out to get him as he said, "The danger of violence and disturbances is that those organizing them generally look to foreign assistance and in the present condition of the world today, there is always a danger that once any disturbance occurs, outside powers will attempt to intervene."[6] This was a correct assessment of possibilities except that it did not address the more fundamental question: Why in the first place should there be substantially discontented groups in the country seeking a remedy outside the law? To provide measures to deal with consequences of discontent was like treating symptoms instead of the disease itself. The heart of the subversion, as discussed elsewhere, was that government repression bred discontent in the first place. Rather than put emphasis on more repressive measures, the correct approach should have been to permit a meaningful role in the exercise of power to the opposition groups instead of legislating them out of existence. The problem was accentuated by sycophants whose jobs seemed to be carrying to the extreme any repressive measure government proposed. Thus W. C. Aduhene could tell Parliament that the prime minister was "too kind" and that if he were the prime minister, he "would have all the members of the Opposition shot and killed" (uproar); or "when opposition members were taken away they should be given a special diet until they wither away."[7] But the response of the opposition was natural and characteristic, foreshadowing the dilemma that often follows repression, namely resistance and defiance, which spark yet further repression and a vicious cycle is produced.

J. A. Braimah (UP, Gonja East) made the opposition stand clear: "The law of retaliation is fundamental. . . . Demonstrations of power by military march past and the police will not prevent an oppressed people from taking actions calculated to free themselves." The parliamentarian then observed the bitter irony and shame that had followed after colonial rule.

For the 112 years that the people of this country had been under imperialist rule, they had never been threatened with detention without trial. All

persons whose actions were considered to be prejudicial to the security of this country were
tried in open court before they were confined
behind bars. The Prime Minister and some of his
colleagues were amongst many who were given a
fair trial. This bill is going to make slaves
of all of us in the land of our birth.[8]

By the end of Nkrumah's rule it is estimated that over
3,000 people had been through preventive detention.
The victims had included many leading Ghanaian nationalists who had struggled for independence no less than
Nkrumah himself. The most famous perhaps, was Dr. Joseph Danquah, the very person who had originally invited Kwame Nkrumah from his studies abroad to help
organize a nationalist party, the United Gold Coast
Convention (UGCC), of which he (Danquah) was head.
Danquah had continued to oppose the rise of autocratic
power in Parliament and the law courts. In 1964, he
was the defeated opposition candidate against Nkrumah
for the presidency. He was frequently detained and
released until his last detention when, overcome by
sickness, he died miserable in jail. Perhaps nothing
speaks more eloquently of the evils of such repression
than this eulogy to him delivered by another contemporary, leading African Nationalist Nnamdi Azikiwe, then
president of the Federal Republic of Nigeria: "I am
of the considered opinion that if independence means
the substitution of alien rule for an indigenous tyrant, then those who struggled for the independence
of former colonial territories have not only desecrated
the cause of human freedom but they have betrayed their
peoples."[9] Preventive detention had failed through
extensive misuse in attempting to foster the "stability"
and "national consciousness" it was supposed to promote.

EMASCULATING THE JUDICIARY

Even with a Parliament predominantly for the executive incumbent, the rigors of a dictatorship could
have been mitigated by an impartial and fearless judiciary offering the last sanctuary of justice to the
ordinary citizens. But the law courts themselves were
not immune from the politicizing influence of the CPP.
True, there had been some courageous stands by judges,
as already noted, and individuals charged with crimes
against the state could be acquitted because there
was no proof of their guilt. Such independence, however, was destined to bring President Nkrumah and the
judges into conflict. The climax came in 1963. Ten

individuals were indicted for attempting to assassinate him, and their trial was conducted in two phases. The first phase resulted in the conviction of five persons who were duly sentenced to death. In April the court resumed the trial of the remaining five, three of whom were acquitted on 9 December. But Nkrumah could not countenance the acquittal of these men (Tawia Adamafio, Ako Adjei, and Cofie Crabbe) who had been his close supporters in government and the CPP. Acting within his vast powers, he dismissed the chief justice on 11 December to signify his displeasure. On 23 December, Parliament met to enact the law of Criminal Procedure Act (Amendment No. 2) that empowered him on 25 December to declare the judgment of acquittal void. With characteristic sycophancy, the leading Ghanaian Times welcomed the dismissal of the chief justice, because he had "failed in his duty, let his leader down, and betrayed his country" by not telling Nkrumah beforehand what the verdict would be! This example was calculated to intimidate other judges and it did have the effect desired.

In October 1961, another legislation, the Criminal Code Act (an amendment) had been passed to establish a special Criminal Division of the High Court, to try such cases of subversion and from which there was no appeal. It was a long-time associate of Nkrumah and deputy leader of the CPP who, having fallen out with him, exposed the implications of this law in his attack:

> If we are to learn from experience (of the abuse of the Preventive Detention Act), this is a Bill which when passed into law would soon show that the liberty of the subject is extinguished forever. Today, there are many people whose hearts are filled with fear -- fear even to express their convictions. When we pass this Bill and it goes on the Statute Book, the low flickering flames of freedom will be forever extinguished. We may be pulled out of bed to face the firing squad after a summary trial and conviction.[10]

It was to this new court that Adamafio, Cofie Crabbe, and Ako Adjei were now brought for another trial because Nkrumah had failed to have them convicted in the regular courts. The twelve jurors were all CPP members, picked from Nkrumah's Ideological Institute at Winneba. They returned a verdict of guilty and the three accused were sentenced to death. In appreciation, each of the jurors was thereafter appointed to a special office, some becoming district commissioners -- just as Obote in Uganda was to reward those UPC

supporters who gave fabricated testimony against his
detained ministers with influential posts in local
governments, such as secretary-general of a district.

Danquah, having failed to stop the passage of the
Preventive Detention Act in Parliament, waged his campaign against it in the law courts beginning in 1959.
But in August 1961, the Supreme Court put the matter
to rest by upholding the constitutionality of the act.
The judges advanced their own arguments in its support.
They pointed out Ghana was not the first nation in the
world to enact a preventive detention act in peacetime.
The government was justified in invoking special detention powers where the basis of the law is thought to
be undermined, and attempts are made to create a state
of affairs that will result in its disruption and make
it impossible for normal government to operate. On
this most critical test, therefore, the judiciary had
abdicated its responsibility, probably to save itself,
and abandoned the people to repression. Once, the
judges attempted to take a stand against the exercise
of this arbitrary presidential power which Nkrumah had
acquired, allowing him to dismiss them summarily. But
among the judges were Nkrumah's informants who, hoping
for promotion or appointment to the vacant posts of
dismissed fellow judges, passed on to Nkrumah the con-
tents of all their secret deliberations. It was consequently not possible for the judiciary to confront
the executive with unanimity and decisiveness. Thus,
through the pressures of intimidation, persuasion,
bribery, and self-interest, the judiciary's capability
to protect the individual citizen against the autocratic power of the executive ceased to exist.

THE RUBBER-STAMP LEGISLATURE

On independence in 1957 the Ghana Parliament with
its government and opposition parties (seventy-one to
thirty-three) was both vigorous and responsive to the
people. People's complaints, fears, and needs could
still be aired on the floor of the National Assembly
without fear of consequences. But once the CPP idea
caught on that opposition was anathema to good government and steps were taken to eliminate it through
measures discussed earlier, the National Assembly became a willing rubber stamp, sanctioning whatever
measure Nkrumah proposed, without the slightest resistance. As was to happen in Uganda and elsewhere, when
the parliamentary majority of the CPP sat to enact
such measures, seldom did it cross their minds that
those very laws were later to be used against them

after they had eliminated the opposition. The critical
idea that it was in the best interests of all the people, including themselves, to ensure a humane minimum
set of rights for every individual whether in or out
of government was consequently absent. But Gbedemah,
a former Nkrumah protege who knew him well, was to
warn parliament: "Today, we may think that all is well,
it is not my turn, it is my brother's turn [to be detained or punished arbitrarily] , but your turn will
come sooner than later. (Hear, hear.)"[11] Gbedemah
himself fled the country after this statement before
he could be detained and lived in exile until Nkrumah's
fall from power. Several former Nkrumah leading ministers were disgraced, accused of attempting to kill him,
and detained, such as Tawia Adamafio, Cofie Crabbe,
and Ako Adjei. The very "political court" which Adamafio had advocated to be set up to try political opponents without a chance of acquittal in 1961 was later
to try and sentence him to death for allegedly trying
to kill Nkrumah.

By 1960, CPP members of Parliament could no longer
be said to be fairly representative of the electorate.
The last election had been held under colonial rulers
before independence in 1956. The last contested by-
election was at the end of August 1960. After this,
party candidates would be selected and approved by the
CPP central committee and then would be declared elected unopposed without anyone of them having tested his
acceptability to the people through a free and fair
general election. This meant that rather than being
answerable to the electorate, the parliamentarians
owed their positions directly to the president who as
life chairman of the Central Committee, which he appointed, would have been responsible for nominating
them as parliamentary candidates. The National Assembly, as a legislative organ reflecting the will of the
masses, had consequently ceased to exist. In September
1962, by overwhelming majority it supported a resolution to establish Ghana as a one-party state, although
de facto it had already become one. Was it conducive
to good government to emasculate Parliament? Was the
best way to unify Ghana, to ensure its stability and
development, to muzzle the representatives of the
masses? Evidence clearly indicates as we shall later
relate that the contrary was the case.

In addition, the CPP monopolized all other national organizations that touched the daily lives of ordinary people. The farmers were organized under the
United Ghana Farmers Council and unless a farmer was
its member it was almost impossible to get government
assistance for agriculture. All the workers came under

a single Trade Union Congress, which was considered
a wing of the CPP. Women and the youth were similarly
organized as arms of the party. The outward total
control of the entire society by the CPP was accordingly unmistakable.

To enhance this control -- although the effect
was in fact counterproductive -- Nkrumah created for
himself a personality cult. His political views became embodied in what came to be called "Nkrumahism,"
which was described as being "basically socialism
adapted to conditions in Africa and African tradition,"
and seeking "to adapt socialist ideas to the evolution
of an African society which has emerged from colonial-
ist domination."[12] An Ideological College was established to propagate this philosophy and none of the
high officials of government were too important to
attend it. Monuments proliferated in the country to
honor the "Father of the Nation."

THE AUTOCRATIC PRESIDENCY

To the immense executive authority that Nkrumah
had hitherto assumed was to be added even more power
under the Republican Constitution that came into effect
in July 1960. In April of that year a plebiscite was
held in Ghana to decide on the acceptability of the
Republican Constitution and the choice of the first
president under it. The opposition put up Danquah to
oppose Nkrumah. Although the official results seemed
impressive with a 90 percent vote for Nkrumah and the
new Constitution, there was considerable suspicion
that the voting had been heavily rigged. For instance,
take the Ashanti rural constituency of Atwima Nwakiag-
yia. In the 1956 general election the results had
been:

	Votes	Registered Electors	Poll
NLM (Opposition)	8,334		
CPP	1,390		
Total Votes	9,724	13,937	70%

But in the plebiscite, the figures were:

	Votes	Registered Electors	Poll
Danquah (Opposition)	137		
Nkrumah (CPP)	22,676		
Total Votes	22,813	25,461	90%

In all previous elections this area was consistently
and clearly an opposition stronghold. In the local
government election of 1959, the opposition candidate
had obtained a substantial vote. It was therefore
most unlikely that Danquah, even if he were outvoted
here would have polled a mere 137 votes. Such electoral malpractice did not, as we discussed elsewhere,
endear those in power to the people. But be that as
it may, the Republican Constitution that came into
being vested Nkrumah's presidency with awesome powers
and downgraded other institutions of the state, like
the legislature and judiciary, which would have acted
as restraining influences.

Part X of the constitution gave him "special powers" as the first president. He could, whenever he
considered it to be in the national interest to do so,
"give directions by legislative instrument. An instrument made under this Article may alter whether expressly or by implication, any enactment other than
the Constitution." The powers of legislation thus
conferred were to be as those conferred on Parliament.
The president by section 51(2) was now empowered to
exercise the powers of appointment, promotion, transfer, dismissal, and disciplinary control of members
of the entire public services of Ghana, consisting of
the Civil Service, the Judicial Service, the Police
Service, and the Local Government Service. Similarly,
as commander in chief, he was not only vested with
the control of the defense forces, including the right
to order them to engage in operations for national
defense, for the preservation of public order, for
relief in cases of emergency, or for any other purpose,
but likewise he had power to appoint, promote, or dismiss any member of the armed forces.

Nkrumah, therefore, singlehandedly could literally
do or undo anything within the state -- however mistaken, objectionable, or detrimental to his people --
without any institutional restraint. Having unfettered
power to appoint, promote, or dismiss any officer in
the state in a society where government was by far the
greatest employer; having rendered the legislature his
mouthpiece, filled with his nominees; having also directly assumed legislative powers to pass more repressive laws if he needed them, with the judiciary cowed
and compliant; and having the police and security apparatus dictated by CPP supporters, there was built
up a more formidable, awesome, autocratic rule than
independent black Africa had ever seen before. Unfortunately, Nkrumah could not realize nor accept that
the natural consequences of this assumption and misuse
of absolute power, in which the multiethnic society

was denied a meaningful part in government, would be
to try to eliminate his rule.

THE CONSEQUENCES

    The overt opposition had helped keep the CPP uni-
ted. When its existence was eliminated with the establishment of a one-party state, the CPP leaders turned
against each other with the same ferocity they had
used against the UP members. The infighting at the
top was enhanced by the need solely to appear to be
an ardent Nkrumah supporter, it no longer being necessary to cultivate the good will of the electorate.
This meant that competition and intrigue in the top
echelons closest to the president were very intense.
Some of the cofounders of CPP, like Gbedemah, fell out
with Nkrumah. To meet their challenge Nkrumah promoted
junior men who had very little personal support and
whose authority as a result depended on a profuse use
of his name and the promotion of his personality cult.
Disillusioned, some CPP members began consciously to
retreat to their primordial ethnic or regional connections. In 1962, the revised party constitution had to
admit that the CPP leadership "is faced with the danger
of being swamped by tribal, regional and other communal
ideological influences which are penetrating the ranks
of the more backward party membership."13
    Nkrumah's further response to these challenges
from within the CPP was to assume its total control.
To his post as life chairman of the party he now added
that of secretary-general. And yet it was physically
impossible for him to administer the country and the
party efficiently alone without sharing his power meaningfully with subordinates, even if this meant his
retaining ultimate control. But repression by a dic-
tator tends to breed mistrust in him even of close
subordinates, and the winner-take-all practices discourage a sharing or devolution of power. The clandestine unrest that was gripping the country, therefore,
could not be arrested by a single individual with
concentrated authority. Rather than diminishing the
unrest, his powers promoted it.
    Those opposed to his rule could not hope to re-
move him peacefully through a general election or
through resignation. Besides being chairman for life
of the CPP, section 55(s) of the Republican Constitution made him in effect president of Ghana for life.
As in the case of most rulers who decided to remain
in power at all costs, therefore, the only means of
removing him, however risky, devious, or protracted,

was either physical elimination or a military coup
d'etat. Evidence that Ghanaians were thinking in these
terms soon became manifest. For example, there was an
attempt on his life on 1 August 1962 at Kalugungu as
he was returning from a meeting with President Yameogo
of Upper Volta. A hand grenade was thrown at him and
although he escaped serious injury, a schoolboy and a
policeman were killed and over fifty people were injured. It was widely believed that almost all his
ministers and party leaders had been tipped off that
some imminent danger awaited the president on this
trip. To prove this it was pointed out that those who
usually flanked him like Adamafio, Cofie Crabbe, and
Ako Adjei had avoided him and kept at a distance on
the entire trip, including the time of the explosion.
It was this incident that led to the disgrace and the
trial of Adamafio and his colleagues, discussed earlier. This incident was to be followed by several
more attempts to assassinate him, although it is alleged that some of them had been faked by Nkrumah to
provide an excuse for crippling and eliminating the
opposition. But several were real attempts.

On 2 September 1962 an explosion took place in
the middle of a crowd outside Flagstaff House, the
main presidential quarters. A girl of eleven was killed and sixty-three people were injured. The immediate
reaction was to suspect his former close colleague,
Adamafio, and the sycophants demanded his blood. The
CPP party was tearing itself apart. On 2 January 1964
a police constable who was on duty at Flagstaff House
fired five shots at Nkrumah as he was leaving his office for lunch. The shots missed Nkrumah but killed
his security guard. As often happens after such
events, the commissioner of police, E. R. T. Madjitey,
his assistant, and eight other senior officers were
dismissed. Several leading citizens were detained.

However, these threats of desperate people could
not detract Nkrumah from his "mission." He continued
to be preoccupied with continental and international
affairs. The Third World accorded him the respect
and approbation he seemed to deserve as one of its
foremost freedom fighters against colonialism and imperialism. We shall discuss his efforts towards African unity later. But few in the world outside Ghana
paused to consider the plight of Nkrumah's own nationals who were caught up in the tragic, painful paradox
of being denied the very freedoms he championed for
others in distant lands. Yet, sometimes distance truly
lends enchantment. For those who never experienced
his repression, for families who never wept or disintegrated because their breadwinners had been indefin-

itely detained without trial by his presidential fiat,
it seemed impossible that such cruelty could coexist
with such majestic ideals in a single individual. But
to the Ghanaians there could be no deception. The
winner-take-all philosophy of the president and his
CPP left them no choice but to engineer the coup d'etat
that toppled him from power on 24 February 1966.

In what ways had his overcentralization of power
assisted in unifying the diverse ethnic groups? To
what extent was the CPP effective in managing communal
conflict? While it can be said that this party under
Nkrumah's leadership eliminated overt, centrifugal
forces and ensured the apparent unity of Ghana, it is
misleading to conclude that this meant elimination of
ethnic identity or communal, tribal loyalties or even
that it developed systems to manage interethnic competition and conflict. Indeed, it was significant
that towards the end of his regime when he was obsessed
with personal safety, Nkrumah himself named only fellow
Nzimas (his ethnic group) to head both special intelligence units and military intelligence operations. The
president's own Guard Regiment, which was his elite
bodyguard, contained a preponderant number of Nzimas.
Intraparty conflict having weakened party loyalty, the
more fundamental pulls of ethnicity became important
pegs of support and security, not only for the president but for his ministers, too, even though tribalism
officially was condemned and its existence often down-
played.

One can conclude, then, that if ethnic competition
or conflict appeared nonexistent it was primarily because the repressive one-party state eliminated open
political contest through which they would have been
manifested. This meant that the competition and conflict were driven underground to surface as discontent-
ment in different areas that eventually led to the demise of the CPP and Nkrumah's rule.

THE BUSIA ADMINISTRATION

On 1 October 1969, after three and one-half years
in office, the National Liberation Council (NLC, discussed later), which had overthrown Nkrumah, handed
over power to a civilian regime headed by Dr. K. Busia
after a fairly contested election. Busia was in turn
overthrown by another military regime, the current
rulers of Ghana, on 13 January 1972. It is not intended here to discuss in detail the causes of Busia's
fall, but it is relevant to consider the significance
of ethnic identity that surfaced vigorously in the

Ghanaian politics that put him in power, disproving those claims that ethnic politics had been eliminated by the CPP under Nkrumah's centralism.[14]

When the NLC permitted politics, two political parties were formed: the Progress Party (PP), headed by Busia, a long-time opponent of Nkrumah and former leader of the opposition; and the National Alliance of Liberals (NAL), led by K. A. Gbedemah, a one-time deputy to Nkrumah in the CPP until they fell out and he fled the country. Pro-Akan influence among the NLC had tried unsuccessfully to disqualify Busia from standing for elections. The political campaigns that ensued when people were free to express their political beliefs for the first time since the 1956 preindependence elections were decisively influenced by ethnic considerations. Consequently, Busia, an Ashanti of the large Akan group, won 85 percent of the votes in the Akan-dominated Brong region, 77 percent in the Akan-dominated Ashanti region, and 71 percent in the Akan-dominated central region. Thus, the PP won all seats in Ashanti, Brong Ahafo, and central regions, all Akan-speaking people. The only Akan area where the PP lost was in the Western region where it lost two seats. It was Nkrumah's ancestral home and Busia was clearly resented. For the opposition, Gbedemah's NAL received overwhelming support from his Ewe ethnic group where it polled 77 percent of the votes and won all the seats. The final results were 101 seats for the PP and 39 seats for the NAL in the new National Assembly.

While Nkrumah's repressive centralism that had stifled self-expression of the different ethnic groups had contributed to building the pressure that eventually toppled him, Busia's acceptance of overt ethnic politics contributed to his fall. He did not deal with competing ethnic demands fairly but rather sought to exploit them to enhance sectional interests. True, his regime was incomparably more liberal than Nkrumah's. There was no preventive detention law. Although the opposition was unfortunately harassed it was not outlawed. Steps were taken by the Local Administration Act of 1971 to give a more meaningful role to local governments so that different ethnic groups could feel involved in the management of their affairs and the nation. The traditional rulers and chiefs were to be given a more useful role in regional and district governments, although this experiment was cut short by the coup. These were sound reforms.

It was in the handling of ethnic competition and conflict at the center that Busia made great mistakes and created problems. Having heightened ethnic con-

sciousness through the political campaigns, Busia
neglected to include representatives of his principal
rivals, the Ewe, in his cabinet. Responding to pressures of adverse economic conditions, he dismissed
568 civil servants and policemen in February 1971.
Because Busia gave no specific grounds for doing this
and the majority of those dismissed were Ewe, the Ewe
experienced a heightened sense of victimization. However, the Ewe had been the principal plotters of the
coup that toppled Nkrumah. When those dismissed challenged government authority, the Supreme Court declared
their dismissals wrongful. In a defiance of the judiciary that was so reminiscent of Nkrumah, Busia -- who
had been Nkrumah's foremost critic -- simply ignored
the court ruling and insisted that his government would
not reemploy the Ewe. The clash of tribal cleavages
could no longer be masked.

In attacking these dismissals, an Ewe spokesman,
Dr. Godfrey Agama, called Busia a tribalist. A leading
paper, the Daily Graphic, observed that, "Tribalism was
being glaringly brandished through dismissals, transfers, postings, dispensation of development votes,
contracts, licenses, and the like."[15] Responding to
these opposition charges for the government, Victor
Owusu, an Ashanti (Akan) and then foreign minister,
countercharged that the Ewe were themselves notorious
for their tribalism.

It is a fact that when a particular member (of
the Ewe tribe) was put in a responsible position
as manager of the Ghana National Trading Corporation, approximately 80 percent of employees became Ewes overnight. . . . It is also a fact
that when a member of his tribe was made head of
CID (Criminal Investigation Department), 80 percent of the staff of CID became Ewes. I can go
on ad nauseam with these examples.[16]

But this countercharge could not absolve Busia's
government from partiality. The allocation of government funds and development projects rightly increased
Ewe fears of victimization. For instance, while the
rate of government-financed community water projects
nearly doubled in the country as a whole, they declined
in the Ewe region by 30 percent during the first two
years of Busia's government.

There had been serious economic and financial
problems that hampered Busia's rule and contributed
to his fall. The enormous national debt inherited
from Nkrumah (which external creditors were pressing
to be repaid), the uncertainty of cocoa prices, and

the relative decline of sources of foreign investments
to invigorate the economy were among such problems.
Would these alone, without the exacerbation of interethnic rivalry and conflict, have been sufficient to
overthrow his government? Would the ethnic cleavages
in the absence of acute economic problems have done
so? The degree to which each of these forces contributed to Busia's fall may remain a moot point but,
as I argue later, it is my belief that the exacerbation
of interethnic conflict through the policies of winner-
take-all is a much more unsettling experience. It is
this that intensified the unfairness of the economic
difficulties and inequalities in the perceptions of
the different national groups, and Busia's administration suffered because of it.

9
Nigeria: The Effects of Winner-Take-All Policies

Despite the presence of powerful regional parties and the absence of a monolithic one-party state, as in Ghana, the winner-take-all philosophy was applied in postindependence Nigeria with devastating consequences. Nigeria became independent in October 1960, with a coalition government between the predominant, conservative NPC and the more nationalistic NCNC, with Tafawa Balewa of the NPC as federal prime minister and Dr. Namdi Azikiewe of the NCNC as governor-general. Later, after the introduction of the Republican Constitution, Azikiewe became president of the country. The Action Group (AG) of the West formed the opposition in the federal Parliament. The euphoria of independence had hardly subsided when a bitter struggle for power among the national leaders ensued within a short space of two years. Let us look at a few of the struggles that best illustrate the winner-take-all philosophy.

THE ELIMINATION OF ACTION GROUP OPPOSITION AND LEADERSHIP

As we observed earlier, the North, because of its size and population, was assured permanent domination in the federation. Its party, the NPC, had returned more members to the federal House of Representatives than any of the rest. Despite this assurance, which should have generated self-confidence and self-restraint, the NPC/NCNC federal government was still discontented about having a regional government in the West (under the AG) opposed to it. Thus, soon after independence, the federal government began moves to harass and, if possible, destroy it. Chief Awolowo, who had led the AG regional government on independence, moved to center as leader of the opposition and left

the western region under the charge of his second-in-
command, Chief Festus Akintola. Intraparty differences
between leaders are not unusual, and they broke out
between the AG leadership. On the one hand, Awolowo
espoused a socialist ideology and very much wished one
day to form a national government under the AG, while
Akintola, on the other hand, represented the entrepre-
neurial interests in the West. He favored making a
deal with the NPC that would guarantee that the AG was
assured permanent control of the western region in
return for not aspiring to unseat the NPC in the federal Parliament and ceasing support for minority parties in the North and East. Akintola's view appealed
to the federal coalition government as it assured it
of a monopoly of power, and both groups forged an opportunistic alliance to undermine and eventually eliminate Awolowo's leadership. In justifiable indignation at this interference with the AG's internal
matters, Awolowo launched a peaceful, political battle
against Akintola in 1962. In February 1962 in Jos,
northern Nigeria, Awolowo denounced Akintola at an AG
party congress, after which Akintola openly fraternized
with the Sardaunan of Sokoto, who was the real head
of NPC. On 19 May, the AG executive committee called
on Akintola asking him to resign but he refused. Awolowo then asked the regional governor of the West to
convene the western House of Assembly to debate a vote
of no confidence in Akintola. The governor refused,
whereupon Akintola appealed to the federal prime minister to revoke the governor's appointment. In a purported exercise of his powers, the governor in turn
wrote to Akintola revoking his appointment as regional
premier, appointing in his place Alhaji D. S. Adagben-
ro, an Awolowo supporter.[1]

On 25 May, the West's Regional House of Assembly
was convened to approve the appointment of the new
premier. Deliberately, most probably because they
expected to lose, parliamentary supporters of Akintola
violently disrupted the proceedings. Shortly after
the session began, a supporter of Akintola jumped on
his desk, lifted a chair, and struck someone on the
head. Another took the mace and missing the speaker,
broke it in two as he hit a table. One of the ministers was injured badly, having been stabbed with a
knife. In face of these provocations, the anti-Akin-
tola faction with a majority of sixty-six to forty on
the whole showed considerable restraint. Police had
to enter the chamber and restore order. A second
attempt was made to convene the members but it also
ended in an uproar. The police dispersed members with
tear gas and locked up the chamber on instructions from

the federal prime minister. Hitherto, despite the
unbecoming physical disruption of parliamentary proceedings, the process of attempting to change leadership in the West was essentially a normal democratic
political process. It had caused no disorder in the
region and the courts could have resolved whatever
constitutional challenges were brought by Akintola
against his dismissal by the governor.

It was when the federal coalition of NPC/NCNC
used emergency powers to save their friend, Akintola,
control the West, and eliminate Awolowo from the political scene that the beginnings of upheaval in
postindependence Nigeria began. There were no other
legal powers with which to attain this end. There
was no preventive detention act, such as Nkrumah had,
under which Akintola's enemies might have been removed.
There was no executive power at the center to remove
a regional government under normal conditions. The
only alternative therefore was to convene Parliament
and declare a state of emergency, which was done on
29 May 1962.

Under the vast powers thus assumed, the federal
prime minister dissolved the western regional government, and appointed an administrator to manage the
region. Akintola left the AG, was released from the
restriction under which he had been placed, and formed
a new political party, the United Peoples Party (UPP).
With material assistance and government patronage
from the NPC/NCNC coalition, he was restored as regional premier when the emergency elapsed at the end of
the year. Awolowo, who had been detained since the
declaration of a state of emergency, was now charged,
tried, and convicted for treason and was sentenced
to ten years in jail, as were some of his leading
lieutenants, like Chief Anthony Enahoro.

Was it really justifiable to declare a state of
emergency, assume its awesome powers, impose Akintola
on the western region, and dismantle the AG? Emergency
powers, as was pointed out earlier in Uganda's case,
are an essential feature of every sound constitution.
There are cases when they may be truly needed by objective judgment. But they were invoked in this case
when there was no justifiable cause but solely to destroy a political opponent and to ensure the federal
government's permanent domination. It was a case of
overkill as its domination had already been ensured
by an unbalanced federation. Whatever little stability
that had been obtained on independence was due partly
to the predominant ethnic groups having been assured
of substantial regional power. Each region could
choose its own leaders and pursue regional development

without undue central interference. But emergency
powers effectively nullified entrenched clauses in
the constitution, eliminating those aspects of federalism that guaranteed regional autonomy, and empowered
the central government to take over a regional administration, including the choice of its leaders. The
primordial fears of the West therefore could not but
revive with great intensity over the reality of permanent northern domination, not only at the center,
but now also in their own western regional government.

Moreover, bitterness among those adversely affected in the West was heightened because of the discriminatory nature with which the federal government used
strong-arm measures. Shortly after independence there
had been rioting of a most serious nature in the Tiv
division of the northern region where the minority Tiv
were demanding their own separate region. Many lives
were lost and property was destroyed. There was extensive arson and a general breakdown of order. But
Tafawa Balewa, who was already the federal prime minister, never called on Parliament to declare a state of
emergency. Again, at Okrika in the eastern region,
there had been serious riots in which many lives were
lost and property was destroyed. Likewise, no emergency was declared. And yet where there had been no
serious threat to security in the West, emergency
powers had been invoked and parliamentary government
was revoked when Balewa appointed an administrator.
The conclusion was inescapable: emergency powers were
never invoked in the North and East, however justifiable it would have been to do so, because the federal
coalition government came from those two regions; and
they were applied in the West to eliminate the opposition. The laws of the land, therefore, which were to
apply to all citizens without distinction, were now
manifestly given discriminatory operation. The result
could only be to discredit the institutions of the
young state and to make those adversely affected think
in terms of extralegal methods as the only alternative
for achieving justice. Indeed, the fears of westerners
were enhanced by rumors among highly placed federal
government ministers that after the midwestern region
was created from the West, the remaining portion in
Awolowo's allegation was "to be regarded by the Federal government as not legally constituting a region under the Constitution."[2] In other words, the West would
cease to exist. When Awolowo asked the federal prime
minister for an explicit statement that the western
region would remain, Tafawa Balewa did not help allay
suspicion, mistrust, and anger by publicly refusing
to give it.

THE STRUGGLE TO CREATE MORE REGIONS

If the British had been responsible for creating and bequeathing an unbalanced federation, what did the independence leaders do to correct it? In the first place, even before independence, it had been because of the persistence of indigenous leaders, especially from the North, that Lugard's structure had been maintained. After independence, the demands by minority ethnic groups for separate regions was intensified. This was partly the result of a natural desire for each ethnic community to have an area under its own exclusive jurisdiction, but in addition this was partly -- and perhaps especially -- the result of the fact that regional governments, functioning as de facto one-party states, monopolized power and its benefits to the detriment of their minorities.

All that the Independence Constitution had done to meet these demands was to provide a complex procedure under which a new region could be created. A new region could only be created if two-thirds of both houses of Parliament, two of the three existing regions, and 60 percent of the registered voters in the proposed region agreed that it should be created. Under Chief Awolowo's leadership, the AG had probably been the most consistent advocate of creating more states based on linguistic and ethnic identity. For this reason the western House of Assembly had passed the necessary resolution in December 1955 initiating the eventual formation of the fourth region, the Midwest, which had been carved out of the western region. Unfortunately, the NPC and the NCNC supported the creation of this new region not because it helped to establish a more logical, acceptable constitutional framework for the federation's diverse peoples, but principally because by reducing the West in size and population, it contributed to the strongly desired goal of weakening or destroying the AG. Consequently, when Awolowo was proposing a federation of nine regions in his endorsement for the creation of the Midwest region, the NPC/NCNC coalition had to reject the proposal.[3]

As a result of a United Nations plebiscite, the Trust Territory of Northern Cameroons decided to join Nigeria in February 1961. In an unambiguous step of a winner-take-all administration, the new territory was added to the already preponderant North, when the most logical thing might have been to make it a nucleus for another separate region to improve the balance of the federation. The result was that the NPC had an additional seven representatives from the Northern Cameroons in the federal House of Representatives and

it now obtained absolute majority in the federal Parliament. Able to govern by itself, the NPC no longer
"courted" the junior partner in the coalition, the
NCNC, and the alliance was destined to disintegrate,
just as it was to happen between the UPC and the KY
in Uganda once the UPC had obtained an absolute majority.

But the demands for the creation of more states
intensified. As we said, among the Tiv in the North
there was considerable disorder, and the army had to
be called in to restore peace. The more restive the
minorities became, the more the majorities in control
responded with repressive measures, both in the regions
and at the center, clearly promoting generalized, un-
stable conditions throughout the federation. We discuss elsewhere the actions of subsequent military
rulers of Nigeria after the 1966 coup d'etat. However,
it should be noted here that one of the causes for the
elimination of General Ironsi was his promulgation of
Decree 34 in May 1966, which abolished the federal
structure and established a Unitary Constitution for
all the 250 ethnic groups. The military like the
civilians before them had misjudged the power of ethnic
identity and the desire of the diverse groups to have
a say in matters peculiar to themselves. While the
minorities had been deprived of this right, the federation could stagger on because the majorities still
controlled their regions. But when the army denied
this right to the majorities by establishing a unitary
structure, the northern majority responded with hitherto unprecedented violence, which led to the elimination
of Ironsi and the installation of General Gowon as the
new federal military ruler. The violence took a terrible toll on human life during a bitter civil war
(1966-1970) before it was realized that the desire for
more states could no longer be denied as an inalienable
right of the diverse peoples and as the best way to
achieve peace and stability in the federation. But by
the time General Gowon restored the federal system and
created twelve regions in place of the previous four,
it was already too late to prevent the imminent civil
war launched by the East's bid to secede, as we recount
elsewhere. There must be a point beyond which demands,
such as for the creation of more regions, become counterproductive and against the national interest, leading to excessive fragmentation. However, such a point
has to be established on empirical evidence for each
particular state. It is significant that the federal
military government of General Murtala Mohammed, which
overthrew General Gowon in July 1975, created a further
seven regions, making the total nineteen as compared

with Lugard's original three. Some hypothetical questions will probably remain unanswered. For example,
even given the federal imbalance on independence,
would the demands for more regions have been so strong
if the federal and regional majorities had consistently
and consciously paid due regard to minority interests
in sharing power and all it involves? Probably the
leaders of the minorities would have still demanded
separate regions to give them their own control, but
it seems debatable that, once assured of fair play
within a particular region, the ordinary citizens
would still have insisted on separate regions.

CONTROL OF THE PUBLIC SERVICE

Associated with though distinguishable from the
demands for more regions was the problematic issue of
hiring public servants in a country where the government, both at the center and in the regions, was by
far the biggest employer. As already observed, the
North had a genuine grievance and handicap as the
region least prepared for independence. The most logical redress for this deficiency should have been a
crash program in education at all levels, as much as
possible comparable with the other regions, to produce
appropriate manpower. The issue that caused great
controversy concerned the best policy to follow.
In unambiguous words and actions, the government
of the northern region preferred employing in their
regional government non-Nigerians from overseas to
Nigerians from the South. The attitude dated from
colonial times. As one leading parliamentarian had
said in 1955, "We do not agree with giving a high post
to a Southerner in the Northern region. We do not
trust them. We prefer a European or a Northerner because the Europeans are always ready to improve the
North."[4] The more northern leaders offered jobs to
aliens when qualified southerners went unemployed, the
greater the resentment grew, especially among the enlightened southerners. Leaders suffered a credibility
gap. Tafawa Balewa made repeated appeals for unity
of all Nigeria, such as the New Year's Eve broadcast
at the end of 1964, "It will be a very good idea if
we all make it our resolution this new year wherever
we may be to think and act in terms of belonging to
one and only one Nigeria." But as was pointed out by
a southerner, while he made this speech, Balewa's own
northern region had, "applied to India through their
Chief Justice Prasad Sinh for lawyers to fill vacancies
in the judicial service of Northern Nigeria, whereas

there are excess lawyers in Eastern Nigeria readily
available."[5]

A leading Nigerian academic and parliamentarian,
Professor Kalu Ezera, expressed the indignation that
was widespread in the South:

> I would rather not be a citizen of a country where
> I am regarded as a second class citizen. We know
> it to be a fact that in some parts of this Federa-
> tion citizens of this country are not regarded as
> citizens but rather as expatriates; Pakistanis,
> Ceylonese, and other nationalities are given pre-
> ferential treatment. I am not saying that the
> Northernization policy, giving preference to Nor-
> therners, is a bad thing as such, but where Nor-
> therners are not available other Nigerians should
> be given preference to expatriates, if we are
> sincere about our advocacy of Nigerian unity.

Such had the tensions become that Professor Ezera
then proposed, "If all these are not acceptable, then
I would suggest that we agree to disagree and break up
the Federation."[6]

CENSUS CONTROVERSY: THE STRUGGLE FOR MORE NUMBERS

One of the incidences that illustrates the effect
of winner-take-all policies was the falsification of
census figures by the regional and federal governments.
Ordinarily a periodic census taken every decade or so
is useful to assist in planning for all aspects of a
country's development, especially in economic and social spheres. A region with more people may claim more
funds and amenities from the federal government; this,
therefore, became an incentive for each region to in-
flate its census figures. But by far the most critical
reason for inflating population figures (or deflating
an opponent's) was that they determined the number of
parliamentary seats each region was to have in the
federal Parliament which in turn determined who controlled the federal government. The more people a
region could claim the more parliamentary seats it
could demand and thus the greater was the prospect of
at least sharing power at the center. Because all the
parties practiced winner-take-all policies, either at
the center or in regional governments, the idea of
being in a minority and on the losing side -- because
it meant losing everything -- held such depressing
prospects that it had to be avoided even if it meant
falsifying one's regional population to do so. It may

be more correct to say that all the major parties
shared blame for this.

All attempts at an impartial national census have
failed. The first postindependence count in 1962
caused a storm. The federal minister of economic development, Alhaji Wazir Ibrahim, had announced that
the population count for the North, East, and West was
21, 12, and 10 million, respectively. But then he
suddenly retracted those figures, saying that the government could not release any figures, as he charged:

> Figures recorded throughout the greater part of
> Eastern Nigeria during the present census are
> false and have been inflated. . . . The figures
> for the five divisions -- Awka, Brass, Degema,
> Eket, and Opobo -- which have recorded increases
> of over one hundred and twenty percent can cer-
> tainly be rejected out of hand.[7]

The count in the West was said to have been organiza-
tionally poor. It was only in his region, the North,
that the census allegedly had been well done. And
yet, ominously, the northern regional government, after
the figures of other regions were known, nullified its
original count and began a second one with the obvious
aim of adding more numbers that did not exist. The
1962 census figures were, therefore, rejected by the
NPC federal government causing considerable anger in
the South.

In February 1964, the federal government published figures for the second census, held in 1963, with
two profound political consequences. First, on the
basis of its population, the North alone could now
form a national government without reliance on any
southern party. Second, the East was no longer larger
than the Midwest and West and consequently felt vulnerable. There was bitter and widespread protest in the
whole South against these results and the abolition of
the NPC/NCNC alliance became unavoidable. The political implications of this census were not only that the
North's ascendancy was confirmed in the federation,
but also that no new states could be created without
its cooperation, as a two-thirds majority would be
required in Parliament, which it controlled. The northern insistence of its territorial indivisibility, therefore, could not but enhance frustrations and bitterness
of those who wanted their own regions. The federation
was in danger as some southerners now began to think
of secession as the best alternative.

LAST ATTEMPTS AT RECOVERY: THE DECEMBER 1964 ELECTIONS

To the southerners there was just one last chance
of containing the winner-take-all preponderance of the
North and that was in the first postindependence general election of 30 December 1964. Although the North
had an absolute majority in Parliament, this could
theoretically be eliminated or reduced by the South's
championing minority parties in this region. To counter this, the North also sought to reduce southern
power even more by alliances with their minority opponents. For this general election, therefore, two
alliances were forged. First there was the Nigerian
National Alliance (NNA), consisting predominantly of
the Northern Peoples Congress (NPC), the Nigerian
National Democratic Party, the Midwest Democratic
Front, the Niger Delta Congress, and the Dynamic Party.
Second was the United Progressive Grand Alliance (UPGA),
consisting of two erstwhile rivals, the principal
southern parties of the NCNC of the East and the AG
of the West, together with the United Middle Belt Congress, which under Tarka was seeking to carve out their
own region from the North.

The election manifesto of the UPGA and its other
declarations promised nationals a list of corrections
within departments where the NPC winner-take-all policies had been most acutely felt:

1. The Senate, where representation was by region
   and not by population, was to be given concurrent powers with the House of Representatives
   when the North was assured of a preponderant
   majority. This would enable minority regions
   in the South to influence legislative measures.
2. The president, hitherto a purely ceremonial
   position, was to be given executive powers
   over the electoral commission that dealt with
   the conduct of elections, the public service
   commission, census, and government audit. He
   would set up a permanent vital statistics
   commission to collect figures of births and
   deaths over a period of up to twenty years to
   ascertain the correct population figures and
   avoid census controversies.
3. A permanent judicial commission was to deal
   with tribalism, discriminatory practices, and
   violations of fundamental human rights.
4. All police forces were to be brought under the
   inspector-general of police. The abuse of
   police powers to victimize political opponents
   had been a practice of all regional governments.

Indeed, the AG itself had set up a new post of superintendent-general of native authority police throughout western Nigeria, which in effect sought to undercut the police authority of the federal government. This step had been vigorously attacked in 1961. But perhaps it was in the North where police powers were most used unashamedly in concert with the judiciary to intimidate political opponents. It was therefore felt that for the good of all, regional power over police matters should be centralized.

5. Discriminatory types of courts were to be eliminated and a uniform system of justice was to be established. One of the great problems heretofore had been the existence of certain Islamic courts of the North, called Alkali, in which non-Moslems invariably received poor justice. They became a real instrument of intimidation for the NPC to use against political opponents, and their public perception was totally negative among southerners.

6. National political parties were to be provided for and tribal and regional parties were to be discouraged. Although this was aimed at the NPC, all the southern parties were also de facto regional and one could say tribal as well, despite appeals of a national character. One had only to look at the preponderant membership of the leadership and rank and file of each to confirm this.

7. In order to court northern separatists, more regions in the federation were to be created.[8]

Such a reformist political platform, if implemented honestly, would go a long way to heal the sickness of the republic. But there were two impediments. The first, which eliminated the prospect of the second, was that the dominating NNA rejected these proposals because of its vested interest in the status quo it had helped create. The second obstacle, although it was never put to the test, was the doubt of the extent to which the UPGA alliance would have honestly gone to implement these proposals, had they won. Objective evidence indicates its principal allies, the NCNC and the AG, were also practitioners of winner-take-all politics and policies where they were in control. The question therefore validly remains as to whether they genuinely wanted these reforms to ensure fair play to all, or whether, if they had won the election, they would not also have fulfilled the North's fundamental fears of a southern domination. But it must be admitted the proposals were sound and it was disastrous for the NNA to reject them.

The campaigns were intense. Although the UPGA initially hoped for victory or a close race, by the end of November they were overwhelmed by disillusionment and their leaders now began to think and talk of secession. The reason for this change was largely the ruthless and arbitrary manner with which the NNA victimized UPGA candidates and campaigners in the North. Hired thugs and goons violently attacked them and disrupted their campaigns, and there was no protection in the northern courts or from the police. Forty candidates of the UPC were arbitrarily put in jail, and twenty others were denied registration there. In contrast, a total of eighty NNAs were returned unopposed. An eastern Nigerian parliamentarian expressed the prevailing frustration and anger in the South:

> It is very disturbing to the people of this country...to hear that lawyers [who were defending UPGA supporters] are being arrested and dragged to Alkali courts, refused bail, handcuffed and dragged along naked in the streets by the Native Authority Police of Northern Nigeria. These lawyers were made to be tried by the Alkalis who have no legal knowledge whatsoever.[9]

A region that was so overwhelmingly strong should have found it easy to be magnanimous and fair. Instead, it used all its preponderance to crush the rest through patently unfair means. The UPGA decided to withdraw from the elections and boycotted them.

Dr. Michael Okpara, premier of eastern Nigeria, again threatened secession. Dr. Azikiwe, the ceremonial head of state from the East, in the aftermath of an election contested by one group, tried to persuade the heads of the army, navy, and police to give him allegiance as president to enable him to assume executive powers. He refused to call on the victorious Balewa to form the government. As with Mutesa when he was Uganda's president, Azikiwe had been confronted with the difficulties of a ceremonial incumbent in attempting to arrest a national crisis caused by the misdeeds of a ruling party. But the security forces refused on the ground that they had been legally advised that the president had no such powers. Later, after tottering on the brink of collapse, the federation was given a respite by a compromise between Azikiwe and Balewa, who had again assumed the federal premiership. More NCNC ministers were appointed in

Balewa's new government. But as the fundamental ills
of the federation still remained, the southerners
could not rest assured until they were redressed.

REGIONAL ELECTIONS IN WESTERN NIGERIA, OCTOBER 1965

There was just a slim hope among southerners
that, even though they had lost at the center in the
general election, if they could control the western
region by winning the October 1965 elections to the
western Regional House of Assembly, they might be
able to have enough members in the Senate to check
the preponderance of the North in the federal House
of Representatives. As already discussed, the predominant party of the West, the AG, had been pushed
out of the regional government through emergency powers and a minority under the patronage of the NPC had
been installed, led by Chief Akintola. The campaign,
with all the accumulated frustrations and grievances
the AG had suffered from 1962 through the fraudulent
1964 general election, was waged with unprecedented
intensity on all sides. People generally will know
who the winners are by voting time, especially if the
winning margin is decisive. It can, for instance, be
readily observed by noting the relative numbers of
crowds addressed by competing parties in all the constituencies and their responses to the candidates.
There was not a shadow of a doubt that the candidates
supported by the central coalition of the UPGA would
win. The conduct of Akintola and the unparalleled
extent to which he misused power to win these elections
remain an outstanding example of winner-take-all policies in practice. Under no circumstances was he prepared to concede defeat by the ballot box and he used
executive power to commit every conceivable trickery
and deception to remain in office. Let us look at
some of the malpractices:

1. Several NNDP candidates (Akintola's party)
   were returned unopposed because electoral officers, having accepted their nominations,
   absented themselves to prevent some of the
   UPGA candidates' being nominated in time.
2. Some electoral officers simply refused to accept nomination papers of UPGA candidates.
3. Substantial ballot papers were unlawfully distributed to Akintola supporters before polling
   day, despite purported security precautions
   to prevent it. This meant an individual could
   enter a polling booth not with the one ballot

he receives there, but with scores of ballot
papers in his pocket.

4. Some potential UPGA candidates were arrested
and falsely imprisoned to prevent their filing
nomination papers, as had happened in the
North in the 1964 general election.

5. Party agents of UPGA candidates were deliberately denied identification labels for use at
polling and counting stations. Consequently,
under the pretense of lack of identity they
were excluded or ejected from these stations
to permit the NNDP supporters to cheat without
eyewitnesses to their misdeeds.

6. By Section 46(1) of the Electoral Regulations,
the results of elections had to be announced
at the counting stations immediately after
counting the votes. This would mean immediate
declaration of the winner. But, as if all the
malpractices before and during voting were not
enough, Akintola gave instructions not to announce electoral results according to this law
but to transmit the results for announcement
to the government first so that further falsification, if necessary, could be made before
announcing the winner.

7. The chairman of the Electoral Commission, Esua,
reported that during this whole electoral process, the western Nigerian local government
police proved to be "nothing but thugs in their
operation," as they harassed and intimidated
UPGA supporters.

8. In heavy Awolowo precincts, polling places
mysteriously ran out of ballots.[10]

The results of such unfettered cheating were as
predictable as they were tragic. Akintola announced
he had won the election and with that unleashed spon-
taneous widespread violence. The UPGA had been pushed
hard against the wall, as all rules of fair play were
violated by the dominant alliance ultimately under
Balewa's NPC. The stage was set for extralegal recourse for redress. An eastern parliamentarian accurately noted the effect of this winner-take-all operation:

In less than five years we have seen that entrenched sections of the constitution are not
operating. It is noteworthy that in spite of all
these things in the West, nobody, no political
party has considered it fit to go to court. In
other words, they have no confidence again in an

independent and impartial judiciary. I think the
road to revolution in this country is the only
way back to free and fair elections. If the people can no longer trust the ballot box, these
people are bound to get out and shoot, because
you can oppress some people some times but you
cannot oppress them all the time.[11]

Many lives and properties were lost in the West
as the majority of the region rejected the unfair electoral victory of Akintola. The East vigorously pleaded
for the Awolowo supporters and Dr. Okpara, their premier, to put the responsibility for what was happening
squarely on Balewa. Meanwhile, leading northern politicians began to say that the NCNC had instigated chaos
in the West. As a result, they felt, the East itself
might come under a state of emergency which, irrespective of whether or not this was true, heightened the
tensions between those involved. Rumors circulated,
for example, that after declaring a state of emergency,
a preventive detention act -- which Nigeria had rejected in 1961 -- would be introduced to round up leading
southerners from the West and East.[12] Considering the
violations that the NNDP had committed, such rumors
became credible, and violence escalated in the West to
the point of a total breakdown of law and order. Yet,
no matter how much Prime Minister Balewa was pressed
to declare a state of emergency in the West to contain
the situation, he refused on the patently preposterous
ground that the situation in the West did not warrant
the federal government's intervention. The injustice
was all the more acute because Balewa had declared a
state of emergency in the same region in 1962 when it
was not warranted, simply to save Akintola and destroy
the AG. Now, when it was manifestly needed, he refused
to invoke it because his protégé had rigged elections
and won amidst violence and disorder. Equality before
the law and all the fine clauses of fundamental rights
in the constitution had been rendered meaningless by
the power of the example of the winners who consistently stood above the law to which they ruthlessly subjected the losers. It was in these circumstances that
the young majors of the Nigerian army launched their
coup d'etat on 26 January 1966. Federal Prime Minister
Tafawa Balewa, his finance minister, and the Sardaunan
of Sokoto, among others of the NPC, were assassinated
(as was Chief Akintola in the West), and the Nigerian
army under General Ironsi took power until he was himself overthrown six months later for reasons discussed
in a later chapter. Civilian leaders had failed.
While there were fundamental and long-term problems in

the federation, some of which dated from colonial times, it is clear that the winner-take-all philosophy held and practiced by the national leaders was decisive in leading the country to chaos. The NPC had been uninhibited in its quest for perpetual and total domination. The NCNC had been exceedingly opportunistic. By joining the NPC to destablize the West, by installing Akintola, and by eliminating Awolowo in 1962, the NCNC had created conditions that made it likely for the instability later to threaten its own region, the East, with catastrophic results. By the time the NCNC/AG alliance was formed in 1964, so many rules of fair political conduct had been broken since independence that honesty seemed incongruous amid rampant deceit and massive misuse of power.

10
Poverty, Subversion, and Instability

I began by arguing that of all causes that have contributed to the instability in postindependence Africa, the imperfections of the colonial legacy and the policies of winner-take-all practiced by the independence leaders among their multiethnic states rank foremost. It is conceded that there are many other causes of the instability, but it is debatable whether these are secondary, catalytic in nature, or whether they are primary. Two of these causes deserve special mention because of the persistence with which they have been advanced as basic causes, partly by academics and partly by fallen leaders.

POVERTY

There is no question that the poverty of these African states exacerbates other conflicts and helps promote instability. The colonial experience developed unbalanced economies that were geared principally to benefit their metropolitan states and only consequentially the African colonies.[1] These state economies depend on subsistence agriculture or on the export of a few minerals, all of whose prices in turn depend on global economic forces over which the African governments have no control. Consequently, they are the constant victims of price fluctuations of the raw materials they produce. These states have conducted a vigorous new diplomatic offensive with the rest of the Third World for a more equitable global economic order. This has been met (and will probably continue to be) with considerable resistance from the developed nations, which have vested interests, and multinational corporations. Whatever positive economic results that accrue from the international system, therefore, are likely to take a long time in coming, possibly several decades.

221

Meanwhile, however, one can reasonably assume that the
African states are likely to continue to be relatively
poor and, except where a state hits a prized commodity
like oil, no dramatic rise in material well-being will
be accomplished in a few decades.

Because of this basic economically adverse condition, it is constantly argued, more often by observers
and academics from the developed world, that disorder
and instability must be expected in these states.[2]
Nothing could be more harmful or misleading. What
level of economic development, what income per capita
is regarded as the point beyond which, according to
such arguments, poverty ceases to be a cause of instability? Although it is not stated specifically,
it is probably assumed to be comparable to the economy
of a developed Western nation. The difference in the
standards of living is indicated in the sample in
Table 10.1. To accept this view, given the great disparity in income and wealth between the Western and
African nations, is to conclude that for many decades
to come it should be accepted or expected as a normal
condition to have pogroms, massive arbitrary detentions,
and general political upheavals in the African states
because of the struggle over the control of scarce
resources by some group or groups within the states.
Africa cannot afford to accept this sentence of chaos
and death. Between now and the time the African states
do reach an acceptable level of wealth, there need not
necessarily be chaos among them, for such upheavals
themselves may perpetuate the condition of poverty by
negating optimum conditions for purposeful, dynamic
development.

It does not follow that in times of scarcity members of society must tear each other to pieces fighting
over limited resources. Scarcity is not new to Africa.
In absolute terms, most Africans are materially richer
now than four decades ago, although they may not be
conscious of it. They are certainly richer than they
were in precolonial history. In those days of long
ago, it was natural to share vital resources peacefully
within most communities during hard times. Among cul-
tivators, when crops failed by drought or another calamity, unaffected groups within the clan or ethnic group
shared food with those who were adversely affected.
Similarly among people who kept livestock, kinsmen
within the group whose animals survived a sickness,
such as rinderpest, took in and assisted those whose
animals were destroyed. Wars or upheavals to control
limited resources within a particular group hit by hard
times were seldom, although they may have occurred frequently between groups. There is in Africa's past,

TABLE 10.1 Some Social and Economic Indicators of the Contrast Between Some Developed Countries and 15 African States

Country	GNP per capita US $	EDUCATION			HEALTH				NUTRITION	
		Public Expenditure per capita US $	School age population in school % (ages 5-19)	Literacy (representing % of adults over 19)	Public Expenditure per capita US $	Infant mortality (under 1 yr per 1,000)	Life Expectancy Years from birth	Population per Hospital bed	Calories per capita (per day)	Protein per capita (per day)
A. Developed Western										
United States of America	6,154	348	90	99	171	18	71	135	3,330	106
Canada	5,318	452	85	94	319	17	72	105	3,180	101
Belgium	4,785	323	71	98	191	17	73	121	3,380	95
Denmark	5,520	420	67	99	243	13	74	120	3,240	93
France	4,938	286	70	99	209	15	73	97	3,210	105
West Germany	5,635	254	68	99	259	20	71	87	3,220	89
Netherlands	4,487	331	62	99	206	12	74	84	3,320	87
United Kingdom	3,084	181	83	98	131	17	72	106	3,190	92
Sweden	6,111	489	80	99	398	10	73	63	2,810	86
B. African										
Burundi	83	2	15	10	1	150	39	746	2,040	62
Cameroon	251	10	41	10	3	93	41	323	2,410	64
Chad	84	3	14	6	1	160	38	656	2,110	75
Ghana	309	10	44	25	3	156	44	796	2,320	49
Guinea	134	7	20	10	2	216	41	569	2,020	45
Ivory Coast	517	36	39	20	1	164	44	499	2,430	56
Kenya	181	10	39	25	3	135	50	805	2,360	67
Malawi	109	3	24	22	1	119	41	647	2,210	63
Senegal	365	11	27	10	4	159	40	755	2,370	65
Nigeria	177	3	20	25	1	180	41	1,952	2,270	63
Somalia	87	2	7	5	1	177	41	566	1,830	56
Tanzania	123	4	21	18	2	162	44	625	2,260	63
Uganda	158	5	21	25	2	160	50	676	2,130	61
Zaire	133	6	46	12	2	160	44	343	2,060	33
Zambia	418	28	53	40	11	157	44	294	2,590	68

Source: Adapted from "World Military and Social Expenditures 1976." Figures refer to 1973 data. Published by Arms Control Association, 11 DuPont Circle, Washington, D.C.

therefore, tradition and proof that the presence of
scarcity or limited resources within a state or community did not necessarily produce instability, official
violence, or disorder.

As a source of instability, poverty does become
very relevant primarily because of the winner-take-all
philosophy and practices of postindependence leaders,
exacerbated by the existence in most cases of diverse
ethnic groups who may feel acutely alienated. It is
true that the campaigns for independence had led to
exaggerated expectations among the masses of what
freedom would bring, as competing politicians sought
to outdo each other in promises. Those who won (certainly in most of the states where there have been upheavals) systematically set out to monopolize the power
and benefits it brought to the permanent advantage of
their supporters but to the detriment of the rest in
their state.

Because the resources are limited, the winner-
take-all policy leaves too little for others. The
basic point is, however, that if the government sets
out deliberately to be fair in apportioning the scarce
resources to all sections of society, there is little
probability that disorder will ensue. Of course,
several grounds could be advanced by "realists" to
demonstrate the difficulties of determing what is fair
or to argue that politics must necessarily have a system of patronage, all of which tends to find governments incapable of sharing limited resources fairly.

Yet, when the nationalists from different groups
came together within a colony to demand freedom and
promise the masses justice and equality in all respects,
there was no ambiguity or double standard in their
minds. When Obote or Balewa took a stand against the
British colonialists in order to provide their nationals with equal opportunity and when Nkrumah and his
colleagues promised a socialist program to establish
equality and fair play, there were no double standards.
Simply stated, all benefits and burdens were to be
fairly shared by all. Simple men will understand fair
play when they see it. Similarly, no rhetoric of
equality by leaders can prevent ordinary citizens from
understanding attempts to monopolize power, jobs, patronage, and resources by one group within a state.
Instability came, then, partly because leaders broke
their original promises to the people, and the people
through their representatives reacted to redress matters as the government attempted to impose its unfair
practices upon them by force and deceit.

Moreover, those who are in power and seek to monopolize it for all time do not do so necessarily because

they are poor. Invariably within their state they are
either from among the most educated (the professional
classes) or from among the successful businessmen.
If they were poor when they took power, they became
fairly wealthy within a few years, relative to the
rest of society. It is, therefore, not a full explanation to allege that the majority of these leaders
monopolize power because they have no viable alternative livelihood outside government. It may be more
correct to say that they persevere because of greed
for material possessions and power and, unless subjected to a higher moral, spiritual, or ideological
precept, this tends to feed on itself. The more they
acquire in office the more they want and, therefore,
the stronger the temptation they feel to retain power,
thus creating a great contrast between the leaders and
the masses. Given this basic background, it is rare
for a government that practices a policy of winner-
take-all to remove from public consciousness the inequality of its policies, despite all its attempts
outwardly to promote fair or progressive programs.

A Ugandan example is a case in point. In its
manifesto for independence the UPC espoused a socialist
policy for an independent Uganda that would aim at
removing inequalities in society and promote controlled
and evenly distributed programs without destroying
individual freedom. However, in this country, where
the yearly income per capita was less than $150 and
where the majority of the citizens were under- or unemployed, "socialist" Prime Minister Obote had a state
wedding within a year of independence for which a conservative figure of $45,000 was paid from public funds.
His annual gross income from the state was over $21,000
per annum. In contrast, this sum of money could have
constructed five medical aid posts in rural areas to
serve tens of thousands of peasants who lacked medical
care.[3] The prime minister in addition proceeded to
reserve for himself all of the four palatial residences
that had previously been used by the colonial provincial commissioners, one in each of the four regions.
His justification was that he would use each when he
toured the particular region -- which would be only a
few days a year. Obote could have thrown them open
for government or public use, there being scarce acco--
modations, but rather he reserved them to himself all
year round largely for the use of personal friends who
seldom were connected with government.

After Obote assumed the presidency and merged the
two posts, he had an additional five palatial residences in Kampala and Entebbe alone, although dozens
of public servants or international experts in the

service of Uganda had to spend months with their families in expensive or inconvenient hotel accommodations
without personal quarters. It would, of course, be
ridiculous to equate the needs of a head of state with
those of an ordinary countryman. He has to entertain
state guests and meet many important local and foreign
leaders and public officers; more resources are needed
to do this. The critical issue, however, is how great
the resources should be. There is a limit beyond
which the result is sumptuous living. This will generally be easily identifiable amid the simple livelihood of the country.

In October 1969, Obote launched his "move to the
left," alternatively called a "new political culture,"
a full-fledged socialist program to promote the equality and fair sharing of wealth within the society.
That there was a need for such a move, there can be
no doubt. The economy of the country was effectively
controlled by aliens, either Asian merchants and indus-
trialists or expatriate firms, in many cases subsidi-
aries of foreign-based companies. The loss of capital
and profits in this manner constantly drained the
nation of badly needed money. Obote then published
his political manifesto, the Common Man's Charter,
which incorporated a considerable body of sound principles, even if some were unrealistic. Among its main
goals were:

1. Bridging the gap between the rich and poor
2. Correcting inequitable distribution of income
   because it hindered the development of resources
3. Controlling foreign and local investments to
   ensure that they are channeled into priority
   schemes
4. Nationalizing in the interest of the people any
   privately owned enterprises, <u>mailo</u> or freehold
   land, and all productive assets or property[4]

The means of production and distribution were to
be in the hands of the people as a whole. The charter
then made a noble affirmation: "We cannot afford to
build two nations within Uganda, one rich, educated,
African in appearance but mentally foreign and the
other, which constitutes the majority of the population, poor and illiterate. . . . People tend to look
to their immediate family when there is opportunity
for employment. If action is not taken now to change
this situation, it may be too late to avoid violence
in future years." The UPC leadership, however, was
the worst offender with respect to nepotism, and Obote
was its leading example.

On 1 May 1970, he made the celebrated Nakivubo announcements implementing the Common Man's Charter to mark May Day for the workers.[5] The following industries were to be taken over by the state to the extent indicated:

1. Import and export, 100 percent state ownership
2. The oil companies, 60 percent state ownership
3. Public transport, 60 percent ownership by Kampala City
4. All other transportation, 60 percent ownership by the district administrations and the cooperative unions based in regions where they operate
5. Kilembe Mines, Ltd., the largest mining concern, 60 percent state ownership
6. Insurance companies, 60 percent state ownership
7. Commercial banks, 60 percent state ownership

These were far-reaching proposals and they were clearly calculated to promote a badly needed base of popular support. It was an effort to erase public consciousness of the administration of government for the few who cared little about how unevenly the resources of the state were distributed to the many.

But, for the nationals whose land or property might be affected, there was considerable anxiety and anger. With the exception of the foreign-owned sector, there was really no African capitalist class. The majority of indigenous people who had at great sacrifice and effort built small houses, farms, or businesses consequently considered the measures too sweeping and inconsiderate. What was even more infuriating at this stage was the open manner in which Obote's ministers were grabbing wealth in all directions. The prime minister himself had just built a multimillion shilling residence on Kampala's exclusive summit view. Through the Obote Foundation, which for all practical purposes he owned, he had branched out into several important areas of business, including a projected 200,000-acre cattle ranch that was about to be formed in Bulemezi County of the Buganda region in partnership with the Commonwealth Development Corporation. The Obote Foundation would own 51 percent of the equity, the initial cost being about $3 million. Almost all government bureaucrats were equally busy developing private business interests. There was consequently an awareness among the people of a double standard. One set of rules exempted those in power from being subject to another set of rules to which they sought to subject the rest. The embryonic entrepreneurial group of

indigenes especially saw itself directly or potentially
threatened by the government. The poor became more
suspicious as they saw the rich devising means to get
richer, with government promises broken as fast as they
were made. Once again, the force of example by the
leaders spoke more eloquently than the published rhetoric. As a leading trade unionist said concerning the
implementation of these proposals, "people are becoming
suspicious, organized labor is becoming suspicious . . .
because even in the implementation nepotism had prevailed."[6] Those who were on top ensured that those
close to them, either a kinsman or another connection,
filled the new directorships and jobs in acquired businesses, although of course this was to be insignificant in comparison with what Idi Amin was to do later.

In criticizing the behavior of those in power, I
do not wish to suggest that it is necessarily wrong
for ministers or bureaucrats to own private businesses.
On the contrary, I support this so long as one's personal ventures are not a result of the abuse of one's
position or the neglect of one's public duties. It
seems to me absurd that a creative and enterprising
person should be penalized by denial of a right that
every other citizen has. To deny one the right to own
personal property in my view sometimes encourages discontent, mediocrity, and paradoxically in some cases
corruption. What is denied a public servant openly
and honestly, may be sought by him clandestinely. The
emphasis should be placed on respecting their position
and on defining the units of property that can be owned.
My criticism of the Ugandan experience, rather, concerns its hypocrisy and dishonesty. Instead of setting
limits on what they did so as to deal honestly and openly with their actions, they pretended to adhere to what
they contradicted in reality and what they sought to
subject everyone else in the state to, a rigid socialist commitment.

Implementation and acceptability of the Common
Man's Charter and the Nakivubo pronouncements were
handicapped from their inception by two principal factors within the UPC itself. First, as stated above,
there was considerable skepticism, even cynicism, a-
mong party supporters regarding the government's capability and integrity to implement them. In an independent, scientific study of the acceptability of these
reforms, Tertit Aasland reports: "In between praise
and general support of the Charter itself, many delegates [at the UPC conference that adopted it] gave air
to critical remarks on ministers owning buses and other
businesses; on feudalism in the cabinet, in companies
and parastatal bodies; on nepotism in district admin-

istration; on nepotism and corruption in cooperative societies, i.e. all aspects of actual behavior in glaring contrast to the principles of the Charter." The study cites further adverse opinion among the UPC constituency chairmen who would have been vital in assisting to implement the proposals: "The constituency chairmen most often brought out the question of implementation. Some chairmen who were in favor of the charter expressed skepticism towards the possibilities of implementation because of lack of devoted leadership (often with reference to ministers owning bus companies, etc.)."[7]

The second factor that detracted from the value of the proposals was that persons having vested interests were asked to implement a socialist program. A leading millionaire in East Africa, Jayant Madhvani, was appointed managing director of the import/export business, most of which had been privately handled by his Asian kinsmen and had now been acquired 100 percent by the state. Madhvani was competent and likeable but it was both imprudent and unfair to him and to the state to ask and expect him to faithfully implement a program that was directed against his own material interests. Within the Cabinet itself, opinion was deeply divided for and against the reforms. The minister of defense (also the secretary-general of the UPC) was openly against them and for more private enterprise. The minister of commerce who was to oversee their implementation was a leading businessman. Speaking about the fear the proposals had struck in the Ugandan business elite, a parliamentarian observed, "I was glad to note people with the size of elephants shrink in a matter of 24 hours, including the Minister of Commerce and Industry."[8] It is not an exaggeration to say that not one minister in the Cabinet was not actively committed to developing personal private enterprise. Party officials outside of government were no exception. To quote Aasland again about UPC constituency chairmen, "some perceived the Charter as clearly socialist and approved it on that basis. There were, however, more chairmen who disagreed with the charter on that ground, and who did it frankly with reference to their own position as capitalists."[9] Neither at the top, nor in the hierarchy of the UPC and its government, therefore, was there really a demonstrable commitment by example to a socialist development. Yet it was preached profusely. Why? Partly to share the limelight of the more genuine pioneers in that field, like Julius Nyerere of Tanzania, and partly to demonstrate independence from the "capitalist mentality" associated with the colonial exploitation of

the past. But perhaps it was preached more especially
to hoodwink and misdirect the poor masses into feeling
that something tangible was being done for them so
that in return they would not vigorously attack the
rapid and often unfair self-enrichment of the UPC elite.
Another important -- though unstated -- reason was to
deny actual or potential critics independent means of
livelihood in order to silence or subdue them. It is
generally true that, if people have to depend on government to earn a living or if the state makes it a
rule to acquire most of their private means of income,
they become more amenable to government and may desist
from criticizing its mistakes. Nevertheless, few people were fooled. The question that assumed more serious proportions and implications was: to what extent
would it really be justifiable for a national leadership to advocate and impose upon its population fundamental precepts and practices in cultural, political,
or economic spheres, while they place themselves above
these same ideals?

The problem of corruption is universal in its
scope, affecting both developed and developing countries, from the lowest to the highest echelons of state.
But one can say it is accentuated in African politics
because the winner-take-all practices reduce the inhibitions that would act as restraints. It was impossible after Obote's fall to determine the extent of
corruption because, although several commissions of
inquiry were set up to examine it, the nature of President Amin's administration became so incoherent that
these commissions were unable to conclude their work.

Several deposed heads of state in other African
nations have not escaped censure. For example, in
Sierra Leone, Sir Albert Maghai, a former prime minister now living in exile, was ordered to pay the sum
of ₤771,037 to the state as a result of the findings
of a commission, headed by Justice Foster, which probed
corruption during his rule. In Upper Volta, President
Maurice Yameogo went on trial charged with embezzling
₤212,000 during his tenure of office.

We can learn comparable lessons from Ghana. President Nkrumah had launched a bold, socialist program
and was probably one of the greatest and most articulate critics of capitalism and its evils. But how
much was he really a socialist? To what extent did he
practice what he preached to his people? No one should
desecrate the hallowed memory of what Kwame Nkrumah
did for all Africa, and indeed, for the whole Third
World. He opened the door to freedom and retrieved
the pride and honor of the black race. For this, if
for no other reason, his name is assured a distinction

in Africa's troubled history. In spite of this, we
should not deny ourselves the opportunity of learning
some lessons from any mistakes Nkrumah may have committed, if only to guide our future leaders. After
Nkrumah's fall from power in February 1966, the National Liberation Council set up a commission of inquiry
into his wealth, under the chairmanship of a respected
Ghanaian judge of the Supreme Court, Justice Apaloo.
The commission established that when Nkrumah first
assumed office in the then Gold Coast on 8 February
1951 he was worth "practically nothing." However, by
the time of his fall in February 1966 after fourteen
years in power, he was worth ₤2,322,000 in cash, property, and in the accounts of organizations that he in
fact controlled. Justice Apaloo found that most of
this money was "earned dishonestly." The commission
found that the "contingency fund" in the president's
office was used for his personal purposes. In 1965-
1966 alone it was ₤2 million. As president, he drew
₤12,000 yearly, tax free, and an annual pension of
₤2,400 as a former prime minister.

By the time of his fall, he had in Ghanaian banks
a total of ₤454,000. Yet, Ghana's income per capita
was less than ₤100. There had been many attempts in
the country to stamp out corruption, including commissions of inquiry in 1954 and 1956, which had absolved him. In 1961 he made his celebrated broadcast at
dawn against corruption when he himself already had
₤250,000 on his Ghanaian bank account that could not
be accounted for.[10] His close followers were not
blind to his example. They followed suit and so did
their own followers down the line throughout the
country. Nkrumah's leading ministers were not exempt.
There was the well-known case of Krobo Edusei's wife,
who bought a golden bed and caused a sensation by such
a flamboyant display of wealth. Such practices are
at the heart of the failures of many economic reform
programs among many African states. The added danger
is that the masses become cynical because of the vast
credibility gaps of their governments. It is argued
here that such behavior by leaders, betraying their
teachings and promises, leads to resentment, unpopu-
larity, and consequent attempts to reform or remove
such governments. This in turn leads invariably to
instability since government will not voluntarily quit.
This instability is not necessarily due to the people's
poverty, but rather it is due to the practice of a
winner-take-all policy by their leaders, which accen-
tuates disparities in their multiethnic states beyond
the level of tolerance.

EXTERNAL SUBVERSION AND LOCAL INSTABILITY

Accusations by Third World leaders that they are
subverted by developed nations are a daily occurrence.
Internal upheavals or instability is linked to covert
operations of some external power. What is subversion?
For our purposes, subject to a variation discussed
later, we define it as the act of attempting to influence, control, or change a government by unconstitutional means, generally through a conspiracy between
local leaders, with or without external prompting and
aid. It may or may not succeed; it may not be -- but
often is -- violent. It may stop short of overthrowing
a government by merely weakening or controlling it.
Yet there is a wide range of issues labeled subversive
that objectively could not be. For instance, are
external attack, censure of local repression, or inhuman treatment of people subversive? When the government of a state systematically terrorizes its citizens, denies them their basic human rights, or slaugh-
ters them by the thousands, the matter ceases to be
a domestic issue and should rightly concern the whole
international community. If therefore some foreign
country or international bodies, like those associated
with the Human Rights Commission of the United Nations,
condemn a particular government for perpetrating such
acts, it cannot be reasonably called subversion. It
is for this reason that South Africa has correctly
been vigorously attacked by the outside world for its
inhuman apartheid policy, despite the fact that ordinarily it might have been an exclusively internal
matter under Article 2(7) of the Charter of the United
Nations.

In 1974, in a singular act of compassion at the
urging of African diplomats, the United Nations General
Assembly called upon the Ethiopian military government
to exercise restraint and observe the right to life of
its citizens after over sixty leading officials of
former Emperor Haile Selassie had been shot by a firing
squad in Addis Ababa. Amnesty International, a private
organization having consultative status with the United
Nations, has pleaded with governments all over the
world -- in developed and developing countries, capitalist and communist alike -- for the freedom of prisoners of conscience, men and women imprisoned by their
governments because of their political or religious
beliefs. In a comprehensive indictment, the International Commission of Jurists charged the Idi Amin
government of Uganda with the killing of many thousands
of its citizens, which the government angrily and lamely denied. These are not subversive acts by outsiders,

even if they may embarrass or irritate a particular
regime that may label them so.

Real subversion, nevertheless, does exist, and
it is a global phenomenon even if at times leaders
"cry wolf" for their own reasons. Two former employees
of the U. S. Central Intelligence Agency (CIA), Victor
Marchetti and John Marks, published a revealing book
about how the CIA subverts foreign governments.[11] So
revealing was it that by a court order some portions
had to be struck out and the book was published with
numerous blanks. The most scathing indictment of CIA
activities in African states is a book, In Search of
Enemies, by John Stockwell, former chief of the CIA
task force in Angola. He concludes that clandestine
operations are on balance a liability and counterproductive. Stockwell's book is a very revealing account
on how an intelligence operative functions in the
field, particularly in Africa. If there was any doubt
about the existence of such subversive actions, at
least on the part of the United States, it has been
authoritatively removed by the hearings and findings
of the United States Senate Select Intelligence Committee under Senator Frank Church, which investigated
the activities of the CIA. With unprecedented candor
this committee revealed wide-ranging activities of the
CIA that were often intended to subvert foreign governments through covert actions. Covert action was
defined as "the attempt to influence the internal
affairs of other nations in support of United States
foreign policy in a manner that conceals the participation of the United States Government."[12] The committee established that the CIA had conducted over 900
major or sensitive covert operations in addition to
several thousand smaller ones since 1961. A number
of foreign national leaders had been targets of attempted or successful assassination, ranging from Fidel
Castro in Cuba to former President Sukarno of Indonesia
in the 1950s, and more lately to the coup that deposed
and killed the Chilean Marxist president, Salvador Allende Gossens, in 1973. It was confirmed that an
effort was made to assassinate the first Congolese
prime minister, Patrice Lumumba, by a specially prepared poison, though Lumumba was killed by his other
enemies before he could be poisoned. Nevertheless,
those local politicians who murdered him were friends
of the CIA and must have shared a common opinion of
Lumumba.

Covert operations have involved a wide range of
activities. There have been paramilitary and other
covert operations sponsored by the CIA in Asia, Latin
America, and, as John Stockwell has recently brought

to light, in several African states, including Zaire
(formerly the Congo Kinshasa)., Ghana (under Nkrumah),
Burundi, and more recently Angola -- this list being
hardly exhaustive. At another level, there have been
extensive publications of propaganda. As the committee
found, "The Central Intelligence Agency attaches a
particular importance to book publishing activities as
a form of covert propaganda." Prior to 1967, the CIA
sponsored, subsidized, or produced over 1,000 books,
approximately 25 percent of them in English. In 1967
alone, the CIA published or subsidized over 200 books,
including books on African safaris and wildlife and
other publications in Swahili, for example. Indeed,
covert or clandestine operations seem to cover an
infinite range of variety.

While it is highly commendable that responsible
U. S. opinion, having been outraged by the excesses
of the CIA, moved to expose and eliminate them, it is
important to note that there has been complete unanimity between the president and Congress on the necessity of continuing covert operations on a global scale.
The Church Committee noted that "United States interests and responsibilities in the world will be challenged, for the foreseeable future, by strong and
potentially hostile powers. This requires the maintenance of an effective American intelligence system."
It was further stated, "The committee has found that
the Soviet KGB (i.e., the Soviet equivalent of the
CIA) and other hostile intelligence services, maintain
extensive foreign intelligence operations for both
intelligence collection and covert operational purposes.
These activities pose a threat to . . . the interests
of the United States and its allies." It was then
charged there are over 400 Soviet spies in the United
States.

None can seriously think that because other great
powers have not exposed their covert operations as the
Americans have that they, therefore, do not undertake
comparable activities. The unfortunate truth is that
interference in other countries' internal affairs is
widespread and real and is conducted by most states,
especially the great powers -- capitalist and communist alike -- against each other, and clearly against
developing countries. To acknowledge the existence
of subversion, of course, is not to condone it, as it
deserves the severest condemnation. We merely do so
in the same way we acknowledge the existence of sickness or death, or any other unpleasant but real fact
of life.

Have Third World states been free from subverting
each other themselves, independent of alien subversion?

Have African states? In any grouping of states (in
Asia, Latin America, and Africa) there have been serious acts of subversion over the past two decades between some neighboring states. In Africa, for example,
before the formation of the Organization of African
Unity in 1963, the Monrovia group of states consistently accused the Casablanca group of using subversion of
neighboring states as an instrument allegedly for
promoting African unity. In 1964, I represented Uganda at an extraordinary ministerial meeting of OAU in
Lagos, Nigeria, summoned to resolve a bitter dispute
between Ghana and her French-speaking neighbors who
were accusing President Nkrumah of subverting and attempting to overthrow their regimes, and the evidence
was cogent and credible. For several years, Somalia
supported Kenya's Somali population in the northern
frontier district with arms to fight and break away
until the dispute was "settled" by the mediation of
President Kaunda of Zambia. The struggle between
Somalia and Ethiopia for Ethiopian Somali-speaking
areas is well known, and it later erupted in a brutal
war between the two. Currently, some Arab states,
including some in OAU, are financing and arming Erit-
rea to secede from Ethiopia by force of arms. In
1972, Obote, with supporters who were harbored, trained,
and armed by neighboring Tanzania, attempted a desperate suicidal invasion of Uganda to overthrow the military regime of Idi Amin and regain the presidency,
leading to a terrible loss of life. Among themselves,
then, African states are not immune from subverting
each other, even though tragically and undeniably
foreign subversion takes advantage of and exploits
such intra-African conflicts.
     Indeed, we may say that subversion is merely a
symptom of a more fundamental sickness in the international body politic. So long as there is no effective world government to which all nations owe higher
loyalty and so long as nations remain distinct, each
with its own national interests, they will continue
to pursue selfish sectional goals, if necessary to the
detriment of others. There exists a real crisis facing
all humanity caused by a fundamental clash of values
among nations, due in part to the advanced technology
that has vastly reduced distances between nations and
their finite resources, which have caused them to become more and more interdependent than at any time in
recorded history. Common words mean different things
to different people in different countries. Wealth
and poverty mean one thing to an American but another
to an African or Asian. A patriot fighting for his
freedom, say in Southern Africa, is termed a terrorist

by the apartheid regime and some of its external supporters. The concepts of justice, freedom, and democracy become perverted as each is defined by vastly
different social systems. International law and practice lack the force and universality to which they
aspire, as they as well are constantly distorted by
the selfish, particularistic interpretations of individual states. The only global organization that might
harmonize world conflict, the United Nations, is denied
the authority to do so by the very nations that attack
it for its incapacity. Under such circumstances, subversion, sadly but logically, becomes an essential
tool of the states that have the means to undertake
it to promote their national interests.

What steps can African states take to deal with
subversion in such a setting? The fallen leaders who
alleged that subversion was the cause of their political demise argued that it was largely aimed at stopping
them from implementing measures to assert their political and economic independence, and that, because of
the superior wealth of the foreigners behind the subversive activity, it was relatively easy to buy the
support of local politicians, bureaucrats, or army
leaders in order to overthrow them.[13]

Quite often, these allegations are only partially
true. There is evidence to show that covert activities
do support dissidents or local enemies of a regime.
But the assertions are incomplete as they omit acknow-
ledging that, independent of the foreign subversion,
there existed in the country substantial numbers of
disgruntled citizens who were already plotting to overthrow or subvert the regime. These claims tend to
attribute to foreign powers greater control over local
events than they possess and are psychologically detrimental to the state involved. They totally overlook
the intensity and power of genuine discontent and
opposition of an indigenous population against an oppressive and unjust government to effect a forcible
change. Generally speaking, therefore, to the extent
that subversion is a factor in the destabilization
of African governments, it seems it is so largely because it exploits already existing conflicts and differences within the state, such conflicts being rooted
either in the history of the country or in the unjust
policies of its rulers.

Perhaps the assistance of Idi Amin by the Israelis
to overthrow Obote is as good an illustration of this
as any. After the daring Israeli rescue of Jewish hos-
tages from Entebbe Airport in July 1976, a former head
of the Israeli military mission in Uganda, Colonel
Baruch Bar-Lev, publicly admitted he assisted Idi Amin

in overthrowing Obote who had become unfriendly to
Israel. According to Bar-Lev, Amin confided in him
that he was worried because he and Obote had fallen
out and only Obote's army supporters were around the
capital. Obote, Amin felt, might order his arrest and
execution before his supporters stationed up-country
could come to his rescue. Correctly aware of the
power of ethnic identity, Bar-Lev advised Amin to sta-
tion in Kampala (the capital) a military contingent
from his tribe. The contingent included paratroopers,
armor, and jeeps. Its firepower was such that 600 to
800 men could overcome 5,000. This contingent had
been largely trained by the Israelis, and was crucial
in defeating pro-Obote forces. Although Israeli officials denied any responsibility in ousting Obote, it
is significant that Amin never contradicted Bar-Lev's
story, which was published in the New York Times of
17 July 1976. Moreover, there was further circumstantial evidence to indicate the closeness between Amin
and Israel shortly after he toppled Obote. Not only
were Israeli diplomats the most visible and perhaps
the most influential in the capital, but Israel was
the first country to which Amin hurriedly paid a state
visit as president.

Two important facts emerge from this experience.
The most important one is that Amin and Obote had become enemies, had divided the army, had been plotting
against one another, and basically had posed a threat
to the stability of the state for reasons predominantly
rooted in domestic intrigue. The second fact is that
the advice from an alien power (Israel) was solicited
by one of the parties to the indigenous conflict seeking to outmaneuver his local enemy. Even if the Israelis or anyone else had declined to advise Amin, the
sheer compulsion to survive would still have moved
him and his supporters to take some violent action to
save themselves from Obote. Alternatively, if it had
been the pro-Obote forces who had moved to liquidate
Amin and his supporters without the aid of any external
power, the likelihood of a violent upheaval in the
Ugandan army, and consequently the country, would still
have been very great. Whatever foreign subversion
there was, therefore, was essentially supportive or
catalytic and not the basic cause of the 1971 revolution.

After many years of suspicion, allegations, and
denials, the truth is now reliably known that the CIA
was deeply involved in the overthrow of President Kwame
Nkrumah. A dependable source described its role to
the New York Times (9 May 1978) as having been pivotal.
Stockwell reports that local CIA operatives, contrary

to the directives of their superiors not to interfere,
became deeply involved with those Ghanaians who were
plotting Nkrumah's fall.[14] Immediately after his fall,
Nkrumah himself bitterly accused the CIA of toppling
him. Yet it must not be overlooked that the CIA was
exploiting an already existing domestic conflict. Independent of the alien subversion, there were already
existing in the country substantial groups of the population who, having been alienated by some of Nkrumah's
policies, were ripe to plot (or were already plotting)
to overthrow him. True, one could persuasively argue
that without the expert advice of the CIA, the coup
might not have materialized. Yet the country would
have continued with tension and uncertainty as the
alienated groups continuously attempted to eliminate
Nkrumah. Indeed, as we saw, there had already been
several attempts to assassinate him before the coup.
    If the premise is substantially true that foreign
subversion thrives on domestic discord, I should like
to suggest the following approaches as possible realistic means of curbing or successfully frustrating it.
    First, the state might shut itself off totally
from the outside world and thus deny entrance to would-
be subversives. This is what China did after the Communist takeover. However, no African state is so
self-sufficient that it can attempt to do this without suicide. Even China is abandoning it. In any
event, in a world that becomes smaller all the time
and where inhabitants become more interdependent, this
seems no longer to be a practical alternative. African
states need the technology and the assistance from the
outside world that is necessary for their development.
The compromise, then, may be to regulate the activities
of resident aliens to make it impossible or at least
difficult for them to subvert the country if they
should want to. This is a very limited solution, although it is useful in conjunction with other safeguards.
    Second, the most effective alternative by far, in
this writer's view, is for the government to adopt
policies that do not alienate significant segments of
its society, that give every citizen -- irrespective
of his ethnic, regional, ideological, or religious
background -- a feeling that he belongs to the state
and has a real stake in nation building and stability.
This would mean discarding the winner-take-all philosophy and practices. This approach would involve
practicing all or many of the principles discussed in
the last chapter. It would deny potential foreign
subversives easy access to powerful, alienated groups,
since fair play would tend to eliminate or diminish

their existence. Otherwise, how can there be real loyalty to a regime that reduces many of its citizens to the level of nonpersons or second-class citizens; that indefinitely and arbitrarily locks up blameless people, without fair trial, leading to the destruction of their families; or that carries out an extensive, brutal slaughter of its innocent countrymen? In cases where there are alienated people (who have as much right to the country as its incumbent, unjust rulers) there is no loyalty felt to the regime. They consider it patriotic -- not treasonous -- to plot to remove the government. These are the people foreign subversion or influence may effectively seek out, aid, or provoke into subverting a government. With the presence of alienated people, the stage is set to overthrow a regime with or without external support. The Nigerian chief of state, General Olusegun Obasanjo, made a most timely and pertinent statement on this matter before the African heads of state meeting in Khartoum, the Sudan, in July 1978, which heatedly discussed foreign intervention: "We African leaders must realize that we cannot be asking outside powers to leave us alone while in most cases it is our actions which provide them the excuse to interfere in our affairs. We can no longer hide behind real or imagined foreign machinations for our own failing."[15] Such perceptive and courageous self-assessment from a leader of the most powerful black state may give grounds for hope that there may perhaps be more mature and correct perspectives forming about some of the major causes of our upheavals since independence.

One must caution also that the attempts of foreign powers to topple a local tyrant are not often without risk or price. Beyond sharing a common distaste for the regime (which is sometimes for different reasons), it is unlikely that the interests of the local conspirators are identical with those of the foreign power whose support they enlist to overthrow a government. Since the support of such a power is often given with some advantage in mind, it may turn out that the price is too high for the new regime to pay after a successful coup. If the new regime pays the price, it risks incurring the displeasure of its citizens. If it refuses to pay it, obviously, it also risks the enmity of the foreign patron who assisted it to power. In either case, it risks creating conditions for fresh subversion between another combination of local and foreign forces. However unavoidable it may seem to enlist foreign support to overthrow a tyranny, therefore, it is most prudent to consider the cost first, to measure whether one can live with it afterwards,

and defend it if necessary. It is an exceedingly difficult and sensitive issue to resolve.

There are two exceptions to consider. First, it
is conceivable that despite sound and just policies of
a government, there might still be a few discontented
groups whose leaders might attempt to subvert the regime, with or without external covert support. Indeed,
it can exist only in theory that at any given moment
under a good government there are no minor malcontents
attempting to upset the state. In such a case, the
government is surely justified to move sternly against
such groups. The issue of whether there exist such
unreasonable groups and whether a government was justified in taking stern measures against them must be
objectively determined on a case-by-case basis. The
temptation is ever present that a government could act
sternly on the basis of exaggerated or nonexistent,
fabricated grounds from which it might reap further
problems.

The second exception involves one of the worst
forms of foreign subversion. This obtains where foreign agents find a country at peace with itself but
seek to sow discord through a whole range of dirty
tricks in order to bring about domestic conflict. It
is not enough to loudly condemn such acts whenever they
occur, since those who perpetrate them may be imper-
vious to our cries. The response to such a form of
subversion is to take immediate and long-term action
on many different fronts, both domestic and international. The state must obviously do its best to survive. It is imperative for the family of nations to
earnestly seek a universal minimum of global values
under which all states, great and small, can live in
relative security without the constant fear of being
subverted. If the powerful think -- and continue to
act -- as if they are above the restraints which they
loudly proclaim others must observe, then one can confidently though sadly conclude that there can be no
enduring global peace, that detente between the super-
powers is a mere prelude to what the Chinese leaders
have consistently claimed was inevitable, a global
holocaust.

Having subverted us in our weakness during uninhibited and cruel competition, the great powers may
find it exceedingly difficult not to fight each other
over what remains of us and in the end none would benefit. It seems to me that whether or not the human race
ultimately endures or self-destructs may well depend
to a significant degree on whether the powerful nations
acquire an enhanced degree of empathy for the poor and
weak nations that constitute the majority of mankind,

or whether they opt to continue or intensify preying
upon them. By preying upon the weak and helpless, the
powerful may be forfeiting their right to endure, demonstrating an absence of that heightened sensitivity
for others and that restraint that must surely be part
of any preconditions for a lasting enjoyment of the
blessings of a technical civilization.

We can identify yet another type of subversion:
one which does not seek to overthrow a regime but instead seeks to perpetuate it, however reprehensible
and oppressive such a regime may be. What matters to
the subverting, patron power is the survival of the
client regime and not necessarily the well-being of
its people. Such regimes are spread all over the world.
That of Idi Amin in Uganda was a clear example because,
as is later shown, despite such horrendous inhumanity
to its citizens, Amin's government continued to attract
some big power support, openly or covertly. There is
an urgent challenge for those great powers that help
create or sustain such regimes to desist -- however
attractive may seem the short-term advantages.

With regard to subversion as a cause of African
upheavals since independence, therefore, we can reasonably conclude that it has been significant but that its
success hitherto has been largely because it exploited
an already serious domestic conflict. Its success
seems more pronounced generally where regimes, through
reckless domestic policies, alienated significant segments of their societies, making them receptive to foreign intrigue and collaboration. But any discussion
of clandestine foreign subversion must be necessarily
provisional and incomplete, because by their nature
covert operations are secret and we remain uninformed
unless someone makes public privately known information
or they are exposed by other governments. Nevertheless,
there is sufficient information now available on how and
why subversive activities are operated, to enable us
to map out a sound strategy -- if not to end them altogether, then to minimize their dangers.

THE APPARENT EXCEPTIONS TO INSTABILITY

Even though I attribute the rampant instability
in Africa to a combination of defective colonial legacies and winner-take-all policies, there have been
exceptions to the usual consequence. There have been
states where these defects existed in varying degrees
but where the regimes have survived and the countries
have acquired a measure of stability. They range from
socialist Tanzania to moderate Kenya, the Ivory Coast,

Botswana, and Zambia. Their existence may lead one
to fault my thesis on the causes of instability since
they share more or less the basic elements for upheaval
but have instead avoided it. Let us examine these
cases more closely.

Assuming that their stability is real and enduring,
their cases simply form the exception that often proves
the general rule. In spite of similarities in history
and to some extent the one-party characteristic, these
states have enjoyed leadership by men of outstanding
quality who, each in his way, has made the difference
between order and chaos. Let us compare Uganda and
Kenya to illustrate this point. Informed political
observers had given Uganda a better chance for stability than its neighbor, Kenya, after independence. Although Uganda had had political problems, they were
relatively minor as compared to those of Kenya, which
had fought a vicious civil war. There is little doubt
that the ability and quality of Mzee Jomo Kenyatta's
leadership was the most crucial single factor among
other variables that stabilized Kenya and confounded
the prophets of its chaos. The outcome for Uganda was
completely opposite due to the quality and nature of
Obote's leadership, which led Uganda into its present
state of chaos and tragedy. The human factor of individual leaders, therefore, can make the difference,
even where other variables for unrest exist, although
this assertion cannot be without obvious limits.

There are those who may persuasively argue against
the claim that there has been genuine stability in
these states. It is true that these states have had
their own domestic conflict. Each has had its share
of attempted coups and trials of persons charged with
treason. But by comparison these nations have been
able to contain their problems. What can justly be
said is that it may be too early to be categorical
about the durability of their stability. The oldest
nation among this category of states is less than two
decades old at the moment of this writing. Except in
Kenya, none of the others has yet smoothly and successfully undertaken a transfer of power from the great
independence leaders to their successors, often a hazardous phase. For the sake of Africa one hopes they
will succeed; however, one cannot lightly dismiss those
who reserve final judgment for a later date on the nature of this stability.

Finally, it should be understood, as has already
been indicated, that I do not claim that once the twin
causes of colonial defects and winner-take-all policies
exist, upheavals must necessarily follow speedily. A
brutal regime or one slightly less so could endure for

many years, despite the existence of these characteristics. Amin was in power for eight years. What I
argue, rather, is that once these twin causes exist
in an African multiethnic state, conditions are created
that sooner or later lead to instability or upheaval.

Part 3

The Future: Some Lessons and Some Basic Principles

11
Alternatives for Africa

If, as it is hoped, a case has been made for the
erroneous policies of a winner-take-all philosophy,
ruthlessly imposed on diverse nationals, as one of the
twin pillars of the most serious causes of postindependence instability among African states, what principles
can we advance as likely corrective measures to reduce
or eliminate such policies and enhance the general prospect for national stability? What institutional and
philosophical underpinnings can we consider as most
appropriate? When we talk of fostering stability,
we do not suggest the kind that unprogressive and sta-
tic regimes can manifest, such as those of General
Franco in Spain and Salazar in Portugal. The type of
stability we mean permits and contains creative tensions that must necessarily be the result of Africa's
attempts at rapid modernization and change. It can
only be attained by each state establishing a dynamic
equilibrium among all its nationals in the process of
sharing the power and experience of nation building.
No serious account of Africa's future in the sphere
of government and politics can afford to ignore the
examination of two preeminent postindependence developments: the one-party system and military rule. Let
us look at these first before proceeding to other fundamental principles.

THE ONE-PARTY SYSTEM

Of the more than forty-eight independent states
on the African continent (excluding South Africa and
Rhodesia for different reasons), only two states have
a multiparty system of government: Gambia and Botswana,
(Senegal is trying to establish a formal opposition).
The rest, whether ruled by civilian or military leaders, are de jure or de facto one-party states. So

swift in its adoption and sweeping in its scope has
been the one-party system that it has become a revered
form that many people dare not question, else they
might be branded enemies of the "African Revolution."
But we should not be deterred by clichés because its
ubiquity has not been synonymous or coexistent with
good government. To determine the suitability of the
one-party system it seems necessary to examine the extent to which it has succeeded or failed in meeting
the goals it was supposed to attain, a few of which
are presented next.

Fostering Stability and Unifying the New State

By far the most persuasive and urgent reason for
the proliferation of the one-party system has been the
desire of each African leader to hold the new state
together by eliminating or minimizing the centrifugal
tendencies that seem more often than not to character-
ize multiparty politics. This was and still remains
a genuine fear. For those who equated democracy with
multiparty systems, the divisive and devastating experience of multiparty politics that led to the civil
wars in Nigeria and Zaire indicated that the Western
type of parliamentary multiparty government might be
unsuited to African needs. Numerous parties seemed
to exist and prosper not by appealing to universal
unifying ideals, even though they tried to give such
impressions through profuse rhetoric, but more by
exploiting particularistic ethnic or intraethnic sentiments, which could be done in most cases only at the
expense of the higher ideal of overall unity in the
young state
Consequently, the one-party system seemed to present the best alternative as the instrument through
which not only to maintain stability by minimizing
dissent but also to put in motion schemes for the "or-
ganic" unification of the different ethnic or religious
groups within each state. Yet even the moderate success of the one-party states in attaining these goals
was to depend on the manner in which it came into existence. We can distinguish between two broad cate-
gories.[1]
The first category of one-party states came into
being through democratic and fair elections where the
overwhelming majority of citizens in the state voted
for a single party and whatever opposition there was
seemed insignificant. Such was the case of Tanganyika
(Mainland Tanzania) under President Julius Nyerere and
of Tunisia under President Habib Bourguiba. In such
cases the one-party system began with a fair chance of

success as it was by the consent of the governed. Indeed, if the Tanganyika African National Union (TANU)
has seemed to have relative success to this date in
establishing stability and minimizing interethnic conflict, it is partly because of the relative freedom
to express dissent within this one party that its
leadership has permitted. Numerous TANU candidates
compete in generally open elections and the masses
are given an opportunity through their chosen representatives to shape and influence local and national policy. Part of the legacy that President Nyerere leaves
behind will be his demonstration that a one-party system can function and attain the objectives that multiparty representative democracy aspires to, although
whether the TANU will maintain this indefinitely remains to be seen. However, Nyerere, by example, has
discouraged the practices of winner-take-all among his
nationals, especially those in the party hierarchy who
might be tempted to monopolize power.

Nevertheless, even where one party was originally
established by consent, it may be highly doubtful
whether now, a decade or so later, it is still maintained by popular consent. People change their minds
about leaders and policies. The African experience,
unfortunately, clearly indicates that leaders and
parties in power on independence expected their initial
election by the masses to be irrevocable, even if the
masses later wished to opt for other alternatives. In
such cases there could be no stability or unity as people would be forced to devise extralegal remedies to
change their governments.

The second and principal method in which the one-
party state has been established was through sheer
ruthless suppression of opposition parties, ostensibly
to maintain stability and to promote national unity.
Leading examples in this category are Ghana and Uganda
(which were discussed earlier), Mali, the Central African Empire, Chad (under the late Francois Tombalbaye),
Niger, and the Upper Volta. But the forcible elimination of opposition in these states, rather than promoting stability and unity, has produced subversion, plots,
and some upheavals as those denied a fair say in running the affairs of their state have sought to change
incumbent regimes by force. For instance, after several assassination attempts at Kwame Nkrumah, he was
later overthrown by his army and police in Ghana in
1966. In Uganda, following several abortive plots and
an attempt on his life in 1969, Obote was similarly
toppled in 1971. Modibo Keita in Mali and later Tombalbaye in Chad suffered similar fates after numerous
unsuccessful attempts. There was a coup in Togo in

1963 when it was a one-party state. Those regimes in this category that survive continue to experience the pressures of subversion within. The latest, in the Central African Empire, involved two serious attempts on Emperor Bokasa's life in 1979. The Ivory Coast uncovered two serious plots in 1963 and others later. There have been numerous attempts to subvert or over-throw President Sékou Touré in Guinea. One could go on. While there have been diverse reasons in each particular case combining to unleash such instability or a threat of it, one constant and perhaps decisive reason has been the hostile, clandestine activities of the several political groups within each state that were outlawed and thus denied a meaningful say in running local and national affairs. At best, there-fore, the claims of the suppressive one-party government that it stabilizes and unifies the state are debatable and unproven. By this we do not argue necessarily in favor of multiparty systems, which as we said have not functioned that well in Africa. But we strongly argue for any system, whether one-party, coalition, or multi-party, that permits all diverse national groups to participate in the all-embracing activities of nation building. The definite attempts to monopolize power by many postindependence leaders raises the question of whether the true motives of establishing the one-party state were the laudable objectives of national stability and national unity, or whether in fact the motive was the establishment of absolute rule for which they took the only available avenue, regardless of the consequences. The distinction between these two ob-jectives is crucial in understanding the reasons for the brutal excesses of several one-party systems. Where the true objective was as declared, to foster national unity and stability once the system was estab-lished and from there to proceed with nation building, it has not been misused and has certainly been rela-tively democratic. But where a leader has been resol-ved to seize power at all costs, never yielding even when rejected by his people, then the one-party system by providing the means to that absolute power becomes an end in itself and is not an instrument to attain higher ideals.

For the future, therefore, one cannot say without qualification that the one-party system is the African panacea for unity, stability, and development. It is more fitting to acknowledge that fundamentally one-party systems are neither bad nor good by themselves but assume their particular character according to the use to which they are put by the leaders. What is crucial, whatever system is chosen, are ideals that

are intended to be achieved and the principles on
which the state is to be run. These are discussed
later.

Promoting Rapid Economic Development

It is generally argued that unlike divisive multiparty systems the one-party system is better able to
mobilize the masses and to facilitate more economic
development so desperately needed by every African
state. But this claim is as hotly disputed as it is
advanced. One can point to some of the impressive
development projects under Nkrumah's CPP, initiated
when Ghana was for all practical purposes a de facto
one-party state. Such impressive schemes include the
Volta River Dam and its associated projects, the creation of Tema township and facilities including Tema
harbor, an impressive program of road construction,
the elimination of the swollen-shoot cocoa disease,
housing schemes in many parts of the country and a
rapid expansion of higher education, including building
two new universities, technical, secondary, and primary
schools. It could be argued that by mobilizing the
masses, the CPP was able to galvanize them into responding to the government's call for support and involvement in these schemes. This, however, would be a
rather one-sided view, because there is definitely a
negative aspect to Ghana's one-party system in which
it could be said to have adversely affected Ghana's
economic development. For example, while it is true
that the republic entered independence with a surplus
of over ₤200 million in reserves, the CPP government
was within a decade to deplete the treasury and leave
at the time of Nkrumah's overthrow in 1966 ₤300 million
of debts. Certainly, the fall in world prices of cocoa
-- Ghana's leading export -- while affecting the country adversely, was not principally responsible for this
adverse economic condition. The real cause seemed to
be that having eliminated all meaningful criticism outside and inside the CPP, there was no longer an effective check on how public finances were spent. Consequently, the wrong priorities attracted vast public
funds as the sycophants applauded each scheme as the
work of a genius and no one dared point out that Ghana
was becoming bankrupt.

The best way in which the one-party system could
promote rapid economic development would seem to be by
providing increased national capital through taxation.
It is estimated that African states need to raise 15
to 20 percent of national income in taxation so as to
provide adequate public services and contribute towards

capital formation.[2] Most African states raise less
than 10 percent (excluding oil producers). Several
single-party regimes have been threatened or overthrown partly because of massive resentment against
increased taxes. Nkrumah tried to raise taxes in Ghana
in 1965 and the response was riots and strikes in Tak-
oradi and Sekondi by workers. Although the tax increases were repealed, they left a legacy of resentment
among those affected against the CPP one-party government. In 1963 when the one-party government of President Maga of Dahomey introduced a harsh budget, it
alienated trade unions and led to his overthrow. Similarly in Upper Volta and in the Central African Republic where one-party regimes introduced austerity bud-
gets affecting those highest paid in the state, like
civil servants, the regimes were overthrown. Not long
before his fall, President Obote had cut down on the
privileges of public servants, including denial of
loans to buy cars. On the other hand we have already
noted the contrast that existed between the economic
power of those in government and the plight and discontent of the masses in the case of the one-party
governments of Ghana and Uganda. Before the 1965-1966
coup in Dahomey, salaries for public servants made up
two-thirds of the country's meager budget. Such examples could be multiplied manifold. Consequently,
the argument that the one-party system is an essential
precondition for African rapid economic development
cannot be sustained. This is by no means to say that
it is not possible to attain rapid economic development
under a single-party system. It is simply argued that
the majority of those one-party states hitherto formed,
based as they are on repression and their consequent
preoccupation with survival, more often than not are
incapable of total commitment to development even when
they honestly wish to be.

The "Africaness" of the One-Party System

     To clothe the one-party system with legitimacy,
practically all the leaders who adopted it have persistently argued it was rooted in the African culture.
The existence of opposition parties has been rejected
as alien, capitalistic, and a relic of imperialism.
With his unquestioned eloquence, President Nyerere of
Tanzania has cited the analogy of how African elders
in the traditional society sat under a tree and discussed issues jointly until they agreed.[3] But the
relative success of Nyerere's one-party state is not
so much because it is based in the African culture as
it is because it has permitted room for the more than

120 ethnic groups to have a meaningful role in their
government. If problems should later beset him they
will more likely be from other areas, like the economy,
rather than be caused by repression. But how correct
is the claim that we should adopt the one-party system
because it is indigenous?

It cannot be seriously contested that there was
not a single African political culture operating on
a political party basis in precolonial history, and
therefore that the one-party system is as un-African
as the multiparty one. As one African writer rightly
says, "if there was any system in the nature of a political party, it was a no-party system."[4]

But even if one were to accept the one-party system as African, which is contested, one would be hard
put to cite an example of where such a system operated.
The 2000 ethnic groups that inhabited the continent
had vastly diverse systems of government. Some knew
no central authority, an overwhelming characteristic
of the one-party state, as they were administered by
heads of extended families. Others stopped at clan
heads in the collective consciousness. Still others
had established relatively sophisticated kingdoms with
a centralized and well-ordered administration. There
were even empires, loosely held together by a central
kingdom that exacted tribute and loyalty but permitted
considerable autonomy to outlying regions. As colonial
powers arbitrarily and forcibly gathered together within a single colony numerous groups operating on one or
the other of these systems, it must follow that within
each African state, on the basis of purely African
heritage, there were numerous different methods of
government. If any leader were to claim to be practicing the one-party system as an indigenous African
system, he should candidly and logically answer the
question, which one? For instance, what type of African one-party system, assuming one existed, did Obote
impose on Uganda? If he were to base his concepts in
the Langi traditions of his kinfolks, he would almost
automatically alienate the majority of his countrymen
whose systems, like that of the Baganda or even other
northern groups, differed from his. Which one-party
system did Nkrumah, a Nzima, operate in Ghana among
his diverse nationals? The claim of the legitimacy
of one-party states as based on Africa's past, therefore, is impossible to substantiate.

Moreover, while it has always been said that the
concept of opposition is contrary to African ideas of
government, it has totally been ignored that the multiethnic states of Africa today are quite different from
the relatively more homogeneous and generally smaller

states of Africa's precolonial history. It is true
that at the time of colonization numerous groups even
when ethnically the same shared no concept of common
identity or nationality. For instance the Yoruba in
Nigeria or the Banyankole in Uganda were unified for
the first time in their history by the colonial experience. Despite this reservation, one can still validly
say precolonial societies were more homogeneous than
the present multiethnic states. Where a people (for
example, the Baganda or Acholi in Uganda or the Ashanti
in Ghana) are quite homogeneous, where their culture,
their values, and their concept of justice are consequently so harmonious, and where the society at the
time is simple, it was possible to dispense not only
with political parties but with institutionalized opposition in precolonial times. But the modern African
states are comprised of diverse multiethnic groups that,
while sharing some basic values and similarities, are
characterized by even more diversity in their primordial, traditional cultures. It would be disastrous,
therefore, to cling to the simplified forms of government of the precolonial societies. Any good government
of these multiethnic states that would enable them to
stand up and take their place in the complex twentieth
century must surely require of its African leaders the
willingness to innovate, to borrow, and to adapt new
systems -- from outside if necessary -- without feeling
any inhibitions of inadequacy or inferiority. Civilizations and cultures that have thrived throughout history have done so by enriching themselves through a
combination of their own original systems and borrowed
ideas from others. Thus, the Greeks learned a lot from
the Egyptians, as did the Romans from the Greeks. Many
European cultures borrowed from one another as did the
Japanese from the West. The massive borrowing of technology and other knowledge by developing nations from
developed nations is self-evident. One day we might
even come to know on a much grander scale that planetary civilizations survive by borrowing from others on
a galactic scale, even if this may seem like science
fiction now.[5] If the one-party system, un-African as
it is, appears the best suited (which it could be under
conditions discussed later), by all means let us adopt
it purely for its utilitarian function, and not because
it makes a unique claim -- falsely -- of roots in the
African heritage.
     We cannot conclude this brief discussion of the
one-party state without examining the claim of its
advocates that it provides enough room for dissent and
constructive criticism and therefore eliminates the
need for institutionalized opposition parties. Theo-

retically this proposition is feasible. In reality,
however, barring very few exceptions, the vast majority
of one-party states are notoriously intolerant of criticism. The first, which seeks to run down every action
of government irrespective of its merit, is obviously
negative and should have no room in whatever party system is adopted. But there is another type, which seeks
to expose the failings of government or the misuse of
power and consequently acts as a check on bad government. Such criticism is surely a must, even if it
embarrasses the rulers. Where formal opposition has
been outlawed, such criticism has often not been permitted within the ruling party. The same intolerance
that led to the elimination of opposition parties, is
continued within the ruling party. Those who seek to
check excesses or mistakes of government, as we illustrated in the case of Uganda and Ghana, are ruthlessly
eliminated.

If the one-party system is to have a constructive
role in Africa's future development, therefore, it
seems it will have to be genuinely open to all the diverse nationals, it will have to permit a healthy measure of self-examination and criticism without which
advancement is impossible. Certainly, it will have
to cease being used as a vehicle by a few groups to
monopolize political power and its benefits in perpetuity to the exclusion of other nationals under the
smokescreen of profuse but empty rhetoric on nation
building.

MILITARY RULE

In the space of less than a decade and a half,
there have been thirty-eight successful coups d'etat
in African states and many more unsuccessful ones.
In some states there have been many, such as in Benin,
formerly Dahomey, where there have been as many as six
successive military takeovers, and Nigeria, where there
have been three with a serious abortive one that took
the life of the chief of state, General Murtala Mohammed, in 1976. Few of the African independence leaders
would have dreamed the army was to assume such pre-
eminence in its challenge of civilian rulers, even
though military intervention in politics was rampant
in the Middle East and Latin America. Beginning with
Togo in January 1963, the military swept through most
of French-speaking Africa and created the false impression that former British Africa was immune from coups
until those in Nigeria and Ghana in 1966 shattered this
illusion. What has been the cause of this rampant

military intervention in such a short space of time?
What is the likelihood of its continuation? To what
extent if any are the armed forces of these new states
better able to govern than the civilian rulers they
supplanted? These must surely be some of the most
urgent questions in the minds of African leaders and
interested observers, and we shall attempt to answer
them below with specific examples.

The Major Causes of Coups in Africa

Scholars have written extensively about the probable causes of armed forces taking over governments.[6]
These causes have included (1) the failure of the elite
to resolve economic problems; (2) incipient tensions
from development due to mobilization policies; (3) corruption, government inefficiency, and interelite strife;
(4) tampering with the corporate interests of the military; and (5) the individual interests of the coup-
makers themselves. Undoubtedly, combinations of these
factors in varying degrees have contributed to the
overthrow of these governments, although it may often
be difficult to identify the precise degree to which
each contributes to the final act. Nevertheless, I
would argue that the most fundamental, constant basis
of an African coup d'etat lies invariably in the un-
resolved interethnic tensions, in failures by government to formulate fair and effective methods to regulate or contain ethnic rivalries and conflict. Since
the tendency is to view most major issues affecting
the young state "through ethnic eyes" and because the
majority of the independence governments tended to
monopolize power through unfair means, the result was
that the diverse ethnic groups who felt cheated out of
the independence bargain could seek effective redress
only by taking measures outside the law. To maximize
support toward this end it became a common sense strategy to exploit whatever current failings or difficulties the incumbent regime might have. These failings
encompass many of those factors already mentioned,
like corruption, economic problems, etc. This does
not mean that once serious ethnic conflicts exist the
regime will necessarily be overthrown. (The Obote
government lasted five years under serious interethnic
stress before it was toppled.) It does mean that the
foundation exists for the regime to be overthrown
abruptly should an immediate cause present itself,
which may or may not tangentially relate to ethnic
conflict or rivalry. Thus the soldiers and policemen
who toppled Nkrumah could exploit the economic difficulties into which Ghana had fallen, capitalize on the

corruption of the civilian rulers, and those who overthrew Tombalbaye in Chad in 1975 could exploit his
economic failures when the decisive issue was basically
a racial/ethnic one.

To what extent is it likely to overthrow a regime
that plays fair to all its diverse nationals but meets
serious economic problems or other grave impediments
unrelated to ethnic conflict? Theoretically, while
it is conceivable to have this situation, it may be
more difficult to overthrow the government because in
such a case there is tolerance. Indeed, this situation
may be outside the African experience, for it is not
easy to identify a government that has fallen by forcible means exclusively because of causes unrelated to
ethnic conflict. The coup-makers have tended to play
ethnicity down as a cause and to give prominence to
other conventional, stereotyped grievances.

The Suitability of Military Regimes as Rulers

It is true that the armed forces in Africa have
played an important and useful role in intervening to
rid society of discredited and undesirable regimes,
many of them civilian independence leaders. Such particularly was the case, for example, in Ghana, Nigeria,
Uganda, Mali, and Chad. Equally of crucial importance,
in countries like Zaire and Nigeria, the army has held
the state together in the face of serious divisive
civil wars. Indeed, while the universal role of the
armed forces is to defend the state against external
danger, the predominant preoccupation of most African
armies has been the maintenance of internal order.
Notwithstanding these commendable roles, the question
must still be asked, to what extent are military regimes better able to govern than civilians?

Once again theoreticians have extolled the relative virtues and advantages the military have over
civilian rulers. For example, Dennis Austin says that
they display those military virtues of courage, honor,
discipline, and loyalty not easily found among their
civilian predecessors. Further, he states that they
work more closely with the civil service than the former leaders did because of a common professionalism;
that they have the advantage sometimes of starting
with a clean slate, not being committed to a particular group interest; and that they were therefore free
to make decisions in the national interest.[7] Ernest
Lefever claims, "African armies tend to be most detri-
balized, integrated and cohesive institutions in their
respective states."[8] The truth unfortunately contra-
dicts this glowing tribute and few if any of these

claimed advantages exist in fact. African armies like
the politicians they replace are exposed and respond
to all the pressures and cleavages that affect the
societies from which they are drawn. If the country
is adversely affected by ethnic rivalries and conflict,
these will penetrate the army no less than they do
other departments of the state or political organizations in the society. If at any time African armies
had these attributes it was during colonial rule,
partly because Africans were marginal participants in
the government of their states, partly because most
armies were drawn from the least politically conscious
ethnic groups (as they were in Ghana, Nigeria, and
Uganda), and partly because of the colonial tradition
to insulate the public service and the armed forces
from political activity. But this was an artificial
state of affairs that crumbled swiftly with the demise
of colonial rule. As soon as civilian independence
rulers took over, their first cardinal mistake was to
politicize the army and police force in the belief
that this was the safest way to ensure their loyalty.
As most politics were intimately connected with ethnic
grouping and loyalty, this invariably meant promoting
the leader's trusted kinsfolk to strategic commands
and recruiting primarily those groups whose loyalty
was considered reliable largely because of ethnic com-
patibility. Almost inevitably, this tampered with
the impartial professionalism of the military and enhanced ethnic consciousness among the excluded groups
who became discontented and apprehensive. A symbiotic
relationship always developed between the opposing
political groups and their corresponding ones in the
security forces. The suppression of opposition parties
invariably led to active though secret courting of
potential allies by oppressed politicians among the
discontented and alienated groups within the army.
Thus, the soldiers became as fragmented as the politicians, despite the external semblance of cohesion that
perhaps became misleadingly enhanced by common uniforms.
The account on the fragmentation of the Ugandan army
given previously, rather than being unique, is indeed
typical. One need only look at other states.

Sir Albert Magai, having politicized and divided
the Sierra Leone Army while prime minister, after being
defeated in a 1967 election asked Brigadier General
David Lansana (his trusted army commander) to take over
the government rather than have the opposition party
of Dr. Siaka Stevens form the next government. The
general in fact did intervene but was in turn overthrown by military supporters of the opposition, who
clearly had a more just cause. This attests to the

division of the Sierra Leone Army along the same lines on which civilian leaders had been split.

In Nigeria Tafawa Balewa significantly always reserved the portfolio of defense for an influential northern politician, first Ribadu then Inuwa Wada. The fact that Balewa gave the army command to Brigadier General Ironsi, an easterner, instead of Brigadier General Maimalari, a fellow northerner, was merely a tactical step and not an evenhanded attempt at equalization of opportunity (just as Obote had first appointed Opolot and not Idi Amin). The desire by the northern groups in the NPC to dominate the army at the expense of the southerners was unmistakable even if initially they had a just claim to increase their officers. The more the NPC suppressed the opposition groups among the politicians, the more apprehensive became the southerners in the army about a similar fate. When Balewa deployed the army to intervene and support his protege in the west, Chief Akintola, after an unparalleled fraudulent election, the divisions in the army approached the bursting point and troops had to be hastily withdrawn from the west although the political damage that sparked the first coup had already been done.

It cannot be accidental that, of the six inside planners of the coup against Balewa, five were Ibo, even if the grounds on which they moved were supported by a nationwide cross section of the population. The political conflict unleashed by attempts to monopolize power that we discussed with regard to Nigeria had, therefore, inevitably split the army. In such coup operations soldiers sometimes took commands not from their superiors, as army discipline dictates, but from their kinsfolk. This is a common practice even though there are exceptions. The troops that supported the coup against Ironsi disobeyed orders from southern superiors and took them instead from kinsmen NCOs of lesser rank from the North. During the coup led by Amin, his supporters similarly defied their superiors known to be pro-Obote and took orders from strong pro-Amin subordinates. Discipline as well as all the theoretical attributes of army unity and purpose thus tend to collapse and loyalty to ethnic group or political faction transcends in such a crisis.

What about Ghana? Afrifa's book, The Ghana Coup, makes it plain that President Nkrumah's humiliation of the once powerful Ashanti was a real contributing cause of his overthrow.[9] There are two further facts that are more than coincidental: (1) Nkrumah had omitted influential Ewes from his government since he fell out with Gbedemah in 1961, and (2) that the principal

plotters against him in the army and the police force,
Major General E. K. Kotoka and Commissioner of Police
J.W.K. Harlley, were both Ewe. Indeed, from his exile
in Guinea, Nkrumah was bitterly to observe that these
two could plot against him because they came from the
same tribe.[10] There was an attempt to play down and
minimize the role ethnic conflicts and rivalries had
played in Ghana's first coup. Yet to appreciate their
significance one had only to see the effort that had
to be taken in constituting the National Liberation
Council (NLC), which assumed government, so that it
reflected the ethnic, regional, and religious diversity
of the country.[11]

The similarities between civilian and army regimes
are indeed undeniable once soldiers are in power. We
later discuss more fully the Ugandan case under Idi
Amin, but let us briefly look at Ghana and Nigeria
under their previous military governments.

Military Rule in Ghana

The combination of the army and police officers
who overthrew President Nkrumah and formed the NLC in
1966 to govern the country had aroused great expectations among the masses who had enthusiastically welcomed the coup. It is true that the NLC can be credited with real positive measures. Although political
activity was banned, the repression of Nkrumah's era
was largely gone. The new rulers paid close attention
to conciliating the demands of competing interest
groups. They reintroduced participation of communities in their respective local governments and looked
more kindly on traditional institutions and chiefs.
In a singular act of self-denial most worthy of praise,
after three and one-half years in office, the NLC
handed power back to civilians true to their promise,
through a fair general election.

Yet, soon after the honeymoon with the public,
the real problems of competing communal interests invaded with some negative consequences. Many Ashantis
and other Akans began to suspect the NLC of being an
Ewe-Ga bastion, partial to the interests of these two
groups. The Akans alleged that the Ewes and Gas (who
dominated the NLC) were favored when officers were
appointed to key military positions. In this atmosphere of suspicion, the Ewes in turn suspected that
the abortive counter coup of 1967, which took the
lives of General Kotoka and other Ewe officers, had
been a plot by Ashantis and Fantis to take over control
of the NLC from the Ewes and Gas.[12] With the approach
of civilian rule, ethnic tensions in the NLC increased

as its members lined up behind their kinsmen among the
politicians competing for power. Afrifa, supporting
the candidacy of his fellow Ashanti, Dr. K. Busia,
took steps to have Busia's rival, K. A. Gbedemah, an
Ewe, disqualified from the race on the ground that he
had once been Nkrumah's minister, all Nkrumah's ministers having been disqualified. But Gbedemah had fallen
out with Nkrumah in 1961, as we saw, had fled Ghana,
and like Busia lived the remainder of Nkrumah's rule
in exile. Predictably and rightly, all the Ewe members
of the NLC vigorously opposed this attempt to disqualify him from competing for political power. We have
already discussed the effect of this ethnic rivalry on
Dr. Busia's government, which succeeded the NLC.

On other counts, such as combating corruption,
economic difficulties, etc., they fared no better. An
eloquent Ghanaian writer titled his novel, which dealt
with the continuation of these ills under the NLC, The
Beautyful Ones Are Not Yet Born.[13] The military rulers, who had set up elaborate commissions to expose
these evils under Nkrumah's rule, continued them. Indeed, the first chairman of the NLC, Lt. General J. A.
Ankrah, was forced to resign because he had taken money
from foreign corporations to promote his political ambition in shady circumstances.

Military Rule in Nigeria

Although it had been bloody, the coup that toppled
Tafawa Balewa might still have stabilized the state if
his successor, General Ironsi, had initiated imaginative nationwide reforms of all the ills for which the
civilians had become notorious. But Ironsi fell victim
of most ill-conceived strategies that exacerbated interethnic conflict and led to his own liquidation six
months later. Rather than pose and be seen as a center
of national reconciliation by drawing close advisers
from all the significant groups, particularly in the
North, he surrounded himself with a small group of his
fellow easterners from the military and civil service.
This could only heighten the belief among the preponderant northerners that the coup that removed Balewa
was designed to foster Ibo domination. This belief
was irrevocably reinforced when in the most ill-conceived move of his brief career, Ironsi abrogated the
federal constitution and established Nigeria as a
unitary state with the promulgation of Decree 34 on
24 May 1966. To the northerners this meant the ful-
fillment of what they had historically dreaded: their
domination by the more developed South.

The stage was now set to avenge the death of the

leading northern leaders who had perished in the first
coup, including the Sardaunan of Sokoto, Tafawa Balewa,
and leading northern army officers. Within five days
after the announcement of Decree 34 there was an extensive slaughter of Ibos in northern towns. Within
the army, divisions were now intense as the northern
junior officers and other rank became openly hostile
to the Army Officer Corps, now more than ever dominated
by the Ibo. In July, under Colonel Murtala Mohammed
and Major T. Y. Kanjuma, the northerners unleashed
their own vengeful coup, killed Ironsi, took power,
and replaced him with General Yakubu Gowan. The army
under Ironsi had hopelessly failed, principally because
either it did not properly understand the problems it
faced or if they did, its leadership lacked the will
to impose the most just and logical solutions in a
diverse, bitterly divided multiethnic state.

Although Gowan restored the federal structure and
its regional autonomy to the regions, the bitterness
that was soured by the escalating bloodshed meant he
could no longer hold Nigeria together by constitutional
government. The Ibo, fearful of genocide from the
North, declared the East the new republic of Biafra,
and in a bitterly fought civil war sought to secede
from Nigeria. The military leadership of General Gowan
justly deserves praise for the magnanimity with which
it soon reconciled a defeated Biafra and took steps to
integrate it once more into Nigeria. But if the army
takes credit for having saved the unity of the state,
it cannot escape its share of blame in having contributed to the bloodshed that threatened the state since
they alone possessed and used the means of massive organized violence. On the other hand, by creating more
regions (nine under Gowan and nineteen under his successor Murtala Mohammed) they have creatively come to
terms with the unyielding tenacity of diverse local
communities, including minorities, to have a more
equitable say in the running of their affairs, unlike
the civilians who had irrationally defended the indivisibility of their regions in an unbalanced union.

However, the military record under Gowan was mixed
in other areas. The regime proved unequal to the task
of moving from reconciliation to reform. Corruption
continued as it had done under the civilians, with its
attendant evils of inefficiency and slow development.
The army became a privileged class with the accusations
against civilians forgotten. Notwithstanding his positive contribution, General Gowan, like the politicians
he deposed, decided to stay in power and refused to
hand it over to an elected civilian government as originally promised when the time came to do so. Whatever

legitimacy he had had now seemed to have disappeared
and once again the stage was set for another coup which
overthrew him and installed General Murtala Mohammed
from the predominant Hausa group as the new chief of
state in July 1975. General Mohammed was himself assassinated in an abortive coup within less than a year
of taking power.

The foregoing is merely to demonstrate that African armies are as vulnerable to the divisive ethnic
and regional rivalries and conflicts as the politicians
they overthrew, and they are no better on this count.
There are two other important limitations that have
tended to hamper several military regimes that took
power and we should mention them briefly.

Inadequate Legacy of Colonial Rule for African Armies

The insufficient training in senior cadres that
had characterized other departments of African administrations during colonial rule was equally reflected
in the African armies, as we mentioned regarding Uganda. True, on the whole the French had been less discriminatory towards their African armies than the
British and Belgians. And yet, though French African
troops had seen active service in most major French
foreign conflicts in the nineteenth century (including
Napoleonic wars and the Crimean war), by 1956 there
were only seventy-five African officers in the entire
French African empire. Nevertheless, perhaps nowhere
was the neglect of training an African officer corps
more manifest as it was in British Africa. First of
all, the British deliberately based the colonial army
in each territory on a narrow ethnic base among the
least-developed and hopefully least-politicized groups,
systematically omitting other groups, especially those
from the more developed areas. This was so in Ghana,
Nigeria, and Uganda. The general pattern was that in
each colony the whites would compose the officer corps
to command native troops. Even during World War II,
when African armies fought heroically in the Far East,
North Africa, and Ethiopia against the Italians, the
highest rank that able Africans could aspire to was
a mere warrant officer, class one.

The British Army Council in 1948 continued the
practice of limiting the ranks of African officers in
colonial armies, the idea of allowing the African genuine officer status being long resisted. Such had
been the downgrading of the African that it was believed he could not manage even some basic NCO responsibilities, such as orderly room sergeant, regimental
and company quartermaster sergeant, signals sergeant,

and vehicle mechanic.[14]   Seldom were Africans permitted
to have powers of discipline over these ranks.   With
such a philosophy, therefore, real training of an efficient, knowledgeable officer corps among Africans was
delayed far too long.   British West Africa did not begin regular officer training until 1953 at the Teshie
Training School, and the East African armies did not
begin a comparable program until 1958.   In Central
Africa the first local course began at Ndola in 1964.
The first few Nigerian and Ghanaian officers trained
abroad were not commissioned until 1947.   The first
East Africans went to Sandhurst in 1959 when this
region was contemplating independence within two years.
Table 11.1 clearly shows the inadequacy of the African
officer corps on independence in a number of states.

TABLE 11.1 Army Africanization on Independence

Country	Year of Independence	Approximate Size of Army on Independence	Commissioned Officers		
			European or Asian	African	% African
Uganda	1962	1,000	50	14	21.9[a]
Tanganyika	1961	2,000	58	6	9.4
Malawi	1964	750	40	9	8.4
Zambia	1964	2,200	134	1	0.7
Nigeria	1960	8,000	320	57	15.1
Ghana	1957	7,000	184	27	12.8
Sierra Leone	1961	1,000	50	9	15.2

[a] Half of these Ugandan officers were trained at Sandhurst or Mons military academies in England. The others were, like Amin, promoted from the ranks.

Source: J. M. Lee, *African Armies and Civil Order* (New York: Frederick A. Praeger, 1969), p. 44. It should be noted several of the commissioned officers had risen from the ranks.

If the Africans were neglected and deprived at
the higher combat ranks in their armies, they were
worse off in the specialized fields, important posts
in every well-integrated army.   There were virtually
no corps of engineers, doctors, communications experts,
or pilots in most armies by independence.   When these
armed forces found themselves compelled to take over
governments a few years after independence, therefore,
they were too inadequately prepared to handle the complex, wide-ranging problems that faced their states.
Like the civilians they ousted, they had been denied
the opportunity to wield real decision-making power,
having been accustomed always to taking orders from
colonial officers.   Where they have done well as rulers
it has often been through their use of more knowledgeable civilian bureaucrats and other specialists.   While

it is true that crash programs to train these armies
were launched after independence, the results were not
always positive as newly qualified officers found important positions already filled by upgraded NCOs who
looked at them with suspicion. In any case, a decade
and one-half is a short time to build up expertise,
even in the best circumstances. It is largely because
of such inadequacy and consequent inability to do better than the politicians that there have been -- and
are likely to be -- successive coups d'etat in several
nations, with new groups within the army toppling or
attempting to topple their fellow incumbent officers
from power.

The Limited Nature of the Army's Mandate To Govern

We have already indicated that when the army intervenes to seize power, more often than not it is
because of serious conflict among civilian politicians
to which the soldiers themselves are not immune. It
is seldom if ever that the army intervenes as a unified
organization. What generally happens is that there
are several rival groups within the army that mirror
the civilian conflict. One of these boldly seizes
power (ostensibly in the name of the entire armed forces) to save the country, and immediately moves to impose its will on rival groups by methods that range
from their discharge and imprisonment to outright
physical liquidation, as is discussed later. Admittedly, there is often widespread support for most coups
from a broad cross section of the people because of
public relief at the demise of some detested unpopular
regime, as in the examples already discussed. But the
truth of the matter is that the soldier's mandate is
the barrel of his gun, his monopoly of violence in
society, and his consequent capacity to impose his will
on the general population.
It is therefore fair to say that army rulers generally start with a more limited popular base of support in comparison with the independence civilian
regimes at the time they were first popularly elected.
Since both groups are similarly susceptible to the
divisions that afflict their societies, both can become equally unpopular. The army's advantage of the
monopoly of arms becomes weakened because of its fragmentation and consequently the likelihood that another
faction of it may overthrow the incumbent group.
But it seems inescapable in the African situation
to conclude that in spite of these shortcomings, the
armies of Africa are destined for a significant role
in government for a long time to come. (See Table 11.2

TABLE 11.2 Black Africa: Occurrence of Coups, 1963–1978

Country	Year of Independence	Population (millions) by Mid-1975	Number of Coups	Dates of Coups
Botswana	1966	0.7	0	
Burundi	1962	3.8	2	Nov. 28, 1966; Nov. 2, 1976
Cameroon	1960	6.4	0	
Central African Republic	1960	1.8	1	Jan. 1, 1966
Chad	1960	4.0	1	Apr. 14, 1975
Comoro	1976	0.0	1	May 13, 1978
Congo/Brazzaville	1960	1.3	2	Aug. 15, 1963; Aug. 4, 1968
Benin (formerly Dahomey)	1960	3.1	6	Oct. 23, 1963; Nov. 29, 1965; Dec. 22, 1965; Dec. 17, 1967; Dec. 10, 1969; Oct. 26, 1971
Equatorial Guinea	1968	0.3	0	
Ethiopia	—	28.0	1	Sept. 12, 1974
Gabon	1960	0.5	0	
Gambia	1965	0.5	0	
Ghana	1957	9.9	3	Feb. 24, 1966; Jan. 13, 1972; June 4, 1979
Guinea	1958	4.4	0	
Ivory Coast	1960	4.9	0	
Kenya	1963	13.3	0	
Leosotho	1966	1.1	0	
Liberia	1847	1.7	0	
Malagasy	1960	8.0	1	May 18, 1972
Malawi	1964	4.9	0	
Mali	1960	5.7	1	Nov. 19, 1968
Mauritania	1960	1.3	1	July 10, 1978
Niger	1960	4.6	1	Apr. 15, 1974
Nigeria	1960	62.9	3	Jan. 15, 1966; July 29, 1966; July 29, 1975
Rwanda	1962	4.2	1	July 5, 1973
Senegal	1960	4.4	0	
Seychelles	1976	0.06	1	June 5, 1977
Sierra Leone	1961	3.0	3	Mar. 21, 1967; Mar. 23, 1967; Apr. 18, 1968
Somalia	1960	3.2	1	Oct. 21, 1969
Swaziland	1968	0.5	0	
Tanzania	1961	15.4	0	
Togo	1960	2.2	2	Jan. 13, 1963; Jan. 13, 1967
Uganda	1962	11.5	2	Feb. 22, 1966; Jan. 25, 1971
Upper Volta	1960	6.0	2	Jan. 3, 1966; Feb. 8, 1974
Zaire	1960	24.5	2	Sep. 14, 1960; Nov. 25, 1965
Zambia	1964	5.0	0	

[a]Total number of coups since independence = 38.

Source: Samuel Decalo, Coups and Army Rule in Africa: Studies in Military Rule (New Haven, Conn., Yale University Press, 1976), pp. 11-12, Table 1.2 with adaptations.

for the occurrence of coups since independence.) Those
who think their incidence will be shortlived have to
note that after about one and one-half centuries of
independence, most Latin American states are still
dominated by the military. To be sure, instability
might still continue as one armed faction deposes the
other. As Edmund Burke so eloquently observed when
pleading for the American Colonies, "The use of force
alone is but temporary. It may subdue for a moment,
but it does not remove the necessity of subduing again:
and a nation is not governed, which is perpetually to
be conquered."[15] Whether it is the civilians or the
military who govern, therefore, it would still be vital
to do so on the basis of sound principles if instability is to be avoided or diminished and real development
is to have a fair chance of success.

The Prospects for Nigeria and Ghana

If we lament at the proliferation of violent upheavals in postindependence Africa, we cannot fail to
take heart at the insistence with which countries so
adversely affected have courageously tried to reestab-
lish representative, democratic government. It is in
this hopeful context that the efforts of Nigeria and
Ghana to revert from military rule to civilian government should be viewed. True, in Ghana no formula has
yet been devised for carrying this out. Yet so strong
is the desire that when the former military head of
state, Ignatius Achempong, tried to maneuver the army
into a position of permanent political power by advocating "union government" he was swiftly deposed with
popular approbation.
Nigeria offers the greatest hope so far for political redemption. No one can minimize the complexity
of operating a democracy here considering the diversity
of its people and the nature of its history. But
equally, none should deny the sincerity of the present
military rulers to return Nigeria into the hands of a
democratically elected government. Under a carefully
planned and executed program, steps have been taken
towards holding a national election and choosing a
president, taking special care that every political
party and presidential candidate has national and not
merely regional commitment and support. One most fer-
vently wishes Nigeria to succeed. If this most populous black state demonstrates successfully that it is
feasible to return to civilian rule, it could well set
an example for several militarily dominated states.
No doubt there are cynics who say it will not last,
the same people who predicted chaos for Kenya after

Kenyatta's death. But there are enough people of good
will around the world who realize that the establishment of a stable democratic rule in Africa is a necessary component for those who truly aspire to global
peace.

Yet the civilian successors have been amply warned
both by recent history and specifically by the military
rulers. Africa is replete with examples of leaders
who were toppled because of bad government. In Ghana,
where the army had commendably handed power over to
the elected government of Prime Minister Busia, it in-
tervened later (as we saw) and overthrew him on charges
of bad government. The current Nigerian head of state,
General Olusegun Obasanjo, has clearly warned civilian
successors against a repetition of the failings that
plunged Nigeria into costly bloody turmoil. What one
can say at this moment is that there is greater awareness among the aspiring political leadership of what
would or would not disrupt the country in the exercise
of political power, more than there was certainly at
the time of independence.

12
The Military Regime
of Idi Amin in Uganda

No regime in Africa demonstrated the failings of
military rule at their worst as did that of Idi Amin
in Uganda. All the shortcomings we have thus far considered are manifested here in a clearly extreme form.
Yet when Amin deposed Obote on 25 January 1971, his
coup was welcomed with intense joy in most parts of
Uganda. The masses of people who greeted Obote's fall
in the capital and other areas of the country exceeded
those who had gathered to celebrate independence, both
in numbers and emotional release. I witnessed both.
There had been a general expectation and hope that the
military regime would remove the ills of Obote's civilian dictatorship and offer the country another chance
for a new start. Sadly, however, it is a matter of
incontrovertible record that within a short period of
time Idi Amin's regime had become so utterly tyranni-
cal, so sadistic, and so incompetent that by comparison
it made Obote's dictatorship seem mild and humane.

It would, however, be unjust and misleading to
regard Amin as representative of African military rulers; despite their handicaps, some of them have in
fact rendered invaluable service to their states.
Amin was exceptional and clearly magnified whatever
actual or potential shortcomings military rule might
manifest in general. The ignorance and brutality with
which he faced the task of governing the country were
unmatched by any government that independent Africa
has thus far produced.

Often, Amin boasted that the military were more
competent to govern than civilians. He asserted how
army governments can act more speedily and decisively
than their civilian counterparts. But what in actual
fact was his rule like? How far did he fall short of
his claims? Let us consider the following brief record of his rule.

THE DEVALUATION OF HUMAN LIFE

The function of any government, by whatever name, is to protect and enhance the sanctity of human life. But Amin repudiated this fundamental purpose with the most brutal and comprehensive methods that Uganda had ever known. These activities were in three basic areas.

Eliminating the Rule of Law and Basic Rights

In March 1971, Amin's government granted extensive powers of arrest to all the security forces.[1] The practical effect of these powers was widespread repression by the army -- and especially by his personal security units -- whose personnel stood above the law to which they ruthlessly subjected the nationals they were supposed to protect. Preventive detention of citizens, which Amin had cited as one of the reasons to justify removing Obote, was now reenacted as Decree No. 7 in March 1971. Its purpose was to give the military rulers power to arrest and detain political suspects. But its safeguards were without exception ignored. Thousands were to be detained and then slaughtered using this legality.

By Decree No. 8 of 8 May 1972, Amin empowered security forces to shoot to kill -- or, as he said, "Shoot on sight" -- anyone they suspected of being kondo, a local word for "robber." Under this license, his henchmen slaughtered thousands of people in the name of combating robbery. By the time the decree was repealed, considerable loss of innocent life had already occurred.

Decree No. 8 of May 1972 was one of the most significant decrees. This granted the government immunity from any court proceedings as a result of any of its actions or those of its security forces, dating from the eve of the coup against Obote until a date never specified. (Obote had sought similar immunity in 1966 to excuse the excesses of his own revolution, as has been described.) This meant that armed forces personnel could commit unwarranted arrests, mass murders, and ill treatment of their citizens without challenge in a court of law. As the International Commission of Jurists correctly noted in its objective indictment against Amin, "The armed forces are placed outside the law. In the most literal sense, the rule of law has been abandoned."[2]

But there was no more tragic symbol of the eclipse of the rule of law than in the brutal murder of the chief justice of Uganda, Benedicto Kiwanuka. He had strenuously stood for the rights of the individual against their widespread abuse by the security forces and especially by Amin's killer squads. (He had taken the same stand against Obote's dictatorship while leading the DP, for which Obote had detained him without trial.) On 8 September he ruled in favor of a foreign businessman who had been arbitrarily detained. Firmly, he stated that "the military forces of this country have no powers of arrest of any kind whatsoever." Within two weeks, on 21 September, the chief justice was arrested in the morning hours in his chambers by armed men of Amin's security forces who escorted him to a waiting car in the presence of petrified witnesses and subsequently murdered him. Of course, Amin promptly denied any hand in the crime and blamed the guerrillas, who had nothing to do with it. No judge or magistrate, with this brutal crime as an example, could ever again defy the military regime regarding its massive abuse of people's rights and lives. The rule of law was both symbolically and literally destroyed.

Widespread Loss of Human Life

The most terrifying aspect of the absence of the rule of law was the unparalleled scale of mass killings of Ugandans at the hands of the security forces, particularly Amin's killer squads. It is impossible to give a proper estimate of lives lost. Ordinarily, such information can only be gathered through the administrative machinery of the state. Since Amin's government did not permit anyone to do this, the exact number of the dead will never be known, especially where 90 percent of the people were rural. The difficulty in ascertaining the number is reflected in the wide range of estimates. For example, the International Commission of Jurists estimated the number killed by May 1974 to be between 25,000 and 250,000. Tens of thousands of others are estimated to have been killed later in the massacres that took the life of Archbishop Janan Luwum and particularly those of February/March 1977, when Amin allegedly was foiling a plot against his own life. How many others lost their lives before the end of his rule is anyone's guess.

The fact is that Amin found physical liquidation of supposed enemies the simplest and the most efficient form of dealing with them. But for everyone he killed, he increased the number of his potential enemies manifold. He therefore had to continue killing in order to stay alive and in power. As long as he stayed alive, no numbers were too staggering to slaughter as it seemed to him the only way to preserve himself or to preside over what is now the ruin of Uganda.

There is no method of unlawfully taking human life that should be considered preferable. Yet the sordid manner in which Amin's killer squads disposed of their victims has shocked most human beings around the world. Consider these examples: Some like Francis Walugembe, former mayor of Masaka, had their genitals cut off, stuffed into their mouths, and then were dragged through the town tied to a Land Rover. The decapitated head of Basil Bataringaya, former minister of internal affairs, was driven around and put on display in the garrison town of Mbarara. Hundreds of prisoners, especially at the notorious Makindye prison, were lined up and given heavy hammers to blow their neighbors' brains out, only to have the survivors themselves shot by drunken troops. But it seems the standard practice of eliminating the thousands of unwanted soldiers, especially from Acholi and Lango, was to decimate them in military exercises, particularly on the border with Tanzania. Others are known to have been locked up in buildings, which were then blown up with explosives. The range of methods of killing was as wide as it is revolting and bizarre. Each time Amin had an explanation. If it was not outright denial of responsibility for the deaths, the blame was put on the guerrillas, or it was said that those missing had simply gone into exile, when everyone else -- including their families -- knew they had been murdered. Amin even set up a phony commission of inquiry, which predictably absolved him of all blame. Admittedly, there have been deaths committed by Amin, his agents, or by others through deliberate misinformation from one Ugandan against another, or (as is believed) committed by foreign agents on their own fishing expeditions in our turbulent waters. But these cases cannot objectively excuse, let alone absolve, him of direct responsibility for the general loss of life.

Crippling or Destroying National Institutions

Obote had abolished the opposition, deviously evaded elections, and downgraded participatory democracy on the local and national levels. But Parliament, though cowed, still remained, and political activity, though stifled, still somehow persisted within the UPC. One of Amin's first acts, however, was to abolish Parliament and all political activity. By Decree No. 3 of 4 February 1971, he was given the sole power to promulgate all decrees. The result was to vest himself of all legislative, executive, and military powers. Decree No. 2 dissolved all district and

municipal councils, which had been so closely tied to
serving the people at the grass roots. Thus, the
national institutions of representative government,
which Uganda had had since the commencement of the
first legislature in 1921, were now declared extinct,
without any substitutes. On 23 March 1971, by Decree
No. 14 all political activities were suspended, decep-
tively "as a temporary measure to allow the military
government time to reconstruct the economy, reorganize
the administration, and restore public order and tran-
quility." None of these were achieved; the ban on
political activity became permanent; and Idi Amin proclaimed himself president for life.

The judiciary did not fare much better. We out-
lined the repudiation of the rule of law and the murder
of the chief justice. Another vivid illustration of
the intimidation of the judiciary is cited by the
International Commission of Jurists, and I quote it
in full:

> During the allocation of businesses left behind
> by expelled Asians, Mr. Samson Ddungu, a business-
> man, had acquired a cinema together with an army
> man. This army man later alleged that Ddungu had
> stolen 50,000 shillings from the business.
>
> Mr. Ddungu was arrested by one of Amin's security
> units, the Public Safety Unit, and was taken to
> court for theft. He engaged a Kampala lawyer,
> Mr. Enos Ssebunnya, who defended him successfully
> and secured his acquittal. Immediately, the sec-
> urity head of the Public Safety Unit attempted to
> arrest Ddungu in the courtroom, but the magis-
> trate warned that the acquitted man should not be
> arrested.
>
> When Ddungu's lawyer, Ssebunnya, left the court-
> room, he was arrested and taken to Naguru prison
> where, for some days he was interrogated as to
> why he had defended criminals. The advocate was
> badly tortured and beaten up. The Uganda Law
> Society protested strongly to the attorney general.
> Eventually, Mr. Ssebunnya was released with ser-
> ious bruises. Realizing that he would eventually
> be arrested and killed he has since fled Uganda.
> Meanwhile, in Buganda Road Court, in the center
> of Kampala, when Ddungu left the courtroom he was
> chased and fired upon. He hid in the nearby YWCA
> hostel but was pulled out and shot to death.[3]

In February 1973, the judiciary complained to Amin
that "members of the security forces turn up in court

and demand that someone be sent to jail or that someone be prosecuted. Very often members of the security
forces, when called to give evidence, fail to turn up
and no explanations are given. At times when they do
turn up they refuse to answer questions put to them."[4]
    There were two further reasons that accounted
for the decline of the judicial system under Amin.
The first was an almost complete ignorance of the function and processes of the legal system and its value
to the stability of society. Having been placed above
the law, the killer squads under Amin saw no point in
the judicial process, especially as most of those involved in its abuse did not understand it anyway.
The second reason was that the increasing tendency to
entrust (or to threaten to entrust) military tribunals
with all the serious crimes in the state usurped the
criminal jurisdiction of regular courts and as a consequence it demoralized and emasculated them.
    Amin's increasing preference for military tribu-
nals was because they took a very short time to try
people. The rules of evidence were completely violated, and the rights of the accused were rendered nonexistent. No one who appeared before these military
tribunals was ever acquitted. As far as is known, the
sentence on conviction was always death by the firing
squad. Still, as gross an abuse of the legal process
as this was, military tribunals functioned relatively
few times. The reason was simply that it was useless
to go through any legal process at all (even a false
one) if there was no credible evidence to be used
against a person, a person who could simply be murdered
without any fear of retribution. Ignorance, arbitrariness, and murder, therefore, were at the heart of the
destruction of the judicial process.

CHAOTIC FOREIGN POLICY

    The diverse nations of this planet -- communist
and capitalist, developed and developing -- manage to
live together because basically, despite serious imperfections noted in this book, they have established a
set of rules by which international relations are conducted. It is possible for leadership in a country to
repudiate some of them, for instance if its vital interests are prejudiced, but even then it is according
to rules. When Amin took over the dictatorship of
Uganda, however, he was totally ignorant of these rules
and their attendant diplomacy. His ignorance was reinforced and maintained by his instinctive will to
survive against the local and external hostility that

his wild conduct had unleashed. To him, no laws or rules literally existed, domestically or internationally, except those that coincided with his whims, however outrageous such whims or ambitions were to the rest of mankind.

As a result, Amin alienated most of his former friends. In East Africa he antagonized Kenya by claiming extensive parts of its territory, slandered its leaders, and threatened its security, despite the fact that Kenya had supported his overthrow of Obote. Since Uganda is a landlocked state and largely dependent on the Kenyan port of Mombasa, an angry Kenyan government began to put economic pressures on Uganda, with devastating effect. Suddenly, for example, railroad cars on the East African railway line passing through Kenya began to disappear, until at one time, by Amin's own admission in 1977, there were 2 million tons of coffee (Uganda's chief export) in Uganda that could not be sent through to the Kenya port of Mombasa.

It is true that shortly after taking power, Amin had a good case against President Nyerere's efforts to return Obote to the Ugandan presidency, having given Obote refuge after his ouster. With all his idealism and humanity, Nyerere seemed totally uninformed about the reality of the situation concerning Obote, that he had lost support in Uganda and was responsible for the tragedy that was beginning to unfold. Although Nyerere's condemnation of Amin's tyranny was a most welcome voice to Ugandans, the majority of them were not prepared to exchange Amin for Obote as there was so much linking both of them to Uganda's misfortune. Yet, even when Amin might have had a good case in the first year of his rule to attack Tanzania's efforts to depose him, he lacked the political skill and diplomatic approach to win sympathy for his side. Instead, he blundered about, attacked President Nyerere, and called him unprintable names, which no self-respecting head of state seeking international credibility and stature would have done.

Internationally he fared no better. He created too many powerful enemies in quick succession without the slightest idea of their retaliatory capabilities. By insisting on the expulsion of tens of thousands of British Asians, he was creating a considerable problem for Great Britain. But Uganda was still tied to Great Britain more than to any other country, especially in all aspects of modernizing development. When, in addition to the expulsion of the Asians, Amin expropriated British properties without compensation, Britain retaliated by waging diplomatic and economic harrassment on Uganda through her extensive contacts,

the consequences of which further depressed the Ugandan economy and development. Amin knew of the friendship between Britain and Kenya, for example, but he
did not consider how it might be turned against him
until it actually had happened.

His first move against traditional friends had
been the expulsion of Israelis and the takeover of
their businesses. The Israelis had been very close
to Amin, had trained him and part of his army, and
were undertaking several projects in Uganda. But he
turned against them with an intense bitterness that
astonishingly exceeded that exhibited by Arab heads
of state who have long been the traditional enemies
of Israel. He could thus publicly praise Hitler, in
a cable to the secretary-general of the United Nations,
for having exterminated Jews. Months later, to the
embarrassment of the Soviet diplomats who were hosting
a reception in Kampala to mark the Russian revolution
-- at which Amin was guest of honor -- he stated that
he was going to erect a monument to Hitler in south-
western Uganda. Amin did not know that the Soviet
Union had lost more people fighting Adolf Hitler than
any other country in the world. Under normal circumstances his remarks would have been highly objectionable, but the Russians who had become his patrons
swallowed the utterance and simply pointed out that
Hitler had been a bad man because he caused so much
suffering to so many people. Amin then said he understood, and claimed to have fought in World War II,
which Hitler had unleashed -- a false claim.

The alienation of Britain and Israel, which Amin
did not try to resolve, meant its spread in varying
degrees to most Western countries that had supported
the Ugandan economy and development. The United States
closed down its embassy in Kampala and ceased its aid.
Canada, which was offering substantial support for
development projects in the country, cut off most of
its aid, partly in retaliation for having had to help
Britain absorb thousands of Asians.

There developed in the West an undeclared commitment to cripple the Ugandan economy, even if it did
not go as far as most Ugandan enemies of Amin wished.
In response, Amin sought alternative patrons. The
Soviet Union promptly replaced Israel in training and
equipping the security forces. A few new Arab friends,
particularly Qaddafi of Libya, became generous finan-
ciers who often bailed him out of impending economic
ruin. But these new-found friends could do no better
than his old ones in helping the recovery of Uganda's
national development. As it had been with Israel and
Britain, so it was now with the Soviet Union and others:

the basic problem remained Amin himself -- his ignorance compounded by an erratic and violent temperament
that had crippled or ruined the infrastructure of the
state and destroyed national development.

ECONOMIC AND SOCIAL RUIN: EXPELLING ASIANS AND CONFISCATING THEIR PROPERTY

Apart from the extensive slaughter of his citizens,
none of Idi Amin's measures was as controversial as his
abrupt and ruthless order to expel Asians from Uganda
and take over their wealth.

The Asian community had come to East Africa from
the Indian subcontinent at the end of the last century
when both areas were ruled by the British. Having
helped to construct the railway from Mombasa to Uganda,
they were encouraged by the British to settle in the
country and develop its commerce and trade. They did
it well, and the modern sector of Uganda's economic
development owed much to their skill and enterprise.
So successful were they that although there were fewer
than 70,000 Asians in a country of more than eleven
million they controlled more than 80 percent of Uganda's commerce and trade. However, throughout the era
of colonial rule there had consequently grown considerable resentment among the majority of Africans that
their wealth should be controlled by a small immigrant
community. There were violent boycotts by Africans of
Asian shops in colonial times that had been suppressed
without an attempt to meet their grievance of being
kept out of the commercial life of the country. The
independent government of Milton Obote was constantly
faced with the problem of how to bring the African into
the modern sector of the economy, but the results of
its efforts were minimal. To aggravate the disparity
in wealth that accentuated the differences in race,
the majority of the Asian community kept to themselves
socially. In addition, most of them, although offered
an opportunity to apply for Ugandan citizenship, chose
to retain British nationality. Nevertheless several
thousands, especially the poorer and younger ones, had
opted to become Ugandan nationals. When Idi Amin took
power early in 1971, therefore, the historic problem
of integrating the Asian community and Africanizing
commerce and industry still awaited an equitable solution.

Amin has claimed that his order to expel the
Asians and expropriate their property was a directive
from God in a dream. That is nonsense. Two basic
reasons were foremost for his expulsion of the Asians.

The first was rooted in his experience during the
Zaire civil war. Having fought and taken part in
the capture and looting of several towns in East Zaire,
he had vividly realized how the use of sheer violence
easily brought wealth overnight. The shops, the mines,
and the banks in some of these towns had provided in-
stant affluence. The idea was then born to apply the
same principle to the helpless but much wealthier
Asian community within his domain. The method of re-
distributing wealth through the conventional use of
legislation, compensation, etc., was too laborious,
too complicated, and certainly would have taken far
too long for his restless nature. There was only one
viable option to him: use the guns to expel the aliens
and take over their wealth.

The second reason for expelling the Asians played
on Amin's first disposition to loot. It was Amin's
increasing need to appease mounting opposition against
him in the army by distributing this undreamed of
wealth to his troops, thus keeping them loyal. This
applied equally to the civilian population who were
becoming disenchanted with his rule. If he could dis-
tribute some of this wealth to many of the individuals
in all the towns throughout the country, he shrewdly
calculated the move would give him a renewed surge of
popularity. He had judged correctly. The disillusionment and resentment that was to set in at a later stage
should not obscure the fact that the vast majority of
Ugandans welcomed the expulsion of the Asian community,
whose economic dominance they had long resented but
had been helpless to change. With a rigid deadline of
three months, Amin expelled the Asian community, who
departed with deep heartbreak, most of them almost des-
titute.

Faced with a fait accompli they had no power to
change, many of Amin's civilian advisers tried to cush-
ion the impact and harshness of his moves. For example, as his ambassador to the United Nations, where
Britain assailed the move, I insisted that to be credible Amin's expulsion order had to comply with at least
three basic principles: (1) both those who left and
others who remained were to be free from threats to
their lives; (2) there would be fair compensation paid
to those whose properties were expropriated, in due
course; and (3) Asians who were citizens of Uganda were
to remain and be accorded all the rights of Ugandan
nationals. I delivered these as Amin's undertakings
to the General Assembly of the United Nations.

Several ministers tried their best to ensure that
the exercise was carried out as humanely as possible.
They also exerted pressure so as to make it untenable

for Amin to expel Asians who were Ugandan citizens.
But as the exercise got under way and by the time the
expulsion came to a close, it was clear that most of
the undertakings had been repudiated in action. Amin
decided to expel all Asians including Ugandan citizens,
and to my mind this was one of the very worst aspects
of the tragedy. It is within the power of every sovereign state if necessary to expropriate property on
payment of fair compensation or to expel resident
aliens if it is deemed in the national interest. Sri
Lanka (formerly Ceylon) had expelled several million
resident aliens from the Indian subcontinent who had
settled there, and had taken over and compensated them
for their properties. Ghana had expelled a million
Nigerians. In both these cases it was essentially for
economic reasons. But, it is unmitigated brutality
for a government to expel thousands of its own citizens, thus rendering them stateless, as Idi Amin did
to those Asians who had genuinely taken Ugandan citizenship. In a real sense it devalued our nationality
both inside and outside the country.
     Apart from the hardship to the Asians, there was
an immediate and calamitous hardship placed on the
economy of the country. Amin had made no contingency
plans for keeping the economic activity of the country
going once those who operated it were abruptly removed.
Asian businesses were distributed to Africans who, in
most cases, were totally unfamiliar with them. For
example, a new owner would suddenly take over a shop
or factory without the slightest idea of where his
stock came from, how to order replacements, and how
to keep accounts. Invariably, such new owners sold
off all the goods in the business (sometimes worth
millions of shillings), locked up the empty shop, returned its keys to the Ministry of Commerce, declared
that they were no longer interested in the business,
and left as very wealthy persons. Only a few of the
Ugandan entrepreneurs who had the capability of running
such businesses were given one. The initial jubilation
of the masses over the expropriations soon developed
into mixed feelings, envy, and outright anger as the
system of allocating the Asian businesses to nationals
became manifestly unfair. Amin had initially set up
committees in his predominantly civilian cabinet of
competent men for allocating the businesses to Ugandans
on merit. On balance, they tried to do so, but his
military cronies were outraged because they demanded
the lion's share of these businesses. New allocation
committees were consequently formed, which were dominated by soldiers, with the result that in a good many
cases people were given business enterprises they were

totally unequipped to manage.

Two fundamental problems arose from these massive expropriations. The first problem concerned whether the state or private individuals should have taken over all businesses. Rightly, most of the large businesses became state-owned. Yet quite a number that might have been better if state-managed still went to individuals who Amin favored, even if they had no idea how to run them. As a result, one of the necessary tasks of the post-Amin government is to review the entire disposition of the Asians' goods. This task is not made easier by the fact that a lot of valuable property has disappeared without a trace. Another unavoidable problem is that a fair price will have to be paid for every property left by the Asians. It is incredible that no one who took this wealth has paid for it. Even when solid, bonafide Ugandan citizens were ready and expecting to pay, they were never required to do so. No sound government can tolerate arbitrarily distributing hundreds of millions of dollars in free grants to a few nationals and aliens. Indeed, one by-product of Amin's seizure of property was that under his rule the legal title to property, however small, was almost meaningless. Throughout the country, when an Amin favorite fancied any citizen's property he simply dispossesed the owner, however secure his title. Often, in such cases if the owner was not killed, he was intimidated to flee the country so that the looter could enjoy the booty in peace. Might made right.

Within a few months, the adverse effects of the so-called economic war were already stamped on the republic. The production and distribution of goods, formerly dominated by Asians and currently unreplaced with qualified people, were now in total disarray. Scarcity of the most basic commodities that nationals regarded as necessities of life soon became chronic. Foreign exchange, so necessary for external trade, increasingly became limited to military appropriations and to a small clique of Amin's favorites. The professions (especially medicine, law, teaching, and construction), which had been significantly manned by Asians, were now badly crippled. Because of the breakdown in social services (such as medical care), diseases that had for decades been unknown or had declined returned with a vengeance to afflict rural and urban populations alike. Infant mortality dramatically rose.

As of 1977 the economy, resilient and basically sound as it was, was on the brink of collapse. Consider these stark facts about Uganda's industries.

o Coffee. The nation's number one export had
  fallen by at least 30 percent from an average
  200,000 tons a year, and its quality had declined. About 25 percent of it was smuggled
  through Kenya under circumstances so wild and
  daring as to match a fiction thriller.
o Cotton. Traditionally the second most important crop, cotton had fallen to about one-half
  of what it was in 1972, then averaging 80,000
  tons a year. Ugandan cotton yarn was sold to
  Libya at well below world prices.
o Copper. The third most important source of
  revenues, copper had declined sharply. From
  the 20,000 tons mined yearly through 1974, it
  is now less than 1,000 tons.
o Tea. Close to copper in importance, tea had
  declined by about 25 percent from over 20,000
  tons annually. What was produced was of poor
  quality due to lack of fertilizer, inadequate
  storage, and transportation problems.
o Tourism. One of the best sources of foreign
  exchange had fallen to nothing from 100,000
  visitors in 1972.
o Nyanza Textiles. This is the oldest and largest mill in East Africa. Formerly exporting
  40 percent of its production to Kenya and Tanzania, its output had fallen by 25 percent and
  its exports had ceased. Other mills were running at 30 percent capacity.
o Sugar. The production of sugar had fallen by
  at least 30 percent. There was no longer enough
  local supply of sugar and no surplus for export.[5]

In addition, the following key industries were in
varying degrees of disintegration and decline: Lango
Development Corporation, Tororo Industrial Chemicals
and Fertilisers, Uganda Meat Packers, East African
Distilleries, Uganda Metal Products, Uganda Grain Mill-
ing Corporation, Crane Estates, African Ceramics Corporation, United Garment Industry, Uganda Fishnet Manu-
facturers, oil mills, soap works, and Uganda Fish
Marketing Corporation. The decline in quality and
quantity of leading exports like coffee is made up by
the rise in world prices and the willingness of traditional buyers of Ugandan produce to continue business
as usual.

No one really knows how much of these revenues
Amin spent on the defense budget. But two indicators
show it was disproportionately high. First, in 1976
he ceased publishing the defense budget with the usual
yearly national budget on the grounds (by his own

admission) that he did not want the people to see the figures lest they think they were too high. Second, despite the fact that the country still got substantial revenues from coffee, there was not a single development project except in the armed forces, and government aid was scarce for ordinary people because it had to pay for military hardware. The defense budget was put at between 60 and 70 percent of all foreign earnings. Yet there are persistent rumblings that part of it went into his secret bank accounts abroad. Because he ran the country as a personal estate, there is little likelihood of this being an exaggeration. Under Amin, the economy and the infrastructure that supported it stood on the brink of total collapse without the slightest chance of recovery while he squandered Uganda's scarce resources on sophisticated military hardware that did not fight disease or underdevelopment.

In the long run, however, I have little doubt that his "economic war" will ultimately be beneficial to Uganda. Even in the chaos and brutality of his rule, there developed a substantial group of Ugandan entrepreneurs who were never there in the sixty-eight years of colonial rule or in Obote's nine years of independent government. This development is likely to be irreversible. Amin's unforgiveable sin is that he did not need to cause so much human misery and widespread loss of life to Africanize the Ugandan economy.

WHY AMIN SURVIVED

At the time of this writing, Amin has finally been deposed; however, the question still remains relevant as to why he could terrorize the population and ruin Uganda's economy and still survive the numerous attempts to remove him for so many years. An understanding of his survival may forecast what is in store for several African states, not in an academic, abstract sense but as a distinct possibility where internal and external forces combine to impose a tyrant on a citizenry.

Basically, there were four reasons -- both internal and external -- contributing to why Amin survived. The first was his own character, a combination of guile, buffoonery, and utter ruthlessness in killing off anyone even remotely suspected by him or his subordinates of being unfriendly. This characteristic, initially operating on a trusting, innocent, if not naive population, went a long way to eliminate most

of those in the armed forces who could have credibly
challenged him without arousing nationwide alarm and
resistance. He adopted a method of liquidating his
suspected opponents on the slightest hunch, with the
assumption that it was better to err on the side of
excesses than to take the risk of giving suspects the
benefit of the doubt or keeping them under surveil-
lance.

The second and basic domestic reason was the deep
divisions, rivalries, and jealousies among Uganda's
diverse ethnic groups, especially among their leaders.
These indigenous divisions have often precluded serious
joint efforts to resist tyranny even when it threatened
most of these groups. In this way Amin was able to
liquidate one group's leadership at a time, often while
other groups looked on unconcerned, with indifference,
or even with secret satisfaction, until their own turn
came and they were too exposed and weak to resist successfully. I first observed this weakness in 1966
when the Obote/Amin axis abrogated the Ugandan Constitution, locked up leading ministers, and slaughtered
some thousands of unarmed Baganda. Many leaders and
their supporters in several different areas of the
country publicly congratulated Obote for his "firm"
leadership. Many, secretly or even openly, celebrated
the destruction of the once proud and prosperous Baganda. Few, pitifully few, paused to consider what it
was like to be on the receiving end of machine-gun fire
or to be left an orphan or widow by such callous actions.

When in 1971 Amin overthrew Obote and began a
systematic extermination of Acholi and Langi on a scale
larger than in 1966, a good many among the other tribes
cared little. Others visibly celebrated because these
two tribes had been Obote's elite corps, which in its
heyday had itself dispensed its own brand of repression. Again, few leaders of other unaffected groups
felt sufficiently outraged or threatened by the tragedy that was overtaking the Acholi and Langi to take
any action. When Amin finished off the effective
leadership of these two groups, he turned on some of
the very tribes that had made it possible for him successfully to overthrow Obote, particularly those of
West Nile. They had helped him to eliminate the other
significant groups but they never paused to consider
the ultimate implications of this tyranny on the state,
much less on themselves. By the time he turned against
them, they were too weak and isolated to resist successfully. By pitting tribe against tribe, religious
group against religious group, Idi Amin was able to
neutralize his enemies, despite the fact that their

combined population and support made his own quite
insignificant. Given such basic divisions in addition
to the secret aid of aliens wanting his survival, it
was relatively easy to establish an extensive, ruthless, and efficient spy apparatus within these very
groups opposed to him, which with success exposed plots
to overthrow him.

Another facet compounding these divisions has been
an obscene and heartless greed on the part of the population to amass wealth at all costs. People from all
walks of life, men and women alike, have sold their
souls, have betrayed their relatives, friends, colleagues, and strangers alike in order to be rewarded
with part of the loot Amin took from the Asians. This
has been all the more tragic because often it has involved the incrimination of innocent victims. The
fact that Amin often later liquidated many of those
he had similarly rewarded did not deter new aspirants
from attempting to lay their hands on that wealth. I
can think of nothing that discredits the concept of
private enterprise more than such a heartless quest
for material possessions, totally devoid of any moral
content or responsibility.

Yet another problem militating against unity was
the unreasonable ambition on the part of some Ugandans, particularly those in exile, who believed they
had a special claim to lead after Amin's fall. In this
way new rivalries were created and old ones were revived or accentuated, as each group in the country or
in exile formed its own shadow cabinet awaiting Amin's
demise. Once the quest for position took precedence
over the actual task of removing Amin, it became extremely difficult to maximize support for it or to
prepare the proper foundations for a just post-Amin
society. This is especially so because the groups
that were left out turned into real or potential rivals
-- to be avoided or opposed -- instead of needed allies. In this way, the disastrous seeds of a winner-
take-all philosophy are sown by future Ugandan leaders.
For example, it was common knowledge among exiles that
there were occasions when Amin was about to be overthrown by one group but was indirectly tipped off beforehand by another group. This was the result of
the first group not including the second group in the
plans or accepting its leadership. In this way, Idi
Amin was assisted and enabled to survive by his enemies. Ugandans' failure to unite in a common cause,
most especially when in peril, has provided the most
solid and plausible ground for the establishment of
a dictatorship even now that Amin is gone. We must
face up to the probable consequences of our faults.

The third principal reason for Amin's long survival was the external support he received in security
and financial matters. Indeed, his support from other
powers, directly or indirectly, is a good example of
the variant of subversion discussed elsewhere whereby
a great power maintains a client regime in spite of
the tyranny the regime imposes on its citizenry. Thus,
the Soviet Union stepped in to be the principal sup-
plier of arms and trainer of Amin's enormously expanded
army. They assisted in the training of his intelligence force and defended him in international forums
where he came under attack. This support by a super-
power greatly boosted the morale of his supporters and
correspondingly depressed his domestic enemies.

Dating from the expulsion of the Asians in 1976
but especially from the brutal murder of the archbishop, one got the impression that the West was up in
arms against Amin, at least diplomatically. Seldom
was a leader of any state so denounced and so ridiculed
as Amin was in the Western news media. Great Britain,
in an unprecedented act, broke off diplomatic relations
with Uganda, a Commonwealth country. The United States
closed its embassy in Kampala. Outwardly, therefore,
the West has angrily and consistently denounced and
not supported Amin. But what about privately?

Alas, there is abundant evidence to show that, in
fact, the West gave Amin the crucial support to survive
by continuing business relations with him. Despite
Soviet arms, Amin might have been toppled sooner had
the West not continued giving him the support with
which to prop up his otherwise ruined economy. The
money he needed so desperately to keep his troops and
bodyguard happy was largely from Ugandan coffee, which
he sold to the West and especially to the United States.
When the Kenyan railroad would not carry the coffee to
the coast, an American airline company, Seaboard Corporation, stepped in to ferry it abroad.[6] By early
1977, the United States was paying Amin more than $20
million a month for this coffee. Between Uganda and
Britain, too, there was a weekly airlift in Ugandan
planes of crucial commodities and merchandise so badly
needed to keep Amin's security men well supplied and
happy. This support ensured that Amin's troops and
bodyguard, who alone could easily have eliminated him,
were contented and insulated from the general deprivation affecting the country. A seasoned observer on
the East African scene reported: "No less a survival
factor are the British and American professionals,
businessmen, and technicians, about 500, who keep
essential services going, and without whom the whole
rickety edifice would have come tumbling down long

ago."7

If the West had really seriously opposed Amin and had genuinely wished for his departure, why in fact did they provide him with the crucial financial and business support to prolong his survival? They might argue that boycotting his business would have only meant his looking for other markets. Yet they should have known this would not have been easy. The economy of Uganda was and is so closely tied to its traditional markets in the West that if there had been a concerted effort the chances were great that Amin would not have survived the crises before he was able to establish alternative trading partners. On the other hand, the West might argue that a total trade embargo against Amin would have punished the vast majority of Ugandans who were innocent of his outrages. Yet it is no secret that the vast majority of Ugandans hardly benefitted from the revenues Amin received from the West. As far as Ugandans were concerned, having already been forced into subsistence living, a trade boycott of Amin would have made no difference. They received nothing anyway from what went on. Actually, there was a whole range of alternatives open to the West that they either neglected, discounted, or half-heartedly attempted. At long last, the U.S. government in August 1978 imposed economic sanctions against the Amin regime. It is worth noting, though, that this was done at the insistence of determined congressmen while the State Department had consistently resisted imposing any type of sanctions against him. The bitter and sobering lesson from all this is that by and large the alien powers, East and West alike, are largely opportunistic, being primarily motivated by their own self-interest. The rhetoric and high-sounding righteousness about human rights when closely examined become merely or largely polemical and propagandistic.

The burden becomes all the greater for the nationals in such a situation to realize that their own salvation cannot come from a mythical, redeeming power but their own sweat and blood. The later dramatic intervention of Tanzania to assist decisively in toppling Amin could not remove the burden of doing so from the nationals themselves.

The fourth basic reason for Amin's survival was that the regrettably different approaches to Amin by Uganda's closest neighbors, Tanzania and Kenya, denied these countries a common policy in working for his overthrow. Though at some stage Kenya quarreled with Amin, later Uganda became an invaluable trade partner and Ugandans began to feel increasing resentment that Kenya had a vested interest in perpetuating Amin's rule. Although Tanzania had been consistent in opposing and denouncing Amin, for some time it was presumed completely committed to Obote's restoration to power. While the majority of Ugandans warmly applauded President Nyerere's denunciation of Amin, they were apprehensive of Obote's return. This meant anti-Amin forces could not be joined in a decisive effort to overthrow him until as late as March 1979.

IDI AMIN IN PERSPECTIVE

Amin has meant different things to different people. As a result, his true nature and that of his rule have often been obscured by misguided though often understandable emotional reaction. To some Africans and Afro-Americans beyond the orbit of his repression, for example, he had been regarded as a valiant fighter against the capitalistic or neocolonial exploitation of the Western white man. His rumblings and uncouth denunciations of Western leaders endeared him to such groups, partly because he articulated their own frustrations. The incessant attacks and ridicule of Amin by the Western news media were taken as a reaction to and evidence of his effectiveness to defy and humiliate the imperialists. The truth, however, is that those blacks who hold this image of Amin are in a minority compared with those who regard him as an acute embarrassment and a nightmare for black Africa. The adulation diminished in direct proportion to the increased knowledge about his actual brutality and appalling ignorance. Mistakenly, it was often taken as a sign of support when many African leaders did not openly denounce him. The fact was that they desisted because of the general fragility or arbitrariness of their own regimes where they might themselves be called upon to take measures deserving public censure. By being mute about Amin, they expected, or hoped, that others would be mute against them should they deserve condemnation. The few who consistently and publicly denounced him -- like presidents Kaunda of Zambia and Nyerere of Tanzania -- deserve very special praise. In actual truth, with the exception of one or two African heads of state, Idi Amin had no genuine support or admiration within the Organization of African Unity leadership. More often than not his fellow heads of state and their top advisers laughed him off lightheartedly only to mask the acute embarrassment he caused them.

To the overwhelming majority of his nationals, Amin took on a definite though dreadful form. He was

as capable of considerable affability and hospitality
as he was, in the twinkling of an eye, of limitless
brutality whose hallmark was a total disregard for
human life. Endowed with native intelligence, he was
nevertheless greatly flawed by this propensity to violence. Having had only two or three years of formal
schooling, he was at the very best semiliterate. As
a result, he conducted government business orally,
having assistants read and write papers or briefs for
him. He had extreme suspicion and fear of educated
people. To rule Uganda he had to understand how its
government functioned. He had therefore to rearrange
everything at a level low enough for his own grasp.
In so doing, all the skilled manpower that took decades to train and who are the preeminent resource of
every modern state became irrelevant because he viewed
them as a threat and their methods of administration
as incomprehensible.

Systematically, he destroyed the public service
that even Obote's dictatorship had had the self-interest to maintain. Those who had not been murdered fled
into exile. If they stayed in the country they were
too terrified to do any useful work. His treatment
of political leaders whose knowledge and support would
have assisted his administration was equally callous.
Most of Obote's ministers were violently murdered on
his order, as were other leading parliamentarians.

On 28 January 1971, Amin released all Obote's
political detainees (in a shrewd move to get mass support from their known followings), most of whom he had
himself assisted, directly or indirectly, in imprison-
ing during Obote's dictatorship. They included the
five ministers who had supported his removal from the
army in 1966, and Benedicto Kiwanuka, a distinguished
leader of the opposition. Neither myself nor Kiwanuka
were eager to serve in his regime. Having accused me
publicly in June 1971 of refusing to become ambassador
to the United Nations, he took me to a public meeting
and appealed to my constituents to prevail upon me to
accept. In the jargon of criminal overlords, he made
me an offer I could not refuse. Reluctantly, I went
to the United Nations and, providentially, by getting
out of Uganda, saved my life. Kiwanuka, who had reluctantly agreed to become chief justice, was then
murdered on Amin's orders within a year and a half of
taking office. An extraordinary claim was made by
Obote that Kiwanuka had agreed to work with him to
topple Amin in the abortive invasion of 1972. I had
talked with Kiwanuka several times after our mutual
imprisonment by Obote and know that he bore nothing for
Obote but contempt and anger, knowing that our tragedy

was a result of his misdeeds. There would simply have
been no basis for supporting Obote as Kiwanuka was
probably the most popular and eligible leader in Uganda after Obote's fall. But of course he was not around
to refute Obote's claim. By Amin's deliberate policy
of eliminating technocrats and enlightened political
leaders, he denied himself the only weaponry that in
the final analysis would have sustained him -- their
expertise and following.

One of my first official dealings with Amin was
in 1964. I was leading a Ugandan delegation to discuss
defense matters within the OAU in Addis Ababa. My
delegation consisted of, among others, Idi Amin as my
military adviser. And yet he understood none of the
official languages of OAU, English or French. He
could, therefore, neither read the conference documents
nor participate in the proceedings. Within my own
delegation we could communicate with him only in Swahili or Luganda, both of which he spoke well. But not
only was he handicapped by language -- though we could
always privately translate if necessary -- but even
more fundamentally he had no knowledge of the substantive topics under consideration, which involved complex
geopolitical and economic aspects of the armed struggle
in South Africa. A decade later one can see Amin had
made some improvement and was therefore capable of
learning. But he lacked the sound foundation upon
which to build and it was too much to expect an absolute head of state to have sufficient time to catch
up on what has taken others decades of training and
education. It needs to be emphasized that Amin's
principal shortcoming was not his illiteracy, but his
murderous nature. There were many unschooled men in
the army and outside it who would have made better
presidents. It does not require schooling or ability
to speak foreign tongues before one appreciates that
murder is a heinous crime, that the function of government is to protect life, or that it is necessary
for good government to value skilled and trained personnel. All of us throughout Uganda have illiterate
relatives or friends who would have been much more
humane and reasonable.

Amin was an outrageous fraud. He did not hesitate
to bestow upon himself honors to which he had absolutely no legitimate claim. He coerced Makerere University
to confer a doctorate on him. After receiving another
African president who had a weakness for medals, Amin
promptly awarded himself military honors to the embarrassment of those around him, because they were colonial titles of the British army and could be awarded
only by Britain to someone in combat. But he paraded

them all: the VC (Victoria Cross), the DSO (Distinguished Service Order), and the MC (Military Cross).
He then made himself a field marshall, notwithstanding
the fact that the only war he ever fought in was for
the colonial rulers against the Mau Mau nationalists
in Kenya. Despite the blood of many thousands of innocent people on his hands, he claimed a special relationship with God; having been to Mecca on a pilgrim-
age, he earned the title El Haj. Then, to cap it all
off, he declared himself president for life. All
officers of state and foreign countries were officially
notified that any communication to Amin had to include
all these titles. This, of course, was a vivid illustration of an attempt to compensate for his sense of
extreme inadequacy.

In a thorough and lucid account, his former phy-
sician, a leading Ugandan, Dr. John Kbukamusoke, finally confirmed that Amin's murderous and erratic behavior was partly the result of an advanced syphilitic
condition that afflicted him. It was logical, then,
to expect his condition to worsen and correspondingly
Uganda's ruin to deepen so long as he remained in
power. In contrast, however, many high level officers
of state who served under Amin attested that he was
perfectly responsible for his actions and in full possession of his faculties. His capacity to survive
attempts on his life over several years tended to confirm this.

Idi Amin has been a priceless gift to white ra-
cists. He exemplifies all their distorted beliefs
about the stereotype of a typical black chief: illiterate, brutal, sexually insatiable, and incapable of
any worthy purpose in life. According to this view,
the more publicity given to these negative characteristics the better will the black man's incompetence be
stamped on world consciousness. Also, it will be
easier to justify the excesses of the white minority
regimes against blacks in South Africa, on the grounds
that the African as exemplified by Amin is not capable
of sharing power much less of assuming the sole responsibility for it. This in part explains the extraordinary global publicity given to Amin, although I
know for certain there are governments and people who
seriously cared about what was occurring in Uganda,
even among the countries from which such negative
views are secretly promoted.

Many Africans have increasingly come to believe
that racism is behind Amin's survival. They allege
a conspiracy of sorts, according to which Amin was to
be economically crippled so that no other African
leader could emulate his example of radically African-

izing the national economy. But he was first to be
kept afloat for a while to counterbalance the drastic
measures the minority regimes in South Africa had to
undertake by making them look more humane or no guilt-
ier than Amin. Of course, the Western governments
would indignantly repudiate such allegations, citing
their clearly manifest condemnation of Amin's crimes.
The difficulty would be explaining away that vital
economic nexus from the West that more than anything
else kept him in power. This charge may well be unfounded in fact, but it is so serious that even if
there was only a mere semblance of its being true, we
should consider here whether the promotion and maintenance of an Idi Amin or his type truly assists the
resolution of African problems or promotes the best
interests of any country that does. What is the probable target audience to which such ruthless and
cynical propaganda would be aimed?

First, such propaganda cannot be aimed at the
victims of the tyrant nor the rest of black Africa
where murder has been regarded and punished as the
worst crime in indigenous societies from the dawn of
time. Amin is viewed there as a terrible tyrant who
deserved to be removed. Neither can such propaganda
convince the blacks of southern Africa to accept minority white domination on the ground that their own
leaders would be Idi Amin types. They know better.
Second, the real adversaries of the West in ideological
and military terms who support black liberation movements cannot be moved by this propaganda. On the
contrary, it invariably tends to work to their advantage to abuse or debase blacks thus making them frustrated and hostile to the West. The most important
assistance it gives them, however, is to misdirect by
misinformation enlightened fair-minded Western opinion
that would otherwise constitute a crucial pressure
group in any meaningful effort to bring relatively less
violent change in southern Africa.

Indeed, the Amin propaganda in practical terms
is aimed largely at this enlightened segment of the
West to dissuade it from mounting effective pressure
for change in southern Africa, the type of enlightened
pressure that has in the past ended slavery and the
slave trade and more recently that has made the acceptance of the civil rights revolution for blacks and
other minorities possible in the United States. Assuming that enlightened Western opinion was so emasculated
as to believe that to press for change in southern
Africa was to invite probable Idi Amins, the desired
result would be the maintenance of the status quo in
this troubled region, soothed marginally by cosmetic

ineffectual political, economic, and diplomatic moves.
The probable end result of this would be that the
situation would deteriorate to a point where major
regional violence became inevitable. The real adversaries of the West would then be in a position to move
in with arms to assist what by any objective criteria
was the oppressed masses. At that juncture the West
would have been maneuvered into the painful position
of having to choose between being identified with the
minority incumbent oppressors or the majority who
yearn and struggle for simple justice so manifestly
enshrined in Western philosophy and culture. I do not
wish for such an eventuality; indeed there may be other
less grim scenarios. But none of them can be accomplished by a deliberate policy of secretly or openly
promoting the likes of Idi Amin among African states.

The West has a real reservoir of friendship and
esteem among the vast majority of enlightened African
leaders in every area of society, both in the civilian
and the military segments. If it consciously and vigorously sought to support such types of leaders for
their mutual benefit I believe that a bond would be
forged so strong that no problem, however intractable
(like the southern African one) could not be resolved
by a joint effort to minimize or avoid calamity.

In an exceptional way, the Idi Amin experience
represents proof of my thesis in this book that the
principal causes of African instability are rooted in
a combination of defective colonial legacies and ruthless winner-take-all policies of many independent African leaders. Although the British were in the vanguard
of a global condemnation of Amin's brutal excesses,
they, in fact, materially helped to produce him. If
they had trained an officer corps of educated Ugandans
to lead the army, even if only in the last five years
of their sixty-eight-year rule in Uganda, there would
not have been room for an Amin in the officers rank
when Uganda gained independence in October 1962.

Nevertheless, even if the colonial rulers had
created conditions that made the emergence of Amin
possible, his ascendancy was not unavoidable. The
inevitability of Idi Amin as a power is directly due
to Obote's rigid determination to have him head and
develop the Ugandan army, despite his demonstrated un-
suitability. Obote lavished money and privileges on
Amin and the army. In a consistent and deliberate
manner he encouraged Amin's misuse of defense appropriations for eight years by stifling criticism from
his close colleagues. It was therefore ridiculous
and hypocritical when in the last year of his dictatorship, having decided to remove Amin because he

posed a threat, Obote now gave as the basis for his
proposed action Amin's misuse of public funds. The
bitter enmity between them should not obscure the fact
that at one time and for several years, they were extremely close. In this way, more than any other Ugandan army officer, Amin was closely initiated into the
ruthless Machiavellian methods of political intrigue
and manipulation, which later made it possible for
him to outmaneuver Obote himself once the two fell
out and to survive so many attempts to depose him.
     But even now that Amin is no longer in power, his
legacy to Uganda may endure for a long time to come.
He divided and embittered many groups against one
another on the basis of ethnic group and religion on
a scale unknown in Uganda's history. He brought out
and promoted the worst traits in many of his countrymen and stifled all the worthy attributes that distinguish mankind from beasts. By establishing a rob-
ber-baron type of government, he destroyed or disrupted
the sense of social order and propriety that most Ugandans knew and valued. Because he had to meet all
aspects of Ugandan life at his illiterate level to
understand and to control them, he reversed the country's development -- possibly by several decades.
His policies promoted general instability in East
Africa, creating hostility and an arms race with Kenya
and Tanzania and contributing to a hastened demise of
the much needed East African community. In fairness
to Amin, however, the conflict between the other partners, Kenya and Tanzania, probably was more decisive
in destroying the community. Amin needed the East
African community desperately to compensate for the
internal economic disruption in Uganda. His real contribution to its demise was his providing a plausible
pretext for those who wanted to destroy it and promoting a general sense of insecurity in the region.

UGANDA'S FUTURE

Amin's Overthrow and the Nature of Tanzania's
Involvement

     In October 1978, Idi Amin, in a desperate diver-
sionary tactic designed to prevent his army from de-
posing him, invaded neighboring Tanzania and annexed
over 700 square miles of its territory, which he publicly declared a new administrative district of Uganda.
It proved his undoing. After a slow, careful start,
President Nyerere of Tanzania launched a military
operation fighting along with a few Ugandan exiles

that not only recovered his territory but went on to
overthrow Amin. In some quarters the Tanzanian action
has received ambivalent reaction or criticism. Those
who are unsupportive consider it a dangerous precedent
to set: to go beyond recovering a territory and overthrow a government. The fears are obviously well
founded. Were it to become an accepted policy for one
state to invade another at will, Africa -- and the
world -- could be in a conflagration. I have already
defended this principle of noninvolvement elsewhere.
But I strongly contend the Tanzania-Uganda case constitutes a special case to be judged on its own merits.
Experience in international relations demonstrates
that general principles of international law and practice -- catering as they do to an imperfect, complex
world -- must make exceptions in particular cases
that must be considered on their own merit to permit
justice to be done. Not to concede this is to render
legal norms and principles irrelevant to some of the
interests they are supposed to serve. When legality
is at total variance with reality, it is well known
that reality prevails. It is because of this, for
example, that there have been over 150 wars throughout
the world since the signing of the United Nations
charter (despite contemporary international law for-
bidding recourse to war).

The Tanzanian military action is justified and
excepted on the following cogent grounds. First, it
was an act of self-defense by Tanzania to expel a
barbarous invader who had publically violated its territorial integrity. It would not have been sufficient
simply to recover Tanzania's territory. Amin, by
uncontested universal knowledge was thoroughly unreli-
able, irrational, and reckless -- in addition to being
murderous. There would have been absolutely no assurance that he would not have launched a more devastating
invasion of Tanzania in retaliation against the humiliation of his first repulse. Logic dictated, therefore,
that Amin be pursued and defeated to ensure Tanzania's
secure borders.

The second ground justifying the action is that
the Organization of African Unity failed to act even-
handedly in the war. When it tried to mediate, Nyerere
stipulated certain conditions, one of which was that
the OAU censure Amin for his invasion of Tanzania.
Because it had sadly become a body that could neither
decide nor act when its role was most sorely needed,
the OAU did not censure Amin. Its failure to do this
gave the impression that Tanzania's ongoing self-
defense was a greater wrong than Amin's original invasion, which had caused it all. This was obviously

unfair. In my view Tanzania was justified at that
particular time to pursue a unilateral course in the
defense of its vital interests where neither regional
nor international machinery was able or available to
protect it.

The third reason justifying Tanzania's action is
based on humanitarian grounds. Customary international
law once permitted as a ground for foreign intervention
in the affairs of a state humanitarian reasons, such
as saving a population from genocide. This was superceded by the covenant of the League of Nations, later
by the Charter of the United Nations, as well as other
treaties that forbade unilateral intervention. The
reason was obvious and sound. To permit otherwise is
to sanction possible aggression by a predatory power
under the cover of humanitarian assistance. Unfortunately, though, no ample provision was made for genuine
exceptions in an imperfect world.

Thus, situations do arise that erode the very
purpose of maintaining regional or world peace for
which these principles had been designed. I have already stated how numerous serious wars have been fought
despite these rules. I should like to ask specifically:
would the world have preferred Idi Amin -- who had already massacred nearly half a million nationals -- to
continue the genocide as a price for adhering to the
sanctity of noninterference in Uganda's internal affairs? Or was it to be preferable that a compassionate
neighbor seized an opportunity to actively assist the
nationals to overthrow his tyranny? If you have either
suffered such tyranny or have human sensitivity though
having lived outside it, then the choice for the latter
alternative would be simply compelling. Nyerere's
actions and those of his government and people in actively assisting the overthrow of Amin's tyranny shall
remain a humanitarian act of the greatest kind in the
annals of Africa's turbulent history. Rather than
being condemned, it deserves the highest commendation.
Let those who attack it out of sincere reservation or
mischief pause and consider how they would feel if they
had been the victims of such tyranny. It is the absence of empathy for the weak, the poor, and the oppressed while we are secure and well off that constitutes one of the greatest dangers on this planet.
Anyone who regards Amin as a peculiar example of a
backward African, having nothing to do with the rest
of mankind, is terribly mistaken. The existence, sus-
tenance, and perpetuation of Amin was directly a
symptom of the sickness of the whole world. Anyone
who overtly or covertly condoned, helped, or was indifferent to Amin has within himself some of Amin's

traits, the difference being that he does not show
them -- yet -- or does so by proxy. It is crucially
urgent that mankind realizes how interdependent it is.
Ultimately, we can only survive as a race if we accept
the wisdom in the statement that, despite our diversity, we are each other's keeper on this earth.

There are forces that would like to mar Tanzania's
image, to paint it as an invader that imposed its will
on an unfortunate neighbor in order to create a precedent for its own less lofty, more selfish adventures.
Nothing would be more gratifying to them than to have
Tanzania drawn into imposing individual leaders on
Uganda. If chaos resulted because of local protest,
so much the better. Tanzania could then be accused
quite plausibly of having invaded Uganda in order to
impose a new government of its own choice. Such a
situation would conceivably get Tanzania more deeply
involved in Uganda than it had anticipated. The result would obviously be its diminished involvement in
the liberation of southern Africa, which those who
resent Nyerere's crucial role there would obviously
welcome. But since the disarray that overtook the
Uganda National Liberation Front (UNLF) and its government, I have come to wonder about how much of these
implications are fully grasped in all their complexity
in either Tanzania or Uganda. Time alone can tell.

Uganda deserves and needs to maintain its independence as a sovereign state. During the entire
period from the Moshi meeting to the defeat of Amin,
President Nyerere and his ministers repeatedly assured
us that Tanzania's war effort had absolutely no price
tag. All Tanzania wished was a secure, friendly northern neighbor. This was commendable. But if Tanzania
should change, as many Ugandans have begun to charge,
and it feels tempted to exert undue influence on
Uganda, either by forcing leaders of its own choice
upon Uganda or by dictating the policies such a government should follow, then there can be no doubt that
the relations between the two states will have entered
an unfortunate and difficult phase. All the good and
the decent sacrifice Tanzania undertook to assist in
Amin's overthrow will be jeopardized with uncertain
consequences to all concerned. Neither of the two
countries can afford this to happen. This in no way
prejudices the manifest need for both countries, and
indeed for Kenya as well, to work out closer relationships for their mutual benefit, similar to what they
had before under the defunct East African Communities.

The Transitional Government and Beyond

In late March 1979, twenty-two different Ugandan
groups met in Moshi, Tanzania, and created the Uganda
National Liberation Front. It elected a distinguished
academician and public servant, Yusufu Lule, as its
head. On 11 April he formed the first post-Amin government of which he became president. This transitional government adopted Obote's constitution of 1967
(with some modifications) as the state constitution.
But after barely two months, on 20 June 1979, Lule was
deposed by a faction of the Consultative Council of
the UNLF, with the full backing of the Tanzanian government, whose more than 45,000 troops (still in Uganda
at the time) constituted the ultimate sanction of force
in the state.
     This removal of Lule has to be accepted as an
accomplished fact, even if its aftermath may still
linger with some political reverberations. However,
as an active participant at the Moshi meeting that
formed the UNLF, I can categorically say that Lule's
removal was not done in accordance with the rules for
the removal or replacement of a leader of the UNLF
that we had agreed upon. It was specifically debated
and decided at Moshi that if for any reason a leader
had to be replaced (e.g., because of incapacity, death,
resignation, or no confidence) it could only be done
by the UNLF delegates conference. Categorically, this
right was never delegated to the Consultative Council,
which therefore acted ultra vires in assuming powers
it did not properly have. These points I state purely
for historical accuracy. What is disturbing is not
so much that Lule was removed unjustly (as he was) but
the motives for and the manner in which it was done.
It had been the hope of us all that the UNLF could
form the principal -- and perhaps the only -- party
at election time in two years. But for this to materi-
alize, the UNLF needed the support and loyalty of all
the major political forces in the country. With such
manifest division among the UNLF leaders, this seems
presently unlikely. The result can only be the denial
to the government of the broad political base that it
must have to perform adequately.
     Lule was replaced by Godfrey Binaisa, Q.C., as
the second post-Amin president in over two months.
Binaisa is a distinguished Ugandan lawyer and veteran
politician. To his credit, he was not involved in
the infighting that deposed Lule, although he became

its beneficiary. I will support his leadership and
presidency, although I had been one of Lule's supporters, if he rises to the challenge of making a concerted effort to reconcile the different political groups
in the country (whose bickering could prevent Uganda's
recovery from the ravages of Amin). It is an insult
to him to be called a stand-in for Obote. I have
worked with both men in UPC days and as their colleague
in the independence government of 1962. In my estima-
tion Binaisa will easily make a better leader. Both
men have government experience and are accomplished
politicians, but Binaisa has the advantages of learning
and an absence of complexes such as Obote's, which
contributed so adversely to his style of government.
I believe Binaisa has been treated very unfairly by
those opponents of Obote who regard him as having been
his henchman. He stood up against Obote and quit his
government. It should be remembered that many able
Ugandans served in Obote's government after independence and did a good job. They should not be confused
with, or blamed for, the mistakes of those few whose
actions plunged us into misfortune.

But Binaisa has grave problems to face in taking
over the country. The most central one is the same
one Lule encountered: limited powers and limited mandate as the chief executive of state. If the Consultative Council should demand the right to endorse all
his chief executive actions, it may simply incapacitate
him, resulting in a government that is both slow to
decide and slow to act at a time when the country needs
and deserves sound decisive action. Over-jealous of
their authority, some members of the Council saw the
assumption of more powers as those of a dictatorship,
thus to be resisted. I hate dictatorship. I have
suffered at its hands longer and more than most members of the Consultative Council who decry it. But
I do know what is necessary in practice for a government to function effectively. This is all that is
pleaded for.

Another problem that Binaisa faces are the sharp
divisions within the Consultative Council, often on
narrow grounds but so intensely held that they have
already led to the overthrow of the government under
Lule. How long Binaisa survives must remain to be
seen. He probably has an advantage in that the consequences of Lule's overthrow will inhibit similar
action being taken lightly against him. If only the
Consultative Council members would discover that they
all need each other, that they have to work to accom-
modate not eliminate one another, despite their divergent outlooks on how things should be run. If they

would, then Uganda would have a fair chance to attempt
recovery. Not otherwise.

There was criticism that the transitional government should not be based on Obote's dictatorial constitution of 1967, already fully discussed in this
book. I share in the objections to this constitution;
certainly, if anyone proposed it to be Uganda's constitution after the expected general election, I would
be among those objecting. But it should be realized
that as an interim measure, it was not inappropriate
for the transitional government to use it with some
modifications. Government had to have a state constitution to run the state, no matter whether it was
Lule, Binaisa, or any other person as president. The
constitution of a state is quite different from that
of the UNLF, and I know that a misunderstanding of
this fact by some Consultative Council members contributed to Lule's difficulties.

Among the major tasks of any post-Amin government
is laying the foundations for a just and humane society.
We shall have learned little from our experience if as
a result of our suffering we were to urge our new government to carry out a systematic victimization of all
Nubians, Moslems, and the Kakwa tribe because Amin
used them. I know Uganda well enough to understand
that there are good and bad among these people just
as there are among the rest of the country. Indeed,
while we condemn Amin's people for all that has be-
fallen us, let us not forget that he could not have
survived this long, despite his monopoly on violence,
if he did not have collaborators among every group in
the country, including those who suffered the most.
It would be both unwise and counterproductive for anyone interested in reconciliation and recovery in Uganda to seek to destroy the good and the bad alike, to
punish the innocent for the evil deeds of the guilty.
The inevitable consequence of indiscriminate retribution is profound fear and the escalation of violence.

I, personally, have every reason that would in-
cline any man of flesh and blood to seek retribution
against Amin and his henchmen. After I supported and
campaigned for his removal from the army in February
1966, he was instrumental in supporting Obote's decision to imprison me and my close friends for five
years without trial in a maximum security jail under
the most appalling conditions. After he took over,
his henchmen murdered two of my close cousins, both
of them fine young lawyers. On 8 November 1977 my
only brother, Katabarwa, was hanged and then burned
on Amin's orders. He was one of the first trained army
officers who had tried to resist Obote's imposition

of Amin on the Ugandan army. As a result he had also
been detained without trial in 1966 for four years.
Most of his former comrades have been eliminated. In
addition hundreds, nay, thousands of people from all
regions and ethnic groups who were good friends and
colleagues in our struggle for independence have been
killed. My property in the country has been taken
over and looted by Amin's local cronies. I have been
driven to live in exile, to flee the land of my birth
whose independence I promoted. In addition to this,
tens of thousands of innocent lives have been brutally
extinguished and Uganda lies in ruins. These surely
are reasons enough to move me to seek justice. But
I am profoundly convinced they do not entitle me to
indiscriminately murder everyone remotely connected
with Amin, however guilty of Amin's crimes. When
revenge becomes an end in itself, leading to the count-
less slaughter of innocent lives, a new regime could
easily become engulfed in deepening and uncontrollable
violence. This is the lesson from Amin's indiscriminate massacres of Acholi and Langi. He either did not
know, or completely ignored the fact if he did, that
Obote had real opposition -- political enemies --
among the Acholi and Langi people who would not have
regretted Obote's removal or would not have been
against Amin's seizure of power. All they wanted was
a stable, just government that gave them security.
But Amin antagonized these potential supporters because
he slaughtered them no less than he did his real enemies among them in the army. The situation unavoidably
got out of control. The killing spread to other groups
until there was hardly a village the length and breadth
of Uganda that had not felt his wasting hand or his
destructive forces.

This in no way prevents the punishment of the
guilty. For, indeed, excessive leniency, which is a
weakness, gives a false sense of harmony and leaves
deep grievances unredressed, while effectively punishing the guilty may constitute an effective deterrent
and clearly gives a sense of satisfaction to the previously oppressed. Examples have to be made so that
it is clear to the whole nation that it neither pays
for a leader to commit such heinous crimes nor for a
citizen to serve such regimes. The first challenge
in post-Amin reconstruction, therefore, will be the
difficult but necessary process of defining and limiting the bounds of retribution.

The second task is, of course, the administration
of relief and rehabilitation. Obviously many tasks
in rehabilitation and particularly reconstruction will
go well beyond the two-year period into the era of

elected governments. Probably the greatest item of
rehabilitation needing priority above all others is
that of our values as a society. A restoration of
morality and the norms that Amin's jungle law had destroyed is needed. Without the mental and spiritual
rehabilitation of the people, it will be difficult to
effect material rehabilitation and reconstruction.
But in doing all this the leaders must provide the
example. It is a central challenge.

The whole country will look forward to the general
election with exceptional anticipation. When they last
had an election, Ugandans knew how to vote and loved
it. In the last general election (discussed earlier
in this book), many constituencies polled over 95 percent of registered voters. I believe the electorate
is wiser and will not easily be swayed by empty political slogans. It is of importance, however, that the
government should prevent political organization or
activity for at least a year to enable it to address
the immediate tasks with a united population. To permit political groups sooner is to allow politicians to
scramble for support, thus dividing the people and
making urgent tasks impossible or difficult to perform.

The detailed timetable for an elected government
is not yet complete as I write. But it will probably
follow the usual steps: the establishment of a constitutional commission to determine an appropriate constitution, the election of a constituent assembly to
consider and decide on the constitutional provisions,
demarcation of constituencies, and then a free and
fair general election based on a universal adult franchise.

One cannot really overemphasize the awesome responsibility political aspirants have in restraining
themselves in the competition for power. We must forgive each other for all the wrongs and wounds we have
inflicted upon each other and on the country since
independence. There is no other way if the country
is to heal. But on no account does forgiving each
other mean forgetting what has caused all the suffering
we went through. That is the essence of our experience
and it provides an invaluable lesson of what to avoid.
There is likely to be some ideological diversity; that
is the wealth and reality of our country. What we
need is a fundamental realization that beyond the different parties or ideologies we have a common destiny,
that working together is a source of strength, and
that reckless rivalries and power struggles sap or
destroy our endeavors, as demonstrated already in the
UNLF. I hope we can avoid cheap politics. I remember
when we formed the UPC, whose constitution and social-

ist manifesto I had drafted, we were motivated with
genuine idealism committed to democratic ideals and
social justice. After a few years in power, our practice and preaching became increasingly at variance
with each other. For instance, in a discussion on
personal matters with a distinguished colleague I had
expressed a desire to conduct some business, to set
up a farm, and I needed to borrow money because I had
none. My colleague retorted that he preferred to have
cash, not visible, immovable property. His explanation
was that because we were socialists, we could not afford to be seen owning such businesses. Moreover, he
reasoned that in case there were a civil upheaval, the
money could be easily moved to any place around the
world, where immovable property could not. This was
in 1963. In 1966, and especially since 1971, Uganda
has been through upheavals. I lost almost everything
I had invested in farming as I fled to live poorly in
exile. My socialist compatriot, who fled to exile in
1971, has to my knowledge lived in relative luxury
where he had his inconspicuous wealth transferred.
One could say he was the wiser; but, the hypocrisy of
it all remains saddening. I hold a strong commitment
to social justice and the elimination of exploitative
business practices. Yet life has taught me that to
maximize what we have as a country, we must permit a
reasonable measure of freedom to encourage and motivate
individual effort. The degree of mix as I have stated
elsewhere must be a matter for constant examination
and adjustment depending on the nature of our society.
Let us be honest about it, instead of publishing mani-
festos for the purpose of impressing local or foreign
friends (which we have little intention in our hearts
to keep, both in spirit and letter). We should accept
the challenge that we face now more than at any other
time in our history: to produce men of integrity to
be our leaders.

Finally, on the domestic front I must say that
for Uganda's future to stand a chance of success we
must seriously consider the basic principles in the
last chapter of this book. They seem tailor-made in
many respects for us. In one sentence, let us abandon
the winner-take-all philosophy and all its devious
manifestations. If we do, no force on earth can block
our rapid recovery and triumph. We have the human and
natural resources it takes to make it happen.

Regionally, we have a duty to ourselves and our
neighbors to revive the East African cooperation that
we shared and that had been the envy of the whole
world. Uganda has historically been placed in a position to initiate or actively participate in a new

beginning of such a relationship. Where even the great
powers find security and strength in working closely
together, it would be great folly for us to break off
our association!

13
Some Basic Principles

It would seem that to foster national unity and intergroup cooperation among the diverse nationals of the African states, to ensure an optimum degree of stability that would permit both the leaders and masses to be fully involved in nation building, the following principles are basic to the attainment of these aims, whatever form the government takes: military, civilian, one-party or multiparty, federal or unitary.

THE PHILOSOPHICAL OR IDEOLOGICAL PREMISE OF GOVERNMENT

The philosophy of winner-take-all deserves elimination from the conduct of leaders at all levels in the state. If as it is hoped we have made out a case that this philosophy has been at the heart of African instability, it surely follows that the sharing of power and all the benefits it brings (such as jobs, distribution of development projects, and national resources) should be fair to all groups within a given state and should be seen to be so. Eliminating excessive desires to monopolize power can only come about through an enhanced sense of tolerance between the diverse groups in the state, especially among the most powerful -- those involved in the national government. The issue of whether or not to have this or that ideological commitment has often been a concern of African governments who tend to identify them with one or the other of the powerful capitalist and communist camps. The Third World of which Africa is part is constantly bombarded with big power ideologies, as if it were a tabula rasa or a void to be filled. The West urges us to accept the system of free enterprise as the cornerstone of freedom and the Christian religion and philosophy as constituting mankind's only hope for peace. Yet we know in practice that because

of the profit motive, free enterprise has a tendency
to promote exploitation and inequality and thus dimin-
ishes the freedom of others. As a result, the noble
ideals of the Christian doctrine have often been negated in the name of "freedom."

The Communists boast that their ideology alone
can guarantee human equality and global peace. But
the facts are that, like everyone else, communist powers have the capacity and potential to fight each other
and to threaten global peace, as evidenced by the war
between Cambodia and Vietnam or the serious split and
conflict between the two communist giants, the Soviet
Union and China. H. R. Haldeman, a former principal
aide to President Nixon, has revealed how it was the
United States, ironically, that had to intervene to
stop an imminent Soviet nuclear strike on China intended to destroy her nuclear weaponry capability. We
know, too, that communist dictatorship of the prole-
tariat hinges on the denial of liberty to the majority.
Besides, the manifest denial of the existence of God
by Communism runs counter to some of the most primordial African beliefs in his existence. One can therefore say that, generally speaking, Africans do not need
alien ideologies to confuse them even if there are
some useful lessons and principles that could be selec-
tively adapted from them.

Whatever path of development is chosen, it must
have as its basic aim for society the elimination of
the adverse inequalities and the promotion of a human-
istic, egalitarian life that, while seeking equality
for all, permits and ensures a basic measure of freedom to the individual. Balancing the rights and power
of the state on the one hand with the rights of the
individual on the other is one of the most difficult
challenges among young states. Often there is a tendency either toward excessive monolithic central control or unhealthy laissez-faire, neither of which
maximizes development and national well-being. If
there was advanced genetic engineering that could in
time produce a human race in which all individuals
were identical, it would be both logical and desirable
to organize society on a highly monolithic centralized
basis. But in the absence of this, the attempt to
impose such exclusive monolithic control on diverse
human beings is bound to be problematical.

The best course seems to be an effort to strike
an optimum balance between the rights of the state
and those of the individual. One cannot overstate the
caution, though, that this concession to inherent
human diversity should never be permitted to become
a license for the exploitation of man by man. In

developmental terms, this would mean a mixed economy
where both the state and the individual can have a
sphere within which to operate. I am convinced (and
I believe it is borne out by evidence where it has
been tried) that monopolistic control of the economy
by the state seldom maximizes development. It dis-
courages or inhibits those members of society who have
the creativity, motivation, and business sense from
taking their natural place of leadership in the drive
for economic development. The general result in such
a case tends to promote mediocrity and to discourage
initiative. If one concedes -- as one must -- that
human beings are endowed with different natural apti-
tudes, it must surely follow that a good government
is one that provides for the utilization of such diverse gifts. It is far better to permit, regulate, and
guide this than to cripple or stop it altogether. This
need not, nor should it, diminish the government's
right to have exclusive control of some sectors that
are considered vital to the well-being of the state,
nor should it diminish its right to regulate and ultimately control even the private sector for the good
of society as a whole.

It should also be observed that there has been
widespread conflict between the rural and urban areas
over the limited national resources that has not been
satisfactorily resolved in most African states. Although African populations are overwhelmingly rural
(an average of 80 percent) an alliance of convenience
between the few but vocal urban dwellers and organized
labor has lobbied more effectively for a dispropor-
tionate share of national resources. Since for the
foreseeable future a preponderant percentage of the
population is bound to live on and farm the land, social justice demands that more attention and more resources be given to rural development, in an effort
to make living on the land more worthwhile and to
discourage the increasing and vexing exodus to cities
and towns where there is insufficient employment.

LEADERSHIP

The availability and choice of sound leadership
in the country is of pivotal importance. While it is
undeniable that civilian leaders on independence played
a vital role in the decolonization process and the
emancipation of Africa, it is equally clear that having
attained this independence, a good many became corrupted by power, especially absolute power. Many had been
chosen by their people, not because of their ability

to lead -- because there had been no ample opportunity
under colonial rule to test this -- but largely because
of their anticolonial posture. After a decade and a
half of independence, bad government, and instability
in a number of states largely brought about by poor
leadership, it seems an opportune time for these states
(given the chance) to make a conscious effort to avoid
the costly mistakes of the past and demand better cre-
dentials of their leaders. This choice and care are
just as necessary in conventional representative,
elective government, as in the selection of leaders
by the coup-makers at their secret meetings seizing
power. No effort should be spared to seek and support
leaders with proven integrity and ability.

Fortunately (or unfortunately), mankind is deeply
impressed by example. Consequently, no amount of
propaganda extolling the virtues of a leader through
a controlled news media, as all fallen leaders have
discovered, can have any durable, positive effect if
he is setting a negative example in fact through his
deeds. The quality of leadership is so crucial that,
more than any other single factor, it often makes the
difference between failure and success and between
order and chaos in these states. If leaders are un-
suitable, costly failures may ensue even where the
constitutional framework was viable. On the other
hand, given excellent leaders and weak institutions,
the state could still be stabilized and inevitable
failures could be minimized.

Let us now examine the following illustrations
of the adverse consequences of winner-take-all leadership through certain aspects of its practices.

The Desire To Hold Office Indefinitely

Generally speaking, one can discern several reasons, operating singly or in various combinations,
that explain why leaders may seek to remain in power
indefinitely or for life. First, even among the best
leaders there may be a genuine belief that there is
no successor around who has the acceptability, competence, or similar commitment to carry on what had been
started. Second, for those leaders who may have committed grievous misuses of power, there is the fear
that losing power would mean losing their immunity
from just censure and retribution. Third, there may
be external influences. For example, where a foreign
power has assisted or supported the installation of
a leader, it has a vested interest in his continuation,
expecially if there is no comparable successor in the
state or if such a successor would be hostile to the

foreign power. But in my view, it is the fourth reason, the excessive self-interest aspect of the winner-
take-all philosophy, that has been the single most
important reason why many African leaders have gone
to such costly extremes to remain in power.
It is true that at the inception of a new state,
with its invariably attendant uncertainties, its initial leadership may have to govern for a long time to
permit the new structure to consolidate. This is
especially so if a state is born through a revolution.
Not only are leaders likely to be military or semi-
military but the regime is likely to be a one-party
system. Such was the case in the United States under
George Washington after the War of Independence. It
was also the case among some communist states where
the leaders seized power by insurrection or civil war.
Recently, we have seen it among former Portuguese
colonies in Africa, which took independence by force
of arms. Yet the majority of African states gained
their independence without military conflict but
through peaceful constitutional evolution. In such
cases independence leaders came to power through fair
general elections in most cases, supervised by the
departing colonialists. Despite the rhetoric, therefore, there was no extraordinary circumstance that
compelled every postindependence leader to monopolize
all state power indefinitely. Except where these
leaders were overthrown by force or in the rare cases
where some have died peacefully in office, they still
hold power in all African states, even though in many
cases the ritual of periodic elections is permitted.
It is well known, however, that no serious opposition
candidate could defeat the incumbent. While it is undeniable that several of these independence leaders
have made distinguished contributions to the development of Africa and even the Third World, it is clearly
obvious that not all were Plato's philosopher-kings,
endowed with profound knowledge, wisdom, and justice,
nor were the military rulers who deposed some of them
endowed with the genius of Turkey's Kemal Ataturk or
China's Mao Tse-tung. What has happened in Africa is
that those who take and wield power want to do so in
practice for life, whether or not they are able to
govern reasonably well.
This consequently means that, because there is
no limitation on the leaders' tenure of office, should
they become unpopular or undesirable the only way to
remove them is by revolution. But since the leaders
are aware of this and try to safeguard against it, not
only does it lead to repression but it means the change
of government more often than not has to be violent.

Unquestionably, therefore, one of the grave failures of substantial African postindependence leadership has been the absence of an orderly change of government, a peaceful transfer of power. This has been an unfortunate beginning because it has deprived practically all African states of any precedent of such peaceful transition (except the recent example in Kenya where President Arapo Moi succeeded Jomo Kenyatta, who died in office). It is likely to mean a widespread acceptance of the use of violence, of the coup d'etat with all its potentially unsettling results, as the only viable option available to the people to change their regime. Good government is maintained not only by the laws and institutions of a state but by the sound conventions and precedents that leaders build over a period of time, so that their violation becomes unthinkable. Whatever shortcomings Western systems of government may have, their ideal of peaceful change of leadership is worthy of serious consideration and, emulation.

Take, for example, Sir Winston Churchill. After he had led the British people with distinction through a horrendous World War, they promptly voted him out of power and he bowed to their choice. He did not cite his contribution to the war effort or illustrious ancestry as grounds for calling on the army to keep him in power in defiance of the popular will. President Charles de Gaulle, the greatest French leader in modern times, who did much to restore France's prestige in the world, had to resign when a referendum turned down some of his measures. More than any other Frenchman, he could have defied the results of this referendum, imposed his own measures, and ruled on. Whatever shortcomings former President Richard Nixon of the United States had, there is no doubt that his policy of detente with the Soviet Union and his opening of relations with China were most useful contributions to world peace. And yet this leader of the most advanced nation on earth resigned his office because of accusations made by subordinates about his misuse of presidential power. Star witnesses who led the attack against him, insignificant men like John Dean, did not disappear overnight.

Indeed, the similarity and contrast between Obote in Uganda and Nixon in the United States is a good illustration. Both presidents had been accused of using their authority to cover up their misuse of power, Obote for hiding his unlawful adventures in Zaire's civil war and Nixon for his unlawful spying and harrassment of political opponents in what popularly became known as "Watergate." In both cases the presidents

denied any wrongdoing and sought to stop any probing
by claiming that such inquiries would be prejudicial
to national security (just as "national security" was
to be used in both cases as the reason why the unlawful
acts had been committed in the first place). But when
both were pressed on the allegations, their reactions
could not have been more different. Obote reacted by
abrogating the constitution, seizing absolute power
to obliterate any prospect of proving his derelictions
or his removal from office. When he set up a judicial
commission of inquiry, its members were denied access
to material evidence because he terrorized the witnesses, and consequently the truth remained officially
hidden. In contrast, in the case of Nixon, neither
the congressional members who investigated "Watergate"
nor the numerous witnesses who testified against him
were exposed to comparable threats or risks to their
lives. Rather than remaining in office, in which case
President Nixon would have faced impeachment, he
stepped down, bowed to the manifest demand of most
American citizens, and an orderly transfer of power
to Gerald Ford, the new president, ensued without dis-
rupting the nation. Numerous such examples and contrasts abound that must surely give us reason for
reflection.

The worst thing we could do to ourselves is to
excuse our shortcomings and excesses on the grounds
that our upheavals are "natural" because our states
are too young, need more time to experiment, settle
down, etc. To accept this is to create the necessary
psychological and political climate to perpetuate
instability. The African record to date is appalling.
Within fifteen years there have been over thirty-eight
successful coups d'etat and many more unsuccessful
ones. There have been several stages of insurgency
or rebellion within several states and outright civil
war in about eight. Within eighteen of these states,
eighteen current or former heads of state or government have been assassinated or executed, and nineteen
others have experienced either imprisonment, or have
lived or died in exile. As of 1976 more than a million
Africans were refugees, most in neighboring states,
having fled some domestic upheaval. Consider these
names of national leaders and their fate:

    o Burundi
      Assassinated:
        Prince Louis Rwagasore (First Prime Minister)
        Pierre Ngendandumwe (Prime Minister, 1963-1964
          and 1965)
        Joseph Bamina (Prime Minister)

King Ntare V

In exile:
King Mwambutsa IV

o Chad
Assassinated:
Francois Tombalbaye (President, 1960-1975)

o Congo
Assassinated:
Marien Ngouabi (President, 1968 -18 March 1977)

In detention and later executed:
Alphonse Massamba-Debat (President, 1963-1968)

o Benin (formerly Dahomey)
Condemned to death in absentia and now in exile:
Dr. Emile-Derlin Zinson (President, 1968-1969)

In house detention:
Hubert Maga (President, 1960-1963)
S. M. Apithy (President, 1964-1965)
Dr. Justin Ahomadegbe (Vice-President, 1964-1965)

In jail:
Lt. Col. Alphonse Alley (President, 1967-1968)

o Ghana
Former Ghanaian leaders executed by firing squad
in June 1979:
General Ignatius Achempong
General A. A. Afrifa
General F.W.K Alcuffo

Dead in exile:
Dr. Kwame R. Nkrumah (Leader for Life, 1957-1966)

Living in exile:
Dr. Kofi Busia (Prime Minister, 1969-1972)

o Mali
In detention:
Modibo Keita (President, 1960-1968)

o Niger
In house detention:
Hamani Diori (President, 1960-1975)

o Nigeria
Federal Leaders
Assassinated:
   Sir Abubakar Tafawa Balewa (Prime Minister,
   1960-1966)
   Maj. Gen. Aguiyi Ironsi (Head of the Federal
   Military Government, 1966)
   Gen. Murtala Mohammed (Head of Federal Mili-
   tary Government, 1975)

Regional Leaders
Assassinated:
   Sir Ahmadu Bella (Premier, Northern Region)
   Chief Festus Akintola (Premier, Western Region)

Imprisoned for treason; released by military:
   Chief Obajemi Awolowo (Federal Leader of the
   Opposition and former Premier of Western
   Region)

Living in exile:
   General Yakubu Gowon (Head of Federal Military
   Government, 1966-1975)

o Sierra Leone
Executed:
   Brigadier General David Lansana

Living in exile:
   Sir Albert Margai (Prime Minister, 1964-1967)

o Seychelles
Overthrown and living in exile:
   James R. M. Mancham (President, 1976-1977)

o Somalia
Assassinated:
   Abdirashid Ali Shermarke (President, 1967-1969)

Imprisoned and later released:
   Abdirazak Hussein (Prime Minister, 1969-1973)
   Mohamed Egal (Prime Minister, 1967-1969)

o Tanzania (Zanzibar)
Assassinated:
   Sheikh Abeid Karume (first president of Zan-
   zibar)

o Togo
Assassinated:
   Sylvanus Olympio (President, 1960-1963)

o Malagasy Republic
  Assassinated:
    Col. Ratsimandrava (President, 1975)

o Uganda
  Died in exile:
    Sir Frederick Mutesa II (President, 1963-1966)

  In exile:
    Milton Obote (Prime Minister, later President, 1962-1971)

o Upper Volta
  Imprisoned and later released:
    Maurice Yameogo (President, 1960-1966)

o Rwanda
  In exile:
    King Kigeria (since 1961)

  Under house arrest for some time:
    Gregoire Kayibanda (President, 1961-1973)

o Zaire (formerly Congo Kinsasha)
  Assassinated:
    Patrice Lumumba (Prime Minister, 1960)

  Executed:
    E. Kimba (Prime Minister, 1965)

  Died in exile:
    Moise Tshombe (Prime Minister, 1964-1965)

Although the tenure of office of most of those affected seems to have been generally brief, these leaders have been involved or caught up in intense conflicts of winner-take-all politics or interethnic regional, religious, or ideological rivalries. In any event, those who had the opportunity to stay in office long (like Nkrumah of Ghana, Obote of Uganda, Modibo Keita of Mali, Tombalbaye of Chad, Hamani Diori of Niger, Kayibanda of Rwanda, and Micombero of Burundi) were deciding to rule indefinitely or for life -- if not in law, then in fact. The numbers of government ministers who have met violent death, been jailed, or fled to exile in these states were many times more than that given for the heads of state and government. It seems proper to suggest, therefore, that as one way of stabilizing leadership and ensuring orderly changes of government, <u>the leader, be he president or prime minister, should serve for a limited, specified</u>

term of office. It may be one or two terms, it may
go up to six years in total, but it should be certain
and limited. It may be argued that leaders remain in
power indefinitely partly because they are not sure
their successors can continue their policies. This
need not be so, as the incumbent takes part to influence the choice of a successor. But limiting the term
of office would do much to restore the confidence in
government among the masses that was so manifest at
independence time.

Moreover, the specified term of office is needed
partly because in a state with many ethnic groups it
is important psychologically that each feels it has
the right theoretically to provide a president, a prime
minister, or any other high official of state, even if
in practice it has no chance to do so. It was for this
reason that the issue of holding fair, periodic, general elections was so unanimously and strongly supported by all groups and enshrined in independence
constitutions; it provided an open avenue for all to
participate in or to change their governments. These
electoral provisions were a fundamental contract between the diverse nationals and their government and
their consequent abrogation by most leaders directly
contributed to the instability of the country. Besides, a great effort had been made, as we saw in
Uganda and Ghana, to discredit the legitimacy of traditional rulers, principally because their positions
rested on inheritance, were for life, and were non-
elective. Yet once some of the postindependence
leaders themselves had taken power, they decided to
rule like traditional rulers, not only in style but
also for life. They speedily forfeited the credibility
and legtimacy with which they had started, and shifted
to the use of force and repression as the only basis
of retaining power.

Eliminating Opponents

Once a decision is made by a leader to remain in
power for life, he can seldom behave the same way as
another with a limited term. It often becomes necessary to eliminate any potential opponents, real or
imagined, even when these have not manifested any intention to challenge the leader. This invariably
means the use of draconian laws to buttress one's rule,
which then becomes challenged by those oppressed, and
a vicious cycle is produced with further repression
followed by more challenges, which necessarily become
clandestine. In the examples we gave of Ghana, Uganda,
and even multiparty Nigeria, it is most unlikely that

had the leaders not decided to monopolize power indefinitely or for life they would have gone to the extreme
measures of seeking to eliminate dissent without or
within their groups with such recklessness. If a
leader knows he is in for a limited term it follows
he must envisage a time when he is out of power, living
like an ordinary citizen, and subject to the ordinary
laws of the land, which a ruler for life would never
face. This obviously would tend to restrain him
against excesses since the fear of a future inquiry
by a succeeding regime or a trial for crimes against
the state cannot be ignored. This does not mean that
a limited term for leaders will necessarily produce
perfect ones. You may still have some who are prepared
to ruin the state, loot part of its wealth, and flee
to live comfortably in exile after their term of office.
But it would seem that the tendency would be one of
restraint and tolerance (worth all the effort) once
the concept of leadership for life or an indefinite
term is abandoned. The best safeguard for an enlightened leader would therefore seem to be to treat all
other groups in the state more or less the way he
would like to be treated once he is out of power.

RECOGNITION AND ACCEPTANCE OF DIVERSITY

There seems to be a cogent case for more tolerance
of communal identity, in particular of an ethnic, religious, or regional nature, than has hitherto been
the case. The notion that the best way to stabilize,
unify, and develop these multiethnic states is through
excessive centralization and negation of some basic
group identity has clearly failed. As we saw, Nkrumah
could not permanently repress Ashanti or Ewe identity
merely by banning their parties (the NLM, the TC, and
the UP), because they were to surface again as the new
military rulers in the NLC, who overthrew him. Obote's
abolition of the kingdoms, the KY, and the DP did not
stop these groups from decisively contributing to a
political climate that made his overthrow inevitable
in Uganda. There have been serious errors concerning
the nature of communal (particularly ethnic) identity,
which in turn have led to wrong solutions. The first
error as we saw was to think that excessive centralization of power enforced by repressive measures would
enhance the feeling of common citizenship and diminish
or eliminate ethnic or regional group identity. The
second error was to think that the abolition of some
basic formal institutions of powerful ethnic groups,
e.g., kingship among the Baganda, would necessarily

speed up the demise of ethnic identity and promote
national integration. While there may theoretically
be cases in which this may be conceivable, in the
African reality the effect has been (and for many
decades will continue to be) counterproductive for a
number of reasons. To begin with, common ethnic identity is based on far more diverse characteristics than
on the existence of a single institution like kingship
or chieftainship, however important this may seem. An
ethnic group is bound together by many bonds, such as
a sense of common origin or past, by a wide range of
common customs and traditional values, and often by
a common language. Thus the absence of a kabaka among
the Baganda will not deny them other focal points to
perpetuate a common identity. Such an identity would
more than likely survive and adapt itself to new circumstances. This is perhaps all the more so because
rarely have many national leaders stood above ethnic
politics and cleavages, even when they have repeatedly
claimed to do so. Every African leader comes from a
recognizable ethnic or regional group. More often
than not when he is urging the rest of his diverse
nationals to stop thinking in terms of their groups,
he is in fact encouraging them to do just the opposite
by example as his tendency is visibly to rely more on
and favor his own ethnic group or region. While it
does not follow that the civilian governments that
have survived longest have done so because they are
without blemish, it seems true that on the whole most
of them have endeavored by their actions to stand
above ethnic conflict, avoiding its exacerbation and
moderating its exploitation for political sectional
gains.

No search for future internal stability and harmony, it seems, can avoid the acceptance of communal
diversity in most African states, not as a menace to
be stamped out, but as a fundamental characteristic
that would enrich the state. Paradoxically, experience
seems to show that a reasonable recognition of this
diversity, as was done in the first few years of independence in most states, puts the fears of different
groups at rest and enhances their willingness for a
common nationality with other groups. The degree to
which each community is permitted this, of course,
must depend on the peculiar circumstances of each
state although it should not be so permissive as to
promote centrifugal tendencies. The concept hitherto
adopted by many fallen leaders, that the state must
monopolize the loyalty of all its citizens, as we
stated before, is contrary to human nature, just as
diversity is inherent in all nature. One has only to

take a look around to establish this in any natural
setting. One is struck by the diversity <u>as well as</u>
the harmony of nature's handiwork, except where the
environment is highly artificial. Diversity is not,
need not be, incompatible with harmony, not only in
nature (of which we are a part) but also in the relationships of human beings in organized societies. If
the aim of leaders is to acknowledge this diversity,
it will provide them with the opportunity not only to
emphasize and promote areas of common identity, which
undoubtedly exist, but also to conciliate intergroup
tension and competition in a less strained atmosphere.
It should surely be a sobering thought that communal,
particularly ethnic, religious, and regional identity
is a global phenomenon affecting all countries, developed and developing, communist and capitalist alike.[1]
It manifests itself in the Soviet Union and Yugoslavia
as it does in Canada, the United Kingdom, and Belgium.
Its duration is as old as the states themselves. That
the Welsh and Scots should be seriously demanding their
regional autonomy after centuries of a common nationality with the English and so much shared experience
should provide a warning to those leaders who thought
they could stamp out ethnic or regional identity in
their term of office by simply passing draconian laws
and making martyrs of ethnic or regional group leaders.
After 110 years of independence, Canada is still faced
with the problematical demands for autonomy from its
French citizens of Quebec. The interethnic strains
between the Walloons and Flemish of Belgium after over
a century and a half of common citizenship is another
example. In these cases government, rather than suppressing particular group identity, has sought to meet
it by recognizing its reality and this has provided
an atmosphere within which to consider the problems
and avoid civil wars or major instability. It is of
special significance that even communist states with
their monolithic centralism had to come to terms with
the demands of such diverse ethnic group identity.
It is for this reason that the Soviet Union and Yugoslavia have federal constitutions, for example, per-
mitting each particular group a measure of authority
to run its affairs without weakening the central
structure of the state.
    The experience of some Asian countries, which like
most of Africa were part of European empires, also indicates that those states have experienced relative
stability and have come to terms with their diverse
characteristics. Thus Malaysia has enjoyed orderly
transfers of power because regional or ethnic groups
were assured a place and a role, which the leaders have

been generally careful to honor. The Indian union
recognizes such diversity, and not only because of its
large population. The government of Singapore has been
generally most attentive in not only being evenhanded
to all its different ethnic groups but also in being
seen to be so. A realization that enforced uniformity
is hardly synonymous with desired national unity would
go some way towards realistically creating the atmosphere for resolving intergroup conflicts and competition and making a genuine effort to harmonize rather
than destroy or suppress communal differences based
on the individual's loyalty to his family, clan, ethnic
group, region, or religion.

ACCEPTING THE IDEA OF RESPONSIBLE OPPOSITION

Examples abound in Africa where the elimination
of opposition political parties in the name of national
unity has been a license for repression, as we have
seen. Human experience, whether it be with an individual, a family, an organization, or a state, seems to
indicate that a healthy measure of self-appraisal or
a recognition of valid criticism of oneself by others
is necessary for improvement and progress. How else
can errors be rectified or adverse omissions be countered if a view is held that the leadership of the
state or its government does no wrong? And yet it is
tragically true that often, largely because the leaders wanted it and partly because their sycophants profusely preached it, there has been a tendency to clothe
African leadership with a doctrine of "infallibility"
not unlike that of the pope. Rather than enhance the
interests and popularity of such leaders, this intolerance to criticism has been detrimental, driving all
criticism underground from where it invariably surfaces
through upheavals or coups, or creates a state of permanent apprehension.
As we mentioned previously, whatever system of
government is adopted it should permit room for constructive criticism, for opposition, if you will. But
those opposing have to exercise restraint and responsibility not to abuse this right. We discussed at
length the ruthless elimination of opposition parties
and its adverse results. But it is important to
mention that this does not mean all the opposition
parties were necessarily better than the rulers, that
they were not committed to a winner-take-all philosophy, even if they rightly attacked it when applied
against them. There had been no chance at the national level to determine whether or not, once in power,

they would have permitted opposition themselves. But
in the regions that they controlled they had a monopoly of power no less than that of the national rulers.
The difference was therefore more of scale than of
principle. Thus, for example, in the West of Nigeria,
the AG tended to monopolize power as did the NPC in
the North, or the NCNC in the East. In Uganda, the
KY had a complete monopoly of power in Buganda and was
intolerant of opposition groups. The same was true
for the DP in the district administrations it once
controlled before Obote eliminated it from power. In
Ghana the opposition to the CPP behaved similarly and
the leading opponent of Nkrumah's monopoly of power,
Dr. Busia, was himself to attempt his version of it
when he had an opportunity to form a civilian government after the NLC. It is, however, true that the
magnitude to which this has been done has been far
more pronounced and its evils have been more clearly
manifest among national ruling parties than among
those of the opposition. The prognosis of governments
that brook no constructive criticism, whether at the
center or regionally, must surely be for continued
instability as the suppressed groups take recourse to
extralegal remedies.

It makes sense then that there should be a requirement for all principal parties or groups in the
state to be included at every level of government and
on all committees or commissions of a political nature
that deal with the sharing of power and benefits or
distribution of national resources. Rather than argue
that the one-party system is African, it seems more
accurate to say that it is more African for all groups
in the state to participate in their government. This
may take several forms. An open one-party system that
permits the existence of differing political views
within its membership and carefully seeks to have each
principal group represented at all levels of government
may seem more attractive to those who prefer the one-
party system. Or there may be the ordinary multiparty system within carefully worked-out parameters.[2]
But the executive authority of the national government
seems best served through a presidential system of
government. The presidency facilitates action better
than the cabinet system of government under a prime
minister, in which the executive authority is vested
in the cabinet as a whole. The president, however,
must have clearly defined constitutional checks to
prevent the abuse of power. It is preferable that he
be assisted by a prime minister or vice-president and,
of course, ministers to direct government departments.
The fact that presidential powers have been abused by

autocratic rulers does not mean that the concept of
the presidency per se is flawed.

Professor Lewis suggested the abolition of the
electoral methods inherited from colonial rule because
he regards them as one of the main causes of "winner-
take-all" practices and unsuited to these multiethnic
societies.[3] Yet the fault was not with electoral
systems but in the attitudes of leaders wielding power
who sought to monopolize it. Constituencies in most
of these states had catered to ethnic representation.
What is now needed more than anything else is for
"winners" to permit "losers" to have a meaningful role
in government and the shaping of their common future.
In other words, basic rules of political conduct must
be established in the state that ensure equitable and
humane treatment of the loser of the contest for power.

In addition, there is a duty in all levels of
leadership to speak out when things begin to go wrong
that has been singularly abdicated in many African
states. Most cabinet ministers, parliamentarians, or
bureaucrats chose either to be silent when things went
wrong or shamelessly praised the policies of their
national leader while knowing them to be faulty on
the theory that by so doing they might gain favor or
survive. Yet, the result has generally been tragic
for everyone. Denied the criticism or fearless advice,
the leaders persisted in error until it led to their
downfall. Those subordinates who thought flattery or
silence would buy them fortune or security invariably
became the scapegoats of the leader's wrath when things
began to get worse. Many of them who survived met
harsh retribution at the hands of the new regime for
the collective guilt of their deposed leader. Generally, ultimately nobody benefited. If the enlightened leaders cannot advise or are willing to mislead
the head of government, then it follows that the
masses become helpless and prey on the opportunism of
their rulers. True, standing up against a dictatorship
can be costly, as one can lose one's liberty, livelihood, or life. Yet without the willingness to take
a stand, liberty can easily disappear, as we saw, at
the hands of ruthless autocratic political leaders.

CONSTRUCTING A SOUND, VIABLE CONSTITUTION

There should be a constitution that provides the
fundamental law of the land, defining and establishing
all the main organs of the state (such as the executive, legislative, and judiciary), clearly setting
out their respective powers, and, where appropriate,

defining the nature and degree of the sharing of power
between the center and the regions. It is futile to
set down a blueprint here of a constitutional structure of a particular or hypothetical state. This
would not necessarily be relevant to conditions in
situ for such diverse states as exist in Africa. But
one can usefully discuss fundamental principles that
should be obtained regarding any constitution of whatever state.

Once an appropriate constitution has been drawn
up, the people -- and particularly the leaders -- have
a fundamental duty to protect and uphold it. Because
it is the basic law of the state from which every
other law and all legitimacy derives, its unique place
in society must be preserved. The practice of abrogating or amending constitutions in many African states
(so often by simple majorities or by the leader himself) has meant uncertainty and consequently instability. I admit that many constitutions that ushered
African states into nationhood needed some modifications, but I question the view that most of them were
so bad that they deserved repudiation. There can be
a legitimate distinction made between the failure of
leaders to operate an otherwise viable constitution
on the one hand and the failure of such a constitution
per se on the other hand, even if leaders had the competence to make a good one work. In the case of a
poor constitution, there would have to exist such basic defects, for example, as a conflict of powers or
functions between the organs of government for which
the constitution provides no resolution, or, having
granted some regional autonomy, a denial to the center
of any authority to correct the abuse of such a power.
Thus, while we can fairly say the Nigerian Independence Constitution had fundamental defects, the same
cannot be said of those of Uganda or Ghana.[4] Constitutional limitations on the power of the executive
branch were taken by leaders who sought absolute power
as a basic constitutional flaw, not knowing that the
removal of such checks would invariably lead to the
emasculation of other important organs of the state,
like the judicial and legislative branches, which in
turn would promote unrest among the diverse nationals
who felt helpless and totally exposed to the mercy of
a single, imperfect national leadership that monopolized all power.

The constitution needs to provide a strong center
for governing a modern state, capable of generating
development, and protecting it against external and
internal enemies. But equally, it should recognize
and permit an appropriate devolution of power to the

diverse groups so that through the exercise of running
their own local affairs, they can genuinely feel involved in nation building. The extent of such a devolution must of course depend on each particular case.
It concerns several factors: the nature of communal
diversity, the size of population and land area, and
the resources of the state. Once there is good will
and the principle is conceded, a formula would always
be worked out. If the state is large and wealthy,
such as Nigeria, then a federal constitutional structure seems imperative, as all its rulers have agreed.
Where there are medium-sized states (like Ghana or
Uganda), a semifederal or unitary constitution with
substantial devolution or delegation of authority from
the center seems within reason. The semantics of
"federal" or "unitary" can sometimes be contentious.
The important thing is the substantive division of
powers in the state. It seems a correct conclusion
to say that highly unitary constitutions bearing
excessive centralized power have not proved conducive
to the good government of Africa's multiethnic states.
It is also important to repeat that this does not mean
to propose the opposite extreme, excessive decentralization, which promotes centrifugal tendencies and
weakens or fragments the state. The optimum constitution generally seems to be somewhere between these two
extremes.
     The constitution should also ensure a sound and
impartial legal system, enforced and administered by
law officers who have no fear that they may be dismissed if they ruled against government or its leaders.
It is important that a citizen feels and knows that
the law courts can safeguard his rights not only a-
gainst other individuals but also against the state
and its officials, including leaders of ruling political parties. Should his rights be violated by the
executive or the legislative branches, the judiciary
branch provides his only protection. But if he is
denied such protection even there, for instance because the judiciary has lost its independence and is
subject to the will or threats of the executive (as
we saw in Nkrumah's Ghana, for example), then the
individual has no constitutional remedy within the
institutions of the state. This will inevitably lead
to his seeking justice through illegal actions, which
increases tension or violence. In such circumstances,
ethnicity, because of its strategic efficacy, provides
him the only haven of protection and in this way conflicts or tensions are created or exacerbated, leading
eventually to destabilizing situations ranging from
riots or boycotts to attempts to overthrow the regime

or secession from a particular region or the state
itself.

GUARANTEEING BASIC HUMAN RIGHTS

Few things are as controversial and critical as
the issue of human rights in our contemporary era,
involving all countries, developed and developing,
capitalist and communist alike.[5] With regard to Africa, in order to realize the disillusionment and frustration that has often attended massive abuse of such
rights, one only has to recall the intensity of the
anticolonial struggle, characterized as it was by
demands for greater freedom on the part of the subject
peoples. Nothing bound the diverse communities of
each colony more closely than the desired ideal to be
self-governed, to be freed from the shackles of imperialism, and to have freely chosen their form of government and its leaders, thus to enjoy liberty much
more abundantly and to experience self-fulfillment,
progress, and prosperity.

Yet, as we have shown in our examples, most of
these basic rights were arbitrarily and ruthlessly
eliminated or so restricted as to negate their value
soon after independence was achieved, all in the name
of protecting the state. The winner-take-all philosophy practiced by fallen leaders necessarily meant
denial or excessive curtailment of many if not most
of these rights. To my mind this assault on the basic
fundamental rights ranks as one of the foremost problems these states have to grapple with. One reads or
hears how much Africa's leading priorities must be
economic development, eradication of disease, poverty,
and ignorance. While it is true that these are significant challenges, no effective headway can be made
in meeting them unless there are some reasonably stable
conditions under which to launch a sustained, purposeful program of development in any state. This minimal
order is a fundamental condition necessary to any
effective development. But experience in the last
fifteen years has indicated that this condition of
relative stability cannot be attained if the government
of a state, through repression and systematic denial
of basic human rights in the name of establishing unity
or stability, in fact drives its citizens to acts of
desperation and subversion as they seek to recover
their lost rights or to protect themselves against tyranny. In such circumstances, whatever progress is
made in meeting the other challenges of development,
it is never maximal because the major effort of govern-

ment, despite the rhetoric on development, is geared
to ensuring its own survival. That essential unity
of the government and its nationals in pursuing a
common goal is absent. It must therefore follow that
any rational approach to Africa's pressing problems
has to begin with the issue of guaranteed minimum
human rights and security.

No rational person claims that the individual is
endowed with absolute rights, because in any organized
society there are no rights without limitation or corresponding obligations. A legal system exists within
every state to define the rights of each person; if
they are unlawfully exceeded or misused, the citizen
is duly penalized through the criminal or civil laws
of the land. The controversy, which is exacerbated
by the East/West ideological conflict and rivalry,
concerns the limits of such rights.

The international community unfortunately becomes
impotent in protecting these rights effectively and
the United Nations system demonstrates the difficulties
of ensuring them on a global scale. The preamble of
the Charter of the United Nations reaffirms the faith
of the member states "in fundamental human rights, in
the dignity and worth of the human person, in the
equal rights of men and women and of nations large
and small." Article 1(3) of the charter states that the
aim is "to achieve international co-operation . . . in
promoting and encouraging respect for human rights and
for fundamental freedoms for all without distinction
as to race, sex, language or religion." The United
Nations General Assembly adopted the most comprehensive code on human rights in history when in 1949 it
enacted the Universal Declaration of Human Rights.
Notwithstanding these positive steps, because of the
ideological differences mentioned, it became impossible
to enforce or ensure such rights internationally. Not
only were the great powers to violate them with impunity in regard to their nationals, but they were to
suppress these rights in countries they considered
within their own orbit in their power struggles. Thus,
Soviet tanks crushed the Hungarian and Polish uprisings
in 1955 and 1956, essentially aimed at recovering local
rights, and Alexander Dubcek was suppressed in Czecho-
slovakia in 1968 because he led a reformist government
providing socialism "with a human face." In the West,
the CIA became instrumental in overthrowing the popularly elected Marxist President Allende Gossens of
Chile in 1974 and thus produced an extremely repressive
military regime to replace him, just as it had done to
maintain the unpopular, ruthless military rule in
Greece. In Portugal the United States supported the

repressive regimes of Salazar and Caitano for decades.
With such derelictions it meant that the organs of the
United Nations dealing with abuses of human rights,
especially the Human Rights Commission, became helpless and were reduced to instruments of propaganda.

When the young African states became independent
and fell foul of the abuses of the rights of their
nationals, it followed that there was no effective
international system to help enforce these rights or
check their abuses. The way was consequently open
to sustain these massive violations, which have been
committed consistently by governments hiding their
actions behind exceptions to the rules. Let us illustrate this on an international level. The intervention
of the United Nations on behalf of nationals has been
effectively reduced if not often eliminated by pleading Article 2(7) of the United Nations Charter, which
states that the United Nations is not authorized "to
intervene in matters which are essentially within
domestic jurisdiction of any state." The treatment
of nationals has been argued to fall under this "domestic jurisdiction." Within the state, we can illustrate the process of violation by discussing a specific
right. For example, let us look at the freedom of
expression.

In both the Ugandan and Nigerian constitutions,
the individual was assured the freedom to express his
views on any matter, "to receive and impart ideas and
information without interference," and "freedom from
interference with his correspondence." But as we said
earlier, there had to be qualifications to such a
right. Thus measures were permitted to curtail it if
they were <u>reasonably required</u> under several circumstances, including "the interest of defense, public
safety, public order, public morality, or public
health."6

It is at once obvious that vast discretionary
powers had to be vested in rulers, determining the
circumstances of removal or limitation of such rights.
They alone decided when it was "reasonably required"
to do so; they alone could assess what constituted
"public safety" or "public order," as we saw in our
examples of Uganda, Ghana, and Nigeria. For a leadership committed to monopolizing power, these were en-
ticing loopholes providing legal avenues within which
to negate human rights. I am convinced no amount of
ingenious legal drafting can prevent such opportunities
for the abuse of power if it is at the same time to
provide a viable constitution. The crucial guarantee
for human rights, therefore, has to be ultimately the
ideological or philosophical commitment of the leaders

and their people to uphold and protect them.

The penal laws of the land should be strengthened
to cover all avenues by which those who threaten or
subvert the state or its good government might escape
being brought to justice. However, the arbitrary
preventive detention of people should be studiously
avoided by leaders, however attractive it may seem in
the short run, and circumstances for its application,
if used at all, should be manifestly unavoidable.
Tyranny should not be confused with firmness nor restraint with weakness, because a regime can act decisively against true enemies of the state and still
remain within the bounds of what most of its nationals
consider a good government.

In ascertaining the degree of human rights essential to the enjoyment of life among our citizens,
while external practices can be useful guides it might
be disastrous simply to copy them without adaptation
to our circumstances. I address myself to the reality
that in an average fragile developing state it may not
be possible to enjoy all the basic human freedoms to
the same degree as in a developed state.

There is empirical evidence on a global scale that
those who clamor for the guarantees of human rights
sometimes do so in order to use them to seize governmental power after which time they ruthlessly deny
these rights to anyone else. Both rightist and leftist
dictatorships have sometimes come to power this way.
Nor can it be summarily dismissed that abundant freedom
can provide external enemies of a state the opportunity
to subvert it. One of the contemporary problems of
Western societies is the real danger that freedom can
sometimes degenerate into license. Once this is done,
the basic value of freedom itself becomes endangered.
The crucial issue, always, is gauging the extent of
freedom for the individual that is compatible with the
overall common good and safety of society as a whole.
Young states are perfectly correct to attach great
importance to this relationship. But these reservations should not constitute a license for those in
power to overreact in their effort at self-preservation
and thereby oppress the people. One of the likely
counterproductive consequences of such measures, as
we said, is likely to be subversion and instability.

Let us summarize many of the essential basic
rights as follows: the right to life; a reasonable
degree of free expression, association, and movement;
the right to enjoy property justly earned; the right
to practice one's religion; protection against arbitrary acts of government; and the right to participate
in choosing one's government. In addition, there

should be a comprehensive set of social rights, basically aimed at creating a more just society. These should include the right to equal opportunity in every field and protection against any type of discrimination on the grounds of class, color, race, ethnic group, region, religion, or sex. There should be guarantees for productive work and fair wages in return for honest labor. Where the economy permits it, every child should have the right to a free basic education and all citizens should have access to affordable medical care.

To fortify the legal system and government in enforcing such rights, it may be worthwhile to set up a human rights board, an administrative body that would speedily hear complaints of violations of such rights by governmental administrative actions where the subject matter was not suitable for judicial proceedings. All citizens would have access to such a board and, to be of any value, the government would always have to consider the board's recommendations with great care. Such a board, to carry the prestige it deserves for its task, should consist of a few leading citizens of impeccable integrity who would be directly responsible to the head of government or his ministers.

Given the diversity of Africa's states, no greater guarantee of relative internal harmony exists than the protection and assurance of these rights. Many who held office or served in independence governments failed to realize that, by their consistent violations of the rights of the weak and the disadvantaged in the state, they were providing precedents for other succeeding regimes that they could not later persuasively or morally condemn. It is only when they were thrown out of power and were vulnerable to deprivation by the incumbents that suddenly human rights became worthy of protection. Such a self-centered perspective can never help guarantee human rights. Enlightened self-interest, therefore, seems to indicate that if one is in power, it is to one's own future interest to safeguard the rights of others. One never knows when one may need these same rights for one's own defense.

In conclusion, the function of government, the dream of our independence struggles, was to protect and enhance the enjoyment of human existence on this planet. This fundamental goal can only be realized through a consciously cultivated and jealously guarded system of basic human freedoms. To negate this in the name of whatever lofty objective and by whatever political maneuver is ultimately to provide fertile conditions for instability, which the enemies of Africa would only be too happy to exploit.

PROVIDING "CATCH-UP" PROGRAMS FOR BACKWARD AREAS

Colonial development was unevenly and unfairly spread in almost every colony. The areas of first contact with the colonizers often became the centers of all major development while those acquired last tended to be neglected. Because these different areas were inhabited by different ethnic groups, the disparity in development accentuated the differences among the diverse groups. The result was resentment among the backward areas and accusations of neglect and exploitation. For this reason, such areas constitute sources for potential tension and instability. It seems appropriate and necessary, then, that national governments should move vigorously and demonstrably to correct this imbalance by providing "catch-up" programs for the backward areas over and above the general national development.

There has to be good will and good faith on all sides as government tries to balance the many competing interests. For example, shortly after independence, the Ugandan government enacted special legislation to provide extra comprehensive development schemes for the northeast district of Karamoja, which colonial rulers had grossly neglected. There was no objection from other nationals because the need was so manifest. Where inequalities are not so pronounced, there can be trade-offs. For instance, it might have been more rational and conducive to national unity in Nigeria had Balewa's government had a comprehensive plan that bargained with the developed areas in the South. While northern education caught up in its ability to produce trained manpower, there could have been an agreement to employ southerners in the northern Public Service, instead of recruiting aliens, as was often the case. The options open for bargains to be made in such cases are almost infinite, but they all hinge on the will to be evenhanded to everyone.

EMPHASIZING COMMON INTERESTS

Simultaneous with all the foregoing steps, constant effort should be made to cultivate and emphasize the common nationality and destiny of the diverse nationals in the state. Despite the undeniable diversity, there is a considerable range of truly common ties that bind the citizens. They are Africans. They have shared a common colonial experience in several cases for many generations. They have inherited common institutions of the state, have gone to the same

schools, and have largely shared common values -- even
if political upheavals may tend to negate this. Each
can do little apart but together they can do much.
The leaders can then emphasize such points of common
identity. These points, which colonial rule ignored,
should be an important part of formal education, especially at the early impressionable age. But since
literacy in most of these states is below 30 percent,
(for Ghana, Nigeria, and Uganda it is about 25 percent), it would require extensive informal adult education through community development projects.

Without denigrating the divergent characteristics
of the groups, the leaders at all levels (in the party, government, bureaucracy, trade unions, etc.) need
to set the example, acting as a united people with a
shared destiny, instead of preaching unity and then
proceeding secretly to exploit or exacerbate ethnic
or regional differences.

PROMOTING MEANINGFUL REGIONAL COOPERATION

There are two principal reasons why it should
become a primary goal for every African state to promote regional cooperation with its neighbors. First,
as discussed earlier, their frontiers are artificial
and as a result cause great hardship and inconvenience
to split ethnic communities. Besides, when adjoining
states have not been at peace, such transnational
groups have been used for subversion or repression
across the frontier. The result as we know has been
the increasing border conflicts or wars among such
states. The most tragic and dramatic example of this
is, of course, the bitter war between Somalia and
Ethiopia for the control of ethnic Somali in Ethiopia's
Ogaden region. Yet if there were real interstate communication such split communities could be invaluable
bridges and ambassadors of goodwill across the frontier.

Second, to attain real stability African states
need greater economic and social development. Because so many of them are too small or too poor to be
viable, it is a matter of necessity for attaining that
goal that they must work closely together, pooling
their resources in each particular region. Yet most
regrettably, despite the rhetoric on African unity,
such effective regional cooperation has been minimal
and ineffective. Instead, it is a matter of great concern that even those regional experiments that had real
promise, like the East African Community uniting Kenya, Uganda, and Tanzania, have been dissolved with

enthusiasm. While there are many genuine problems impeding this goal of unity, I consider the most important one to be the reluctance of individual governments or leaders to forgo short-term advantages or personal consequence in return for long-term benefits to all. This was why the worthy effort by Kwame Nkrumah and Sékou Touré to federate Ghana and Guinea (and later, Mali) failed, despite the fact that they were all ideologically compatible. It was also why the much hoped for East African Federation between Kenya, Uganda, and Tanzania, which their leaders had promised to an excited region by the end of 1963, never took place, despite all the factors for mutual benefit that favored it.

Moreover, to attain effective bargaining muscle in international relations and to shield themselves from external undue influence, these poor and weak states simply must interact more intimately and meaningfully. For example, Table 13.1 shows the direction

TABLE 13.1 Ghana: Directions of Import and Export Trade, 1964–1970 (in N₵ thousands)

A. Value of Imports by Region of Origin in Thousands of Ceti

Region	1964	1965	1966	1967	1968	1969	1970
Africa	22,782	13,249	10,753	11,111	11,977	17,644	33,809
Americas	28,982	34,841	44,539	50,033	68,630	77,781	99,517
Asia	23,132	34,867	28,847	35,298	41,943	42,165	48,153
Europe	165,395	233,977	165,087	162,528	188,638	223,869	246,100
Africa's % of Annual Total	9.48%	4.18%	4.31%	4.29%	3.84%	4.88%	7.90%

B. Value of Total Exports by Region of Consignment

Region	1964	1965	1966	1967	1968	1969	1970
Africa	4,662	4,349	4,057	4,620	3,743	3,144	9,226
Americas	52,480	42,099	32,579	44,672	72,382	55,459	89,888
Asia	12,522	11,722	14,864	20,140	27,395	30,378	37,398
Europe	155,502	164,403	135,411	170,536	227,277	235,252	317,358
Africa's % of Annual Total	2.05%	1.95%	2.17%	1.92%	1.13%	0.96%	2.03%

Source: Adapted from: Statistical Year Book 1969-1970 (Accra, Ghana: Central Bureau of Statistics, 1970).

of Ghana's international trade. Africa's share of it
is negligible and it is even more so in the case of
many other African states. In such a case any talk
of a serious, sustained African position on a major
international issue cannot be easily maintained by a
state so manifestly dependent on the very forces with
which it would probably be contending. One would hope,
therefore, that the West African economic community
will grow strong and will escape the tragedy that overtook the East African community.

We should note that since those greater powers
that colonized us have now discovered themselves that
in order to survive they must bury their bitter past
and form the European Economic Community, then it is
great folly on our part, weak as we already are, to
dissolve what little unity we had. The cost will be
bitter and high.

DEVELOPING AN ENLIGHTENED FOREIGN POLICY

A country can have a good government, its people
can be at peace with each other, and yet it still can
be threatened by events occurring on the international
scene, for instance in the economic or political
spheres. It cannot be considered a luxury, therefore,
but a matter of self-interest that African states pursue a foreign policy conducive to their well-being.
But one has to tread with care, for the pursuit of
what may be objectively a just policy may interfere
with the interests of a great power that may then try
to discourage it through diverse methods, ranging from
diplomatic pressure to subversion. It would therefore
be prudent in conducting foreign policy not only to
consider the merit of one's stand, but its likely consequences as well. Nevertheless, the weakness of
African states aside, it seems there are issues about
which no self-respecting human being can remain silent.
I consider three areas particularly important.

First, there is the issue of pressing developed
nations to permit and promote meaningful reforms in
the international economic system that would do more
justice to the developing world than has hitherto been
the case. Intra-African cooperation and involvement
in Third World groupings to sustain creative but non-
disruptive pressure for such change surely needs to
be maintained. Second, it is a responsibility of all
African states to take a sensitive interest in the
search for just solutions to the tragedies of southern
Africa. The likelihood of big power involvement on
a more violent scale remains real if no concerted

effort is made to assist South Africans of all races
to minimize violence. A southern Africa in real conflagration could very well destabilize a greater part
of black Africa. It is in our self-interest to be
involved in the search for just and honorable solutions.
    Third, Africa's voice must always be heard among
those who seek disarmament and a reallocation of the
earth's resources from war tools to the promotion of
a better life for mankind. I do not accept the view
that in the balance of nuclear terror among the super-
powers, mankind has discovered an assured method for
survival. This is merely a most valuable respite that
we should all use to build a structure of enduring
peace on earth. It cannot be done by the manufacture
of more awesome weapons, which we promise each other
we will never use -- thus making mutual fear the principal basis for human survival. Rather, it can only
be accomplished with the imaginative and courageous
development of a set of global values. By creating
a just and equitable world order for all nations, irrespective of ideology or level of development, the basic
causes of the fear that escalates armaments would be
appreciably diminished or removed. Of course, this
is easier said than done. It must especially be painful for those nations that enjoy entrenched privilege
in the status quo, as well as the fact that it also
bears great risk for the human race. But the choice
and prognosis seem reasonably clear. We know that
from the dawn of human intelligence there has never
been a weapon developed that was never used in war
sooner or later. While we can cite the last thirty
years or so in which nuclear weapons have not been
used, we have a longer precedent of millions of years
where weaponry available has been used. Besides,
there is absolutely no assurance that in the continued
conditions of mutual fear another Hitler cannot emerge
among the great powers the way Idi Amin did in Africa,
with vast arsenals at his command.
    Even if there was no prospect of war, the waste
of limited global resources on arms is extraordinary
for the most intelligent species on earth. While 2
billion people of the world go in want, $1 billion
and more are spent on armaments each day of the year
around the world. But it would be hypocritical for
Africans to urge the great powers to disarm when on
their part they are escalating the purchase of conventional weaponry. For example, African expenditure on
arms jumped from $2.01 billion to $3.75 billion within
less than three years (1970-1973). In 1973, the average annual public expenditure per soldier among African states was $3,831, compared with the meager expen-

diture of $11 per capita on education and $3 per capita
on public health.[7]
    Finally, it will be in the interest of us all to
take a wider philosophical view of humanity. I am
quite convinced that beyond earthly man there are vast
powers and intelligences we can little comprehend or
simply relegate to science fiction. The likelihood
of overt contact with them is real and its consequence
to our lives would likely be more profound than anything ever imagined. We do ourselves a great disservice in pretending this is not so. Scientists of
major powers are already engaged in diverse exercises
to determine how to make such contact with them and
what its likely result to mankind would be. One basic
way to condition this earth for such an eventuality
is perhaps to strive more earnestly to establish a
just global order. "Do unto others what we would wish
them to do unto us" is to me not a mere religious
teaching. It could be a cosmic principle by which
those civilizations that survive in the universe abide.
Let not some power from whatever time or space in the
future justify meddling in our planetary affairs overtly by citing our own failings as the precedent or pretext for doing so. This is not to deny the likelihood
that, if human contact with extraterrestrial or other
alien intelligence was made, it could not give us far
greater understanding of our real identity in the cos-
mos as well as a compelling knowledge that our differences and prejudices are meaningless as we face and
deal with this new intelligence. I can think of nothing that could unite the human race more decisively,
hopefully for a better future.

CONCLUSIONS

    There is truly a qualitative difference between
the world under which the European nation-states were
created and consolidated and the present one into which
modern African states have been born. The luxury of a
relatively prolonged isolation permitted formative
Europe, possible before the technological revolution
and its consequent interdependence, is denied present
day African states. They exist in a world that has
irrevocably shrunk because of instantaneous communications between distant nations where everyone, including
the richest and most powerful, lacks self-sufficiency.
    Between now and that longed-for period when all
nations shall abide by a just and equitable world order, there is likely to continue a period of close
proximity among nations where the rich and powerful

may try to take advantage of the weak and poor (as most African states are). It makes eminently good sense that in order to survive under such conditions, an assurance of our domestic harmony and maximum unity is an indispensable requirement in order to face the external hazards. Yet, such a degree of unity and the pursuit of common goals by a national government can never be achieved where the regime, because of repressive or hostile policies, alienates a good portion of its citizens. The existence of avoidable domestic repression invariably promotes disaffection among the population and provides external predatory powers with attractive opportunities to successfully meddle with our destiny to our detriment.

It will surely serve us ill if all we can learn from the upheavals our states have undergone since independence is to put the blame on convenient scapegoats or to seek extenuating circumstances as we absolve ourselves, the dramatis personae, of all blame. We shall be blessed if we can learn the right lessons from our tragedies so that we might minimize their repetition. But to do this we must be candid and true to ourselves.

Some may argue that the guidelines I have advocated as a possible safeguard against subversion are too idealistic and incompatible with the "real world". I have lived and operated in that "real world" at a high level for two decades and my experience convinces me that without a serious commitment to such goals, as opposed to merely paying them lip service, we provide the necessary foundations for continued upheavals. We would have learned nothing from our adversity. To a large extent the choice is ours. That part of our well-being that lies with the great powers imposes on them a responsibility to respect our integrity. It is our right on this planet. Should they secretly or by deed regard us as their prey -- contrary to all their lofty and loud promises -- then they will unwittingly have done everyone, including themselves, a disservice. They will inevitably be preparing the stage for a much more violent world. The critical challenge to these great technological powers is not the attainment of yet other undreamed of scientific feats, but a sincere demonstration that their spectacular technological advance, with all its awesome power, is matched by a demonstrated spiritual and moral growth that would inevitably include an enhanced respect and loyalty to all members of the human race. Without this, every thinking being would have serious reason to worry about the fate of our beautiful planet.

Notes

PREFACE

    1. Arthur Lewis, "Beyond African Dictatorship: The Crisis of the One-Party State," <u>Encounter</u> (August 1965), p. 50.

CHAPTER 1

    1. F.J.D. Lugard, <u>The Dual Mandate in British Tropical Africa</u> (London: Blackwood & Sons, 1922), p. 18.
    2. See "Chiefdoms as Agencies of Local Rule in French Territories," in Lord Hailey's <u>An African Survey</u>, revised ed. (London: Oxford University Press, 1957), p. 544.
    3. Eric Robins and Blaine Littell, <u>Africa: Images and Realities</u> (New York: Frederick A. Praeger, 1971), p. 92.
    4. Jawaharlal Nehru records a similar experience for British India in his book, <u>The Discovery of India</u>, 6th ed. (Calcutta: Signet Press, 1956), p. 412.
    5. Semakula Kiwanuka, <u>From Colonialism to Independence</u> (Nairobi: Nairobi East African Literature Bureau, 1973), pp. 84-88.
    6. David Livingstone, "Exploration and Missionary Work in Southern Africa," in Joan G. Roland, ed., <u>Africa: The Heritage and the Challenge</u> (New York: Fawcett World Library, 1974), p. 139.

CHAPTER 2

    1. F.J.D. Lugard, <u>The Dual Mandate in British Tropical Africa</u> (London: Blackwood & Sons, 1922), p. 17.
    2. F.J.D. Lugard, <u>The Rise of Our East African Empire</u> (Edinburgh: Blackwood & Sons, 1893), vol. 2, p. 580.
    3. Original decision given in Sobhuza II v. Miller

and Others (1926), Appeal Cases (AC), p. 522.

4. On the effect of treaties on contracting parties, see L.F.L. Oppenheim, International Law (New York: Longmans, Green & Co., 1928), vol. 1, p. 829.

5. The Independence Order in Council (1962), S. 26, provided for a plebiscite in two counties (part of this territory) to determine whether or not the inhabitants wanted to remain in Buganda or be part of Bunyoro. Overwhelmingly, they chose the latter.

6. See "The Development of the Legislative Council," in G.S.K. Ibingira, The Forging of an African Nation (New York: Viking Press, 1973), Chapter 3. See also the remarks about this undue delay by Professor K. Ingham, a British colonial historian, in The Making of Modern Uganda (London: George Allen and Unwin, 1958), p. 173.

7. Proceedings of the Ugandan Legislative Council, 1946-1947, p. 5.

8. Quoted in Ibingira, The Forging of an African Nation, p. 36.

9. Proceedings of the Ugandan Legislative Council, 1957, pt. 2, p. 44.

10. Under the Colonial Laws Validity Act, 1865, 28 and 29 Vict. C:63.

11. Full text of the Agreement may be found in Laws of Uganda (Entebbe, Uganda: Government Printer, 1951), vol. 6.

12. Ibid., The Toro Agreement, 1900; The Ankole Agreement, 1901.

13. Ibingira, The Forging of an African Nation, p. 23, and sources quoted therein.

14. C.A.G. Wallis, Report of an Inquiry into African Local Government in the Protectorate of Uganda (Entebbe: Government Printer, 1953), pt. 2, p. 14.

15. See for example, "Colonialism as a System for Underdeveloping Africa," in Walter Rodney, How Europe Underdeveloped Africa (Washington, D.C.: Howard University Press, 1974), pt. 6, p. 203 ff.

16. From Buganda's Independence (Kampala, Uganda: Bugandan Government, 1961), p. 24.

17. Ibid., p. 30. This referred to critical remarks by non-Baganda members of the Legislative Council.

18. For a history of the Uganda political parties, see Donald A. Low, Political Parties in Uganda 1949-62 (London: University of London Institute of Commonwealth Affairs, 1962).

19. See a historical sketch of the KY by Masembe Kabali in Uganda Parliamentary Debates 43 (12 March 1965):1487 ff.

20. The 10 schedules are in the Constitution of

Uganda, 1926.

21. This is a standard definition of federalism. See C. K. Wheare, Federal Government (London: Oxford University Press, 1961), pp. 7, 11.

22. See Ibingira, The Forging of an African Nation, Chapter 8, for more details.

23. Note S. 9, pt. 2, Schedule 7, of the Ugandan Independence Constitution for the immense financial power of the central government.

24. S. 94, the Ugandan Independence Constitution.

25. Ibid., Ss. 80-81; and S. 39 of the Bugandan Constitution.

26. See paras. 1-4, Schedules 2-4, the Ugandan Independence Constitution.

27. See the Local Administration's Ordinance, Schedule 1, S. 24, Laws of Uganda (1962), p. 423.

28. S. 5 (4) of the Ugandan Independence Constitution.

29. Detailed in pt. 2, Schedule 7, in the Ugandan Independence Constitution.

CHAPTER 3

1. See K. M. Buchanan and J. C. Pugh, Land and People in Nigeria (London: University of London Press, 1955) for the diversity of the inhabitants and texts on the subject in the general bibliography for Nigeria.

2. See report by F.J.D. Lugard, The Amalgamation of Northern and Southern Nigeria and Administration, 1912-1919, Cmd. 468 (London: H. M. Stationary Office, 1920), p. 10.

3. Quoted in Nigerian Parliamentary Debates (26 February 1957):col. 256, p. 146.

4. For a detailed account of Nigerian political parties, see R. L. Sklar, Nigerian Political Parties: Power in an Emergent African Nation (Princeton, N.J.: Princeton University Press, 1963).

5. In West Africa Pilot (6 July 1949); also quoted in Joseph Okpaku, ed., Nigeria: Dilemma of Nationhood (New York: Third Press, 1972).

6. The Proceedings of the General Conference on Review of the Constitution as a whole clearly reflect these divisions. (Lagos: Government Printer, 1950).

7. See John Stuart Mill, Utilitarianism: Liberty and Representative Government (New York: E. P. Dutton, 1975), pp. 367-368.

8. These northern grievances had been put clearly by the Hon. Abubakar Tafawa Balewa before a Nigerian constitutional conference. See Proceedings of the General Conference on Review of the Constitution (Lagos: Government Printer, 1950), pp. 64-69.

9. Ibid., p. 62.
10. "Conclusions and Recommendations," Report of the Commission to Enquire into the Fears of Minorities and the Means of Allaying Them, Chapter 14, p. 87 ff.
11. See Prime Minister Belewa's reply to a question in Nigerian House of Representatives Debates (9 September 1957):181 ff.
12. In Nigerian House of Representatives Debates (31 March 1956):991 ff.

CHAPTER 4

1. In Gold Coast Legislative Assembly Debates (30 July - 16 November 1956):col. 19.
2. Ibid., col. 21.
3. In Gold Coast Legislative Assembly Debates (4-17 November 1953). Also quoted by Dennis Austin, Politics in Ghana, 1946-1960 (New York: Oxford University Press, 1970), p. 179. Ghana has thirty-four main ethnic groups, according to David Smock and Audrey Smock, Politics of Pluralism -- A Comparative Study of Lebanon and Ghana (New York: Elsevier Scientific Publishing Co., Inc., 1975), p. 282. For a more detailed account of the ethnic groups in this state, see "Tribes in Ghana," 1960 Ghana Population Census, Special Report E, vol. 5.

CHAPTER 5

1. An expression from Ruth First, Power in Africa (New York: Pantheon, 1970).

CHAPTER 6

1. See, for example, Akena Adoko's book, The Uganda Crisis (Kampala, Uganda: Kampala publisher, 1969); Milton Obote, "The Footsteps of Uganda's Revolution" in East Africa Journal (October 1968), pp. 7-13; and Obote's explanation to the nation of why he seized power in 1966, in Uganda Parliamentary Debates, fourth session (15 April 1966):1-20.
2. The Kabaka of Buganda, King Freddie's, Desecration of my Kingdom (London: Constable and Co., 1967).
3. See report of this statement in Uganda Argus (8 and 9 January 1964); the reply of the opposition groups in Uganda Argus (9, 11, and 22 January 1964). See a discussion of this by A. G. Ginyera Pinycwa, "Prospects for One-Party System in Uganda," East Africa Journal (October 1968).
4. Uganda Argus (11 January 1964).
5. It is significant that there is a general rule

that neither those politicians who cross over to government from the opposition nor those governments which receive them are ever prepared to hold new elections to test whether or not the voters support the change. The reason is the fear of rejection.

6. See Uganda Parliamentary Debates 18 (3 October 1963):421 ff. See Obonyo's charges in ibid., 53 (13 September 1965):3347.

7. Uganda Parliamentary Debates 18 (3 October 1963):421.

8. Ibid., 10 (1 April 1963):388.

9. Ibid., 18 (3 October 1963):425.

10. Ibid., 34 (8 September 1964):3057.

11. Ibid., 23 (6 February 1964):925.

12. Noted by J. M. Lee in African Armies and Civil Order (New York: Frederick A. Praeger, 1969), p. 105. Lee seems to accept the "official reasons" for this military expansion.

13. The mandatory provision to hold the referendum was contained in Section 26, Uganda Independence Order in Council, 1962 (Entebbe, Uganda: Government Printer, 1962).

14. See their complaints, for example, in Uganda Parliamentary Debates 19 (6 November 1963):40; 25 (20 March 1964):1477 ff.; 56 (17 January 1966):565.

15. Lee, African Armies and Civil Order, p. 104.

16. The first appeal to army veteran recruits was broadcast on Ugandan radio on 14 February 1965. See Uganda Argus (15 February 1965).

17. These figures were in my possession by the end of 1963 in a more detailed form, district by district.

18. Quoted from the booklet, Buganda's Independence (Kampala, Uganda: Bugandan Government, 1961), p. 24. For the substantial scale of Buganda's military power, see Arye Oded, Islam in Uganda (New York: John Wiley and Sons, 1974).

19. See Uganda Parliamentary Debates 91 (24 March 1969):1096.

20. See J. W. Nyakatura, Anatomy of an African Kingdom -- A History of Bunyoro-Kitara (New York: Doubleday, 1973).

21. Uganda Parliamentary Debates 14 (2 July 1963): 705.

22. Ibid., 42 (10 March 1965):1313.

23. Ibid., 23 (6 February 1964):954 ff.

24. Ibid., p. 920 ff.

25. Crawford Young points out this confusion in "The Obote Revolution," in Africa Report (June 1966), p. 4. See also Martin Doornbos, "Some Conceptual Problems Concerning Ethnicity in Integration Analysis," in Civilizations 22 (1972):3.

26. Uganda Parliamentary Debates 86 (21 October 1968):4253.

27. See David Martin, General Amin (London: Faber & Faber, 1974), p. 20. David Martin relied heavily on information directly given him by Obote, and his account is clearly one-sided in most parts.

28. Uganda Parliamentary Debates 39 (18 February 1965):737.

29. Ibid., 40 (22 February 1965):803, remarks by E.M.K. Mulira.

30. This account is from sworn affidavits of eye-witnesses given as evidence before the coroner. It was also quoted in the debate. See Uganda Parliamentary Debates 39 (19 February 1965):755 ff.

31. In Uganda Parliamentary Debates 18 (1 October 1963):310 ff.

32. Ibid., 36 (1 December 1964):42.

33. Ibid., 3 (November 1962):623 ff.

34. Ibid., 9 (19 March 1963):19.

35. Ibid., 22 (19 December 1963):746.

36. Ibid., 17 (23 September 1963):7.

37. Ibid., 17 (27 September 1963):202.

38. Quoted from Buganda's Independence (Kampala, Uganda: Bugandan Government, 1961), p. 30.

39. This was confirmed by its first and only secretary-general, Masembe-Kabali. See his statement on the history of the KY in Uganda Parliamentary Debates 43 (12 March 1965):1487 ff.

40. Obote's confirmation, East Africa Journal (October 1968), pp. 11-12.

41. See Uganda Argus (6 and 7 August 1964).

42. Ibid., 2 and 3 August 1964.

43. Ibid., 24 August 1964.

44. Ibid.

45. The name of B. Kirya as a signatory to the ministerial statement was an afterthought for window dressing purposes. Shortly afterward he fell out with Obote and was detained five years without trial.

46. Uganda Argus (24 August 1964).

47. Amos Sempa was one of the central pillars of the Bugandan traditionalist leadership and played a leading role in the isolation of Buganda from the mainstream of nationalist politics.

48. Uganda Parliamentary Debates 43 (17 March 1965):1494.

49. Report of the Relationships Commission (Munster Commission) (Entebbe: Uganda Government Printer, 1961), para. 117.

50. Uganda Parliamentary Debates 56 (14 January 1966):501.

51. Ibid., 86 (21 October 1968):4254.

CHAPTER 7

1. This was his elaborate "political and constitutional report" to the UPC Annual Delegates Conference
held in 1968 at Mbale.
2. Uganda Parliamentary Debates 45 (28 May 1965):
1919.
3. Ibid., 46 (3 June 1965):2090.
4. Quoted by G. Oda in ibid., 42 (10 March 1965):
1312.
5. Uganda Parliamentary Debates 58 (4 February
1966):1014.
6. Constitutional and Political Report to the UPC
Delegates Conference, 1968, p. 26.
7. Uganda Parliamentary Debates 58 (4 February
1966):1018.
8. Ibid., p. 1021.
9. Ibid., 56 (18 January 1966):731.
10. Ibid., 59 (15 April 1966):15. Obote's whole
speech is the most important and authoritative statement of his reasons for the 1966 revolution.
11. Uganda Parliamentary Debates 59 (15 April
1966):7.
12. The Evidence and Findings of the Commission
of Enquiry into Allegations made by the late Daudi
Ocheng on 4 February 1966 (Kampala: Uganda Publishing
House, 1971), p. 346.
13. Colonel Le'ev Shaham, head of Israel's first
military mission in Uganda, has claimed Amin approached
him with a request to find a market for fifteen tons
of gold that Amin claimed he had captured on five
trucks in the Congo. The proceeds were to be deposited
in a Swiss bank. Colonel Shaham declined the request.
Shaham's account appeared in Newsweek (7 March 1977),
p. 34.
14. The Evidence and Findings of the Commission of
Enquiry, p. 471.
15. S. 78, Republican Constitution of 1967.
16. Ibid., S. 69(3).
17. S. 1(a), The Public Order and Security Act,
No. 20 of 1967.
18. Moreover, the conditions of detention whenever
it was done by colonial governors were considerably
more humane. For example, detainees were invariably permitted to live with their families and permitted relatively greater freedom of movement. Such was
the case with leading nationalists like J. W. Kiwanuka,
B. K. Kirya, and I. Musazi, who underwent colonial
detention. Obote was never detained or jailed by colonial rulers in the struggle for independence.
19. Uganda Parliamentary Debates 73 (3 July 1967):

632 ff.

20. These names include: B. K. Kirya, M. M. Ngobi, G. B. Magazi, Dr. E. M. Lume, W. W. Nadiope, A. K. Sempa, G. S. Ibingira, and C. J. Obwangor, five of whom were founders of the UPC.

21. In Nigerian House of Representatives Parliamentary Debates, 4 (7 August 1963):162.

22. Uganda Parliamentary Debates 73 (3 July 1967): 541.

23. Ibid., p. 1067.

24. This was not drastically different from already existing legislation.

25. Uganda Parliamentary Debates 99 (20 April 1970):10.

26. S. 79(1), Republican Constitution of 1967.

27. Ibid., S. 64.

28. For a clear exposition of the rapid changes in local governments and their adverse consequences, see Hon. B. Byanyima's account, Uganda Parliamentary Debates 68 (7 February 1967):1633.

29. Although the Independence Constitution stipulated that there had to be a periodic general election after every five years, the last general election in Uganda was held in April 1962 before independence. Obote ruled for over nine years without holding a single one.

30. Quoted from Buganda's Independence (Entebbe, Uganda: Bugandan Government, 1961), p. 23.

31. Uganda Parliamentary Debates 73 (3 July 1967): 541.

32. Ibid., p. 607.

33. Ibid., p. 546.

34. Ibid., 90 (13 March 1969):857.

35. In Carl Sagan and I. S. Shklovsky, Intelligent Life in the Universe (San Francisco: Holden-Day, 1966), p. 418. These two leading American/Soviet space scientists estimate that within our Milky Way galaxy alone, there are probably between 50,000 and 1 million technical civilizations substantially in advance of earth.

36. See attack on this suggestion by members of Parliament, for example, by J. H. Obonyo, Uganda Parliamentary Debates 74 (17 July 1974):991.

37. See attack on this and factual evidence in Uganda Parliamentary Debates 83 (28 June 1968):3567.

38. John Agami, The Roots of Political Crisis in Uganda (Denmark: H. P. Tryk Kastrup, 1977), pp. 182-

39. Uganda Parliamentary Debates 75 (21 July 1967): 1086.

40. See the details in A. Milton Obote, "Proposals for new methods of election of representatives of the people to parliament," Document No. 5 on the Move to

the Left (Kampala, Uganda: Obote Foundation, 1970),
paras. 35-45.

CHAPTER 8

1. Ghana Parliamentary Debates, 1st series, 5 (6
March 1957):col. 16.
2. Ibid., col. 43.
3. Legislative Assembly Debates (4 February 1954):
col. 129.
4. Ghana Parliamentary Debates 2 (July-September
1958):col. 432.
5. For this debate, see Ghana Parliamentary Debates (3 November 1958):col. 407 ff.
6. Ghana Parliamentary Debates (July 1958):col.
407.
7. Ibid., col. 495.
8. Ibid., col. 416.
9. T. Peter Omari, Kwame Nkrumah, The Anatomy of
an African Dictatorship (New York: Africana Publishing
Corporation, 1970), pp. 212-213.
10. Ghana Parliamentary Debates (16 October 1961).
11. Ibid.
12. Kofi Baako, quoted by Omari, Kwame Nkrumah,
p. 194.
13. David Smock and Audrey Smock, The Politics of
Pluralism -- A Comparative Study of Lebanon and Ghana
(New York: Elsevier Scientific Publishing Co., Inc.,
1975), p. 232.
14. Ibid., p. 247. Originally from Ghana Parliamentary Debates 3 (17 June 1970):878-880. For example,
see Maxwell Ourisu in Uses and Abuses of Political
Power: A Case Study of Continuity and Change in the
Politics of Ghana (Chicago: University of Chicago
Press, 1970), p. 329.
15. Smock and Smock, The Politics of Pluralism,
p. 248; Daily Graphic (25 March 1975), p. 9.
16. Ghana Parliamentary Debates 3 (17 June 1970):
878 ff. Also quoted by Smock and Smock, The Politics
of Pluralism, p. 247.

CHAPTER 9

1. For Prime Minister Balewa's full chronology
of these events, see Nigerian Federal Parliament Debates (29 May 1962):1100 ff.
2. See Awolowo's response, ibid., p. 1102 ff.
3. Nigerian Federal Parliament Debates (22 March
1962), p. 30.
4. Northern House of Assembly Debates (12 March
1955):1.

5. Eastern Nigerian Assembly Debates (March-November 1965):col. 118.

6. Nigerian House of Representatives Debates (16 March 1964):97.

7. Nigerian Federal Parliament Debates (5 December 1962):22. See objection in Eastern House of Assembly Debates (13 November 1962):30.

8. See Moyibi Amoda, "Background to the Conflict: A Summary of Nigeria's Political History from 1914-1964," in Joseph Okpaku, ed., Nigeria: Dilemma of Nationhood (New York: Third Press, 1972), p. 62 ff. See also Eastern House of Assembly Debates (2 April 1965): 200.

9. Eastern House of Assembly Debates (2 April 1965):165.

10. See the discussion of this issue in the Eastern Nigerian Assembly Debates (March-November 1965):cols. 239-240.

11. Ibid., remarks by Hon. M. E. Ogon (NCNC, Ikom East), col. 244.

12. Related by Ruth First, Power in Africa (New York: Pantheon Books, 1970), p. 168.

CHAPTER 10

1. See, for example, Walter Rodney, How Europe Underdeveloped Africa (Washington, D.C.: Howard University Press, 1974).

2. See, for example, Anton Bebler, Military Rule in Africa: Dahomey, Ghana, Sierra Leone, and Mali (New York: Praeger Publishers, Inc., 1973).

3. See Kabaka Mutesa's comment on this marriage expenditure in Desecration of My Kingdom (London: Constable and Co., 1967).

4. A. Milton Obote, The Common Man's Charter (Kampala, Uganda: Uganda People's Congress Headquarters, 1969), proposals for Document No. 1.

5. See Uganda Argus (2 May 1970). See also The People (2 May 1970).

6. Uganda Parliamentary Debates 104 (5 October 1970):165, remarks by Humphrey Luanda.

7. Tertit Aasland, Research Report No. 26 on the Move-to-the-Left in Uganda, 1969-1971 (Uppsala: Scandinavian Institute of African Studies, 1974), p. 10.

8. Uganda Parliamentary Debates 104 (5 October 1970):180, remarks by N. Bisamunyu.

9. Aasland, Research Report No. 26, p. 44.

10. See West Africa (21 January 1967), p. 90. See also the detailed account of Kwame Nkrumah's will in Appendix D of T. Peter Omari, Kwame Nkrumah, The Anatomy of an African Dictatorship (New York: Africana

Publishing Corporation, 1970), p. 215.

11. The CIA and the Cult of Intelligence (New York: Alfred A. Knopf, 1974).

12. Quoted in New York Times (27 April 1976), pp. 21-24. See U.S., Congress, Senate, Detailed Senate Select Committee, Alleged Assassination Plots of Foreign Leaders, Rept. 94-465, 1 vol., 1976, and Foreign and Military Intelligence, Rept. 94-755, 2 vols., 1976.

13. See, for example, Kwame Nkrumah's charge in Dark Days in Ghana (New York: International Publishers, 1968), p. 49.

14. In Search of Enemies (New York: W. W. Norton & Co., 1978), pp. 160, 201.

15. Time (31 July 1978).

CHAPTER 11

1. On one-party systems in Africa, see Julius Nyerere, "Democracy and the Party System," Freedom and Unity/Uhuru na Umoja (New York: Oxford University Press, 1967), pp. 195-203; Ruth Schachter Morganthau, "Single-Party Systems in West Africa," The American Political Science Review 55 (1961):294-307; and Benyamin Neuberger, "Has the Single-Party State Failed in Africa?", African Studies Review 18 (April 1974):177 ff.

2. Professor Lewis' comment is shared by many economic experts. See "Beyond African Dictatorship: The Crisis of the One-Party State," Encounter (August 1965). See also S. E. Finer, "The One-Party Regimes in Africa: Reconsiderations," Government and Opposition 2 (July-October 1967):491.

3. Nyerere, "Democracy and the Party System," pp. 195-203; and Nyerere, "Guide to the One-Party State Commission," in Freedom and Unity, p. 261 ff.

4. Ndabaningi Sithole, "The One/Two Party Systems," in Roland, Africa, The Heritage, p. 342.

5. Many leading scientists believe this a real likelihood among advanced space civilizations. Ronald Bracewell, The Glactic Club, Intelligent Life in Outer Space (San Francisco: W. H. Freeman & Co., 1974), p. 28. See also Carl Sagan and I. S. Shklovsky, Intelligent Life in the Universe (San Francisco: Holden-Day, 1966), Chapters 32-33.

6. See, for example, Ernest W. Lefever, Spear and Scepter (Washington, D.C.: Brookings Institution, 1970), p. 28 ff., for a discussion of types of coups and their reasons. Samuel Decalo summarizes these reasons in "Military Coups and Military Regimes in Africa," The Journal of Modern African Studies 11 (March 1973):105-127; and Aristide Zolberg, "The Structure of Political Conflict in the New States of Tropi-

cal Africa," The American Political Science Review
62 (1968):70-87.

7. Dennis Austin, "The Underlying Problem of the
Army Coups d'etat in Africa," Optima (March 1966):
70-71.

8. Lefever, Spear and Scepter, p. 20.

9. Col. A. A. Afrifa, The Ghana Coup (London:
Frank Cass & Co., 1966), pp. 33, 115-117.

10. Kwame Nkrumah, Dark Days in Ghana (New York:
International Publishers, 1968), p. 49.

11. There were three Ewes, two Gas, one Ashanti
and one Fanti. Of these, two were Presbyterian, two
were Roman Catholic, one was Methodist, one was Angli-
can, and one was Moslem. See Lefever, Spear and Scepter, pp. 60-61. But see also David Smock and Audrey
Smock, The Politics of Pluralism -- A Comparative
Study of Lebanon and Ghana (New York: Elsevier Scientific Publishing Co., Inc., 1975), p. 240, who point out
a clear ethnic imbalance in the NLC and the subsequent
strains resulting therefrom.

12. Smock and Smock, The Politics of Pluralism,
p. 240.

13. Ayi Kwei Armah, The Beautyful Ones Are Not Yet
Born (New York: Collier Books, 1969).

14. J. M. Lee, African Armies and Civil Order (New
York: Frederick A. Praeger, 1969), pp. 39-42.

15. From a speech, Conciliation with America, in
1775. Oxford Dictionary of Quotations, 2nd ed., (New
York: Oxford University Press, 1953), p. 100.

CHAPTER 12

1. Quoted in the International Commission of
Jurists' Report, adopted as a United Nations document
and published 27 May 1974, p. 14.

2. Ibid., p. 19.

3. Ibid., p. 20.

4. Ibid., p. 22.

5. New African Development, May 1977, p. 383.

6. Reported in the New York Times, May 25, 1977,
p. A3.

7. Arnold Raphael, New African Development, May
1977.

CHAPTER 13

1. See a highly perceptive statement on the durability and strength of ethnic nationalism by Professor Walker F. Connor, "Nation-Building or Nation-
Destroying," in World Politics (24 April 1972), pp.
318-355.

2. But see Sir Ivon Jennings on the difficulties of coalition governments in Cabinet Government (New York: Cambridge University Press, 1936), pp. 205-207.

3. Arthur Lewis, "Beyond African Dictatorship: The Crisis of the One-Party State," Encounter (August 1965), p. 8.

4. For discussions on these constitutions, see Kalu Ezera, Constitutional Developments in Nigeria (New York: Cambridge University Press, 1960). Oluwole Idowu Odumosu, The Nigerian Constitution, History and Development (London: Sweet and Maxwell, 1963) argues the northern preponderance was undesirable for the federation. For Uganda, see G.S.K. Ibingira, The Forging of an African Nation (New York: Viking Press, 1973); Henry Francis Morris, Uganda: The Development of Its Laws and Constitutions (London: Stevens, 1966). For Ghana, see S.A.R. Bennion, The Constitutional Laws of Ghana (London: Butterworth, 1962).

5. Some texts on human rights are John Carey, International Protection of Human Rights (Dobbs Ferry, N.Y.: Oceana, 1968); Arthur Robertson, Human Rights in National and International Law (New York: Oxford University Press, 1971); Urmilla Haksar, Minority Protection and International Bill of Human Rights (New York: Paragon, 1974).

6. S. 26(2) of the Ugandan Independence Constitution, 1962. There was an entire chapter in the Constitution detailing human rights and their limits, Sections 17-33. These provisions had been copied from the Nigerian Independence Constitution of 1960 almost word for word.

7. Ruth Legar Sivard, ed., World Military and Social Expenditures, 1976 (Leesburg, Va.: World Military and Social Expenditures Publications, 1976), p. 28.